VOLUME 635

THE A

of The American
and Social S

D1529215

DATE DUE

Young Disadva

Families, Po

S_

TIMOT
University

IRW
Col

RO
Col

Los Ang
Singa

The American Academy of Political and Social Science

202 S. 36th Street, Annenberg School for Communication, University of Pennsylvania,
Philadelphia, PA 19104-3806; (215) 746-7321; (215) 573-2667 (fax); www.aapss.org

Origin and Purpose. The Academy was organized December 14, 1889, to promote the progress of political and social science, especially through publications and meetings. The Academy does not take sides in controverted questions, but seeks to gather and present reliable information to assist the public in forming an intelligent and accurate judgment.

Meetings. The Academy occasionally holds a meeting in the spring extending over two days.

Publications. THE ANNALS of The American Academy of Political and Social Science is the bimonthly publication of the Academy. Each issue contains articles on some prominent social or political problem, written at the invitation of the editors. These volumes constitute important reference works on the topics with which they deal, and they are extensively cited by authorities throughout the United States and abroad.

Membership. Each member of the Academy receives THE ANNALS and may attend the meetings of the Academy. Membership is open only to individuals. Annual dues: $94.00 for the regular paperbound edition (clothbound, $134.00). Members may also purchase single issues of THE ANNALS for $18.00 each (clothbound, $27.00). Student memberships are available for $52.00.

Subscriptions. THE ANNALS of The American Academy of Political and Social Science (ISSN 0002-7162) (J295) is published bimonthly—in January, March, May, July, September, and November—by SAGE Publications, 2455 Teller Road, Thousand Oaks, CA 91320. Periodicals postage paid at Thousand Oaks, California, and at additional mailing offices. POSTMASTER: Send address changes to The Annals of The American Academy of Political and Social Science, c/o SAGE Publications, 2455 Teller Road, Thousand Oaks, CA 91320. Institutions may subscribe to THE ANNALS at the annual rate: $788.00 (clothbound, $889.00). Single issues of THE ANNALS may be obtained by individuals who are not members of the Academy for $142.00 each (clothbound, $160.00). Single issues of THE ANNALS have proven to be excellent supplementary texts for classroom use. Direct inquiries regarding adoptions to THE ANNALS c/o SAGE Publications (address below).

All correspondence concerning membership in the Academy, dues renewals, inquiries about membership status, and/or purchase of single issues of THE ANNALS should be sent to THE ANNALS c/o SAGE Publications, 2455 Teller Road, Thousand Oaks, CA 91320. Telephone: (800) 818-SAGE (7243) and (805) 499-0721; Fax/Order line: (805) 375-1700; e-mail: journals@sagepub.com. *Please note that orders under $30 must be prepaid.* For all customers outside the Americas, please visit http://www.sagepub.co.uk/customerCare.nav for information.

Printed on acid-free paper

THE ANNALS

Editorial Office: 202 S. 36th Street, Philadelphia, PA 19104-3806
For information about membership* (individuals only) and subscriptions (institutions), address:
SAGE Publications
2455 Teller Road
Thousand Oaks, CA 91320

For SAGE Publications: Allison Leung (Production) and Lori Hart (Marketing)

From India and South Asia,
write to:
SAGE PUBLICATIONS INDIA Pvt Ltd
B-42 Panchsheel Enclave, P.O. Box 4109
New Delhi 110 017
INDIA

From Europe, the Middle East,
and Africa, write to:
SAGE PUBLICATIONS LTD
1 Oliver's Yard, 55 City Road
London EC1Y 1SP
UNITED KINGDOM

*Please note that members of the Academy receive THE ANNALS with their membership.
International Standard Serial Number ISSN 0002-7162
International Standard Book Number ISBN 978-1-4522-0539-7 (Vol. 635, 2011) paper
International Standard Book Number ISBN 978-1-4522-0538-0 (Vol. 635, 2011) cloth
Manufactured in the United States of America. First printing, May 2011.

Please visit http://ann.sagepub.com and under the "More about this journal" menu on the right-hand side, click on the Abstracting/Indexing link to view a full list of databases in which this journal is indexed.

Information about membership rates, institutional subscriptions, and back issue prices may be found on the facing page.

Advertising. Current rates and specifications may be obtained by writing to The Annals Advertising and Promotion Manager at the Thousand Oaks office (address above). Acceptance of advertising in this journal in no way implies endorsement of the advertised product or service by SAGE or the journal's affiliated society(ies) or the journal editor(s). No endorsement is intended or implied. SAGE reserves the right to reject any advertising it deems as inappropriate for this journal.

Claims. Claims for undelivered copies must be made no later than six months following month of publication. The publisher will supply replacement issues when losses have been sustained in transit and when the reserve stock will permit.

Change of Address. Six weeks' advance notice must be given when notifying of change of address. Please send the old address label along with the new address to the SAGE office address above to ensure proper identification. Please specify the name of the journal.

THE ANNALS

OF THE AMERICAN ACADEMY OF POLITICAL AND SOCIAL SCIENCE

Volume 635   May 2011

IN THIS ISSUE:

Young Disadvantaged Men: Fathers, Families, Poverty, and Policy

Special Editors: TIMOTHY M. SMEEDING
IRWIN GARFINKEL
RONALD B. MINCY

Introduction

Substantive/Descriptive Surveys of Fatherhood

FORThCOMING
Patrimonial Power in the Modern World
Special Editors: JULIA ADAMS and MOUNIRA MAYA CHARRAD

INTRODUCTION

Young Disadvantaged Men: Fathers, Families, Poverty, and Policy

By
TIMOTHY M. SMEEDING,
IRWIN GARFINKEL,
and
RONALD B. MINCY

This introductory article opens this special issue of *The Annals of the American Academy of Political and Social Science* on young disadvantaged men by explaining the purpose of the conference and its overall contribution to our understanding of poverty and disadvantage. We start by explaining how young men are doing in the face of low educational achievement, joblessness, out-of-wedlock childbearing, incarceration, and in the face of the Great Recession as a way to frame the problems that this volume addresses (see also Peck 2010).

We begin with the fact that by age 30, between 68 and 75 percent of young men with a high school degree or less are fathers (see National Longitudinal Survey of Youth [NLSY], U.S. Bureau of Labor Statistics 1997; National Survey of Family Growth [NSFG], U.S. Centers for Disease Control 2002) (see Table 1). Becoming a teen father reduces the likelihood of a high school diploma and GED receipt instead of a normal degree but has no positive effect on net earnings (Fletcher and Wolfe 2010). Only 52 percent of all fathers (21 percent of black fathers) under age 25 were married at the birth of their first child.[1] Men among this group who become fathers at older ages are more likely to be married by age 30. Sixty-five percent of all

NOTE: The authors thank several sponsors, while dissociating all of these organizations from the conclusions and analyses presented in this article. We thank the Institute for Research on Poverty at the University of Wisconsin–Madison, operating under funding from the Assistant Secretary of Planning and Evaluation at the U.S. Department of Health and Human Services. We also thank the Columbia University Population Research Center and the Center for Research on Fathers, Children and Well-Being, also at Columbia University, for financial and staff support. Special thanks are given to Callie Langton, Becky Pettit, Andrew Weinshenker, and Ty Wilde for help with data preparation. We also thank Deborah Johnson for editorial assistance and Dawn Duren for graph and table preparation. We assume full responsibility for all errors of omission and commission.

DOI: 10.1177/0002716210394774

first-time fathers were married when their first child was born (but only 31 percent of all black men under 30 who were first-time fathers were married at the time of the first birth).[2] In addition, far fewer young fathers continue their education post–high school (29 percent of fathers age 30 and younger compared with 41 percent of all men age 30 and younger according to the NSFG). Finally, 62 percent of fathers with a high school degree or less earned less than $20,000 in 2002, suggesting that most young men with little education, low skills, and poor employment records have acquired family responsibilities that they find difficult to meet (see Table 1).

Another way to consider parenthood at young ages is to look at birth patterns for men and women by age, education, and for completed cohort fertility (see Table 2). The estimates suggest that younger women and men who have less education are most likely to be parents. Less-educated mothers tend to give birth for the first time when young, and the fathers of these children tend to be slightly older than their partners. Mothers with less than a high school degree are most likely to have the greatest number of children (highest total fertility) over the

Timothy M. Smeeding is director of the Institute for Research on Poverty and Arts and Sciences Distinguished Professor of Public Affairs, La Follette School of Public Affairs, University of Wisconsin–Madison. His research interests include the economics of public policy, especially social policy and at-risk populations; poverty and income distribution, income transfers, and tax policy; and health economics. In 1983, he founded the Luxembourg Income Study (LIS), an independent nonprofit research center and cross-national database of income, wealth, labor market, and demographic information of citizens from more than thirty countries; he directed the LIS project until 2006 and is now director emeritus. His most recent book is Wealth and Welfare States: Is America a Laggard or Leader? *(with Irwin Garfinkel and Lee Rainwater) (Oxford University Press 2010).*

Irwin Garfinkel is the Mitchell I. Ginsberg Professor of Contemporary Urban Problems and codirector of the Columbia Population Research Center at Columbia University. A social worker and an economist by training, he has authored or coauthored more than 180 scientific articles and twelve books on poverty, income transfers, program evaluation, single-parent families and child support, and the welfare state. His research on child support influenced legislation in Wisconsin and other states, the U.S. Congress, Great Britain, Australia, and Sweden. He is currently the coprincipal investigator of the Fragile Families and Child Wellbeing study. His most recent book is Wealth and Welfare States: Is America a Laggard or Leader? *(with Timothy M. Smeeding and Lee Rainwater) (Oxford University Press 2010).*

Ronald B. Mincy is Maurice V. Russell Professor of Social Policy and Social Work Practice, coprincipal investigator of the Fragile Families and Child Wellbeing study, a faculty member of the Columbia Population Research Center, and director of the School of Social Work's Center for Research on Fathers, Children and Family Well-Being at Columbia University. His research interests include economic and social mobility, child support, income security policy, responsible fatherhood, low-wage labor markets, and urban poverty. He is a member of the MacArthur Network on the Family and the Economy. He is also an advisory board member for the National Poverty Center, University of Michigan; Technical Work Group for the Building Strong Families and Community Healthy Marriage Initiatives; the African American Healthy Marriage Initiative; Transition to Fatherhood, Cornell University; the National Fatherhood Leaders Group; the Longitudinal Evaluation of the Harlem Children's Zone; and the Economic Mobility Project, Pew Charitable Trusts.

TABLE 1
Percentage of Young Men Who Are Fathers by Education
and Percentage of Fathers Who Earn Less than $20,000

	By Age 22	By Age 30
All	21	56
Less than high school	38	73
High school degree only[a]	32	64
Bachelor's degree and higher	3	38
Fathers earning less than $20,000	—	62

SOURCE: Callie Langton from 2002 NSFG (for this volume; 2010).
NOTE: Dash indicates data were not available.
a. Includes GED holders.

mothers' lifetime, with 2.6 children per woman in the 1960–1964 birth cohort (see Table 2). High school graduates with no additional education have a total of 1.9 children per woman and begin motherhood and fatherhood only a year or two later than dropouts. This is in contrast to the college educated, who have many fewer births (1.6 per woman) and at older ages, and a growing fraction (26 percent of this cohort) are likely not to parent children at all. Taking into account the number of women in each of these categories, we find that 48 percent of all births in the United States to this cohort were to mothers with a high school education or less by age 40. In the beginning of the twenty-first-century economy then, almost half of all kids are being raised by at least one parent with a low educational background and a poor expected economic future.

Social and Economic Forces Facing Young Fathers: The Perfect Storm

At least four major forces help to shape social and economic outcomes for young men who are fathers and for their partners and children: employment and earnings prospects; multiple-partner fertility; incarceration; and public policy, especially as it is reflected in the income support system and the child support system. We briefly review these factors to set the context for our volume, before moving to our introduction of the articles.

Undereducated youth and the labor market

Even for men with full-time work, median earnings for 16- to 24-year-olds fell by 19 percent between 1979 and 2008 to $461 a week; and for 25- to 34-year-olds, median earnings fell to less than $700 per week. But only about 20 percent of low-educated men had regular full-time work in 2008. If the poverty line for a family of three is considered the minimal amount needed to begin a family, a man

TABLE 2

Birth Patterns of Women and Median Age at First Birth for Men and for Women by
Level of Education, Women in 1960–1964 Cohort Who Are Observed in 2004

Level of Education	Percentage with First Birth by Age 25[a]	Percentage with First Birth by Age 40[a]	Average Number of Children Born by Age 40[a]	Median Age at First Birth[b]		Completed Fertility: Percent of All Children Born[a]
				Women	Men	
Dropouts	78	86	2.6	19	22	16
HS grads[c]	64	83	1.9	21	23	32
Some college	49	81	1.8	23	24	28
College graduate	20	74	1.6	28	29	24

a. Data on age at first birth for women based on Ellwood, Wilde, and Batchelder (2009) using annual CPS files 1960–2004. Percentage of total children born, Ty Wilde, private e-mail correspondence (2009).
b. Callie Langton using 2002 NSFG (for this volume; 2010).
c. Includes GED holders.

needed a pretax income of $17,400 in 2008 to support a partner (wife) and a baby. Far less than half of younger men in our target group earn that much by age 30. Indeed, poverty rates among workers grew between 2007 and 2008 as employment, wages, and hours slipped during the recession. For individuals who worked at all during 2008, poverty rates grew from 5.7 to 6.4 percent; from 2008 to 2009, the percentage of these workers in poverty increased to 6.9 percent. The number rose mainly because the share of all workers who could not work full-time, year-round increased, and the rise in poverty among these workers went from 12.7 to 13.5 percent between 2007 and 2008 (Acs 2009; Smeeding et al. 2010) and from 13.5 to 14.5 percent between 2008 and 2009 (DeNavas-Walt, Proctor, and Smith 2010). Almost all analysts expect a significant increase in poverty in 2010 and beyond (Monea and Sawhill 2010).

The forces of the recession and its effect on joblessness among young undereducated men are hard to overstate. The data shown in Figures 1 and 2 indicate changes in employment for various education and age groups from the fourth quarter of 2007 through the third quarter of 2009 (Engemann and Wall 2010). Overall employment fell by 4.7 percentage points over this period. Men, single persons, and minorities all lost employment to a much larger degree (6.3 to 7.0 percentage points). Employment fell most precipitously for the youngest workers (ages 16 to 24, the majority of whom were not in school), while employment actually *rose* by 4.0 percent for those over age 55 (no doubt a reaction to the capital market recession) (see Figure 1). Employment also fell most for workers who were high school dropouts (a 7.5 percentage point drop) and those with a high school diploma only (a 6.8 percentage point drop). Employment for college graduates and those with higher degrees also actually ticked up by 0.4 percentage points over this period (see Figure 2). The recession has therefore been hardest

FIGURE 1
Employment Changes by Age Group, 2007 (Q4) to 2009 (Q3)

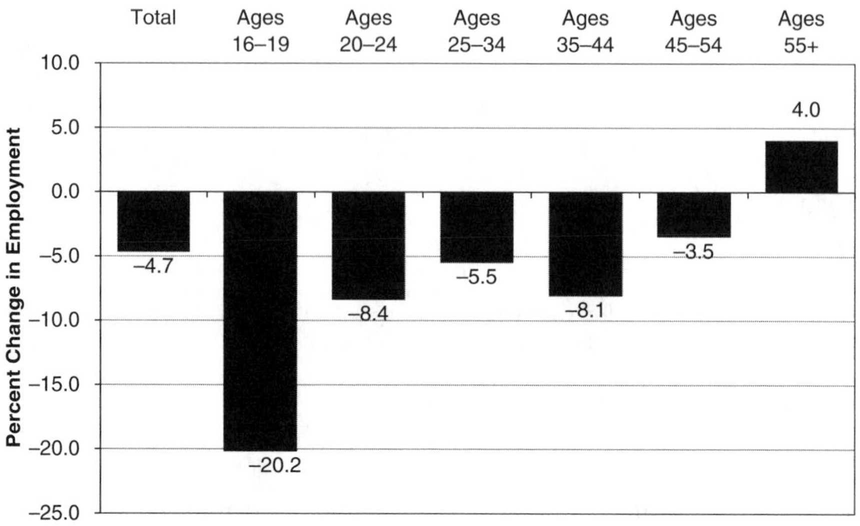

SOURCE: Engemann and Wall (2010).

on young undereducated men, especially minorities. More than 40 percent of black teens and more than 30 percent of young black men ages 16 to 24 were officially unemployed in 2009 and 2010, and that does not count those who have given up on finding work and dropped out of the labor force (Sum et al., this volume; Peck 2010). Unemployment rates for young undereducated men are higher now than they were in the Great Depression—the rates stood at nearly 30 percent in December 2009. Long-term unemployment is at an all-time high, with 46 percent of the unemployed out of work six months or longer; and it has reached nearly every segment of the population, but some have been particularly hard-hit. The typical long-term unemployed worker is a white man with a high school education or less (Murray 2010).

In summary, young undereducated men face both long-term structural issues and cyclical recession-related losses. Structurally, the economy is changing and penalizing lower- and middle-skilled, less-educated male workers, especially younger ones who need training and retraining to be successful (Autor and Dorn 2009a, 2009b; Autor 2010; Goldin and Katz 2008; Smeeding et al. 2010). These structural factors are further compounded by the recession with excessively high unemployment and underemployment, especially high among low-educated younger men who are at the end of the labor market queue and whose job prospects are unlikely to improve greatly within the next five years, leading to fears of a new "disconnected" jobless underclass (Rampell 2010; Bell and Blanchflower 2010).

FIGURE 2

Employment Changes by Education Level, 2007 (Q4) to 2009 (Q3)

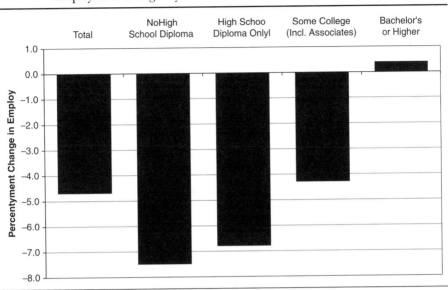

SOURCE: Engemann and Wall (2010).

Incarceration

There exist no national estimates for fathers ever in prison by age and education, but the data we do have is extremely suggestive. The cumulative risk of imprisonment grows steadily for all types of men, and at all levels of education, for men observed in 1979, 1989, 1999, and 2004 (Pew Charitable Trusts 2010). By age 30, more than half of all black men, and more than 25 percent of other men, all of whom are high school dropouts, will have been in prison, on parole, or on probation at least once. For all non–college attendees (including high school graduates and GEDs), the fractions ever in prison or jail are up to 30 percent of all black men (Western and Wildeman 2010, Table 1).

More than half of state prisoners and almost two-thirds of prisoners in federal penitentiaries in 2007 had children under the age of 18 (Glaze and Maruschak 2009). Many of these inmates (42 percent of male inmates with children and 60 percent of female inmates with children) lived with their minor children prior to their incarceration. Among those children born in 1990, one in four black children, compared with one in twenty-five white children, had a father in prison by the time the child was age 14. The risk is even more concentrated among black children whose parents are high school dropouts; fully half of these children had a father in prison, compared with one in fourteen white children with parents who dropped out (Wildeman 2009).

Looking at these three forces together is difficult, but again, the facts we do have are highly suggestive. If two-thirds to three-quarters of low-educated (i.e., high school degree or less, including GED) men are fathers by age 30, and if incarceration rates (ever incarcerated) are 28 percent overall, then at least a fifth of all young fathers will have been incarcerated, which means that they will face severe hurdles in the job market, in parenting, and in supporting their children. Furthermore, most low-educated young men who have children with a young, undereducated mother do so outside of marriage, in unstable relationships, *and* with more than one partner by age 30 (see below). These numbers are much higher for black men.

Multiple-partner fertility

Today, more than 40 percent of all live births are out of wedlock (28 percent for non-Hispanic whites, 72 percent for non-Hispanic blacks, and 51 percent for Hispanics according to Hamilton, Martin, and Ventura 2009). And the majority of first births before age 25 now occur outside of marriage (58 percent of all first births for men; higher for minorities).[3] The chances an unmarried biological father and mother will go on to have a child with different partners, and thus give their child a half-sibling (one or more children with another partner), are 50 to 65 percent, and are likely higher once completed fertility is observed (Cancian, Meyer, and Cook forthcoming; Carlson and Furstenberg 2006). Indeed, evidence from the Fragile Families and Child Wellbeing study (a sample of urban births in the late 1990s) indicates that in 59 percent of unmarried couples, either the mother or the father *already* has a child by another partner at the time of the focal birth, compared with 21 percent of married couples who were in such a situation (Carlson and Furstenberg 2006). By the fifth year of the study, the number of couples who had at least one child with another partner was up to 75 percent.[4] In the 2002 NSFG, which covers the entire population, nearly a third of all fathers under age 25—47 percent of black fathers in that group—had children with multiple partners.[5] Moreover, these young men are highly likely to have additional children with other partners as they age. Based on this same dataset, more than one-third of poor black men ages 35 to 44 report having had children with two or more mothers, and 16 percent report children with three or more mothers (Guzzo and Furstenberg 2007). And clearly these are underestimates as they are for men only (excluding multiple-partner fertility among women). The results for fathers' relationships and involvement in their children's lives are extremely disheartening (Tach, Mincy, and Edin 2010). Research also suggests that complex family structures are more likely for children of parents who are younger or have low earnings and for those in larger urban areas. Children who have half-siblings on their mothers' side are also more likely to have half-siblings on their fathers' side, and vice versa, contributing to very complex family structures—and potential child support arrangements—for some children (Cancian, Meyer, and Cook forthcoming).

Raising a child early on in life, before finishing education and finding a job or a career, is difficult enough when one man and one woman are involved in a stable relationship and have one or more of their own children. But when the competing needs of other partners, parents, and children are thrown into the mix, the situation becomes even bleaker and far less stable. And our public policies have not yet adjusted to this phenomenon.

Policy

Public income support policy in the United States has more or less ignored young unmarried men and fathers for several decades. And when policy does touch their lives, it is usually in the form of a court-issued child support order announcing that they are in arrears for child support owed, rather than a hand up with earnings adequacy (e.g., a larger single-person Earned Income Tax Credit [EITC], as in Edelman et al. 2009). Moreover, child support arrears build up when unemployment or incarceration reduces earnings to zero. Absent young fathers (those not living with their children on a regular basis) are not eligible for the EITC even when they pay their child support. But up to 65 percent of their legal earnings or tax refunds can be garnisheed for child support (Haskins and Sawhill 2009).

The American Recovery and Reinvestment Act (ARRA) of 2009 and further legislation has extended unemployment insurance (UI) to up to 99 weeks and beyond for the long-term unemployed (with higher benefit levels, income tax breaks for UI, and generous health insurance subsidies to maintain the most recent employer's health insurance according to Burtless 2009). But unemployed men under age 30 make up 39 percent of all men who are unemployed but only 20 percent of all UI recipients. Therefore, two-thirds of all young unemployed men missed out on more than $120 billion in UI aid in 2009 and a greater amount in 2010. Indeed, the only income support program generally available to help younger single men is the Supplemental Nutrition Assistance Program (SNAP) or food stamps.

Summary

A perfect storm of adverse events is now being experienced by younger under-educated men, their children, and the mothers of their children. The Great Recession of 2008 to 2010 has severely limited legitimate work opportunities, reflecting longer-term structural as well as cyclical employment issues. High rates of incarceration further limit job opportunities and keep fathers from their children. Most men (and women) who have children early on in life out of wedlock have at least one more child with another partner, and marriage rates are low while divorce rates are subsequently high. Public policy allows child support obligations to build while fathers are in jail or out of work. Few income maintenance programs serve this population. As a result of all these forces, young men are suffering rising poverty; their families are extremely unstable; and these fathers, mothers, and children are in desperate economic and social situations. In this context, the articles in our volume deepen the description of these situations and offer hope for policy changes to help these men and their families.

Articles in the Volume

Descriptions of young fathers' lives

The first four articles in our volume more clearly illustrate these themes by describing economic and family life for young fathers. They outline the economic status of low-income men and fathers, paying attention to the social context in which they live, as well as how they fare as fathers and in relationships with partners, children, and families. These articles help us to understand the intricacies of low-skill employment, low pay, and unstable families and how they, in total, affect fathers, partners, and children.

Andrew Sum, along with Ishwar Khatiwada, Joseph McLaughlin, and Sheila Palma, contribute a cleverly titled article, "No Country for Young Men," where they carefully establish how the economic fortunes of the young have diverged substantially since the 1970s, especially for young adult men without postsecondary degrees who are not living with their families. In fact, a number of policy monographs on the deteriorating labor market and economic conditions of these workers were written in the 1980s and 1990s, for instance the so-called *Forgotten Half* and *When Work Disappears* (William T. Grant Foundation 1988; Wilson 1996), warning the country of the need to invest in their education, training, and employment to help to restore broad-based prosperity. It turns out these pronouncements were about 15 to 20 years too early according to this article. Sum and colleagues find terrible labor market experiences for many groups of young inexperienced men in recent years. These labor market developments in turn have had a number of adverse impacts on young men's criminal justice behavior, on marital behavior, on family formation, and on out-of-wedlock childbearing among young women, all topics addressed in detail later in this volume. A variety of actions on an array of macroeconomic and microeconomic fronts will likely be needed to bolster the employment, wages, earnings, and marriage prospects of the nation's young men. Without such sustained improvements in their real earnings, the future outlook for these young workers, young families, and their children is quite bleak.

Lawrence Berger and Callie Langton next review the existing literature on young disadvantaged fathers' involvement with children from the fathers' point of view. They first outline the predominant theoretical perspectives regarding fathers' involvement among resident (married and cohabiting) biological fathers, resident social fathers (romantic partners of unrelated children's mothers), and nonresident biological fathers. They also present a brief discussion of the ways in which fathers contribute to child rearing. Finally, they describe the socioeconomic characteristics of men who enter fatherhood at a young age, highlighting that they tend to be economically disadvantaged, and they review the empirical research on both antecedents of fathers' involvement and patterns of involvement across types of fathers. They find that younger, less advantaged, and unmarried fathers are less involved with their children than are older, more advantaged fathers and those who are (or had been) married to their children's mother. In addition, whereas most prior work has found that resident biological fathers are more involved with children than resident social fathers, recent evidence from the Fragile Families and Child Wellbeing study, a sample of relatively disadvantaged families, suggests considerable investments on the part of (particularly married) social fathers.

Laura Tach and Kathryn Edin provide insight into the romantic partnerships of disadvantaged men using recently available data, revealing still higher levels of instability and complexity, but also of commitment, than previously understood. They explore the relationship dynamics between young disadvantaged men and their partners, finding that these men are often involved in casual romantic relationships that result in pregnancy. When this happens, most men remain involved with the mother, expressing optimism about the future and a commitment to being involved in their children's lives. But then a series of forces work against these relationships, such as economic disadvantage, incarceration, conflict, and mistrust, which undermine their stability. Most of these partnerships end within several years after the birth. New romantic relationships begin shortly thereafter, creating complex family structures. Tach and Edin argue that, with our growing understanding of the presence of fathers in nonmarital households, policy-makers must adapt their policies to support, rather than undermine, these fragile unions.

Finally, Marcia Carlson and Katherine Magnuson review the literature on low-income fathers' influence on children. They argue that fathers ideally represent an important resource for children, by investing the time, money, and emotional support that contribute to healthy child development. As mothers are increasingly likely to be employed outside the home, fathers' roles have expanded from primarily that of a "breadwinner," who provides economic support, to multiple other roles. These roles include provision of additional caregiving as well as emotional support, provision of moral guidance and discipline, protection to ensure the safety of the child, coordination of the child's care and activities, and guidance to connect the child to their extended family and community members. With the broadening of paternal roles, there has been growing attention to how fathers affect child well-being. The cumulative evidence these authors uncover points to the benefits of high-quality father-child interaction and authoritative parenting, but this is more likely to occur within marriage and among middle-class parents.

In contrast, a number of other recent studies find that nonresident fathers' involvement (especially for those with infrequent contact) has essentially no effect on children's outcomes. Indeed, it is unclear whether fatherhood programs that encouraged paternal involvement generally would, in fact, benefit children. Carlson and Magnuson conclude that interventions and programs should strive to encourage nonresident fathers' positive and engaged parenting as opposed to merely increasing the quantity of time fathers spend with their children.

Commentaries

These four descriptive summaries of the evidence on young fathers are followed by three shorter, cross-cutting comments on culture (Al Young Jr.), race (Devah Pager), and family functioning and longer-term relationships (Frank Furstenberg).

Young reminds us that cultural differences across racial and ethnic lines help to describe and define the patterns of partnering and fathering that we see among low-income men. Pager notes that the social and economic progress of black men since the early 1980s has been relatively stagnant, and so poor prospects for low-income black men have consequences that extend well beyond those for the individuals themselves. These young men's fortunes affect the women they partner with and the children they father. Pager goes on to emphasize the relevance of race and incarceration in thinking through these important problems.

Furstenberg writes on family life among low-income men and their partners and children, drawing on his more than 40 years of research on this topic. He first distills what we have learned during the past several decades, particularly about the role of men in family formation and child rearing, before turning to the consequences of paternal involvement in its myriad forms. He argues that these consequences have only become more varied and intricate as family production has become de-standardized and exceedingly complex. He contends that the micro-level effects in the descriptive articles, important as they are, pale in comparison to the macro-level impacts that changing labor markets, marriage, and kinship practices are having on stratification in American society. He concludes that the prospects for improving family life for such groups are challenging, to say the least, and have become more so with the passage of time. Furstenberg also concludes that however difficult it is to increase human capital and reduce unplanned parenthood among disadvantaged children and youths, it is far more feasible to implement these policies than to accomplish the alternative approach of altering parenting practices within fragile families (see also Furstenberg 2010).

Policy papers

Following the commentaries, five policy papers focus on child support policy; school-to-work transitions, dropouts, and work training; incarceration; family functioning, relationships, and parenting; and income-support policy. In the first article, Maria Cancian, Daniel Meyer, and Eunhee Han write about child support when parents do not live together. The child support policy arena raises a complex set of questions about the relative rights and responsibilities of nonresident fathers and resident mothers and the role of government in regulating, or substituting for, parents' contributions to their children's support. The formal child support system, largely regulated by family law, articulates the expectations for the private financial support expected of nonresident fathers. Public income support programs, especially welfare (Temporary Assistance for Needy Families [TANF]), provide cash assistance, in-kind supports, and tax credits to poor children, primarily those living in single-mother homes. To a large extent, "private" and "public" child support have therefore been substitutes rather than complements.

Recent public policy changes have both strengthened the private child support system and reduced access to public support—welfare. Cancian, Meyer, and Han conclude that the current work-focused safety net, which aims to require and help to enable disadvantaged mothers to work, creates a context in which government should similarly require and help to enable all fathers, even those who are disadvantaged, to work and pay child support. However, a series of reforms are needed to make this a realistic expectation, given many fathers' limited employment options and the complex families of many disadvantaged parents.

Carolyn Heinrich and Harry Holzer write about how to improve education and employment prospects for disadvantaged young men. They begin with the phenomenon called "disconnection," by which low high school graduation rates and sharply declining employment rates among disadvantaged youths have led to an increasing number of young men who are disconnected from both school and work. They ask, What programs and policies might prevent these disconnections and improve educational and employment outcomes, particularly among young men? They review the evidence base on youth development policies for adolescents and young teens; programs seeking to improve educational attainment and employment for in-school youth; and programs that try to "reconnect" those who are out of school and frequently out of work, including public employment programs. They identify a number of programmatic strategies that are promising or even proven, based on rigorous evaluations, for disadvantaged youths with different circumstances. They conclude that policy efforts need to promote a range of approaches targeted explicitly to engage and reconnect youth with jobs, along with ongoing evaluation efforts to improve our understanding of what works, including which program components, and for whom.

Steven Raphael writes about incarceration and prison reentry issues. He observes that U.S. states and the federal government have increased the frequency with which incarceration is used to sanction criminal activity, and increased the length of the sentences imposed and ultimate time served for specific offenses. As a result of myriad sentencing policy changes and changes in postrelease supervision, the nation's overall incarceration rate has increased to an unprecedented level. For less-educated men, and especially less-educated minority men, the likelihood of serving prison time is extremely high, and the challenges faced by former inmates attempting to reenter noninstitutionalized society are vast. Many have tenuous housing arrangements. Most former inmates have poor job skills and face stigma associated with their criminal records. Many of these reentrants fail and are sent back to prison, often for violating the conditions of their supervised release but sometimes for the commission of new felony offenses.

Raphael discusses the reentry–policy challenges faced by an increasing number of low-skilled men who are released from prison each year. Low formal levels of schooling, low levels of accumulated labor market experience (in part due to cycling in and out of correctional institutions), and employer reluctance to hire former inmates are among these barriers. He further reviews the research pertaining to how employers view criminal records in screening job applicants. He reviews the existing evaluation literature on alternative models for aiding the reentry transition of former inmates. Transitional cash assistance, the use of reentry plans, traditional workforce development efforts, and transitional jobs for former inmates and their impacts on postrelease employment and recidivism highlight potentially fruitful policy options.

Virginia Knox, Philip Cowan, Carolyn Pape Cowan, and Elana Bildner assess policies that strengthen fatherhood and family relationships, noting that children whose parents have higher income and education levels are more likely to grow up in stable two-parent households than are their economically disadvantaged counterparts. These widening gaps in fathers' involvement in parenting and in the quality and stability of parents' relationships (including but not limited to marriage) may reinforce disparities in outcomes for the next generation. What can be done to level the playing field? Fatherhood programs have shown some efficacy at increasing child support payments, while relationship skills approaches have shown benefits for the couples' relationship quality, coparenting skills, fathers' engagement in parenting, and children's well-being. They conclude that the research evidence suggests that parents' relationship with each other should be a fundamental consideration in future programs aimed at increasing low-income fathers' involvement with their children.

Ron Mincy, Serena Klempin, and Heather Schmidt write the last article, on low-income men and noncustodial fathers, to highlight four key income-security policy areas where changes are needed to meet the challenge of getting disadvantaged fathers more involved with and supportive of their children. These include relaxation of payroll taxes, expanding the EITC, revamping unemployment insurance, and, most important, changing child support enforcement. Working together, these policies have contributed to increases in employment for young less-educated women and reductions in child poverty, but rarely have the joint implications for less-educated men been considered. They note that each strategy, including unemployment insurance, is predicated on work and sometimes faces a world without work for these men. The provisions of the ARRA are being used in part to increase employment among less-educated men, including nonresident fathers, but they are not enough to change the employment and earnings of disadvantaged men. Finally, they indicate responses needed not only by government, but also by the independent sector—through targeted philanthropy for related research and programming. Engagement by these critical actors will be necessary to make any income-support policy reforms work for young men.

Overall Summary

Most of all, young undereducated and disconnected men need help acquiring skills as well as finding and keeping jobs. As we know from experience, a strong macroeconomic employment policy leading to an era such as that experienced in the late 1990s would allow these men to more easily get and keep good jobs. Unfortunately, the length and depth of the Great Recession suggest that we will be a long way from full employment for many years to come, especially for undereducated younger men.

In the throes of such a poor economic situation, the policies we might adopt for young men are also tempered and shaped by the trade-offs they face. Our conference discussants, Martha Coven, Sheri Steisel, and David Pate, all pointed to difficult policy decisions by federal, state, and local actors whose fiscal resources are diminishing as needs rise. Policies that would extend income support to men may dull incentives to work. Greater public support for low-income women and children reduces the need for men to pay child support. Early-release programs may put public safety in danger. And for those young men who actually pay child support, the question of reimbursing the public sector or passing through benefits to mother and children arises. Forgiveness of arrears may increase the willingness of fathers to pay support, but it also may lead them to believe that future child support orders can be ignored. The discussants suggest that while fathers are a policy priority, additional support for their needs is likely to be both subjugated and deferred in the current policy environment. Because of space limitations, we were not able to focus on several additional important policy levers. These include broader-based education policies, including efforts to keep kids in school, and policies to avoid young fatherhood and motherhood (Smeeding and Carlson forthcoming).

In the end, we believe that public policy regarding disadvantaged young men and their families needs to be addressed directly and not neglected or subjugated. Such policies should emphasize increased employment, training, and education and spur on a more progressive incarceration policy for young offenders. In addition, better efforts to support the incomes and employment of young men would allow more of them to support their families and meet their child support obligations. And finally, we need programs that are effective in preventing young and unintended out-of-wedlock births as well as measures for dealing with consequences of bad decisions.

In this bleak fiscal environment, we must redouble our efforts to help young men who face difficult circumstances. Policy should provide more incentives and rewards for good behaviors and support the incomes of young men through employment and subsidies to make work pay; and most of all, it should try to maintain and strengthen relationships between fathers, mothers, and their children. The articles in this volume suggest both the desperate circumstances of young men and how far we are away from adequate social and economic support of the next generation of children, nearly half of whom are growing up in ever more desperate straits.

Notes

1. Callie Langton, 2002 NSFG and 1997 NLSY data runs conducted specifically for this volume (2010).
2. Ibid.
3. Ibid.
4. Marcia J. Carlson, Fragile Families data runs shared with the authors (2010).
5. Callie Langton, 2002 NSFG and 1997 NLSY data runs conducted specifically for this volume (2010).

References

Acs, Gregory. 2009. Poverty in the United States. Washington, DC: Urban Institute. Available from www.urban.org/UploadedPDF/901284_poverty_united_states.pdf.

Autor, David. 2010. The polarization of job opportunities in the U.S. labor market: Implications for employment and earnings. Paper prepared for the Center for American Progress and the Hamilton Project,
Brookings Institution. Washington, DC, April. Available from http://www.americanprogress.org/
issues/2010/04/pdf/job_polarization.pdf.

Autor, David H., and David Dorn. 2009a. Inequality and specialization: The growth of low-skill service jobs
in the United States. National Bureau of Economic Research Working Paper 15150, Cambridge, MA.
Available from www.nber.org/papers/w15150.pdf.

Autor, David H., and David Dorn. 2009b. "This job is getting old": Measuring changes in job opportunities
using occupational age structure. *American Economic Review* 99 (2): 45–51.

Bell, David, and David G. Blanchflower. 2010. Youth unemployment: Déjà vu? Institute for Labor
Working Paper 4705, Bonn, Germany. Available from http://ftp.iza.org/dp4705.pdf.

Burtless, Gary. April 2009. The "Great Recession" and redistribution: Federal antipoverty policies. *Fast
Focus*. Available from www.irp.wisc.edu/publications/fastfocus/pdfs/FF4-2009.pdf.

Cancian, Maria, Daniel R. Meyer, and Steven Cook. Forthcoming. The evolution of family complexity
from the perspective of nonmarital children. *Demography*.

Carlson, Marcia J., and Frank F. Furstenberg Jr. 2006. The prevalence and correlates of multipartnered
fertility among urban U.S. parents. *Journal of Marriage and Family* 68 (3): 718–32.

DeNavas-Walt, Carmen, Bernadette D. Proctor, and Jessica C. Smith. 2010. U.S. Census Bureau, Current
Population Reports, P60-238. *Income, poverty, and health insurance coverage in the United States:
2009*. Washington, DC: U.S. Government Printing Office.

Edelman, Peter, Mark Greenberg, Steve Holt, and Harry Holzer. 2009. *Expanding the EITC to help more
low-wage workers*. Washington, DC: Georgetown Center on Poverty, Inequality and Public Policy.
Available from www.stateeitc.com/pdf/Georgetown_ExpandingEITC_0902091.pdf.

Ellwood, David, Elizabeth T. Wilde, and Lily Batchelder. 2009. The mommy track divides: The impact of
childbearing on wages of women of differing skill levels. Russell Sage Foundation Social Inequality
Working Paper, New York, NY.

Engemann, Kristie M., and Howard J. Wall. 2010. The effects of recessions across demographic groups.
Federal Reserve Bank of St. Louis Review 92 (1): 1–26.

Fletcher, Jason, and Barbara Wolfe. 2010. The effects of teenage fatherhood on early outcomes. Available
from http://ssrn.com/abstract=1622084.

Furstenberg, Frank F. 2010. The challenges of finding causal links between family characteristics and
educational outcomes. Available from https://xteam.brookings.edu/rrac/Documents/outcomes
_furstenberg.pdf.

Glaze, Lauren E., and Laura M. Maruschak. 2009. *Parents in prison and their minor children*. Washington,
DC: U.S. Department of Justice, Office of Justice Programs. Available from http://bjsdata.ojp.usdoj.gov/
content/pub/pdf/pptmc.pdf (accessed 8 January 2010).

Goldin, Claudia, and Larry Katz. 2008. *The race between education and technology*. Cambridge, MA:
Harvard University Press.

Guzzo, Karen Benjamin, and Frank F. Furstenberg Jr. 2007. Multipartnered fertility among American
men. *Demography* 44:583–601.

Hamilton, Brady E., Joyce A. Martin, and Stephanie J. Ventura. 2009. *Births: Preliminary data for 2007*.
Hyattsville, MD: National Center for Health Statistics.

Haskins, Ron, and Isabel Sawhill. 2009. *Creating an opportunity society*. Washington, DC: Brookings
Institution Press.

Monea, Emily, and Isabel Sawhill. 2010. *An update to "Simulating the effect of the Great Recession on
poverty."* Washington, DC: Brookings Institution. Available from http://www.brookings.edu/
papers/2010/0916_poverty_monea_sawhill.aspx.

Murray, Sarah. 2 June 2010. Chronic joblessness bites deep: Long-term unemployment hits new high, cuts
across income levels, demographics. *Wall Street Journal*.

Peck, Don. March 2010. How a new jobless era will transform America. *The Atlantic Monthly*.

Pew Charitable Trusts. 2010. *Collateral costs: Incarceration's effect on economic mobility*. Washington,
DC: Pew Charitable Trusts.

Rampell, Catherine. 14 January 2010. A growing underclass. *New York Times*. Available from http://economix
.blogs.nytimes.com.

Smeeding, Timothy M., and Marcia J. Carlson. Forthcoming. Family change, public response: Social policy in an era of complex families. In *Social class and changing families in an unequal America*, eds. Marcia J. Carlson and Paula England. Stanford, CA: Stanford University Press.

Smeeding, Timothy M., Jeff E. Thompson, E. A. Levanon, and E. Burak. 2010. The changing dynamics of work, poverty, income from capital and income from earnings during the Great Recession. Stanford Poverty Conference on the Great Recession, June, Stanford University, Stanford, CA.

Tach, Laura, Ronald Mincy, and Kathryn Edin. 2010. Parenting as a package deal: Relationships, fertility, and nonresident father involvement among unmarried parents. *Demography* 47 (1): 181–204.

U.S. Bureau of Labor Statistics. National Longitudinal Survey of Youth, 1997. Available from www.bls.gov/nls.

U.S. Centers for Disease Control. National Survey of Family Growth, 2002. Available from http://www.cdc.gov/nchs/nsfg/nsfg_products.htm#cycle6.

Western, Bruce, and Christopher Wildeman. 2010. The black family and mass incarceration. *The Annals of the American Academy of Political and Social Science* 621 (1): 221–42.

Wildeman, Christopher. 2009. Parental imprisonment, the prison boom, and the concentration of childhood disadvantage. *Demography* 46 (2): 265–80.

William T. Grant Foundation. 1988. *The forgotten half: Pathways to success for America's youth and young families*. Washington, DC: William T. Grant Foundation.

Wilson, William Julius. 1996. *When work disappears: The world of the new urban poor*. New York, NY: Random House.

Substantive/Descriptive Surveys
of Fatherhood

No Country for Young Men: Deteriorating Labor Market Prospects for Low-Skilled Men in the United States

By
ANDREW SUM,
ISHWAR KHATIWADA,
JOSEPH McLAUGHLIN,
and
SHEILA PALMA

The labor market fate of the nation's male teens and young adults (ages 20–29) has deteriorated along most employment, weekly wages, and annual earnings dimensions in recent decades. The employment rates reached new post–World War II lows in 2009, with the less well educated faring the worst. The deterioration in the labor market well-being of these young men has had a number of adverse consequences on their social behavior. Less-educated young men, especially high school dropouts, are far more likely to be incarcerated than their peers in earlier decades. They are considerably less likely to be married and more likely to be absent fathers, with gaps in marriage rates across educational groups widening substantially since the 1970s. The decline in marriage among less-educated young adults, high assortative mating among younger married couples, and growing gaps in earnings across educational groups have contributed to a substantial widening in income and wealth disparities among the nation's young families.

Keywords: economic fortunes; young men; social impacts; male earnings

Changes in the economic well-being of workers and families in the United States have varied substantially both over time and across key demographic and socioeconomic subgroups since the end of the so-called "Golden Era" in 1973. Among the groups whose economic fortunes have diverged substantially from those of the Golden Era are young adult men without postsecondary degrees and their families. In the late 1980s, a number of policy monographs on the deteriorating labor market and economic conditions of these workers (the "forgotten half") and their families were produced, warning the country of the need to invest in their education, training, and employment to help to restore broad-based prosperity (William T. Grant Foundation 1988; Johnson and Sum 1987; National Center on Education and the Economy 1990; Ford Foundation 1989). Despite these warnings, few systematic public policy actions were undertaken in the 1980s or

DOI: 10.1177/0002716210393694

early 1990s to improve the labor market and income prospects of young workers or their families. A few policy initiatives were passed in the early years of the Clinton administration, including the School-to-Work Opportunities Act, which expired in 2000; and the expansion of the federal Earned Income Tax Credit (EITC) in 1993. By the mid-1990s, however, few positive outcomes for young workers or their families had taken place, and a new set of analyses called attention to the continued deterioration in the labor market situation of most members of the forgotten half and their families (Sum, Fogg, and Taggart 1996; Halperin 1998; Johnson, Sum, and Weill 1992/1994). Several of these reports referred to the "vanishing dreams" of America's young families.

From the mid-1990s through the end of the decade, the American economy performed quite strongly, with substantial gains in employment, a move to full employment in the nation's labor markets, and rising labor productivity and real

Andrew Sum is a professor of economics and director of the Center for Labor Market Studies at Northeastern University in Boston. He has authored or coauthored numerous articles, monographs, and books on regional, national, and state labor markets and on the labor market behavior and problems of young adults and the role of education, literacy, and training in influencing the labor market experiences of adults. Among his publications are the books Confronting the Youth Demographic Challenge *(Sar Levitan Center, John's Hopkins University 2000) and* State of the American Dream in Massachusetts *(The Massachusetts Institute for a New Commonwealth 2002); the book chapters "Young Workers, Young Families, and Child Poverty" in* Of Heart and Mind *(Upjohn Institute Press 1996) and* From Dreams to Dust *(Sar Levitan Center, John's Hopkins University 1996); the journal articles "The Case for a Young Adult Jobs Creation Program" in* Indicators: The Journal of Social Health *(2003), "The Great Age Twist in National Employment Rates" in* Challenge: The Magazine of Economic Affairs *(2005); and "The Wealth of the Nation's Young" in* Challenge: The Magazine of Economic Affairs *(2009).*

Ishwar Khatiwada is a senior research associate at the Center for Labor Market Studies at Northeastern University. He has authored and coauthored numerous research reports and monographs on U.S. labor market problems, poverty and wealth issues, and the economic and social costs of dropping out of high school. Among his publications are the reports Mass Economy: the Labor Supply and Our Economic Future *(MassINC 2006);* Mass Jobs: Meeting the Challenges of a Shifting Economy *(MassINC 2007); "Employment Prospects in Information Technology Jobs for Non–College Educated Adults" in* Challenge: The Magazine of Economic Affairs *(2007); and the article "The Wealth of the Nation's Young" in* Challenge: The Magazine of Economic Affairs *(2009).*

Joseph McLaughlin is a senior research associate at the Center for Labor Market Studies at Northeastern University. While at the center, he has researched youth labor market issues and problems and worked on program evaluations, including analyses of the employment and educational outcomes of school-to-work programs. He has coauthored "Historically Low Summer Employment: The Case for a New Youth Jobs Program" in Challenge: The Magazine of Economic Affairs *(2010) and "The 2007–2009 Recession's Effects on African-American Males" in* Communities & Banking *(2010).*

Sheila Palma is a senior administrator at the Center for Labor Market Studies at Northeastern University. She has coauthored many research reports on labor market experiences of young adults and teens.

wages. Most young workers and their families benefited considerably from these developments, which unfortunately came to an abrupt end in the early months of 2001 when the national economy entered a recession and then underwent a nearly two-year-long jobless recovery. Even during the labor market recovery from the late summer of 2003 through the fall of 2007, few teens and young adult males without college degrees (ages 20 to 29) benefited much from the expansion; and during the Great Recession of 2007 to 2009, they experienced steep declines in their employment and earnings opportunities. No demographic group of American workers has been as adversely affected by the recession as young adult men under 30 years old, with all educational and racial/ethnic groups experiencing historically severe labor market difficulties, but less-educated males have fared the worst.

This article focuses on the changing labor market fate of young male workers (16 to 29 years old) over the past few decades in the United States and especially since the end of the labor market boom in 2000. It also highlights associations between this group's labor market experiences and their marital behavior, out-of-wedlock fathering, criminal justice experiences, and the level and distribution of young family incomes. Our story begins with a careful review of key employment developments among various age, educational attainment, and racial/ethnic groups of younger males over the past decade and provides comparisons with findings for earlier decades. This is followed by an analysis of the weekly wage and annual earnings experiences of young men since 1979, with an emphasis on changes in real wages and earnings by educational attainment and racial/ethnic groups.

The Extraordinary Decline in the Employment Rates of Male Teens and Young Adults since 2000

During the national labor market boom years from 1993 to 2000, male teens and young adults (20 to 29 years old) in all major racial/ethnic and most educational attainment groups experienced rising employment rates, lower unemployment rates, and improving real weekly earnings and annual earnings. Since the end of the labor market boom in 2000, however, young males have fared quite poorly in the labor market (Edelman, Holzer, and Offner 2006; Mincy 2005; Sum, McLaughlin, and Palma 2009a; Sum, Mangum, and Taggart 2002). Young adults experienced above average employment declines in the recession of 2001 and in the largely jobless recovery from November 2001 to late summer 2003. Male teens obtained limited to no employment gains during the jobs recovery from late summer 2003 through late fall 2007, and since then have incurred severe job losses in the Great Recession of 2007 to 2009.

Of all the male age groups, the nation's male teens (ages 16 to 19) have experienced a massive depression in their labor market conditions since 2000 (Sum, McLaughlin, and Palma 2009a, 2009b). In the first six months of 2009, the

FIGURE 1

Trends in the January to June Employment Rates for Male Teens
(16 to 19 Years Old) in the United States, Selected Years between
1978 and 2009 (Seasonally Adjusted, in Percentages)

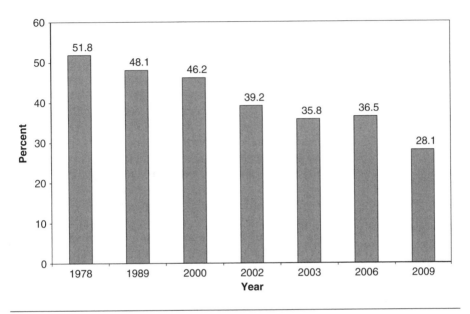

SOURCE: U.S. Department of Labor, Bureau of Labor Statistics, "Labor Force Statistics: Current Population Survey," available from www.bls.gov.

employment rate of the nation's male teens fell to 28.1 percent, the lowest employment rate by far for male teens during the first six months of any year over the past 61 years (see Figure 1). At no time in the country's entire post–World War II history had the January to June employment rate of male teens ever fallen below 30 percent, and at no time prior to 2002 had the January to June employment rate of male teens fallen below 40 percent. In the first half of 2000, 46 percent of the nation's male teens were employed, as were 48 percent of those near the peak of the cyclical boom in 1989 and 52 percent of those in 1978, when federal job creation programs for teens under the Comprehensive Employment and Training Act (CETA), the Youth Employment and Demonstration Projects Act, and CETA public service employment programs were at their peak enrollment levels (Hahn and Lerman 1982). The employment rate of male teens in the first six months of 2009 was only slightly more than one-half as high as it was in 1978 and 18 percentage points below its value in the first half of 2000. This truly constitutes a labor market depression for male teens in the United States, including both in-school and out-of-school youths, whose transitions to the labor market are being significantly delayed.

Male teens do not only work far less in any given month than they used to, but they also work less on a year-round basis. A growing number of male teens in recent years report being jobless all year, especially blacks, low-income youths, and high school dropouts—the groups most in need of substantial employment opportunities. This work experience is a form of human capital investment that affects future employability, wages, and earnings. The steep loss in cumulative work experience during their early teen years, especially among those not going on to obtain a four-year degree, will have adverse effects on their employment and earnings positions as they reach their late teens and early 20s (Bartik 2001; Sum, Fogg, and Mangum 2000; Zhao 2008). Teen employment also is highly path-dependent; that is, the employment experiences of teens today will influence their work experiences in future time periods (Sum, Taggart, and Khatiwada 2007; Sum, Khatiwada, and McLaughlin 2008). The costs of reduced work among male teens today are, thus, not limited to the present. They will also reduce their employment, wages, and earnings in the future; lower labor productivity; and reduce the future real output potential of the U.S. economy. Jobless, economically disadvantaged male teens are more likely to drop out of high school, less likely to attend college, and more likely to become involved with the criminal justice system (Sum, Fogg, and Mangum 2000). Today's American male teens have become a lost generation, frequently off the radar screens of the nation's and states' economic policy-makers.

Employment rates of the nation's male teens have declined considerably over the past nine years in each major racial/ethnic group, but large gaps in employment/population (E/P) ratios persist across these different racial/ethnic groups. During the January to June period of 2009, the employment rates of male teens have ranged from a low of slightly under 14 percent for black males to 24 percent among Hispanics and to a high of 30 percent among white males. Within each group, out-of-school dropouts fare much worse than their peers with a high school diploma; and among high school students, low-income youths are the least likely to be employed.

The ability of male teens in nearly all racial/ethnic groups and in all household income groups to obtain some employment during the year declined considerably between 2000 and 2007. The fraction of male teens with any paid employment during the year fell from slightly more than 54 percent in 2000 to 41 percent in 2007. The reductions in these employment rates ranged from under 3 percentage points among Asians to 14 percentage points among black and white teens. Only one of four black male teens reported any paid work during 2007, before the national recession got under way.

The declines in the work experience rates of male teens were quite substantial in every household income group but were particularly severe among those youths living in low-middle- to middle-income families with annual incomes between $20,000 and $80,000. The incidence of paid work experience among male teens in 2007 varied markedly across household income groups, rising steadily and strongly with household income until the very top of the income distribution was reached. The work experience rates of male teens in 2007 ranged from a low of 28 percent among youths in the lowest income households (under $20,000) to a high of 54 percent among those residing in families with an annual income between $100,000 and $150,000. Taking both the racial/ethnic characteristics of those male teens and their household incomes into account yields even wider disparities in their work experience rates. In 2007, they ranged from a low of 20 percent among black male teens in the lowest-income families to 40 percent among white teens in low-middle-income families to highs of 55 to 57 percent among Hispanic and white male teens in upper-middle- to high-income families ($80,000 to $150,000).

While male teens have experienced the equivalent of a great depression from 2000 to 2009, the steep drops in male employment rates since 2000 unfortunately have not been confined to teens. The employment rates of young male adults ages 20 to 34 years old also have plummeted sharply to historic lows during the first six months of 2009 (see Table 1). Among 20- to 24-year-old men, the average E/P ratio during the first six months of 2009 was only 65.1 percent versus the 76.8 percent average during the same six-month period in 2000, a drop of nearly 12 percentage points. Among 25- to 34-year-old males, the E/P ratio in the January to June period of 2009 averaged only 81 percent, down by nearly 10 percentage points from 2000.

To place these comparatively low E/P ratios for these three groups of young males into historical perspective, we compared them with the values for the same six-month period for every year from 1948 to 2009. For each of these three age groups of men, their employment rates during the first six months of 2009 were the lowest in post–World War II history. The employment rate of the nation's 20- to 24-year-old males had never fallen below 70 percent during the first six months of any year until 2009. The average E/P ratio of 65 percent in the first six months of that year marked an overwhelming, new historical low. Among 20- to 24-year-old males, blacks have fared the worst in the labor market, and both high school dropouts and high school graduates with no postsecondary schooling have incurred very steep declines in their employment rates. Among 25- to 34-year-old males, a major part of their steep declines in employment since 2000 have been felt in the past two years. Their all-time previous low employment rates were established during 1982 and 1983 during and shortly after the very severe national recessions of 1981 to 1982 and in 2003. Among these 25- to 34-year-old males, job losses have been particularly steep among those 25 to 29 years old, those with no completed years of postsecondary schooling, and those in blue-collar occupations.

In contrast to the very sharp reduction in the employment rates of male teens, 20- to 24-year-olds, and 25- to 34-year-olds since 2000, older males (55+) experienced substantive gains in their employment rates over this same nine-year period, rising from 39 percent in 2000 to nearly 44 percent in the first six months of this

TABLE 1

Comparisons of the January to June 2000 and 2009 Employment/Population
Ratios of Males, Ages 16–19, 20–24, and 25–34 and the Ranking of their 2009
E/P Ratios from 1948–2009 (Seasonally Adjusted in Percentages)

Age Group	January–June 2000	January–June 2009	Percentage Point Change, 2000–2009	Rank of January–June 2009 E/P Ratio	Years of 2nd, 3rd, and 4th Lowest Rankings
16–19	46.1	28.2	−17.9	Lowest in 61 years	2008, 2005, 2007
20–24	76.8	65.1	−11.7	Lowest in 61 years	1983, 2008, 2005
25–34	90.5	81.0	−9.5	Lowest in 61 years	1983, 1982, 2003
25–29	88.8	77.8	−11.0	Lowest in 61 years	
30–34	91.3	82.9	−8.4	Lowest in 61 years	
55+	39.1	43.5	+4.4	Highest since 1980	

SOURCE: U.S. Bureau of Labor Statistics, Current Population Survey, National Employment Series; tabulations by authors.
NOTE: E/P ratios for 25- to 29- and 30- to 34-year-olds are not seasonally adjusted.

year. Recent research by the authors on the employment rates of 16- to 20-year-olds in the United States has revealed that there has been some displacement of young workers in jobs by the age 60 and older male population in recent years. The higher the relative increase in the size of the 60 and older male labor force in a state, the lower the expected probability of young male adults being employed.

The Great Recession of 2007 to 2009 has substantially reduced demand for labor in most of the occupations and industries in which males with no substantial postsecondary schooling find employment. In addition, young males, especially teens and 20- to 24-year-olds, have faced severe competition for available jobs from older native born males (60+); young less-educated immigrants, including many undocumented immigrants (Borjas 2003; Camorata 1998; Jaeger 1998; Smith 2007); and their slightly older male counterparts (24 to 29), including recent college graduates who have faced growing problems in finding jobs in the traditional college labor market. In the first six months of 2009, less than half of all male bachelor degree holders age 25 and under were employed in a college labor market job. Among young black and Hispanic male college graduates, the ratio of those with college labor market jobs was only one-third. Bumping down the hiring queue of these somewhat older and better-educated males has further curtailed job opportunities for younger, less well-educated males in the United States.

The Deteriorating Employment Picture among 20- to 29-Year-Old Males by Racial/Ethnic Group and Educational Attainment

To identify the degree to which the adverse labor market conditions for young adult men have affected employment opportunities for racial/ethnic and educational subgroups of 20- to 24-year-old and 25- to 29-year-old men, we compared their employment rates in 2000, 2008, and the first six months of 2009.

The magnitudes of the declines in the employment rates of 20- to 24-year-old men over the 2000 to 2009 period were in the 12 to 13 percentage point range for black, Hispanic, and white males; while Asian men experienced a more moderate 7 percentage point decline (see Table 2). Across educational groups, the job losses were far more considerable among those men with no postsecondary schooling. The E/P ratio of male high school dropouts fell by more than 18 percentage points, and that of high school graduates dropped by 15 percentage points. In contrast, young men with a bachelor's or higher degree experienced a more modest but still substantial drop of 7 percentage points in their employment rate, but their "mal-employment" (working outside of one's field of education or training) problems also worsened.

Estimates of the 2009 E/P ratios for 20- to 24-year-old males by educational attainment and racial/ethnic group varied quite considerably. They ranged from a low of 31 percent among black high school dropouts, to highs of 80 percent to 81 percent for white and Hispanic males with one to three years of college, to nearly 87 percent for white males with a bachelor's or higher academic degree. Among black and white males, employment rates rose steadily and strongly with their level of formal schooling, while the gains from more formal schooling were substantially smaller among young Hispanic males. The relatively high employment rate of young, male Hispanic dropouts was heavily influenced by the employment behavior of young Hispanic immigrants who have a very high rate of employment, considerably surpassing that of native-born Hispanics. Nearly 80 percent of immigrant male, Hispanic dropouts were employed versus only 56 percent of native born Hispanic dropouts.

Time trends in the employment rates of educational attainment groups of 25- to 29-year-old males over the 2000 to 2009 period are displayed in Table 3. Overall, the E/P ratio of these young men fell from just under 89 percent in 2000 to only 77.6 percent in 2009, a drop of more than 11 percentage points. Members of all four racial/ethnic groups experienced very sharp reductions in their employment rates, but Hispanic (–13 percentage points) and black males (–18 percentage points) fared the worst.

The declines in employment rates of these 25- to 29-year-old males varied far more widely across the five educational groups, similar to the findings for 20- to 24-year-old males. The percentage point reductions in the E/P ratios for these men in their mid- to late-20s declined steadily and strongly as they moved up the educational ladder. The declines ranged from highs of 17 percentage points

TABLE 2
Employment Rates of 20- to 24-Year-Old Males in the United States by Racial/Ethnic
Group and Educational Attainment, 2000, 2008, and 2009 (in Percentages)

Group	2000[a]	2008[a]	2009[b]	Percentage Point Change, 2000–2009
All	76.6	69.2	64.0	−12.6
Racial/ethnic group				
Asian	61.4	55.8	54.6	−6.7
Black, not Hispanic	61.4	56.5	49.1	−12.3
Hispanic	82.3	74.7	69.8	−12.5
White, not Hispanic	79.2	71.4	66.4	−12.8
Educational attainment				
College student	57.3	51.4	49.2	−8.1
High school dropout	73.6	62.6	55.2	−18.4
High school graduate	83.6	76.1	68.5	−15.1
13–15 years of schooling, including associate degree holder	89.1	83.1	78.4	−10.7
Bachelor's degree or higher	91.4	87.8	84.4	−7.0

SOURCE: U.S. Census Bureau, Current Population Survey, Monthly Household Surveys, 2000, 2008, and January–June 2009, public use files; tabulations by authors.
a. Findings for 2000 and 2008 are annual averages.
b. 2009 data are for January–June only.

TABLE 3
Employment Rates of 25- to 29-Year-Old Males in the United States by Racial/Ethnic
Group and Educational Attainment, 2000, 2008, and 2009 (in Percentages)

Group	2000[a]	2008[a]	2009[b]	Percentage Point Change, 2000–2009
All	88.9	83.6	77.6	−11.3
Racial/ethnic group				
Asian	85.9	82.0	76.4	−9.5
Black, not Hispanic	79.0	71.6	61.3	−17.7
Hispanic	90.4	86.1	77.7	−13.0
White, not Hispanic	90.7	85.5	87.2	−9.5
Educational attainment				
High school dropout, no GED	83.0	74.5	66.0	−17.0
High school graduate/GED	87.8	81.8	73.2	−14.6
1–3 years of college, including associate's degree	89.6	84.1	79.2	−10.4
Bachelor's degree	92.6	90.1	86.8	−5.8
Master's or higher degree	91.8	87.7	87.1	−4.7

SOURCE: U.S. Census Bureau, Current Population Survey, Monthly Household Surveys, 2000, 2008, and January–June 2009, public use files; tabulations by authors.
a. Data for 2000 and 2008 are annual averages.
b. The 2009 data are for January–June only.

among high school dropouts, to 15 percentage points among high school graduates with no completed years of postsecondary schooling, to lows of 5 to 6 percentage points for those men holding a bachelor's or higher degree. An analysis of the full array of E/P ratios for 25- to 29-year-old men in 2009 revealed that they ranged from a low of 39 percent for black high school dropouts; to 76 percent for Asian, white, and Hispanic male high school graduates; to highs of 88 percent to 92 percent among black and white males with a master's or higher degree. Among whites and blacks, the gaps in employment rates between those with advanced college degrees and high school dropouts were 27 and 53 percentage points, respectively.

Trends in the Real Weekly Earnings of Full-Time Employed Young Adults (Ages 16 to 34) between 1979 and 2008

One of the most important measures of the labor market well-being of employed young adults is their real (inflation-adjusted) weekly earnings (Pond et al. 2002; Sum, Fogg, and Mangum 2000; Johnson, Sum, and Fogg 1996). Widespread growth in real weekly and annual earnings is needed to boost the standard of living of young workers and their families and to achieve key antipoverty goals. The monthly Current Population Survey (CPS) household surveys that serve as the source of the monthly national data on the number of employed and unemployed adults in the United States also collect information on the weekly earnings of both part-time and full-time employed wage and salary workers 16 and older. We focus here on changes in the median real weekly earnings of those young adults between the ages of 16 to 24 and 25 to 34 who were full-time wage and salary workers. The median weekly earnings of workers is that level of earnings that divides the entire weekly earnings distribution of workers into two equal halves.

Our analysis of the weekly earnings data will begin with 1979 near the peak of the 1975 to 1980 business cycle. For men younger than 25, the year 1973 represented a historical peak in their real weekly and annual earnings, especially those without college degrees. The median weekly and annual earnings of young adult men, including high school dropouts and high school graduates with no postsecondary schooling, grew steadily during the 1960s. Toward the end of the 1960s and in the early 1970s, weekly earnings growth slowed as greater numbers of the baby boom generation entered the job market. Despite this increase in labor supply, the real weekly earnings of full-time employed young men still grew by 8 percent between 1967 and 1973. If this moderate rate of real weekly earnings growth of young men had been maintained between 1973 and 2008, their median weekly earnings in 2008 would have been $940 rather than the actual $461 that prevailed that year.

Unfortunately, since 1979, the median real weekly earnings of full-time employed young men have typically declined, with the exception of the labor market boom years from 1995 to 2000, when real weekly earnings grew nearly steadily (Sum, Fogg, and Taggart 1996; Ford Foundation 1989; Levy 1989). Between 1979 and 1996, the median real weekly earnings of young men (younger than 25) fell steeply from $570 to $420, a decline of $150 or 26 percent.

During the second half of the 1990s, as payroll job growth strengthened, labor productivity improved, and the national labor market moved to full employment, young men experienced strong growth in their real median weekly earnings. Over the 1996 to 2001 time period, the median real weekly earnings of young men increased from $420 to $476, a gain of $56 or nearly 13 percent over this five-year period. Rising labor productivity and near full-employment conditions in the nation's labor markets allowed workers to capture a greater share of the productivity gains and steadily boosted the real weekly earnings of young men for the first time since the late 1960s and early 1970s. Unfortunately, since the economic downturn of 2001, the median real weekly earnings of young adults have again declined. Over the 2001 to 2008 time period, the median real weekly earnings of young men fell by $15 or 3 percent (Sum and McLaughlin 2009). Despite the modestly strong and steady gains that occurred from 1996 to 2001, the median real weekly earnings of full-time employed young men in 2008 were still 19 percent below their inflation-adjusted levels in 1979 and 26 percent below their median real weekly earnings in 1973.

In recent decades, as a result of the sharp decline in their own median real weekly earnings and the growth in real weekly earnings experienced by many of the nation's workers 45 years of age and older, younger men have seen their weekly earnings fall relative to their older peers (age 25 and older) since the late 1960s. In Figure 2, young men's median weekly earnings as a percentage of that of older men's (25+) weekly earnings are displayed. In 1967, when the CPS weekly wage series began, the median weekly paycheck (in gross dollars) of young men was about 74 percent as high as that of older men, a relatively high ratio. This relative weekly earnings ratio, however, declined sharply and steadily over the following 15 years, falling to 54 percent by 1982, and it has remained in the 51 to 54 percent range over the past 26 years. Young men's weekly earnings relative to older men's fell to an all-time low of 51 percent in 1996 before improving to 54 percent in 2001 as their real wages improved over the boom years from 1996 to 2000. Over the past seven years, there has been little net movement in their relative weekly wage.

The above findings on weekly wage developments among young males pertained to those who were employed full-time (35 or more hours per week). Over the 2000 to 2008 period, young adult males also found it more difficult to find full-time employment, and they received lower weekly earnings from their part-time jobs. For all employed young men, including the part-time employed, median weekly earnings declined by $18 or just under 5 percent between 2000 and 2008. The declines were highest among high school graduates (–10 percent) and those with some college but no bachelor's degree (–9 to –10 percent). Bachelor degree holders fared the best, but even they experienced a near 7 percent drop in their median weekly earnings.

FIGURE 2

Median Weekly Earnings for Full-Time Employed Young Men (Ages 16 to 24) Relative to Older Men (25 and Older), Selected Years between 1967 and 2008 (in Percentages)

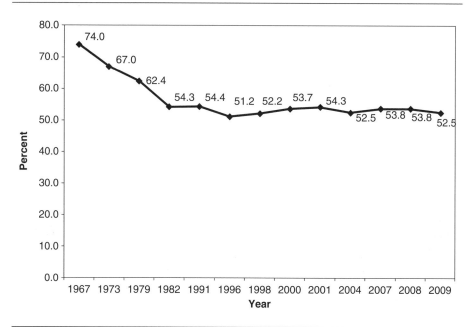

SOURCE: U.S. Department of Labor, Bureau of Labor Statistics, *Monthly Labor Review* (U.S. Department of Labor 1968, 1974); U.S. Department of Labor, Bureau of Labor Statistics, "Labor Force Statistics: Current Population Survey," available from www.bls.gov.

The median real weekly earnings of full-time employed 25- to 34-year-old males followed a similar time pattern to that of the nation's 16- to 24-year-olds over the past 30 years. Between 1979 and 1996, the median real weekly earnings of 25- to 34-year-olds declined fairly steadily and considerably, dropping from $858 to $685, a drop of $173 or 20 percent (see Table 4). Over the ensuing five prosperous years (1996 to 2001), the median weekly earnings of these full-time 25- to 34-year-old men rose by $65 to $750, a gain of 9 percent. Since 2001, however, their real median weekly earnings have once again declined, falling to $704 in 2008. The median weekly earnings of these 25- to 34-year-olds in 2008 was $154 or 18 percent below its median level in 1979.

Similar to the earlier findings for 16- to 24-year-old men, the relative median weekly earnings position of 25- to 34-year-old males also deteriorated relative to that for full-time employed men age 25 and older (see Figure 3). In 1979, the median weekly earnings of the nation's 25- to 34-year-old men was equal to just under 94 percent of those of men 25 and older. By 1989, their relative wage position had deteriorated to 87 percent; it remained fairly stable over the next

TABLE 4

Trends in the Median Weekly Earnings of 25- to 34-Year-Old
Full-Time Employed Male Wage and Salary Workers, Selected Years
between 1979 and 2008 (Annual Averages in Constant 2008 Dollars)

Year	Median Weekly Earnings
1979	$858
1989	$754
1996	$685
1999	$746
2001	$750
2008	$704
Absolute change, 1979–2008	–$154
Relative change, 1979–2008	–18%

SOURCE: U.S. Census Bureau, Current Population Survey, Monthly Household Surveys, annual averages.

FIGURE 3

Ratios of the Median Weekly Earnings of Full-Time
Employed Men 25 to 34 Years Old to All Full-Time Employed Men 25
and Older, Selected Years between 1979 and 2008 (in Percentages)

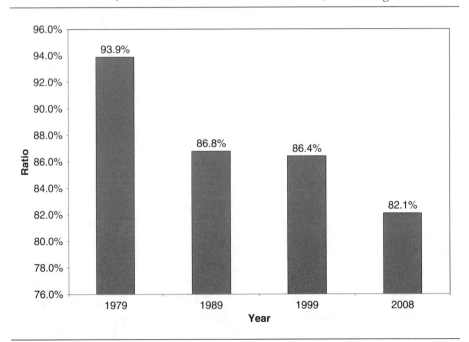

SOURCE: U.S. Bureau of Labor Statistics, Weekly and Hourly Earnings, Current Population Survey, available from www.bls.gov.

decade, then fell again from 1999 to 2008, dropping to 82 percent of the median weekly earnings of all men (25 and older).

The weekly wage structure for males by major age group over the past few decades has changed markedly. While older males (ages 55–64) modestly improved their median weekly wages by about 4 percent between 1979 and 2008, all other younger age groups experienced declines in their real median weekly earnings, with the relative size of the declines widening steadily and strongly as the youngest age groups are reached. Full-time employed males ages 45 to 54 experienced a 4 percent weekly earnings decline versus a 6 percent drop for those ages 35 to 44 and far steeper 18 percent to 19 percent declines for those ages 25 to 34 and 16 to 24, respectively. This was "no country for young men," especially those lacking bachelor or higher academic degrees.

Trends in the Real Annual Earnings of 20- to 29-Year-Old Males, 1979–2007

Perhaps the most important measure of the labor market success of young workers is their real annual earnings from employment. A number of factors will influence a worker's annual earnings. They are the number of weeks worked during the year, the average number of hours worked per week, and their real hourly earnings from employment. Earlier research on trends in the average real annual earnings of young men 20 to 29 years old found a steep decline in the annual earnings of those with no postsecondary schooling from the early 1970s through the late 1980s and mid-1990s (William T. Grant Foundation 1988; Halperin 1998; Sum, Fogg, and Mangum 2000). In their original work on this issue in 1988, the William T. Grant Foundation Commission on Work, Family, and Citizenship referred to this group of young men as "the forgotten half."

Findings on the median real annual earnings of employed 20- to 29-year-old males in the United States for selected years over the 1979 to 2007 time period are displayed in Table 5. Among all employed 20- to 29-year-old males, their median real annual earnings declined by 18 percent between 1979 and 2007. The median real annual earnings of young men in 2007 was estimated to be $23,000 or approximately $5,000 less than the level prevailing in 1979.

The median real annual earnings of these young men declined during the decade of the 1980s and then again through the mid-1990s, falling to slightly below $21,000 that year. During the economic boom period from 1995 to 2000, their median real annual earnings increased by $3,100 due to higher annual hours of work and improved real hourly earnings. This was the only sustained period of real annual earnings growth for young men over this 28-year period.

Trends in the median real annual earnings of 20- to 29-year-olds varied considerably across educational attainment groups. Young men with no high school diploma experienced a substantial 18 percent decline in their median real annual earnings over 1979 to 2007, with their earnings falling from $21,850 in 1979 to only $18,000 in 2007. Young high school graduates with no postsecondary

TABLE 5
Trends in the Median Real Annual Earnings of Employed
20- to 29-Year-Old Men by Educational Attainment and Racial/Ethnic Group,
Selected Years between 1979 and 2007 (in Constant 2007 Dollars)

Group	1979	1989	1995	2000	2007	Absolute Change from 1979 to 2007	Percentage Change from 1979 to 2007
All	28,013	25,076	20,947	24,077	23,000	−5,013	−17.9
Educational attainment							
High school dropout	21,850	17,554	16,323	18,780	18,000	−3,850	−17.6
High school graduate	30,815	25,078	22,308	24,862	22,000	−8,815	−28.6
13–15 years of schooling	31,375	29,359	24,484	28,892	26,000	−5,375	−17.1
Bachelor's degree	37,258	40,123	34,006	41,532	38,000	742	2.0
Master's or higher degree	41,180	41,794	40,808	51,765	50,000	8,820	21.4
Racial/Ethnic group							
White	30,059	26,749	23,123	25,280	25,000	−5,059	−16.8
Black	21,779	20,061	19,094	21,669	18,720	−3,059	−14.0
Hispanic	23,281	19,225	16,323	20,465	20,000	−3,281	−14.1

SOURCE: U.S. Census Bureau, 1980 and 1990 Censuses of Population and Housing, public use files; U.S. Census Bureau, Current Population Survey, March 1996, March 2001, and March 2008 Work Experience Surveys.

schooling experienced an even steeper relative decline in their median real annual earnings following 1979. The earnings of this educational subgroup of workers declined from $30,815 in 1979 to $22,000 in 2007, or nearly 29 percent. Young males with 13 to 15 years of schooling (including associate degree holders) were characterized by a 17 percent decline in their median annual earnings over this time period. In sharp contrast to the findings for young males with a high school diploma or less education, the median real annual earnings of employed 20- to 29-year-old males with a bachelor's degree increased modestly by 2 percent over 1979 to 2007, while those with a master's or higher degree experienced a more rapid 21 percent rate of growth in their median real annual earnings.

The median annual earnings of employed 20- to 29-year-old men declined substantively in each of the three major racial/ethnic groups between 1979 and 2007. The estimated rates of decline in their earnings were quite similar, ranging from 14 percent among black and Hispanic workers to nearly 17 percent among white, non-Hispanic workers. It should be noted, however, that each racial/ethnic group of young males experienced rising real earnings during the economic boom from 1995 to 2000. Since 2000, however, each group has lost ground with young black males faring the worst by far.

Given the highly divergent growth paths of the annual earnings of young men based on their level of educational attainment, the relative gaps in earnings between college-educated and less-educated young males have grown substantially over the past 28 years. In 1979, the median annual earnings of young men with a bachelor's degree exceeded those of young male high school graduates by only 21 percent (see Figure 4). The size of the relative annual earnings gap between four-year-college graduates and high school graduates increased substantially during the 1980s and 1990s. It rose to 60 percent by 1989 and to 67 percent by 2000. By 2007, employed young males with a bachelor's degree had average annual earnings that exceeded those of high school graduates by 73 percent.

The share of young men (ages 20 to 29) with no paid work experience during an entire year also has risen on average in recent decades. In 2006 and 2007, the fraction of young men in the civilian, noninstitutional population with no paid work experience was strongly correlated with their educational attainment, being three to four times higher among high school dropouts than among bachelor degree holders. Declining probabilities of some paid work further depressed the expected mean annual earnings of young men with no postsecondary schooling.

The absolute and relative size of the gaps in the annual earnings of 20- to 29-year-old men across educational groups has widened considerably over the past three decades, owing to rising differences in employment rates, annual hours of work, and hourly earnings. Less-educated males, especially those without any substantive postsecondary schooling, are finding it more difficult to obtain any type of employment, and they earn considerably less when they do find jobs. The steep decline in well-paying, blue-collar jobs in many goods-producing sectors and unionized manufacturing jobs has been a key factor at work in depressing these young men's earnings and contributing to a sharp rise in annual earnings inequality among young men.

These declining annual earnings and employment experiences of the nation's young men without any substantive postsecondary schooling also have had adverse influences on their criminal justice behavior and incarceration rates. Since the mid-1970s, the national jail and prison population has grown substantially, with young men under age 35 dominating the ranks of the incarcerated (Pager 2007; Western 2006). In 1999, both white and black males 30 to 34 years old with 12 or fewer years of schooling were about three times more likely to have spent some time in jail or prison than their similar-aged peers 20 years earlier (Western 2006). Slightly more than 11 percent of white male dropouts and 59 percent of black male dropouts ages 30 to 34 in 1999 had been incarcerated at some point in their lives.

In 2009, the Pew Center on the States revealed that 1 in 100 of the nation's adults (age 18 and older) on average in 2007 was incarcerated during the year (Pew Center on the States 2008, 2009). During 2008, among U.S. native-born males 18 to 29 years old, nearly 4 percent were in jail or prison on an average day. The incarceration rates of these young men by educational attainment ranged from a low of well under 1 percent for those with a bachelor's or advanced degree

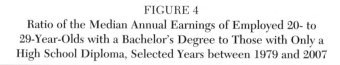

FIGURE 4
Ratio of the Median Annual Earnings of Employed 20- to
29-Year-Olds with a Bachelor's Degree to Those with Only a
High School Diploma, Selected Years between 1979 and 2007

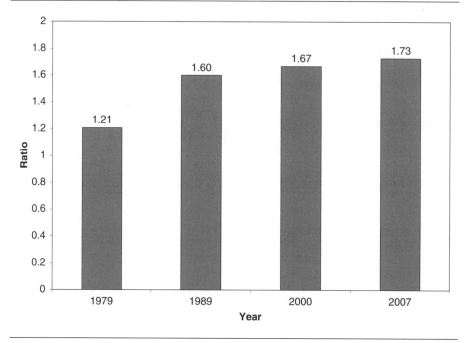

SOURCE: U.S. Census Bureau, 1980 and 1990 Census of Population and Housing, public use files; U.S. Bureau of Labor Statistics, Current Population Survey, March 1996, March 2001, and March 2008 Work Experience Surveys.

to a high of 11.5 percent for high school dropouts. Among blacks, Hispanics, and whites, the incarceration rate of male 18- to 29-year-old high school dropouts was anywhere from 18 to 40 times higher than that of their peers with a bachelor's or higher degree in 2008.

The Changing Marriage Behavior of Young Adult Men in the United States from 1970 to 2007: The Influence of Their Annual Earnings

The number of marriages is greater in proportion to the ease and convenience of supporting a family. When families can be easily supported, more persons marry, and earlier in life.

—Benjamin Franklin, *The Writings of Benjamin Franklin* (n.d.)

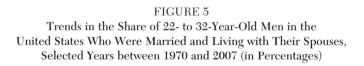

FIGURE 5
Trends in the Share of 22- to 32-Year-Old Men in the
United States Who Were Married and Living with Their Spouses,
Selected Years between 1970 and 2007 (in Percentages)

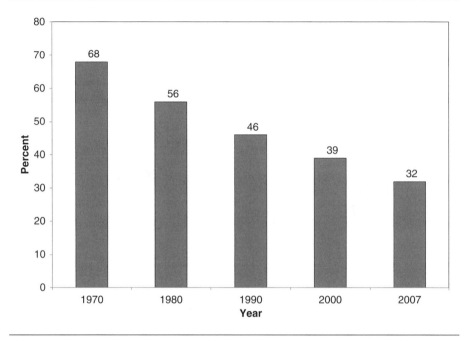

SOURCE: U.S. Census Bureau, 1970, 1980, 1990, and 2000 Census of Population and Housing, public use files; 2007 American Community Surveys, public use files.

The employment difficulties of young men with limited formal schooling and the substantial structural shifts in the levels and distribution of the annual earnings of young adults over the past few decades would be expected to have some adverse impacts on their household formation and marriage behavior. The steep declines in the real annual earnings of many young adult men with no substantial postsecondary schooling would clearly reduce their economic attractiveness as marriage partners.

To track changes in the marital behavior of young adult men (22 to 32 years old) over time, we analyzed the findings of the 1970, 1980, 1990, and 2000 decennial censuses and the 2007 American Community Surveys (ACS). In 1970, slightly more than two-thirds of 22- to 32-year-old men in the United States were married (see Figure 5). Over the next 37 years, their marriage rates declined fairly steadily and steeply, with the rate dropping to 56 percent in 1980, 46 percent in 1990, and 39 percent in 2000. By 2007, fewer than one-third of these young men were married and living with their spouse, a drop of more than half from their marital experiences in 1970.

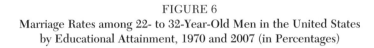

FIGURE 6
Marriage Rates among 22- to 32-Year-Old Men in the United States
by Educational Attainment, 1970 and 2007 (in Percentages)

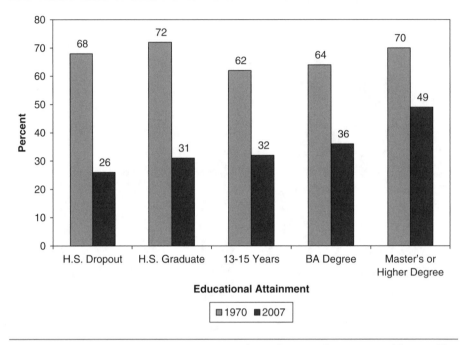

SOURCE: U.S. Census Bureau, 1970 Census of Population and Housing, public use files,
tabulations by authors; 2007 American Community Surveys, public use files.

Partly in response to the important structural changes in their annual earnings
levels, the marriage behavior of young men in different educational groups has
changed at varying rates, declining most among those men with no completed
years of postsecondary schooling. In 1970, the marriage rates of 22- to 32-year-
old men varied only modestly across educational attainment groups. Sixty-eight
percent of male high school dropouts in this age group were married, only 4 percentage points below that of high school graduates and several percentage points
higher than those of their comparably aged peers with 13 to 15 years of school
and a bachelor's degree (see Figure 6). By 2007, the marriage rates of 22- to
32-year-old men had declined considerably in each educational group, but they
fell most among those men with the least education. The best-educated young
men were nearly twice as likely to be married as their peers who failed to graduate from high school (49 vs. 26 percent).

Educational attainment has been distinguishing young males by both their
annual earnings outcomes and marriage behavior much more in recent years
than in earlier decades. The combination of a substantial breakdown in marriage

TABLE 6
Educational Attainments of the Husbands and Wives
in Young Married-Couple Families in the U.S. (2005–2007) (in Percentages)

	Wife's education				
	<12 years, no GED	12 or GED	13–15 of schooling	Bachelor's degree	Master's or higher degree
Husband's education					
<12 years, no GED	56.6	16.8	7.5	1.7	1.4
12 or GED	28.7	52.9	28.9	11.7	6.7
13–15 years of schooling	11.7	23.5	47.6	27.0	18.3
Bachelor's degree	2.2	5.6	13.2	46.2	39.1
Master's or higher degree	.8	1.2	2.8	13.3	34.1
Percentage with a husband with a bachelor's or higher degree	3.0	6.8	16.0	59.5	73.2

SOURCE: 2005–2007 American Community Surveys, public use files; tabulations by authors.

among the less-educated and the high degree of assortative mating (where individuals choose to mate with or marry individuals who resemble their socioeconomic and educational backgrounds) among the best-educated young adult men and women are creating a high degree of economic and social inequality among the nation's young families (McLanahan 2007; Wilson 1987). As Kay Hymowitz has recently argued, "It [the breakdown in marriage] is turning us into a nation of separate and unequal families" (Hymowitz 2006, 3).

The widening of gaps in marriage rates among men and women by educational attainment would have less of an adverse impact on young family income distribution and poverty rates among young families if the mating of young adults was highly random. In reality, however, assortative mating by educational attainment is very high among young married couples in the United States.

To illustrate the heightened degree of assortative mating in the United States among young married-couple families, we analyzed the findings of the 2005 to 2007 ACS, with respect to the educational attainment of the husbands and wives in young married-couple families where the head of the family (husband or wife) was under 30 years old. The distribution of wives in five educational attainment groups across five educational groups of husbands is displayed in Table 6.

Over 2005 to 2007, the vast majority of wives in young families were married to men who had a very similar level of formal schooling. For example, among married women who lacked a regular high school diploma or GED, 57 of every 100 were married to a man who also lacked a high school diploma; 85 of every 100 were married to a man who had no years of completed schooling beyond a high school diploma; and only 3 of every 100 were married to a man who held a bachelor's or higher degree (see Table 6). Among young married women with a bachelor's degree, only 13 of every 100 had a husband who completed 12 or fewer years of schooling, while nearly 60 of every 100 were married to a man who held a bachelor's or higher degree. Among those wives with a master's or higher degree, slightly more than 73 of every 100 had a husband who held a bachelor's or higher degree, and nearly 92 of every 100 of their husbands had completed at least one year of college.

Marriage Behavior of Young Adult Men and Their Annual Earnings Levels in Recent Years

It was too coincidental to be a coincidence.
—Michael Connelly, *Scarecrow* (2010)

The rapidly changing pattern of marriage behavior by young adult men in different educational groups is reflective of our earlier findings on the widening gaps in annual earnings of young men across educational groups. Young men whose annual earnings have declined the most since the late 1970s have experienced the greatest reductions in their marriage rates. The importance of the relative earnings power of young men as a determinant of their marriage potential was emphasized by several of our founding fathers, including Benjamin Franklin and George Washington. Washington provided the following advice in a letter to his step-granddaughter Betcy:

> Do not then in your contemplation of the marriage state look for perfect felicity before you wed. . . . Love is too dainty a food to live on alone and ought not be considered farther than as a necessary ingredient for that matrimonial happiness which results from a combination of causes, none of which are of greater importance than that the object on whom it is placed should possess good sense, good disposition, and the means of supporting you in the way you have been brought up. (Flexner 1972, 197)

To identify the strength of the simple associations between the annual earnings of all 22- to 32-year-old men and their marriage status in 2007, we estimated the marriage rates of these young men in seven annual earnings categories, ranging from those with annual earnings under $10,000 to those with annual earnings of $100,000 or more (see Figure 7). Among all 22- to 32-year-old males, their marriage rates rose steadily and strongly in 2007 with their annual earnings until they leveled off at the very top of the earnings distribution. Only 15 percent of young men with annual earnings under $10,000 were married versus 26 percent of those with earnings between $10,000 and $20,000, just under 50 percent of those with earnings between $40,000 and $60,000, and just under 60 percent of those men with annual earnings greater than $80,000. The most affluent male earners ($80,000+) were four times as likely to be married as their peers with annual earnings under $10,000.

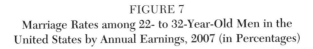

FIGURE 7
Marriage Rates among 22- to 32-Year-Old Men in the
United States by Annual Earnings, 2007 (in Percentages)

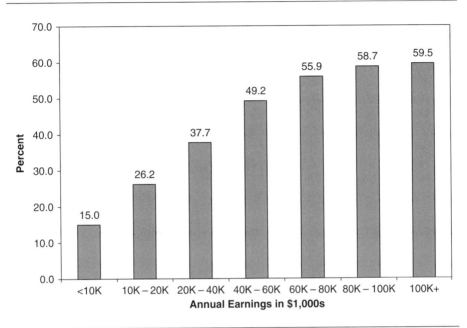

SOURCE: U.S. Census Bureau; 2007 American Community Surveys, public use files; tabulations made by authors.

Highly similar though not identical relationships existed between the annual earnings of young black males and their marriage rates. In 2007, the marriage rates of 22- to 32-year-old black males rose steadily and strongly with the level of their annual earnings up to the $60,000 to $80,000 earnings category. Only 10 percent of those young black men with annual earnings under $10,000 were married, versus 28 percent of those with earnings between $20,000 and $40,000 and 44 percent of those with annual earnings between $60,000 and $80,000.

A second source of national data on the marital behavior of young men in recent years is the National Longitudinal Survey of Youth 1997 (NLSY97), which has tracked a national sample of young men and women who were 13 to 17 years old at the time of the original interview. Findings of the 2006 survey round on the marital status of men were analyzed together with data on their reported annual earnings.

At the time of the 2006 surveys, just under 17 percent of these men were married and living with their spouses. The marriage rates of these men, both overall and in each racial/ethnic group, rose steadily and strongly as their annual earnings

TABLE 7

Estimates of the Independent Effects of the Annual Earnings of Young Men
22–26 Years Old on Their Probability of Being Married at the Time of the 2006 NLSY97

Earnings Variable	Coefficient	Significance Level
$10,000–20,000	.058	.01
20,000–30,000	.105	.01
30,000–40,000	.161	.01
40,000–50,000	.190	.01
50,000–75,000	.294	.01
75,000+	.275	.01

SOURCE: 2006 survey round NLSY97.
NOTE: Other predictor variables in the linear probability model included age, racial/ethnic group, Armed Services Vocational Aptitude Battery test score quintile, educational attainment, and family living arrangements at the time of the initial NLSY97.

increased. Fewer than 8 percent of men with earnings under $10,000 were married, versus 22 percent of those with earnings between $20,000 and $30,000, 32 percent of those with earnings between $40,000 and $50,000, and 42 percent for those with annual earnings over $50,000. Among both white and Hispanic males, the marriage rates of those with earnings at or above $50,000 were four to five times higher than those of their peers with earnings under $10,000. Among black males, the relative difference in marriage rates for these two groups was more than eight times.

The findings of the 2006 survey round of the NLSY97 were used to estimate a linear probability model of the marital status of young men at the time of the survey. A wide array of predictors in addition to their earnings levels were entered into the model (see note at bottom of Table 7). The base group included men with annual earnings under $10,000. As their earnings level rose, *ceteris paribus*, these men were significantly more likely to be married than the base group. The estimated coefficients ranged in size from 6 percentage points for those in the second lowest earnings category to highs of 28 to 29 percentage points among those with annual earnings over $50,000. The annual earnings variables had the strongest independent impact on the probability of marriage. All of the positive effects of schooling on marriage are felt indirectly through their effects on the annual earnings of men.

Can employment and training programs for young men help to boost their marriage rates? One might anticipate that they could do so if they sufficiently boosted the annual earnings of young men and, therefore, increase their attractiveness as marriage partners. Few programs can claim sizable earnings effects. A recent eight-year follow-up of the Career Academies (CA) program undertaken by MDRC in 2007 to 2008 provides the most positive evidence on this issue (Kemple 2008). From years five through eight, the treatment group of men outearned the control group by about $4,300 per year, one of the largest earnings impacts recorded in employment and training evaluations. Eight years after high school graduation, a significantly higher percentage of the men in the CA treatment group were married and living with their spouses (36 vs. 27 percent), and the male treatment group members were significantly less likely to be noncustodial parents than the control group (11 vs. 18 percent).

Trends in Out-of-Wedlock Childbearing among Young Women in the United States

"Definitely a factor of our age," Hazel replied. "It's in Sociology. The nuclear family got nuked."

—Bill James, *Naked at the Window* (2002)

The steep declines in marriage rates among young men and women over the past few decades unfortunately have not been accompanied by anywhere near similar declines in their fertility rates. As a consequence of these fertility developments, in the United States, the share of births among women under age 30 that take place out of wedlock has risen steadily and strongly over the past 46 years (see Figure 8) (Ellwood and Jencks 2006; Sum et al. 2010; Fogg, Sum, and Beard 2009; Uhlenhuth 2008). In 1960, only 6 percent of all births to women under 30 in the United States took place out of wedlock. By 1970, this share had doubled to 12 percent. By 1990, it had risen considerably to 34 percent; it rose further to 44 percent by 2000; and it increased to 50 percent in 2006. In this past year, for the first time in the history of our nation, a slight majority of all births to women under 30 took place out of wedlock—"a dubious milestone," Bob Herbert of *The New York Times* claimed (Herbert 2008). In a June 2008 Father's Day sermon to the Apostolic Church of God in Chicago, then-Senator Obama proclaimed to the congregation,

> Of all the rocks upon which we build our lives, we are reminded today that family is the most important. . . . And we are called to recognize and honor how critical every father is to that foundation. But, we'll admit that too many fathers are missing—missing from too many homes and too many lives. And the foundations of our families are weaker because of it. (Obama 2008)

Out-of-wedlock childbearing among young women in the United States is not a random event but instead varies considerably across educational attainment, nativity, income, and racial/ethnic groups. In 2006, among native-born women under age 30 who gave birth, the share of births that were out of wedlock ranged from a low of 10 percent among women with a master's or higher degree, to 14 percent among bachelor degree holders, to 37 percent among those with one to three

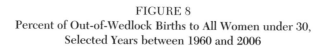

FIGURE 8
Percent of Out-of-Wedlock Births to All Women under 30,
Selected Years between 1960 and 2006

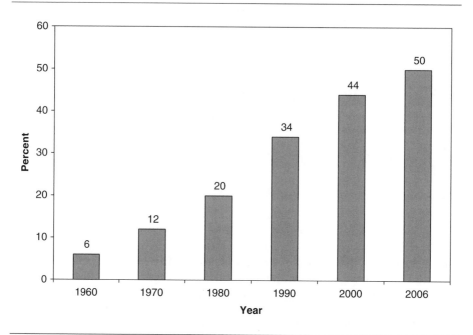

SOURCE: U.S. Department of Health and Human Services, *Vital Statistics Division* (selected years); tabulations by authors.

years of college, to a high of 67 percent among women lacking a regular high school diploma or a GED certificate.

Given the substantial degree of diversity in out-of-wedlock birth rates across the nation's young women in different educational attainment, nativity, and racial/ethnic groups, we estimated the share of all births in 2006 taking place out of wedlock for a matrix of forty different subgroups of women (five educational groups, four racial/ethnic groups, and two nativity groups). The share of births taking place out of wedlock varied extremely widely across these groups. Among foreign-born, Asian women with a master's or higher degree, only 1 percent of births in 2006 took place out of wedlock. The share of out-of-wedlock births remained quite low among highly educated native-born Hispanic women (3 percent) and white, non-Hispanic women with a bachelor's degree (8 percent). The share of births taking place out of wedlock rose considerably as the educational attainment of the mother declined. The share of out-of-wedlock births rose steeply to 62 percent among Hispanic women without a high school diploma and to 90 percent among black, native-born women who failed to graduate from high school.

The Changing Structure and Marital Composition of Young Families and Subfamilies in the United States, 1980–2007

The steep declines in marriage rates among young adult men and women together with the rising share of births out of wedlock and the poor economic prospects of many single mothers, especially those with limited schooling, have had a number of adverse impacts on the living arrangements and the marital structure of young families. Over the past few decades, there has been a rapidly rising share of young families with children that are headed by single parents; and a growing share of these young families with children live as subfamilies in the households of others, including their parents and other relatives (Johnson, Sum, and Weill 1988; Johnson, Sum, and Fogg 1996).

To track the changing living arrangements and marital structure of the nation's young families over recent decades, we analyzed the public use data files of the 1980 census and the 2007 ACS. At the time of the 1980 census, there were slightly more than 11.5 million primary families and subfamilies (related and unrelated) who were headed by an adult under the age of 30. Of this group of young families and subfamilies, approximately 90 percent were primary families (living in their own households); nearly 77 percent were married couples; and among those with a child present in the home, 70 percent consisted of married couples.

In 2007, due to delays in the age of first marriage and independent household formation among the young and a sharp rise in out-of-wedlock childbearing, there were only 9.25 million young families and subfamilies. A higher share of this set of young families (16 percent) was subfamilies, a substantial majority (80 percent) of which were single-parent subfamilies, mostly single mothers. Only a slight majority (52 percent) of these young primary families and subfamilies were married-couple families; and among those families with children present in the home, married-couple families were a distinct minority (43 percent), especially when the mothers lacked any substantive postsecondary schooling.

In 1980, approximately 15 percent of all young families (including subfamilies) were poor, 20 percent were poor or near-poor, and 37 percent were low-income. By 2007, the incidence of each income inadequacy problem among young families had risen. During that year, 20 percent of all young families were poor, nearly 27 percent were poor or near-poor, and 44 percent were low-income (see Figure 9). Among young families and subfamilies with children present in the home in 2007, the incidence of each income inadequacy problem was three to four times as high as that of young families without children. One-fourth of all young families with children were poor in 2007 and a slight majority was low-income (see Figure 9).

Among young families with children present in the home in 2007, the incidence of poverty/near-poverty problems varied markedly by marital status. Among young married-couple families with children present in the home, only 18 percent were poor or near-poor in 2007 versus 45 percent of all single-parent families and just under 50 percent of the single-mother families. The extraordinarily high

FIGURE 9
The Percentage of Young Families/Subfamilies with Children
That Were Poor, Poor/Near-Poor, or Low-Income in 1980 and 2007

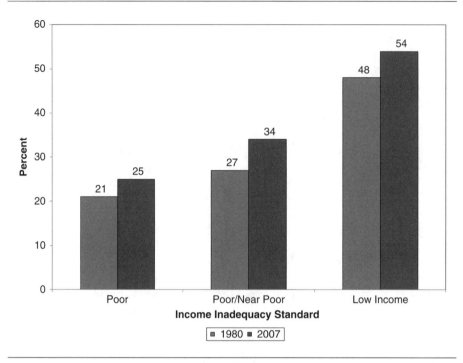

SOURCE: U.S. Census Bureau, 1980 Census; 2007 American Community Survey.

rates of poverty among young single-mother families in the United States is a key
contributing factor to the high rate of poverty among the nation's children (under
age 18) and the sharp rise in the ratio of poverty among children to that among
the elderly.

The Declining Median Real Incomes and Widening Income Disparities of Young Families, 1979–2007

The changing marital composition of the nation's young families combined
with the high levels of assortative mating among young couples and the increasing gaps in annual earnings of young men and women have had adverse effects
on the growth of the median real incomes of young families and widened income
disparities considerably since the end of the Golden Era in 1973 (Sum et al.
2010). From 1949 to 1973, the median real income of the nation's young families
nearly doubled, rising by 93 percent, with strong gains in real incomes for young

TABLE 8
Trends in the Real Annual Incomes of Young Families at Selected Percentiles of the
Young Family Income Distribution, 1979–2007 (in 2007 Dollars)

Percentile	1979	2007	Change in Dollars	Percentage Change
10	11,794	7,320	−4,474	−38
20	21,752	15,251	−6,501	−30
30	29,204	22,369	−6,835	−24
40	36,446	30,198	−6,248	−17
50	43,757	37,621	−6,136	−14
60	50,648	46,772	−3,876	−8
70	58,786	57,019	−1,745	−3
80	67,401	71,175	3,774	6
90	81,701	91,510	9,809	12
95	95,554	111,846	16,292	17
99	139,267	176,920	37,651	27

SOURCE: U.S. Census Bureau, 1980 Census of Population and Housing, public use files, tabulations by authors; 2007 American Community Survey, public use files, tabulations by authors.

families in all family types and in all major educational attainment categories and steep declines in the poverty rates of young families (Levy 1987; Marshall 2000). Since 1973, median real incomes of young families have failed to grow except in brief periods of strong job and real wage growth such as 1995 to 2000, and the degree of inequality in the young family income distribution has widened considerably.

To illustrate the changing economic fate of different groups of young families, we tracked growth (declines) in the real incomes of young primary families at various points along the family income distribution between 1979 and 2007 (see Table 8). Over this time period, the median real income (50th percentile) of young families fell from $43,757 in 1979 to $37,621 in 2007, a decline of $6,136 or 14 percent. The percentage changes in the real incomes of young families varied widely across the income distribution, with extremely steep declines at the bottom of the income distribution from the 30th percentile down to more moderate declines from the 50th to the 70th percentiles and increases in real incomes from the 80th percentile to the very top of the distribution, with the size of these increases rising steadily and strongly as we move up the distribution. Young families at the 10th and 20th percentiles experienced sizable real income declines of 30 percent to 38 percent while those at the 90th, 95th, and 99th percentiles obtained gains ranging from 12 to 27 percent.

The impact of these highly divergent income growth (decline) trends among young families was to considerably widen relative gaps between the high income and the low- to middle-income segments of the income distribution between 1979 and 2007 and increase the share of the income pie captured by the top two deciles. In 2007, the top quintile of young families captured nearly 45 percent of the combined pretax incomes of all young families, up from 38 percent in 1979.

The rising degree of young family income inequality in the United States in recent decades has been accompanied by an extraordinary degree of inequality in their wealth distribution (Sum and Khatiwada 2009).

Summary of Key Findings

And yet, on balance, the school is a weak institution compared with the home. Whatever skills, fortune, and effort it takes to provide a two parent home make as well for better scholars.

—Daniel Patrick Moynihan, *Family and Nation* (1986)

The findings on the labor market experiences of many groups of young men in recent years, especially those with no to few completed years of postsecondary schooling, are quite bleak. Substantial losses in employment and earnings have taken place for key educational subgroups of these young men, and widening disparities in employment and earnings outcomes have taken hold across educational groups.

These labor market developments in turn have had a number of adverse impacts on young men's criminal justice behavior and their marital behavior and family formation, out-of-wedlock childbearing among young women, rising poverty problems among children, and falling real incomes for many young families accompanied by widening income and wealth disparities. The search for effective solutions to these complex problems goes well beyond the scope of this article. Other analysts have proposed a wide array of macroeconomic policies; micro-oriented education and training policies for young adults; job creation programs; wage subsidies; additional Earned Income Tax Credits for young workers and their families; and policies to strengthen incomes, wealth, and marriage among the young (National Center on Education and the Economy 2007; Edelman, Holzer, and Offner 2006; Halperin 1998; Sum et al. 2010; Berlin 2007). A variety of actions on an array of macroeconomic and microeconomic fronts will likely be needed to bolster the employment, wages, earnings, and marriage prospects of the nation's young men. Without such sustained improvements in their real earnings, the future outlook for these young workers, young families, and their children is quite bleak.

References

Bartik, Timothy. 2001. *Jobs for the poor: Can labor demand policies help?* New York, NY: Russell Sage Foundation.

Berlin, Gordon. 2007. Rewarding the work of individuals: A counterintuitive approach to reducing poverty and strengthening families. *The Future of Children* 17 (2): 17–42.

Borjas, George. 2003. The labor demand curve is downward sloping: Reexamining the impact of immigration on the labor market. *Quarterly Journal of Economics* 118 (4): 1335–74.

Camorata, Steven A. 1998. *The wages of immigration: The effects on the low skilled labor market*. Washington, DC: Center for Immigration Studies.

Connelly, Michael. 2010. *Scarecrow*. New York, NY: Grand Central Publishing.

Edelman, Peter, Harry Holzer, and Paul Offner. 2006. *Reconnecting disadvantaged young men*. Washington, DC: Urban Institute Press.

Ellwood, David, and Christopher Jencks. 2006. The spread of single parent families in the U.S. since 1960. In *The future of the family*, eds. Daniel Patrick Moynihan, Timothy M. Smeeding, and Lee Rainwater. New York, NY: Russell Sage Foundation.

Flexner, James Thomas. 1972. *George Washington: Anguish and farewell 1793–1799*, vol. 4. Boston, MA: Little, Brown.

Fogg, Neeta, Andrew Sum, and Allison Beard. 2009. *The family values state: A realistic reappraisal of the evidence*. Boston, MA: Center for Labor Market Studies, Northeastern University.

Ford Foundation. 1989. *The common good: Social welfare and the American future*. New York, NY: Ford Foundation.

Franklin, Benjamin. n.d. *The writings of Benjamin Franklin, Philadelphia, 1726–1757*. Available from www.historycarper.com/resources/twobf2/articles.htm.

Hahn, Andrew, and Robert Lerman. 1982. *What works in youth employment policy*. Washington, DC: National Planning Association.

Halperin, Samuel, ed. 1998. *The forgotten half revisited: American youth and young families, 1988–2008*. Washington, DC: American Youth Policy Forum.

Herbert, Bob. 21 June 2008. A dubious milestone. *New York Times*, A27.

Hymowitz, Kay S. 2006. *Marriage and caste in America*. Chicago, IL: Ivan R. Dee.

Jaeger, David. 1998. *Skill differences and the effect of immigration on the wages of natives*. Washington, DC: Bureau of Labor Statistics, U.S. Department of Labor.

James, Bill. 2002. *Naked at the window*. New York, NY: Norton.

Johnson, Clifford, and Andrew Sum. 1987. *Declining earnings of young men: Their relation to poverty, teen pregnancy and family formation*. Washington, DC: Children's Defense Fund.

Johnson, Clifford, Andrew Sum, and Neal Fogg. 1996. Young workers, young families, and child poverty. In *Of heart and mind*, eds. Garth Mangum and Stephen Mangum. Kalamazoo, MI: Upjohn Institute Press.

Johnson, Clifford, Andrew Sum, and James Weill. 1988, 1992, 1994. *Vanishing dreams: The economic plight of America's young families*. Washington, DC: Children's Defense Fund.

Kemple, James J. 2008. *Career academies: Long term impacts on labor market outcomes, educational attainment, and transitions to adulthood*. New York, NY: MDRC.

Levy, Frank. 1987. *Dollars and dreams: The changing American income distribution*. New York, NY: Russell Sage Foundation.

Levy, Frank. 1989. Recent trends in U.S. earnings and family incomes. In *NBER Macroeconomics Annual*. Cambridge, MA: MIT Press.

Marshall, Ray, ed. 2000. *Back to shared prosperity: The growing inequality of wealth and income in America*. Armonk, NY: M. E. Sharpe.

McLanahan, Sara. 2007. Fragile families and the reproduction of poverty. Princeton University Working Paper 1016, Princeton, NJ.

Mincy, Ronald, ed. 2005. *Black males left behind*. Washington, DC: Urban Institute Press.

Moynihan, Daniel Patrick. 1986. *Family and nation: The Godkin lectures, Harvard University*. New York, NY: Harcourt, Brace, Jovanovich.

National Center on Education and the Economy. 1990. *America's choice: Low skills or high wages*. Washington, DC: National Center on Education and the Economy.

National Center on Education and the Economy. 2007. *Tough choices or tough times: The report of the New Commission on the American Workforce*. San Francisco, CA: Jossey-Bass.

Obama, Barack. 15 June 2008. Remarks of Senator Barack Obama: Apostolic Church of God. Available from www.barackobama.com/2008/06/15/remarks_of_senator_barack_obam_78.php (accessed 8 November 2010).

Pager, Devah. 2007. *Marked: Race, crime, and finding work in an era of mass incarceration*. Chicago, IL: University of Chicago Press.

Pew Center on the States. 2008. *Pew report finds more than one in 100 adults are behind bars*. Washington, DC: Pew Center on the States.

Pew Center on the States. 2009. *One in a hundred*. Washington, DC: Pew Center on the States.

Pond, Nathan, Andrew Sum, Mykhaylo Trub'skyy, and Frank Meredith. 2002. *Trends in the level and distribution of the weekly and annual earnings of young adult men and women in the U.S., 1973–2001*. Washington, DC: National League of Cities.

Smith, Christopher. 2007. Dude, where's my job? The impact of immigration on the youth labor market. PhD diss., Massachusetts Institute of Technology, Cambridge.

Sum, Andrew, Neeta Fogg, and Garth Mangum. 2000. *Confronting the youth demographic challenge: The labor market prospects of out-of-school young adults*. Baltimore, MD: Sar Levitan Center for Policy Studies, Johns Hopkins University.

Sum, Andrew, W. Neal Fogg, and Robert Taggart. 1996. *From dreams to dust: The deteriorating labor market fortunes of young adults*. Baltimore, MD: Sar Levitan Center for Social Policy Studies, Johns Hopkins University.

Sum, Andrew, and Ishwar Khatiwada. 2009. The wealth of the nation's young. *Challenge: The Magazine of Economic Affairs* 52 (6): 96–100.

Sum, Andrew, Ishwar Khatiwada, Neeta Fogg, Joseph McLaughlin, Sheila Palma, and Mykhaylo Trubskyy. 2010. *Vanishing dreams revisited: The deteriorating economic fortunes of young workers and young families from 1973–2008*. Washington, DC: Children's Defense Fund.

Sum, Andrew, Ishwar Khatiwada, and Joseph McLaughlin. 2008. *The declines in the labor force attachment and employment of teens in Massachusetts: The case for a state youth workforce development initiative*. Boston, MA: Center for Labor Market Studies, Northeastern University.

Sum, Andrew, Garth Mangum, and Robert Taggart. 2002. *The young, restless and the jobless: The case for a national jobs stimulus program targeted on America's young adults*. Baltimore, MD: Sar Levitan Center for Policy Studies, Johns Hopkins University.

Sum, Andrew, and Joseph McLaughlin. 2009. *The transition from high school to college and the labor market among the nation's recent high school graduates*. Alexandria, VA: Jobs for America's Graduates.

Sum, Andrew, Joseph McLaughlin, and Sheila Palma. 2009a. *The collapse of the nation's male teen and young adult labor market from 2000–2009: The lost generation of young male workers*. Flint, MI: Charles S. Mott Foundation.

Sum, Andrew, Joseph McLaughlin, and Sheila Palma. 2009b. *The current depression in teen labor markets and the summer 2009 teen job outlook*. Boston, MA: Center for Labor Market Studies, Northeastern University.

Sum, Andrew, Robert Taggart, and Ishwar Khatiwada. 2007. Path dependency in teen employment in the U.S.: Implications for youth workforce development policy. Paper presented to the U.S. Conference of Mayors Workforce Development Seminar, October, Washington, DC.

Uhlenhuth, Karen. 12 September 2008. With out-of-wedlock births topping 50 percent, scholars eye social impact. *McClatchy Newspapers*.

U.S. Census Bureau. 1970/1980/1990/2000. Census of Population and Housing. Available from www.census.gov/prod/www/abs/decennial/ (accessed 8 November 2010).

U.S. Census Bureau. 1996/2001/2008. Current Population Survey, Work Experience Surveys. Available from www.bls.gov/cps/ (accessed 8 November 2010).

U.S. Census Bureau. 2000/2008/2009. Current Population Survey. Monthly Household Surveys. Available from www.census.gov/cps/ (accessed 8 November 2010).

U.S. Census Bureau. 2005, 2006, 2007. American Community Survey. Available from www.census.gov/acs/www/ (accessed 8 November 2010).

U.S. Department of Health and Human Services. Selected years. *Vital Statistics Division*. Washington, DC: U.S. Department of Health and Human Services.

U.S. Department of Labor, Bureau of Labor Statistics. 1968, 1974. *Monthly labor review*. Washington, DC: U.S. Department of Labor.

U.S. Department of Labor, Bureau of Labor Statistics. n.d. Labor Force Statistics: Current Population Survey. Washington, DC: U.S. Department of Labor.

Western, Bruce. 2006. *Punishment and inequality in America*. New York, NY: Russell Sage Foundation.

William T. Grant Foundation. 1988. *The forgotten half: Non-college youth in America*. Washington, DC: Commission on Work, Family, and Citizenship.

Wilson, William Julius. 1987. *The truly disadvantaged: The inner city, the underclass and public policy*. Chicago, IL: University of Chicago Press.

Zhao, Jia. 2008. The training experiences of young adults in the U.S., 2001–2005. Master's thesis, Northeastern University, Boston, MA.

Young Disadvantaged Men as Fathers

This article reviews current theory and empirical evidence regarding young disadvantaged men's involvement with children. It first chronicles the major theoretical perspectives on fathers' involvement among resident (married and cohabiting) biological fathers, resident social fathers (unrelated romantic partners of children's mothers), and nonresident biological fathers. Second, it provides a brief overview of the current and historical role of the father in child rearing. Third, it describes the characteristics of men who become young fathers, highlighting that they tend to be socioeconomically disadvantaged. Fourth, it summarizes the empirical literature on both antecedents of fathers' involvement and patterns of involvement across father types. Finally, it examines the foremost limitations of existing research and draws implications for future research and policy.

Keywords: fathers' involvement; fathering; resident fathers; nonresident fathers; disadvantaged fathers; social fathers

By
LAWRENCE M. BERGER
and
CALLIE E. LANGTON

Both conventional wisdom and existing research suggest that fathers' involvement is beneficial for children's development and well-being. Yet changes in men's roles in family life over the past few decades, coupled with increased diversity in the structure of families, have both reshaped norms and expectations with regard to fatherhood

Lawrence M. Berger is an associate professor of social work and faculty affiliate of the Institute for Research on Poverty at the University of Wisconsin–Madison. His research focuses on the ways in which economic resources, sociodemographic characteristics, and public policies affect parental behaviors and child and family well-being.

Callie E. Langton is a doctoral student in public policy at the University of Wisconsin–Madison and was the 2009–2010 Institute for Research on Poverty's dissertation fellow. Her research focuses on how family characteristics and public policy affect childhood health and well-being.

NOTE: This work was supported by an NICHD grant (K01HD054421) awarded to Dr. Berger. We are grateful to Frank Furstenberg, Irv Garfinkel, Ron Mincy, Tim Smeeding, and participants at the Institute for Research on Poverty Working Conference on "Young Disadvantaged Men: Fathers, Families, Poverty, and Policy" for their excellent comments and advice.

DOI: 10.1177/0002716210393648

ANNALS, *AAPSS*, 635, May 2011

and resulted in many children being exposed to multiple types of father figures. Whereas fathers once primarily functioned as providers or breadwinners, the father's role now encompasses a range of child-rearing activities, many of which require active engagement in children's care (Cabrera et al. 2000). Furthermore, the father figures in children's lives are now likely to consist of nonresident biological fathers and resident social fathers (used here to connote men who are married to or cohabiting with children's mothers but who are not their biological fathers) as well as resident biological fathers. And children born to (particularly young and unmarried) disadvantaged parents are more likely to experience multiple types of father figures than those born to older, more advantaged parents, given high rates of union dissolution, relationship instability, and multipartner fertility among the former (Carlson, Furstenberg, and McLanahan 2010; Meyer, Cancian, and Cook 2005).

In this article, we first review the predominant theoretical perspectives regarding fathers' involvement among resident (married and cohabiting) biological fathers, resident social fathers, and nonresident biological fathers. Second, we present a brief discussion of the ways in which fathers contribute to child rearing. Third, we describe the social, demographic, and economic characteristics of men who enter fatherhood at a young age, highlighting that they tend to be socioeconomically disadvantaged. Fourth, we review the empirical literature on both antecedents of father involvement and patterns of involvement across father types.[1] Finally, we describe the limitations of existing research and provide suggestions for future research and policy.

How Might Biology, Marriage, Coresidence, and Social Selection Influence Father Involvement?

Despite focusing on different aspects of family relationships, sociological, economic, and evolutionary perspectives on fathers' involvement point to three consistent hypotheses, which suggest that, all else equal: (1) biological fathers will invest more in children than social fathers, (2) married fathers will invest more than unmarried fathers, and (3) resident fathers will invest more than nonresident fathers. In addition, young disadvantaged fathers are likely to invest less in children than older and more advantaged fathers both because the former are more likely to be either cohabiting or nonresident, as opposed to married or resident, and because they generally have fewer resources through which to invest. Social selection is also likely to play a significant role with regard to variation in investment in children among fathers who are biological or social, married or unmarried, resident or nonresident, and younger or older. Below, we discuss each of these hypotheses as well as the potential for social selection to influence fathers' involvement.

Hypothesis 1: Biological fathers will invest more than social fathers

Sociological perspectives on fathers' involvement explicitly consider the influence of biological ties, coresidence, and marriage on fathers' investments in children, underscoring that different family types are subject to varying degrees of institutionalization. The degree of institutionalization associated with a particular family type is likely to play an important role regarding fathers' investments. Biological ties are viewed as leading to higher levels of investment than social ties because biological fathers are both legally and normatively obligated to invest in their children; legal and normative expectations of social fathers are less clearly institutionalized or explicit (Cherlin 1978; Cherlin and Furstenberg 1994; Furstenberg and Cherlin 1991).

Whereas sociological perspectives attend to biology, marriage, and coresidence, evolutionary theories primarily emphasize the importance of biological ties for childbearing and child rearing, paying little explicit attention to marriage or coresidence. These perspectives suggest that, given an evolutionary interest in passing on their genes and ensuring their children's success (Daly and Wilson 2000; Emlen 1997), coupled with relatively high (financial and time) costs associated with parental investment, men will inherently strive to provide for their own biological offspring and, by comparison, invest less in social children (Daly and Wilson 1987; Case, Lin, and McLanahan 2001).[2]

Economic perspectives lead to a similar conclusion, but for other reasons. Economic approaches to altruism (Becker 1974, 1991), for example, assume interdependent utility functions between family members, such that the utility of an individual family member is partially dependent on the utility of another family member. This implies that parents' utilities increase with those of their children (and vice versa). While social fathers may engage in some level of altruism toward their partners' children, the role of altruism among social fathers is likely to be more limited than that among biological fathers. Parents are also likely to make fewer investments in children from whom they expect lesser future returns (Becker 1993) or whom they perceive as having lesser endowments, and these expectations and perceptions may differ by biological status (Bergstrom 1997; Case, Lin, and McLanahan 2001). Biological fathers are likely to assume or expect that their relationship with their children will last throughout their lives and that their children will care for them as they age; the extent to which social fathers will share these assumptions or expectations is ambiguous. On average, then, social fathers are expected to invest less in children than biological fathers. In addition, young disadvantaged fathers, both biological and social, may have lesser expectations of future compensation from their children or less sanguine perceptions of their children's endowments than do their older and more advantaged counterparts; if so, then these men may invest less in children.

Hypothesis 2: Married fathers will invest more than unmarried fathers

Sociological theory suggests that (resident) married fathers will invest more in children than cohabiting or nonresident fathers given the institutional strength of marriage. That is, the legal and public aspects of marriage create an "enforceable trust" (Cherlin 2004) such that married parents are encouraged to make joint relationship-specific investments in children (England and Farkas 1986). As such, marriage and child rearing have been said to consist of a "package deal," particularly for men (Furstenberg and Cherlin 1991; Townsend 2002). In contrast, cohabitation is marked by a lack of institutionalization, relatively few formal and legal obligations (Nock 1995), and considerable partnership instability, such that children of cohabiting parents are likely to experience multiple family transitions (Graefe and Lichter 1999) and to receive fewer paternal investments (Hofferth and Anderson 2003). Thus, sociological theory suggests that married biological or social fathers are likely to invest more than their cohabiting counterparts.[3]

Economic perspectives also have implications regarding marriage. To the extent that marriage represents a more formal commitment to an entire family (rather than simply to a spouse) than does cohabitation, married (biological or social) fathers may have a greater sense of economic altruism toward the children, may feel a greater sense of obligation toward them, or may have higher expectations regarding returns on their investments than do cohabiting fathers.

Finally, although evolutionary perspectives do not explicitly address marital status, it is plausible that marriage among biological parents signifies a greater willingness on the part of a father to make long-term investments in a child (particularly if marriage is also associated with greater confidence in paternity) and a commitment to future childbearing with the child's mother. If so, evolutionary perspectives may also, albeit implicitly, suggest that married biological fathers will invest more in children than will cohabiting and nonresident biological fathers (Anderson, Kaplan, and Lancaster 2007).

Hypothesis 3: Resident fathers will invest more than nonresident fathers

Coresidence implies that children will, to some degree, share their fathers' income and quality of life (Case, Lin, and McLanahan 2003). That is, fathers at least partially provide for their resident children simply by providing for themselves. Thus, resident fathers face lower costs of investing in children than nonresident fathers given economies of scale. In addition, coresidence lowers the transaction costs associated with investing in children by reducing the time and money needed to arrange and attend visits, as well as impeding the ability of the other parent to limit access to a child (Carlson, Furstenberg, and McLanahan 2010). Resident fathers may also have greater incentives to invest in children than nonresident fathers given that they are better able to monitor the ways in which their investments are utilized (Weiss and Willis 1985). Finally, with the exception of child support, nonresident fathers are subject to relatively few legally enforceable obligations to invest in their children (although there are now normative expectations—though relatively ambiguously defined—that nonresident fathers play an ongoing role in their children's lives). In short, coresidence lowers the price of investing in children and should thereby encourage investment. Again, both because young disadvantaged fathers are less likely to coreside with their children and because they have fewer total resources than their older, more advantaged counterparts, they are likely to make lesser investments.

The role of social selection

Another possible explanation for variation in investments in children by father type is that the quantity and quality of such investments are driven by differences in the characteristics of the individuals who "select" into particular families (Amato 2005; Hofferth and Anderson 2003). For example, fathers may be more likely to cohabit than to marry or to be nonresident than resident because they are unattractive partners on a range of characteristics, including their willingness or ability to contribute economic resources to the family (see, for example, Smock and Manning 1997); this may be particularly true of young disadvantaged fathers. Likewise, the characteristics of social fathers are likely to differ from those of biological fathers. For example, social fathers may have traits that are associated with lesser investments in children (e.g., problems with violence, drugs, or alcohol) to the extent that men with the most desirable fathering qualities will be in ongoing relationships with the mothers of their own biological children. Alternatively, however, mothers who enter into relationships with social fathers may choose a new partner who exhibits characteristics and behaviors that are likely to benefit their child(ren) (Bzostek, Carlson, and McLanahan 2007).

Prior studies of fathers' involvement have primarily used two strategies to attempt to adjust for social selection factors: controlling for as many confounding covariates as possible and estimating fixed-effects models that adjust for unobserved persistent characteristics while assessing either within-father change (see, for example, Gibson-Davis 2008) in involvement over time or within-father differences (see, for example, Hofferth and Anderson 2003) in investments in different children (e.g., biological and social children). Results suggest that social selection factors explain part, but not all, of the associations among father type and father involvement. Nonetheless, these strategies cannot be assumed to produce causal estimates of the effects of father type on investments in children. For the most part, what we know about social selection into family types suggests that on average, social, unmarried, and nonresident fathers will invest less in children than biological, resident, and married fathers will, based on the preexisting characteristics of men who select into each group. Empirically, however, there are notable exceptions to this general pattern, which we discuss below.

What Do Fathers "Do" for Children?

As families have evolved in both form and nature, so has the social role of father. This role historically consisted primarily of providing financially for children, and until relatively recently, economic contributions were widely viewed as the father's most important input into a household (Crockett, Eggebeen, and Hawkins 1993; McLanahan and Sandefur 1994). Fathers made these contributions in their role as coresident breadwinner or, in the case of absent fathers, through formal or informal child support payments.[4] In recent decades, however, direct and ongoing paternal involvement in child rearing has increasingly come to be seen as important for children of all ages (Hernandez 1993). Thus, today's fathers are expected to engage in a wide range of direct and indirect child-rearing activities (Hewlett 2000). These activities, often referred to as reflecting "investments" in children, have been described as falling into three critical dimensions of fathering: engagement, accessibility, and responsibility (Lamb 1987, 2000; Lamb et al. 1987). As outlined in Lamb (2000), *engagement* generally refers to shared father-child experiences in which fathers directly interact with their children (e.g., helping with homework, feeding them, and playing together); *accessibility* entails the father being physically present and available and able to monitor a child but not actively engaged with the child (e.g., the father is in the same house or room as a child, but they are engaged in separate activities); *responsibility* includes taking an active role in child-rearing tasks and decisions regarding a child's care and well-being (e.g., ensuring, arranging, or providing for children's needs with regard to health, hygiene, and supervision). Fathers may further indirectly invest in their children by supporting (financially, emotionally, or otherwise) their children's mothers, although this aspect of fathers' involvement has received little scholarly attention (Hawkins and Palkovitz 1999; Marsiglio, Day, and Lamb 2000). To date, existing research suggests that children spend considerably more time engaged with their fathers in terms of play, companionship, and personal care than in household work and social or learning activities (Hofferth et al. 2002; Yeung et al. 2001).

Despite relatively sophisticated conceptualizations of fathers' involvement, as discussed below, "most empirical work still employs fairly simple measures of selected aspects of engagement" (Nelson 2004, 434). As such, our knowledge of the range of ways fathers contribute to child rearing—and how fathers' involvement may differ by socioeconomic factors and a father figure's biological, marital, and coresident status vis-à-vis a child and his or her mother—has generally been limited to simple accountings of the amount of time fathers spend with children and the number and types of activities fathers directly engage in with children (Marsiglio et al. 2000). We know much less about fathers' ongoing accessibility to their children; responsibility for their children's care and well-being; or the warmth, sensitivity, and overall quality of their interactions with their children. On the whole, young disadvantaged fathers may have less capacity than older, more advantaged fathers to invest in children across all of these domains, as they are likely to have fewer financial resources to (potentially) devote to child rearing (Danziger and Radin 1990; Furstenberg 1995) and higher levels of social, emotional, and behavior difficulties (Bunting and McAuley 2004).

Who Becomes a Young Father?

The age at which individuals become parents differs considerably by race and ethnicity and is positively correlated with socioeconomic status. Black and Hispanic men are more likely than white men to become young (e.g., under age 25) fathers (Hynes et al. 2008), and young fathers have lower average levels of education and employment, come from lower-socioeconomic-status families, and have greater psycho-emotional problems and levels of delinquent behaviors than men who did not experience early fertility (Bunting and McAuley 2004). In addition, data from the Fragile Families and Child Wellbeing (FFCW) study—the first birth cohort study to collect extensive data on (and from) unmarried fathers—reveal that unmarried fathers are considerably younger and more disadvantaged than married fathers; they are less educated, less healthy, and less likely to be working; they are also more likely to have been incarcerated, to have a substance problem, to be black or Hispanic (and less likely to be white), and to have children by multiple partners (Carlson and McLanahan 2010).

In short, individuals who select into parenthood at young ages tend to be socio-economically disadvantaged (Carlson and McLanahan 2010; Child Trends 2002; Hamilton, Martin, and Ventura 2009; Lerman 1993; Marsiglio 2000),[5] to be unmarried, and to have characteristics that limit their ability to provide for their children economically. These same characteristics are associated with low levels of father involvement (Cooksey and Craig 1998; Danziger and Radin 1990; Furstenberg and Harris 1993; Roggman et al. 2002), suggesting that social selection may well play a role in explaining associations among father type and fathers' involvement. Furthermore, as Nelson (2004) points out, declines in (particularly black) young disadvantaged men's labor force participation and wages over the past few decades (see also Sum et al., this volume) imply that those characteristics that are associated with early entry into fatherhood may be becoming more prominent in the U.S. population. This is likely to have important implications for both public policy and U.S. society given that differences in the socioeconomic characteristics of younger and older parents are likely to be associated with patterns of intergenerational transmission of inequality (McLanahan and Percheski 2008).

What Do We Know about Young Disadvantaged Fathers' Involvement with Children?

In this section, we outline those factors that are associated with men's investments in children. We then describe patterns of fathers' involvement for resident biological fathers, resident social fathers, and nonresident biological fathers.[6] We pay careful attention to what is known about differences in father involvement between married and cohabiting fathers. Whenever possible, we also highlight studies that are particularly relevant to young disadvantaged fathers. Finally, given high rates of incarceration among disadvantaged young men, coupled with the particular difficulties associated with continued involvement with children among incarcerated fathers, we discuss fathers' involvement with regard to nonincarcerated and incarcerated nonresident fathers separately.

Antecedents of father involvement

Prior research points to multiple characteristics of fathers, mothers, children, and mother-father relationships that are associated with fathers' involvement; consistent with what we know about social selection, many of these same factors are associated with age of entry into fatherhood and with father type. Fathers' background characteristics that are positively correlated with involvement include accumulated human capital (e.g., educational attainment and employment) (Cooksey and Craig 1998; Danziger and Radin 1990; Hofferth et al. 2002; Landale and Oropesa 2001; Manning and Smock 2000; Manning, Steward, and Smock 2003), the quality of men's experiences with their own fathers and other male role models (Cabrera et al. 2000; Hofferth 2003), and the extent to which men identify with the fathering role (Cabrera et al. 2000; Rane and McBride 2000). Fathers' psycho-social characteristics such as a history of incarceration or physical violence are negatively associated with both ongoing involvement with children and payment of child support (Carlson and McLanahan 2010; Carlson, McLanahan, and Brooks-Gunn 2008; Ryan, Kalil, and Ziol-Guest 2008), as is paternal repartnering and subsequent fertility (Manning and Smock 2000). Finally, nonresident fathers who make (particularly informal) financial contributions to their children tend to be more involved with them, although the causal direction of this association has not been firmly established (Nepomnyaschy 2007).

Maternal characteristics such as whether a mother and child live with extended family and whether the mother has repartnered or had subsequent children also appear to influence fathers' involvement. Whereas repartnering and new partner fertility are associated with decreased involvement (Tach, Mincy, and Edin 2010), the association between whether the mother lives with kin and fathers' involvement is likely to reflect the quality of the relationship between the father and the mothers' coresident relatives (Bunting and McAuley 2004; Danziger and Radin 1990; Krishnakumar and Black 2003).

Children's characteristics such as age (Hofferth et al. 2002; Lamb 2000), gender (Lamb 2000; Lundberg, McLanahan, and Rose 2005), and health status (Reichman, Corman, and Noonan 2004) are also associated with fathers' involvement. In general, both mothers and fathers are more involved with younger children than with older children; however, the ratio of mother to father involvement with children tends to decrease as children age, suggesting that relative to mothers, fathers spend more time with older than younger children (Lamb 2000). There is also some evidence that fathers are more involved with sons than with daughters (Lamb 2000), although this may only hold for married fathers (Lundberg, McLanahan, and Rose 2005). Finally, fathers appear to be less involved with children who were born low birth weight, are disabled, or have developmental delays (Reichman, Corman, and Noonan 2004).

Involvement on the part of both resident and nonresident fathers has also been linked to the quality of the mother-father relationship and conflict therein (Bunting and McAuley 2004; Carlson and McLanahan 2004; Carlson, McLanahan, and Brooks-Gunn 2008; Ryan, Kalil, and Ziol-Guest 2008). Particularly salient in this regard is maternal gatekeeping, defined as the influence a mother exerts on a father's involvement with children either directly, by controlling access to children, or indirectly, by affecting paternal role identity (McBride et al. 2005), often through encouragement or criticism (Schoppe-Sullivan et al. 2008). Maternal gatekeeping behaviors are closely tied to the relationship quality of mothers and fathers as well as to mothers' perceptions of paternal competence and the father's role within the family (Fagan and Barnett 2003). Research suggests that maternal gatekeeping behaviors heavily influence fathers' involvement among both resident and non-resident fathers (Allen and Hawkins 1999; Fagan and Barnett 2003; McBride et al. 2005; Schoppe-Sullivan et al. 2008).[7]

Fathers' involvement among resident biological and social fathers

The vast majority of resident (biological and social) fathers spend time and engage in activities with children on a relatively consistent basis (see, for example, Child Trends 2002). However, compared with mothers' activities with children, fathers' activities are much more likely to consist of play (including sports) and leisure activities than cognitively stimulating activities. Furthermore, whereas the majority of resident fathers do engage in "rule setting," monitoring activities, and discipline, they do so much less frequently than do mothers (Child Trends 2002).

Most existing research suggests that (particularly married) resident biological fathers are more involved with children than all other father types (see, for example, Hofferth et al. 2007). However, (married) resident biological fathers also tend to have greater human capital than other father types and are typically older (Hofferth and Anderson 2003; Manning and Brown 2006; Manning and Lichter 1996; Smock 2000). A large group of studies has also compared the involvement of married biological fathers to that of married stepfathers. In general, this literature finds that married stepfathers are less involved with stepchildren than are married biological fathers with their biological children (Amato and Sobolewski 2004; Coleman, Ganong, and Fine 2000; Hetherington and Stanley-Hagan 1999; Nelson 2004). Married stepfathers are less likely to participate in activities with children (Cooksey and Fondell 1996; Thomson, McLanahan, and Curtin 1992), express positive feelings toward children (Thomson, McLanahan, and Curtin 1992), be supportive of children (Amato 1987), and exhibit monitoring and controlling behaviors toward (particularly adolescent) children (Amato 1987; Fisher et al. 2003; Hetherington and Jodl 1994).

Far less research has compared the involvement of married biological fathers to that of cohabiting biological fathers or that of married social fathers to that of cohabiting social fathers. Results from the handful of studies that directly compare married and cohabiting biological fathers suggest that the former are more likely to make financial investments in children (Landale and Oropesa 2001), spend more time engaged with children (Hofferth and Anderson 2003; Hofferth et al. 2007), engage more frequently in caregiving activities (Landale and Oropesa 2001), and exhibit slightly more cooperation in parenting with their children's mothers (Berger et al. 2008) than are cohabiting biological fathers. However, they also engage in more frequent spanking (Gibson-Davis 2008). Existing evidence regarding differences in paternal warmth and responsibility for parenting between married and unmarried resident biological fathers has been quite mixed (Hofferth and Anderson 2003; Hofferth et al. 2007).

We are aware of only one study that directly compares involvement in child rearing between married and unmarried social fathers. Berger and colleagues (2008), using data from the FFCW study, find that even after controlling for a wide range of selection factors, married social fathers of young children are reported by mothers as being more engaged with children, sharing more responsibility for parenting, and cooperating more fully in parenting than their cohabiting counterparts. Mothers also trust married social fathers more so than cohabiting social fathers to care for children in their absence.[8]

Finally, a few recent studies have documented differences in fathers' involvement between biological and social fathers, sometimes taking marital status into account. Findings from these studies tend to differ across data sources and by whether analyses are bivariate or multivariate, with multivariate analyses of FFCW study data being most favorable toward social fathers.[9] For example, bivariate analyses of fathers' involvement across five large-scale datasets suggest that married biological fathers have higher levels of engagement than both married and cohabiting social fathers; they also appear to express more warmth than married social fathers (Hofferth et al. 2007). Similarly, Hofferth and Anderson's (2003) multivariate analyses using data from the Panel Study of Income Dynamics (PSID) suggest that, in general, married and unmarried social fathers are less involved with children than are married biological fathers.[10] In contrast, however, Berger and colleagues' (2008) multivariate analyses using FFCW study data suggest that (particularly married) resident social fathers engage in higher levels of shared responsibility for and cooperation in parenting than do resident biological fathers, and Gibson-Davis's (2008) multivariate analyses using FFCW data suggest that cohabiting social fathers have higher levels of engagement and instrumental support and lower levels of spanking than married biological fathers.

On the whole, the existing literature leads us to conclude that biological fathers tend to be more involved with children than social fathers and also that married biological fathers are typically more involved than unmarried biological fathers. However, exceptions to this general pattern are common. In particular, analyses using FFCW data indicate that social fathers engage in relatively high-quality behaviors compared with those of biological fathers. Given that the families in FFCW are more disadvantaged than those in most other national data sources, this may suggest that differences in the behaviors of biological and social fathers are smaller among disadvantaged families than among more advantaged families or that disadvantaged mothers who repartner tend to do so with men who they perceive as investing in their children.

Fathers' involvement among nonincarcerated nonresident biological fathers

For most families, the very nature of nonresident fatherhood means that a father will be less involved in his children's day-to-day lives than will his resident counterparts and that staying involved with his children, particularly in terms of face-to-face contact, will require considerably more effort. Clearly, children spend less time with nonresident than with resident fathers. Although the majority of children with a nonresident father have some contact with him, recent estimates suggest that a substantial proportion—approximately 40 percent—do not. Furthermore, the remaining 60 percent see their nonresident father an average of only 69 days per year (Child Trends 2002). It is important to note, however, that estimates of whether and how much contact children have with their nonresident fathers range considerably across data sources and reporters (Argys et al. 2007). For example, Argys and colleagues (2007), using data from six large studies, report that 45 to 62 percent of white nonresident fathers and 39 to 81 percent of nonwhite nonresident fathers had contact with children five years of age or younger during the prior year.[11]

Current evidence also suggests that patterns of father-child contact tend to be relatively similar across divorced and unmarried nonresident fathers (although children born to unmarried fathers receive slightly less contact) (Argys et al. 2007), that there is considerable variation in involvement patterns within each of these nonresident father types, and that fathers' contact tends to decrease over time for all types of nonresident fathers (Carlson and McLanahan 2010; Lerman and Sorenson 2000). Given that children born to young disadvantaged fathers are disproportionately likely to be born outside of marriage, we focus on studies of fathers' involvement following a nonmarital birth. Estimates from FFCW, for example, suggest that about five years after a nonmarital birth, 63 percent of nonresident fathers had seen their child during (approximately) the prior two years, and 43 percent had seen their child more than once in the past month (Carlson, McLanahan, and Brooks-Gunn 2008). However, whereas most unmarried fathers are substantially involved with their children and their children's mother around the time of the birth, with many engaged in romantic or cohabiting relationships with the mother, the majority of these relationships dissolve within five years. As a result, children born to unmarried parents are likely to be exposed to considerable relationship instability and to decreasing involvement from their nonresident fathers over time (Carlson and McLanahan 2010). Although this pattern is common, it is important to note that there is also considerable variation in involvement trajectories and that many nonresident fathers exhibit steady or even increasing involvement with children over time (Lerman and Sorenson 2000; Ryan, Kalil, and Ziol-Guest 2008).[12]

In addition, nonresident fathers tend to package involvement with formal or informal cash or in-kind support. That is, multiple types of contributions to child rearing are likely to be bundled together such that children who have no contact with their fathers are also less likely to benefit from their fathers' financial support (Nepomnyaschy 2007; Ryan, Kalil, and Ziol-Guest 2008). Such packaging may reflect both fathers' motivations toward rearing their children and mothers' expectations that fathers contribute financially to child rearing as a precondition of access to children (Danziger and Radin 1990; Edin 2000; Edin and Kefalas 2005).

Finally, nonresident father interactions with children tend to be concentrated in "recreational rather than instrumental" activities (Marsiglio et al. 2000, 1184). Much of the time nonresident fathers spend with children appears to be leisure-related;

nonresident fathers are less likely than both mothers and resident fathers to provide cognitive support, monitoring, or supervision to children or to enforce rules (Child Trends 2002; Furstenberg and Cherlin 1991; Hofferth et al. 2002; Yeung et al. 2001). Along these lines, Hofferth and colleagues (2002) report that the majority of nonresident fathers interviewed in the PSID–Child Development Supplement (PSID-CDS) report having relatively little influence over child-rearing decisions (although a fifth report having a great deal of such influence).

Despite considerable variation by data sources, on the whole, current evidence suggests that (1) nonresident divorced and never married fathers have relatively similar levels of involvement; (2) there is considerable variation in both involvement levels and changes in involvement over time among nonresident fathers; (3) on average, children's contact with nonresident fathers tends to decrease over time; and (4) nonresident fathers' activities with children tend to be more leisure oriented than those of both mothers and resident fathers.

Fathers' involvement among incarcerated nonresident biological fathers

Because most existing large-scale data sources are household-based, incarcerated fathers tend to be excluded from their samples (although mothers are sometimes asked about these men's whereabouts, characteristics, and behaviors). As such, we know relatively little about these men's ongoing involvement with their children. Yet they compose an important subset of (particularly young and disadvantaged) nonresident fathers. It is well established that lower socioeconomic status and black men are incarcerated at high rates in the United States. Indeed, whereas approximately 2.3 percent of all U.S. children have an incarcerated parent, black children are seven and a half times more likely than white children to experience parental incarceration (Glaze and Maruschak 2008). And incarcerated men are likely to be absent from children's lives for a considerable amount of time. The majority of incarcerated fathers are expected to spend more than four years in prison, with average sentence lengths of approximately six to seven years among fathers in state custody and eight to nine years among those in federal custody (Mumola 2000).

By definition, the amount of involvement incarcerated men are able to have with their children is limited.[13] Thus, both the criteria used to assess involvement and the normative expectations of involvement for incarcerated fathers are likely to differ from those for other nonresident fathers for multiple reasons. First, simply by being incarcerated, the father has relatively little choice as to how frequently (and when) he can see his children. Second, children may be prevented from visitation by the custodial mother without the father having much (if any) recourse. For example, a mother who has a poor relationship with her child's incarcerated father may be unlikely to arrange visitation (Poehlmann 2005). Third, even if the mother is willing to arrange visitation, there are clear costs associated with doing so, and some mothers may simply be unable to afford much, if any, visitation. Fathers are often incarcerated hundreds of miles from their homes (Mumola 2000). Thus, visitation may require transportation expenses, lodging, and potentially days off work (which may result in lost wages) (Hairston 2001). As such, the distance between an incarcerated father's home and the facility in which he is incarcerated is a strong predictor of any face-to-face contact with his children (Hairston 2008).

These factors suggest that contact between incarcerated men and their children will be limited. This conclusion is supported by existing empirical evidence: Mumola (2000), for example, finds that only 40 percent of fathers in state prison had weekly contact (phone, mail, or visits) with their children and that 57 percent had never had a visit from their children during their incarceration. Glaze and Maruschak (2008) report that approximately 30 percent of incarcerated fathers had weekly contact with their children and an additional 23 percent had contact at least monthly; however, 22 percent had no contact with their children during their current period of incarceration. Furthermore, of those fathers who have contact with their children during incarceration, about only 40 percent receive a face-to-face visit; instead, father-child contact is most commonly accomplished through the mail, with 69 percent of fathers reporting exchanging letters with their children during their sentence (Glaze and Maruschak 2008).

What Are the Major Limitations of Existing Research on Young Disadvantaged Men as Fathers?

As with any body of research, there are limitations to existing studies of fathers' involvement. First and foremost are limitations of the available data. Although national surveys (FFCW, PSID-CDS, National Survey of Family Growth [NSFG], Add Health) have increasingly included interviews with both resident and non-resident biological (and, less commonly, resident social) fathers in recent years, concerns continue to exist regarding the underrepresentation of men—particularly those who are most likely to be young disadvantaged fathers—due to sampling techniques that exclude active military personnel and institutionalized (including incarcerated) populations, as well as the use of households as sampling units (Carlson and McLanahan 2010; Nelson 2004). Furthermore, concerns about systematic nonresponse, attrition, and missing data with regard to fathers are salient when considering estimates of fathers' involvement, particularly if the least involved and most disadvantaged fathers are most likely to be lost from longitudinal studies. There is also evidence that (particularly low-income) men are unreliable reporters of their own fertility either because they do not know they are fathers or due to intentional misreporting (Nelson 2004).[14] Despite these concerns, however, the field has made great strides toward collecting data directly from men, and more datasets are striving to interview both resident and nonresident parents. These efforts should be applauded and expanded. In particular, more studies should interview social fathers in addition to biological fathers.

Second, better measurement of fathers' involvement is necessary. Most studies focus on the amount of time children spend with (or with access to) their fathers and sometimes include the types and amounts of activities in which they mutually engage. Recent studies such as FFCW, Add Health, and the PSID-CDS include somewhat more detailed measures of paternal coparenting, warmth, monitoring, and control. However, information on the "quality" of father-child relationships and interactions continues to lag behind that on mothers and children. Future research would benefit from examining the full range and types of parenting behaviors that have been considered with regard to mothers, including assessments of more "qualitative" aspects of parenting such as nurturance, sensitivity, permissiveness, authoritativeness, authoritarianism, responsiveness, emotional support, and cognitive stimulation. Future research should also investigate the extent to which fathers indirectly support child rearing by emotionally supporting their children's mothers (Marsiglio, Day, and Lamb 2000). These aspects of fathers' involvement have been largely overlooked in existing work.

Third, categorizations of family "type" continue to be insufficient as family configurations are likely more fluid than can be accounted for by existing survey data. There is no common definition as to what truly constitutes a cohabiting relationship as opposed to an intensive visiting relationship. And it is unclear whether it is more important to delineate families by coresidence, marriage, or both. For example, studies often group all nonmarital births together, whether parents are cohabiting, visiting, or not romantically involved. Yet the quality and quantity of father involvement may differ considerably by these factors. Additional theoretical and qualitative work may help to better understand the full range of relationship trajectories families undergo and how they may be related to fathers' ongoing involvement. Such information is difficult to collect via most surveys (which generally conduct interviews a year or more apart); however, there may be utility in asking sample parents to complete "relationship" calendars detailing their romantic relationships and the amount of time various partners spend in their households over time. Similar work history calendars have been used to study labor force participation and may provide a model for how to collect more detailed and reliable information on the fluidity of parental romantic relationships and living arrangements.

Fourth, studies of the determinants of fathers' involvement continue to be plagued by difficulties—if not impossibilities—in being able to identify causal effects. Although existing work has shed a great deal of light on those factors that are correlated with fathers' involvement, in the absence of strong evidence regarding causal relations, caution must be exercised in creating interventions and policies intended to increase fathers' involvement. As such, interventions should be carefully monitored and evaluated for their efficacy in achieving this goal (see Knox et al., this volume).

Finally, there are several important research questions that have received scant attention to date. First, there has been little work on whether all fathers should be encouraged to be involved with their children and, if not, when fathers' involvement should be discouraged (e.g., severe substance abuse or violence) and how. We know little about the circumstances in which fathers' involvement may do children more harm than good. Second, existing research has paid little attention to the effects of fatherhood and various family configurations on men's well-being. A considerable body of work focuses on mothers' relationship trajectories and their influence on both mother and child well-being; a parallel literature related to fathers' relationship trajectories has yet to be produced. Third, single-father families have received little attention in the research literature despite being a growing demographic group. Thus, we know little about single fathers' economic investments in and involvement with their children or about those of their children's nonresident mothers. Fourth, additional research on incarcerated fathers' relationships with their children is warranted, particularly because most interactions between children and their incarcerated fathers do not appear to be face-to-face. Finally, there has been a notable lack of attention to the "full package" of parenting behaviors to which children are exposed. Most studies focus on the behaviors of a particular parental figure rather than attempting to account for the full range of investments children may simultaneously receive from resident or nonresident mothers, resident or nonresident fathers, and various social parents. While it is important to understand the types of investments made by individual parental figures, what may ultimately matter for children is the quality and quantity of the full set of parenting behaviors to which they are exposed and by whom.

What Can We Conclude about Young Disadvantaged Men as Fathers?

Notwithstanding the limitations described above, the existing literature points to several conclusions regarding young fathers' involvement with children. First, young fathers are generally more disadvantaged and less involved with children than are older fathers. Second, married biological fathers are more likely to be involved with their children than their unmarried counterparts (and young disadvantaged fathers are less likely to be married than older, more advantaged fathers). Third, although much of the existing research indicates that resident biological fathers are more involved with children than resident social fathers, this pattern may be less pronounced among disadvantaged families than among more advantaged families. Thus, future research would benefit from more detailed information on the roles of social fathers in disadvantaged households, including information collected directly from these men. Fourth, considerably more research and policy attention are needed around issues of fathers' involvement for incarcerated men. Finally, nonresident fathers' involvement with children is much more focused on recreational activities than is the involvement of both resident fathers and mothers, suggesting that some families with nonresident fathers may benefit from policies and programs to help these men to further develop as supportive parents. To the extent that fathers' involvement benefits children (see Carlson and Magnuson, this volume), it may be important to encourage investments through a range of policy and programmatic options that are described in the subsequent articles of this volume. These include child support policies (Cancian, Meyer, and Han), policies and programs related to education and transitions to work for young disadvantaged men (Heinrich and Holzer), policies and programs that encourage healthy family relationships and strengthen fatherhood (Knox et al.), and income support and labor market policies targeted at young men (Klempin, Mincy, and Schmidt).

Notes

1. For the most part, we exclude financial contributions to child rearing from our discussion because they are covered elsewhere in this volume (see articles by Sum et al. and Cancian, Meyer, and Han). Likewise, we do not discuss the influence of fathers' involvement on child well-being, which is addressed by Carlson and Magnuson in this volume.

2. As suggested by Hewlett (2000), however, this process may be influenced by a host of demographic, ecological, and cultural factors. In addition, it is important to recognize that social fathers may invest in their partner's children in the hope of future childbearing (mating effort) or other positive outcomes (relationship effort) with her (Anderson, Kaplan, and Lancaster 1999). Nonetheless, social fathers' investments in children are likely to be smaller than those of (particularly resident and married) biological fathers.

3. Sociological perspectives on marriage are also careful to differentiate expectations associated with the marriage between a child's biological parents and those associated with parental remarriage. Indeed, Cherlin (1978) describes remarriage as an "incomplete institution" in that normative and legal expectations of step-parents are generally ambiguous: stepparents have limited authority over and obligations toward their partners' children and may also lack a formal parental role in the family (Cherlin and Furstenberg 1994; Furstenberg and Cherlin 1991). Thus, married social fathers are presumed to invest less in children than married biological fathers. However, married social fathers should invest more in their partner's children than cohabiting social fathers given that marriage is more fully institutionalized than cohabitation.

4. An in-depth description of the economic circumstances of young men as well as their (limited) abilities to make economic contributions to their children is presented elsewhere in this volume (see articles by Sum et al. and Cancian, Meyer, and Han).

5. See Nelson (2004) for a discussion of the potential reasons why low-income men are likely to become fathers at younger ages than higher-income men.

6. Before proceeding with this discussion, it is important to point out that, despite the considerable demographic changes of the past half century, at any given point in time most children are living with their married biological (or adoptive) parents. Recent estimates suggest that about 63 percent of children under age 18 live with both of their biological/adoptive parents (60 percent with married and 3 percent with cohabiting parents), 8 percent with a biological/adoptive mother and her married (6 percent) or cohabiting (2 percent) partner, 2 percent with a biological/adoptive father and his married (2 percent) or cohabiting (>1 percent) partner, 23 percent with their single biological mother (20 percent) or father (3 percent), and 4 percent with no biological/adoptive parent present (calculated by the authors from estimates presented in Kreider 2008).

7. Note also that, particularly for young fathers, maternal grandmothers may have substantial gatekeeping power (Krishnakumar and Black 2003).

8. In addition, although Hofferth and Anderson (2003) did not conduct significance tests for differences in involvement between married and cohabiting social fathers, their estimates imply that whereas married social fathers may spend less time with children than cohabiting social fathers, they also engage in more activities with and express more warmth toward them.

9. This may reflect that Fragile Families and Child Wellbeing study mothers who repartner after a nonmarital birth tend to do so (on average) with men who are more socially and economically advantaged than are the unmarried biological fathers in the sample (Bzostek, Carlson, and McLanahan 2007).

10. Hofferth and Anderson (2003) also provides some evidence that social children receive higher levels of fathers' involvement if there is also a biological child of the resident father in their household, suggesting that biological ties to one child in a household may incur spillover effects for a social child.

11. Much of this variation is likely to reflect differences in the characteristics of the particular study samples and whether reports are provided by mothers, fathers, or children. For example, nonresident fathers tend to report higher involvement with children than is reported by resident mothers, though not necessarily drastically so (Argys et al. 2007; Lerman and Sorenson 2000).

12. As noted above, studies of disadvantaged parents also suggest that there is considerable variation in fathers' involvement by mother-father relationship quality and the fathers' financial contributions on a child's behalf (Bunting and McAuley 2004; Carlson and McLanahan 2004; Carlson, McLanahan, and Brooks-Gunn 2008; Edin and Kefalas 2005; Nepomnyaschy 2007; Ryan, Kalil, and Ziol-Guest 2008).

13. Paternal incarceration is also likely to reduce the economic resources available to a child. More than half of incarcerated fathers (54 percent) report being the primary source of financial support for their children prior to their incarceration (Glaze and Maruschak 2008). Furthermore, for fathers who did not live with their children prior to being incarcerated, incarceration is likely to result in unpaid child support (see Cancian, Meyer, and Han, this volume).

14. Furthermore, it is now widely accepted that, in a context in which multipartner fertility is relatively common, mothers may not be aware of their partners' full fertility histories such that maternal reports may be unreliable (Greene and Biddlecom 2000).

References

Allen, Sarah M., and Alan J. Hawkins. 1999. Maternal gatekeeping: Mothers' beliefs and behaviors that inhibit greater father involvement in family work. *Journal of Marriage and Family* 61:199–212.

Amato, Paul. 1987. Family processes in one-parent, stepparent and intact families: The child's point of view. *Journal of Marriage and the Family* 49:327–37.

Amato, Paul R. 2005. The impact of family formation change on the cognitive, social, and emotional well-being of the next generation. *The Future of Children* 15 (2): 75–96.

Amato, Paul, and Julie Sobolewski. 2004. The effects of divorce on fathers and children: Nonresidential fathers and stepfathers. In *The role of the father in child development*, 4th edition, ed. Michael E. Lamb, 341–67. Hoboken, NJ: Wiley.

Anderson, Kermyt G., Hillard Kaplan, and Jane B. Lancaster. 1999. Paternal care by genetic fathers and stepfathers I: Reports from Albuquerque men. *Evolution and Human Behavior* 20:405–31.

Anderson, Kermyt G., Hillard Kaplan, and Jane B. Lancaster. 2007. Confidence of paternity, divorce, and investment in children by Albuquerque men. *Evolution and Human Behavior* 28:1–10.

Argys, Laura, Elizabeth Peters, Steven Cook, Steven Garasky, Lenna Nepomnyaschy, and Elaine Sorensen. 2007. Measuring contact between children and nonresident fathers. In *Handbook of measurement issues in family research*, eds. Sandra L. Hofferth and Lynne M. Casper, 375–98. Mahwah, NJ: Lawrence Erlbaum.

Becker, Gary S. 1974. A theory of social interactions. *Journal of Political Economy* 82:1063–93.

Becker, Gary S. 1991. *A treatise on the family*. Cambridge, MA: Harvard University Press.

Becker, Gary S. 1993. Nobel lecture: The economic way of looking at behavior. *Journal of Political Economy* 101 (3): 385–409.

Berger, Lawrence M., Marcia J. Carlson, Sharon H. Bzostek, and Cynthia Osborne. 2008. Parenting practices of resident fathers: The role of marital and biological ties. *Journal of Marriage and Family* 70 (3): 625–39.

Bergstrom, Theodore C. 1997. A survey of theories of the family. In *Handbook of population and family economics*, eds. Mark R. Rosenzweig and Oded Stark, 21–74. New York, NY: North Holland.

Bunting, Lisa, and Colette McAuley. 2004. Teenage pregnancy and parenthood: The role of fathers. *Child & Family Social Work* 9 (3): 295–303.

Bzostek, Sharon H., Marcia J. Carlson, and Sara S. McLanahan. 2007. Repartnering after a nonmarital birth: Does mother know best? Center for Research on Child Wellbeing Working Paper 2006-27-FF, Princeton University, Princeton, NJ.

Cabrera, Natasha J., Catherine S. Tamis-LeMonda, Robert H. Bradley, Sandra Hofferth, and Michael E. Lamb. 2000. Fatherhood in the twenty-first century. *Child Development* 71:127–36.

Carlson, Marcia J., Frank F. Furstenberg Jr., and Sara S. McLanahan. 2010. The implications of multi-partnered fertility for parental relationships and children's wellbeing. Unpublished manuscript, University of Wisconsin–Madison.

Carlson, Marcia J., and Sara S. McLanahan. 2004. Early father involvement in fragile families. In *Conceptualizing and measuring father involvement*, eds. Randal D. Day and Michael E. Lamb, 241–71. Mahwah, NJ: Lawrence Erlbaum.

Carlson, Marcia J., and Sara S. McLanahan. 2010. Fathers in fragile families. In *The role of the father in child development*, 5th edition, ed. Michael E. Lamb, 241–69. New York, NY: Wiley.

Carlson, Marcia J., Sara S. McLanahan, and Jeanne Brooks-Gunn. 2008. Co-parenting and nonresident fathers' involvement with young children after a nonmarital birth. *Demography* 45 (2): 461–88.

Case, Anne, I-Fen Lin, and Sara S. McLanahan. 2001. How hungry is the selfish gene? *The Economic Journal* 110 (446): 781–804.

Case, Anne, I-Fen Lin, and Sara S. McLanahan. 2003. Explaining trends in child support: Economic, demographic, and policy effects. *Demography* 40:171–89.

Cherlin, Andrew. 1978. Remarriage as an incomplete institution. *American Journal of Sociology* 84 (3): 634–50.

Cherlin, Andrew J. 2004. The deinstitutionalization of marriage. *Journal of Marriage and Family* 66:848–61.

Cherlin, Andrew J., and Frank F. Furstenberg Jr. 1994. Stepfamilies in the United States: A reconsideration. *Annual Review of Sociology* 20:359–81.

Child Trends. 2002. *Charting parenthood: A statistical portrait of fathers and mothers in America*. New York, NY: Child Trends.

Coleman, Marilyn, Lawrence Ganong, and Mark Fine. 2000. Reinvestigating remarriage: Another decade of progress. *Journal of Marriage and Family* 62:1288–1307.

Cooksey, Elizabeth C., and Patricia H. Craig. 1998. Parenting from a distance: The effects of paternal characteristics on contact between nonresidential fathers and their children. *Demography* 35:187–200.

Cooksey, Elizabeth C., and Michelle M. Fondell. 1996. Spending time with his kids: Effects of family structure on fathers' and children's lives. *Journal of Marriage and the Family* 58:693–707.

Crockett, Lisa J., David J. Eggebeen, and Alan J. Hawkins. 1993. Father's presence and young children's behavioral and cognitive adjustment. *Journal of Family Issues* 14 (3): 355–77.

Daly, Martin, and Margo I. Wilson. 1987. Evolutionary psychology and family violence. In *Sociobiology and psychology*, eds. Charles Crawford, Martin Smith, and Dennis Krebs, 293–309. Hillsdale, NJ: Lawrence Erlbaum.

Daly, Martin, and Margo I. Wilson. 2000. The evolutionary psychology of marriage and divorce. In *The ties that bind: Perspectives on marriage and cohabitation*, ed. Linda J. Waite, 91–110. New York, NY: Aldine de Gruyter.

Danziger, Sheldon K., and Norma Radin. 1990. Absent does not equal uninvolved: Predictors of fathering in teen mother families. *Journal of Marriage and Family* 52 (3): 636–42.

Edin, Kathryn. 2000. What do low-income single mothers say about marriage? *Social Problems* 47:112–33.

Edin, Kathryn, and Maria Kefalas. 2005. *Promises I can keep: Why poor women put motherhood before marriage*. Los Angeles, CA: University of California Press.

Emlen, Stephen L. 1997. The evolutionary study of human family systems. *Social Science Information* 36:563–89.

England, Paula, and George Farkas. 1986. *Households, employment, and gender: A social, economic, and demographic view*. New York, NY: Aldine.

Fagan, Jay, and Marina Barnett. 2003. The relationship between maternal gatekeeping, paternal competence, mother' attitudes about the father role, and father involvement. *Journal of Family Issues* 24 (8): 1020–43.

Fisher, Philip, Leslie Leve, Catherine O'Leary, and Craig Leve. 2003. Parental monitoring of children's behavior: Variation across stepmother, stepfather and two-parent biological families. *Family Relations* 52:45–52.

Furstenberg, Frank F., Jr. 1995. Fathering in the inner city: Paternal participation and public policy. In *Fatherhood: Contemporary theory, research, and social policy*, ed. William Marsiglio. Thousand Oaks, CA: Sage Publications.

Furstenberg, Frank F., and Andrew Cherlin. 1991. *Divided families: What happens to children when parents part*. Cambridge, MA: Harvard University Press.

Furstenberg, Frank F., and Katherine M. Harris. 1993. When and why fathers matter: Impacts of father involvement on the children of adolescent mothers. In *Young unwed father: Changing roles and emerging policies*, eds. Robert I. Lerman and Theodora J. Ooms, 117–40. Philadelphia, PA: Temple University Press.

Gibson-Davis, Christina M. 2008. Family structure effects on maternal and paternal parenting in low-income families. *Journal of Marriage and Family* 70:452–65.

Glaze, Lauren E., and Laura M. Maruschak. 2008. *Parents in prison and their minor children*. Washington, DC: U.S. Department of Justice, Bureau of Justice Statistics.

Graefe, Deborah R., and Daniel T. Lichter. 1999. Life course transitions of American children: Parental cohabitation, marriage, and single motherhood. *Demography* 36 (2): 205–17.

Greene, Margaret E., and Ann F. Biddlecom. 2000. Absent and problematic men: Demographic accounts of male reproductive roles. *Population and Development Review* 26 (1): 81–115.

Hairston, Creasie F. 2001. Fathers in prison: Responsible fatherhood and responsible public policies. *Marriage and Family Review* 32:111–26.

Hairston, Creasie F. 2008. *Focus on children with incarcerated parents: An overview of the research literature*. Baltimore, MD: Annie E. Casey Foundation.

Hamilton, Brady E., Joyce A. Martin, and Stephanie J. Ventura. 2009. Births: Preliminary data for 2007. *National vital statistics reports* 57 (12). Hyattsville, MD: National Center for Health Statistics.

Hawkins, Alan J., and Rob Palkovitz. 1999. Beyond ticks and clicks: The need for more diverse and broader conceptualizations and measures of father involvement. *Journal of Men's Studies* 8 (1): 11–32.

Hernandez, Donald J. 1993. *America's children: Resources from family, government, and economy*. New York, NY: Russell Sage Foundation.

Hetherington, E. Mavis, and Kathleen Jodl. 1994. Stepfamilies as settings for child development. In *Stepfamilies: Who benefits? Who does not?* eds. Alan Booth and Judy Dunn, 55–79. Mahwah, NJ: Lawrence Erlbaum.

Hetherington, E. Mavis, and Margaret Stanley-Hagan. 1999. Stepfamilies. In *Parenting and child development in "nontraditional" families*, ed. Michael E. Lamb, 137–59. Mahwah, NJ: Lawrence Erlbaum.

Hewlett, Barry S. 2000. Culture, history, and sex: Anthropological contributions to conceptualizing father involvement. *Marriage & Family Review* 29 (2/3): 59–74.

Hofferth, Sandra L. 2003. Race/ethnic differences in father involvement in two-parent families: Culture, context, or economy. *Journal of Family Issues* 24 (2): 185–216.

Hofferth, Sandra L., and Kermyt G. Anderson. 2003. Are all dads equal? Biology versus marriage as a basis for paternal investment. *Journal of Marriage and Family* 65:213–23.

Hofferth, Sandra L., Natasha Cabrera, Marcia Carlson, Rebekah L. Coley, Randall Day, and Holly Schindler. 2007. Resident father involvement and social fathering. In *Handbook of measurement issues in family research*, eds. Sandra L. Hofferth and Lynne M. Casper, 335–74. Mahwah, NJ: Lawrence Erlbaum.

Hofferth, Sandra L., Jeffrey L. Stueve, Joseph Pleck, Suzanne Bianchi, and Liana Sayer. 2002. The demography of fathers: What fathers do. In *Handbook of father involvement: Multidisciplinary perspectives*, eds. Catherine S. Tamis-LeMonda and Natasha Cabrera, 63–90. Mahwah, NJ: Lawrence Erlbaum.

Hynes, Kathryn, Kara Joyner, H. Elizabeth Peters, and Felicia Y. DeLeone. 2008. The transition to early fatherhood: National estimates based on multiple surveys. *Demographic Research* 18:337–75.

Kreider, Rose M. 2008. *Living arrangements of children: 2004*. Washington, DC: U.S. Census Bureau.

Krishnakumar, Ambika, and Maureen M. Black. 2003. Family processes within three-generation households and adolescent mothers' satisfaction with father involvement. *Journal of Family Psychology* 17 (4): 488–98.

Lamb, Michael E., ed. 1987. *The father's role: Cross-cultural perspectives*. Mahwah, NJ: Lawrence Erlbaum.

Lamb, Michael E. 2000. The history of research on father involvement: An overview. *Marriage and Family Review* 29:23–42.

Lamb, Michael E., Joseph H. Pleck, Eric L. Charnov, and James A. Levine. 1987. A biosocial perspective on paternal behavior and involvement. In *Parenting across the life span: Biosocial dimensions*, eds. Janet B. Lancaster, Jeanne Altman, Alice S. Rossi, and Lonnie R. Sherrod, 111–42. Hawthorne, NY: Aldine de Gruyter.

Landale, Nancy S., and R. S. Oropesa. 2001. Father involvement in the lives of mainland Puerto Rican children: Contributions of nonresident, cohabiting, and married fathers. *Social Forces* 79:945–68.

Lerman, Robert I. 1993. A national profile of young unwed fathers. In *Young unwed fathers: Changing roles and emerging policies*, eds. Robert I. Lerman and Theodora J. Ooms, 27–51. Philadelphia, PA: Temple University Press.

Lerman, Robert, and Elaine Sorenson. 2000. Father involvement with their nonmarital children: Patterns, determinants, and effects on their earnings. *Marriage & Family Review* 29 (2/3): 137–58.

Lundberg, Shelley, Sara S. McLanahan, and Elaina Rose. 2005. Child gender and father involvement in fragile families. *Demography* 44 (1): 79–92.

Manning, Wendy D., and Susan Brown. 2006. Children's economic well-being in married and cohabiting parent families. *Journal of Marriage and Family* 68:345–62.

Manning, Wendy, and Daniel Lichter. 1996. Parental cohabitation and children's economic well-being. *Journal of Marriage and the Family* 58:998–1010.

Manning, Wendy D., and Pamela J. Smock. 2000. "Swapping" families: Serial parenting and economic support for children. *Journal of Marriage and the Family* 62:111–22.

Manning, Wendy D., Susan D. Steward, and Pamela J. Smock. 2003. The complexity of fathers' parenting responsibilities and involvement with nonresident children. *Journal of Family Issues* 24 (5): 645–67.

Marsiglio, William. 2000. Adolescent fathers in the United States: Their initial living arrangements, marital experiences, and educational outcomes. *Family Planning Perspectives* 19:247–50.

Marsiglio, William, Paul Amato, Randall D. Day, and Michael E. Lamb. 2000. Scholarship on fatherhood in the 1990s and beyond. *Journal of Marriage and the Family* 62:1173–91.

Marsiglio, William, Randall D. Day, and Michael E. Lamb. 2000. Exploring fatherhood diversity: Implications for conceptualizing father involvement. *Marriage & Family Review* 29:269–93.

McBride, Brent A., Geoffrey L. Brown, Kelly K. Bost, Nana Shin, Brian Vaughn, and Byran Korth. 2005. Paternal identity, maternal gatekeeping, and father involvement. *Family Relations* 54:360–72.

McLanahan, Sara, and Christine Percheski. 2008. Family structure and the reproduction of inequalities. *Annual Review of Sociology* 34:257–76.

McLanahan, Sara S., and Gary D. Sandefur. 1994. *Growing up with a single parent: What hurts, what helps.* Cambridge, MA: Harvard University Press.

Meyer, Daniel, Maria Cancian, and Steven T. Cook. 2005. Multiple-partner fertility: Incidence and implications for child support policy. *Social Service Review* 79 (4): 577–601.

Mumola, Christopher J. 2000. *Incarcerated parents and their children.* Washington, DC: U.S. Department of Justice, Bureau of Justice Statistics.

Nelson, Timothy J. 2004. Low-income fathers. *Annual Review of Sociology* 30:427–51.

Nepomnyaschy, Lenna. 2007. Child support and father-child contact: Testing reciprocal pathways. *Demography* 44 (1): 93–112.

Nock, Steven L. 1995. A comparison of marriages and cohabiting relationships. *Journal of Family Issues* 16 (1): 53–76.

Poehlmann, Julie. 2005. Incarcerated mothers' contact with children, perceived family relationships, and depressive symptoms. *Journal of Family Psychology* 19 (3): 350–57.

Rane, Thomas R., and Brent A. McBride. 2000. Identity theory as a guide to understanding fathers' involvement with their children. *Journal of Family Issues* 21:347–66.

Reichman, Nancy E., Hope Corman, and Kelly Noonan. 2004. Effects of child health on parents' relationship status. *Demography* 41:569–84.

Roggman, Lori A., Lisa K. Boyce, Gina A. Cook, and Jerry Cook. 2002. Getting dads involved: Predictors of father involvement in Early Head Start and with their children. *Infant Mental Health Journal* 23 (1–2): 62–78.

Ryan, Rebecca M., Ariel Kalil, and Kathleen M. Ziol-Guest. 2008. Longitudinal patterns of nonresident fathers' involvement: The role of resources and relations. *Journal of Marriage and Family* 70:962–77.

Schoppe-Sullivan, Sarah J., Geoffrey L. Brown, Elizabeth A. Cannon, Sarah C. Mangelsdorf, and Sarah Sokolowski. 2008. Maternal gatekeeping, coparenting quality, and fathering behavior in families with infants. *Journal of Family Psychology* 22 (3): 389–98.

Smock, Pamela J. 2000. Cohabitation in the United States: An appraisal of research themes, findings, and implications. *Annual Review of Sociology* 26:1–20.

Smock, Pamela J., and Wendy D. Manning. 1997. Cohabiting partners' economic circumstances and marriage. *Demography* 34 (3): 331–41.

Tach, Laura, Ronald Mincy, and Kathryn Edin. 2010. Parenting as a package deal: Relationships, fertility, and nonresident father involvement among unmarried parents. *Demography* 47 (1): 181–204.

Thomson, Elizabeth, Sara S. McLanahan, and Roberta B. Curtin. 1992. Family structure, gender, and parental socialization. *Journal of Marriage and the Family* 54:368–78.

Townsend, Nicholas W. 2002. *The package deal: Marriage, work and fatherhood in men's lives.* Philadelphia, PA: Temple University Press.

Weiss, Yoram, and Robert J. Willis. 1985. Children as collective goods and divorce settlements. *Journal of Labor Economics* 3:268–92.

Yeung, W. Jean, John E. Sandberg, Pamela E. Davis-Kean, and Sandra L. Hofferth. 2001. Children's time with fathers in intact families. *Journal of Marriage and Family* 63 (1): 136–54.

The Relationship Contexts of Young Disadvantaged Men

By
LAURA TACH
and
KATHRYN EDIN

Recent improvements in data collection offer unprecedented insight into the romantic partnerships of disadvantaged men, revealing higher levels of instability, complexity, and commitment than previously understood. Young disadvantaged men are often involved in casual romantic relationships that result in pregnancy. When this occurs, most men remain involved with the mother, are optimistic about the future of their relationships, and are committed to their children. Economic disadvantage, incarceration, conflict, and mistrust undermine the stability of these relationships, however, and most end within several years after the birth. New romantic relationships begin shortly thereafter, creating complex family structures. We know less about the patterns of interaction between couples that produce unstable partnerships or about the nature of romantic relationships that do not involve children. With our growing understanding of the presence of fathers in nonmarital households, policy-makers must adapt their policies to support, rather than undermine, these fragile unions.

Keywords: poverty; fatherhood; nonmarital childbearing; relationship quality; family instability

Laura Tach received her PhD in sociology and social policy from Harvard University and is currently a Robert Wood Johnson Health and Society Scholar at the University of Pennsylvania. In 2012, she will become an assistant professor of policy analysis and management at Cornell University. Her research examines how social contexts, particularly family structures and neighborhoods, influence the well-being of individuals. She is currently involved in projects studying mixed-income neighborhoods, multiple-partner fertility and father involvement, and the Earned Income Tax Credit.

Kathryn Edin is a professor of public policy and management at Harvard University. Her research focuses on urban poverty and family life. Her most recent publication (with Paula England), Unmarried Couples with Children *(Russell Sage Foundation 2007), is an analysis of a four-year study of fifty unmarried couples. Previous publications include* Promises I Can Keep: Why Poor Women Put Motherhood before Marriage *(with Maria J. Kefalas; University of California Press 2005) and* Making Ends Meet: How Single Mothers Survive Welfare and Low-Wage Work *(with Laura Lein; Russell Sage Foundation 1997).*

DOI: 10.1177/0002716210393680

After reading the scholarly literature on young disadvantaged men, one might conclude that their romantic partnerships are among the least consequential aspects of their lives because very little research has focused on their roles as partners. The near absence of quantitative scholarship on the topic has, until recently, resulted in part from serious data limitations. Household surveys routinely failed to ask questions about young disadvantaged men. Welfare agencies gave household heads—typically girlfriends and mothers—motives to hide these men. Schools failed them, and employers often eschewed them, relegating many to informal or illegal means of employment. The criminal justice system removed growing numbers of them from their families and communities during their prime family-building years. The absence of data on the roles young disadvantaged men played as partners was also evident in qualitative studies. Though earlier ethnographic work contained whole chapters on male-female relationships (Hannerz 1969; Liebow 1967; Rainwater 1970; Stack 1974), more recent treatments focused on their lives as gang members (Venkatesh 2000), drug dealers or petty criminals (Bourgois 1996; Sullivan 1989; Venkatesh 2006), absent fathers (Hamer 2001; Waller 2002), or employees (Royster 2003), or on how they understood their marginalized positions in society (Young 2004).[1]

In recent years, survey data have improved. New longitudinal studies, such as the National Longitudinal Survey of Youth (NLSY), followed cohorts of men from youth through adulthood. We learned much from these new longitudinal studies about the basic demographic facts of young disadvantaged men's lives: they have low levels of schooling and employment; high rates of nonmarital fertility; and low rates of marriage, paying child support, and visitation. Much of the survey evidence we now have about the content and quality of their relationships comes from a new longitudinal survey, the Fragile Families and Child Wellbeing study, which follows a cohort of children born to unmarried parents in the late 1990s.[2] This survey offers of wealth of new information about young disadvantaged men as partners and parents. Via this study and others, we are beginning to piece together a portrait of the romantic lives of young disadvantaged men.

In this review, we focus on the following questions: What are the relationship dynamics between young disadvantaged men and their romantic partners? What makes some romantic partnerships shatter and others cohere? How do families function after romantic partnerships between unmarried parents end? Existing research shows that young disadvantaged men are often involved in casual romantic relationships that result in pregnancy. When this occurs, most men do not flee; they stay involved with the mother during the pregnancy, are optimistic about the future of their romantic relationships, and are committed to being there for their children. Yet these men face a host of barriers to realizing this optimism. Economic disadvantage, incarceration, and mistrust undermine the stability of their romantic relationships, and most relationships end within several years after the birth. New romantic relationships begin shortly thereafter, creating complex family structures and obligations to multiple households. While we have a clear picture of the extent of instability and complexity that characterizes young disadvantaged fathers' relationships, we know much less about the everyday patterns of interaction between couples that produce this instability and complexity and the nature of romantic relationships that do not involve children. It is critically important that scholars and policy-makers understand more about the romantic lives of disadvantaged men because the partnerships they form often do produce children, and stable high-quality partnerships promote child well-being (Beck et al. 2009; Cavanagh and Huston 2006; Cooper et al. 2008; Craigie 2008; Fomby and Osborne 2008; Osborne and McLanahan 2007).

Romantic Relationships and Nonmarital Childbearing

Disadvantaged young men enter into partnerships that produce children unusually early. In the 1990s, 21 percent of men living in poverty reported that they became fathers before age 20, a rate twice as high as for those who were not poor, and the disparity was the same for both whites and nonwhites (Child Trends 2002). While disadvantaged men initiate sex only a little earlier and use contraception only slightly less often than men who are not poor (see Nelson [2004] for a review), there are striking differences by economic status and race in the probability that a young man will father a child within a *nonmarital* relationship (Ellwood and Jencks 2004; McLanahan 2004; Nock 2007). This pattern of early nonmarital childbearing among the least-educated Americans often enrages taxpayers and concerns policy-makers, who note that many women and children end up poor— and dependent on the public purse—as a result. However, only one in five children born outside of marriage in the late 1990s was truly born to a "single" parent; 80 percent of unmarried couples remained together until the time of the birth, and half were living together (Kennedy and Bumpass 2007). The discovery that most births to so-called "single mothers" were in fact to romantically involved mothers and fathers has led to a new term coined to describe them: "fragile families."

In light of this evidence, scholars and policy-makers should understand the relationship contexts in which nonmarital children are conceived and raised. There is very little survey evidence on relationship contexts at the time of conception. The Fragile Families and Child Wellbeing study asks mothers and fathers who were still together by the time their child was a year old about the duration of their relationship. The median length of time married parents had known one another was 5.8 years, compared with only 2.4 years for cohabitors (Osborne, Manning, and Smock 2007). If we subtract the nine months of pregnancy from these figures, the typical unmarried couple who was still together at the first birthday had known one another for only about a year and a half before conception; those who were not living together or who were having their first child had known each other for even less time.[3]

Thus, the typical disadvantaged young man enters into fatherhood for the first time on the basis of a partnership that is relatively short-lived. We know less about the content and quality of these romantic partnerships at the time of conception. One study, based on an in-depth longitudinal qualitative analysis of a subsample of forty-eight unmarried couples from the Fragile Families and Child Wellbeing study, found that although a fair number of unmarried fathers rated their relationships as "serious" prior to conception, fully half described them as "casual," and they were more likely to describe their pre-conception relationships as casual than their female partners were (Edin et al. 2007). Similarly, Kevin Roy (2008), who draws qualitative data from two samples of disadvantaged minority fathers, portrays the partnering process that led to shared children as haphazard (see also Furstenberg 1976).

The children that result from these relationships, then, are seldom explicitly planned. Poor women are more likely to report that a pregnancy was unintended than their nonpoor counterparts (61 vs. 41 percent), and unmarried women are more likely to report an unintended pregnancy than married women (74 vs. 27 percent) (Finer and Henshaw 2006; Henshaw 1998; Musick 2002). Similar patterns hold for men, with 57 percent of men with less than a high school degree reporting that their pregnancy was "wanted," compared with 87 percent of men with a college degree; 70 percent of men who were married at the time of the birth characterized the pregnancy as wanted, compared with just 36 percent of men who were not living with the mother at the time of the birth (Martinez et al. 2006).

Pregnancy intentions are difficult to measure, however. Qualitative evidence suggests that the modal pregnancy is neither fully planned nor avoided (Augustine, Nelson, and Edin 2009; Edin and Kefalas 2005; Edin et al. 2007; see also Waller 2002). In their study of the fertility histories of 183 poor fathers, Jennifer Augustine and colleagues (2009) found that while few men actively planned or consistently took actions to avoid pregnancy, a large minority reported an ambivalent desire to have children and used little if any contraception, even though they knew what might result from such actions. The rest—about half of the total—were not using regular contraception either and said they were just "not thinking" about the consequences of their actions at the time. These results are consistent with those drawn from the fertility histories of the forty-eight unmarried fathers in the qualitative subsample of the Fragile Families and Child Wellbeing study (Edin et al. 2007), in which women were somewhat more likely to describe an ambivalent desire for pregnancy, while men's responses were more likely to fall in the "not thinking" category.[4]

The Fragile Families and Child Wellbeing study shows that an overwhelming majority of unmarried fathers (90 percent) offered financial and emotional support to the mother during her pregnancy, and roughly eight in ten visited her and the child in the hospital (McLanahan et al. 2003). In contrast to popular images, most unmarried men are not eager to flee their parental responsibilities as soon as the child is conceived (Achatz and MacAllum 1994; Augustine, Nelson, and Edin 2009; Hamer 2001; Nelson, Torres, and Edin 2002; Nurse 2002; Waller 2002), though this certainly does sometimes happen.[5] Mounting evidence shows that young men often readily acknowledge paternity rather than contest it (Edin, Tach, and Mincy 2009; Furstenberg 1995; Sullivan 1993; Waller 2002), and many eagerly embrace the role of father, at least initially (Hamer 2001; Waller 2002; Young 2004).

We know little about couple dynamics during pregnancy, as most existing work is based on retrospective data collected after the child was born, and in the case of the Fragile Families and Child Wellbeing study, data were collected in the hospital in the "magic moment" right after the child was born. A few scholars offer retrospective accounts of this pregnancy period, drawing mainly on data from women (Edin and Kefalas 2005; Reed 2008), which suggest that this period may be fraught with turmoil and plagued with serious relationship problems such as domestic abuse and infidelity. Most couples reconcile by the time of the birth because a shared child, though viewed as a poor basis for marriage, offers a strong motive to stay together for the betterment of the child (Edin, Kefalas, and Reed 2004).

In sum, social scientists have produced an increasingly clear portrait of young disadvantaged men as they and their partners enter into parenthood. Rather than fleeing at the news of a pregnancy, most unmarried fathers remain involved and supportive of mothers during the pregnancy, and half of unmarried couples are living together at the time their child is born. Outside of retrospective characterizations offered by fathers gauging the seriousness of their relationships prior to conception, we know little about couples' romantic partnerships prior to conception and during pregnancy. The available evidence suggests that, relative to married couples, the courtship period before an unmarried couple's first birth may be brief, the partnering process haphazard, and the pregnancy period tumultuous.

Relationship Expectations and Commitment

Despite high rates of nonmarital childbearing, marriage has by no means lost its status as a cultural ideal for poor and minority young men and women in the United States (Edin and Kefalas 2005; Gibson-Davis, Edin, and McLanahan 2005). The National Survey of Families and Households (NSFH) asked a nationally representative sample of American women and men whether "it's all right for an unmarried couple to live together even if they have no interest in considering marriage." Only a minority of college graduates disapproved (about four in ten), but fully two-thirds of high school dropouts disapproved or strongly disapproved of the notion (Sayer, Wright, and Edin 2003). The Fragile Families and Child Wellbeing study supports this view among unmarried parents as well—two-thirds of new mothers and three-quarters of new fathers agreed with the statement "it is better for children if their parents are married." They also disapproved of cohabitation as a long-term substitute for marriage (Edin, Kefalas, and Reed 2004; Sayer, Wright, and Edin 2003).

Both unmarried fathers and mothers report strong desires to marry around the time their children are born. The Fragile Families and Child Wellbeing study showed that though most parents were poor or near poor, the majority (80 percent) of romantically involved unmarried parents claimed that there was a "good" to "certain" chance that they would marry one another. Among cohabitors, 86 percent of the mothers and 91 percent of the fathers said that the chances that the couple would marry were good or certain (Center for Research on Child Wellbeing 2003).[6] The majority of mothers and fathers also agreed that a father should have child support obligations, the right to see his children, and the ability to make decisions about how they were raised. When they are romantically involved, mothers and fathers are overwhelmingly in agreement about these rights and obligations, but mothers are less likely to report that fathers should have such rights when the couple is no longer together (Center for Research on Child Wellbeing 2001).

For some couples, the pregnancy serves as a powerful motivation to try to stay together, even if the future of their relationship was in doubt before the conception (Edin, England, and Linnenberg 2003). Some couples solidify their increasing commitment by moving in together after finding out about the pregnancy. The Fragile Families and Child Wellbeing study estimates that, of those cohabiting at the time of the mother's first birth, 15 percent entered into cohabitation in the period between conception and birth.[7] Considerably more couples begin living together in the year after the birth. The survey also reveals that even among those not cohabiting but in a romantic relationship, the overwhelming majority say that they plan to cohabit (Center for Research on Child Wellbeing 2003; McLanahan et al. 2003).[8] Thus, cohabitation is a common response to having a child outside of marriage (Edin, Kefalas, and Reed 2004). While some literature shows that unmarried couples believe that having a child together is clearly a bad reason to marry (Edin and Kefalas 2005; Gibson-Davis, Edin, and McLanahan 2005), it is a good reason to stay together and live together, at least temporarily.

In contrast to the "hit and run" image of young disadvantaged men as eager to flee from family commitments when a child enters the world, a number of surveys have confirmed that unmarried men who are in relationships with the mother—both with and without children—have expectations of marriage at least as strong as their partners' (Brown 2000; Bumpass, Sweet, and Cherlin 1991; see also Hannerz 1969). However imprecisely measured, expectations to marry are strong predictors of future relationship stability, perhaps because they are indirect measures of relationship commitment. Men's expectations are somewhat more consequential for union transitions than women's expectations, though both marriage and relationship stability are more likely when either partner expects to marry (Brown 2000; Waller and McLanahan 2005).

The existing literature shows that men say they value marriage highly and claim, at least around the time of a child's birth, that they are optimistic about their chances of eventual marriage to the child's mother. We know less about mothers' and fathers' expectations for one another—as partners, parents, and providers—in the context of nonmarital relationships. In the next section, we discuss how couples' optimism about marriage clashes with their high economic and relationship standards for marriage and how structural and institutional forces conspire to undermine the stability of their unions.

Relationship Instability

Desires to marry and remain together do not always translate into reality, and nonmarital unions are considerably less stable than marital unions. Though U.S. divorce rates are high relative to those of other industrialized countries, nearly two-thirds of all children born within marriage still live with both parents by age 15, while only about one in five of those born to cohabiting couples do so (Andersson 2002). For children whose parents were romantically involved but not living together when they were born, more than 72 percent see their parents' relationships end by the time they are just five years old (Center for Research on Child Wellbeing 2007).[9] Using data from the 1995 National Survey of Family Growth, Raley and Wildsmith (2004) show that adding transitions into and out of cohabitation to those into and out of marriage increases levels of family instability by about 30 percent for white children and more than 100 percent for black children. These estimates still likely understate the amount of instability children experience, since they include only transitions for the mothers (not the fathers) and consider only residential transitions, not all romantic relationship transitions. Using the Fragile Families and Child Wellbeing study, Beck et al. (2009) found that 83 percent of unmarried mothers experienced at least one relationship transition during the first five years after the child's birth and 50 percent experienced three or more transitions; in contrast, just 24 percent of married mothers experienced at least one transition. Additionally, only 2 percent of unmarried mothers who were single at the time of the birth remained stably single during the child's first five years. Because they capture only transitions from wave to wave, this study also likely misses some transitions.

Sources of instability

There are large socioeconomic and racial differences in the experience of family instability. Cohabiting and marital unions are especially unstable among blacks (Manning, Smock, and Majumdar 2004), whereas marriages are more stable among Hispanics, especially Hispanic immigrants (Bean, Berg, and Van Hook 1996). Low-socioeconomic-status (SES) marriages are also more prone to instability (Graefe and Lichter 1999; Martin 2004). Still, low-SES marriages remain more stable than low-SES cohabitations. Analyses that examine the dynamics of couples' behavior within disadvantaged populations identify men's behaviors as a key source of relationship instability, particularly drug use and physical abuse (Waller and Swisher 2006). M. Wilson and Brooks-Gunn (2001) found that, relative to married fathers, unmarried fathers were more likely to have used illicit drugs, drunk, smoked, or physically abused the mothers of their children. These behaviors were common reasons women cited for ending relationships or failing to enter into new relationships (Amato and Previti 2003; Amato and Rogers 1997; Cherlin et al. 2004; Reed 2007).

Incarceration is also deeply implicated in the romantic relationships of disadvantaged young men, particularly African American men (Western and Wildeman 2009). Relationships are undermined by men's absence from the family and the community, the logistical problems of visitation, and the shame fathers feel as a result of their incarceration (Arditti, Lambert-Shute, and Joest 2003; Arditti, Smock, and Parkman 2005; Edin, Nelson, and Paranal 2004; Roy and Dyson 2005; Waller 2002). Men's absence during incarceration, for example, imposes economic pressures on the men (and their families) and provides opportunities for women to move on to new partners. Even when this does not occur, the physical separation and lack of ability to monitor one another's behavior fuels suspicion and mistrust (Edin and Kefalas 2005). Swisher and Waller (2008) found that couples' relationship quality declined more for non-Latino white fathers following incarceration than it did for Latino and African American fathers, although we know little about the interactions between partners that generated this pattern. Ethnographic studies of the adaptive strategies and dynamic nature of family structures among disadvantaged African Americans suggest a greater adaptability of African American families to the challenges of incarceration (Jarrett 1997; Jarrett and Burton 1999; Jarrett, Roy, and Burton 2002).

Prior incarceration decreases the chances fathers will live with or marry the mothers of their children (Hagan and Dinovitzer 1999; Lopoo and Western 2005; Western, Lopoo, and McLanahan 2004; Western and McLanahan 2000). The Fragile Families and Child Wellbeing study data revealed that men with prison or jail records were 37 percent less likely to be married and 19 percent less likely to be cohabiting than similar men who had never been incarcerated (Western, Lopoo, and McLanahan 2004). We know little about why this occurs. One in-depth study of forty incarcerated men in a work release program (Roy 2005) found that partner relationships were marked by confusion and conflict during incarceration, and deteriorating commitments between partners persisted after the men were released. Other ethnographic work suggests that disadvantaged minority men experience persistent supervision and threat of imprisonment in their communities, which undermines their already tenuous family and romantic relationships (Goffman 2009).

Numerous risk factors limit men's ability to remain in romantic partnerships, despite their stated desire to do so. However, the couples' dynamics that underlie this instability remain largely a black box (Waller 2008). We know little about how disadvantaged men manage to form relationships when many of the factors associated with breakup, such as lack of employment, drug use, and incarceration, are already evident when the women get pregnant. We also know little about how men learn to enact the roles of partner and father. Although we are beginning to learn some of the answers to these questions from qualitative studies, more systematic research is needed to understand how and why unions dissolve.

Getting married

Not all nonmarital unions end in dissolution. While three-quarters of romantically involved couples who do not live together break up by the child's fifth birthday, about one-quarter of those who were cohabiting marry, and another fifth remain stably living together (Center for Research on Child Wellbeing 2007). In-depth qualitative research reveals that the standards low-income unmarried parents of both genders have for marriage closely resemble the standards that their middle-class counterparts hold, even though their chances for meeting them are far lower. For the typical low-income unmarried father (or mother), a prerequisite for marriage is a set of financial assets that demonstrate that the couple has "arrived" economically. Most say that before they can marry, they will need a mortgage on a modest home, a car note, furniture, some money in the bank, and enough left over for a wedding. Without these marks of personal and collective achievement— often called the "marriage bar" by researchers—it would not be right to get married (Edin and Kefalas 2005; Gibson-Davis 2007). Both the in-depth Time, Love, Cash, Care, and Commitment study (TLC3) interviews with forty-eight unmarried fathers and mothers and qualitative work with 115 working- and lower-class cohabitors without children (Smock, Manning, and Porter 2005) found that these views were expressed by both men and women.

Clashing with the reality of poor economic prospects, these standards lead to an indeterminate delay in marriage for many couples. If couples are able to improve their economic prospects, marriage is more likely, while becoming poorer decreases the likelihood of marriage (Osborne 2005; Smock and Manning 1997). However, neither earnings nor income is associated with additional fertility (Gibson-Davis 2009). Men's economic standing is particularly important, and those with less education, low earnings, and weaker attachment to the labor force are less likely to marry (Goldstein and Kenney 2001; Lichter, LeClere, and McLaughlin 1991; Lloyd and South 1996; Manning and Smock 1995; Oppenheimer 2000; Sweeney 2002).[10] The declining economic fortunes of less-educated and minority men may explain some of the decline in marriage rates among disadvantaged groups since the 1970s (Ellwood and Jencks 2004; Oppenheimer 2000).

Many studies have documented a positive relationship between male employment rates and marriage in low-income communities (Lichter et al. 1992; Manning and Smock 1995; Sullivan 1989; Testa et al. 1989). W. Wilson and Neckerman (1986) linked low marriage rates among poor African Americans to the shortage of "marriageable men" in these communities. In this thesis, low male employment rates and high rates of imprisonment depleted the supply of suitable marriage partners for black women in poor urban neighborhoods. Combining Fragile Families and Child Wellbeing study data with data on local marriage market conditions, Harknett and McLanahan (2004) also found that an undersupply of employed African American men could explain some of the racial and ethnic differences in marriage rates *following* a nonmarital birth. In a similar analysis, Watson and McLanahan (2009) found that, conditional on their own incomes, unmarried couples were more likely to marry if their incomes were the same or higher than the median income in the city where they lived. These studies provide further evidence that local contexts in the availability of suitable marriage partners may influence marriage rates among disadvantaged men.

The rules governing entry into marriage are not the same as those governing entry into cohabitation (Reed 2007; see also Hannerz 1969; Liebow 1967). Entrance into cohabitation is often not a deliberate decision; it is more often due to "drift" (Manning and Smock 2005; Reed 2007; Sassler 2004). For unmarried parents, cohabiting sometimes begins in response to a pregnancy, but cohabiting parents do not believe they should marry simply because they have a child together (Edin and Kefalas 2005; Edin, Nelson, and Reed forthcoming). Both men and women view cohabitation as a practical response to parenthood that allows them to coparent and share expenses yet avoid the greater expectations of commitment and more traditional and scripted family roles they associate with marriage (Reed 2008). Cohabitation also allows the couple to remain together in the face of a relationship that is of lower quality than they would consider acceptable for marriage. In fact, such couples often fear that if they were to marry, given their current relationship quality, they would break up (Edin and Kefalas 2005).

Both disadvantaged women and men hold similar standards for marriage but are confronted with a host of conditions that prevent them from meeting those standards. Understanding how men view their roles as partners and the responsibilities these roles entail, particularly in the risky contexts they face, is a fruitful line of future research. The large racial difference in the chances of marriage also suggests that differences in cultural norms and community contexts ought to be considered (Furstenberg 2001; Young and Holcomb 2007).

Family Complexity

High levels of instability in unmarried couples' relationships result in a great deal of family complexity, because after couples break up, they repartner and have new children quickly. International comparisons show that among women with children, the rate of repartnering following the breakup of a nonmarital (cohabiting) union is exceedingly rapid in the United States (Andersson 2002).[11] As a result, almost 60 percent of children born to unmarried new parents in the Fragile Families and Child Wellbeing study had at least one half-sibling at the time of their birth, despite the fact that their parents were, on average, only in their midtwenties (Carlson and Furstenberg 2006). When these parents break up, more than half of mothers and half of fathers repartner, either in a dating or coresidential relationship, by the time the child turns five; likewise, a quarter of mothers and a quarter of fathers have subsequent children from new partners, adding even more half-siblings to the mix (Tach, Mincy, and Edin 2010).

Unmarried mothers who repartner typically do so with men who have considerably more human capital and fewer behavioral problems than their prior partners (Bzostek 2008; Graefe and Lichter 2007), but we know next to nothing about the quality of the subsequent partnerships fathers engage in. Nor do we know much about how stable these subsequent unions are. Drawing on other research showing that complexity is strongly associated with dissolution (Cherlin 1992; Kreider and Fields 2005; National Center for Health Statistics 2002), we can infer that these new pairings are likely quite fragile. Men are more likely to experience multiple-partner fertility when they have a first sexual experience or a first child at a young age or have children outside of marriage, whereas having more than one child with any given partner is associated with reduced odds. There are also racial and economic disparities in the likelihood of multiple-partner fertility. Blacks and Hispanics have greater odds of experiencing multiple-partner fertility than whites, and less-educated men are more likely to experience multiple-partner fertility than highly educated men (Carlson and Furstenberg 2006; Guzzo and Furstenberg 2007a, 2007b; Manlove et al. 2008; Mincy 2002).

Multiple-partner fertility, in turn, has many repercussions for the dynamics of family life. Having children from a previous union reduces the prospects that parents will marry (Carlson, McLanahan, and England 2004; Mincy 2002; Stewart, Manning, and Smock 2003; Upchurch, Lillard, and Panis 2001). Harknett and Knab (2007) have also found that kin networks provide less social support to couples who have children by other partners. Prior partners, who often continue to engage with the mother via child visitation, are a significant source of tension in new couples' relationships, as the prior partner's visits to see the child fuel jealousy from the current partner (Classens 2007; Hill 2007).

The "package deal"

For fathers, multiple-partner fertility means that scarce resources must be spread across several households, and this presents a challenge to maintaining meaningful involvement with all of the households to which they may be obligated. Yet fathers' tenuous ties to both current and former partners are crucial to maintain if fathers wish to remain meaningfully involved in their children's lives. In the American context, fatherhood has traditionally been viewed as part of a "package deal" (Furstenberg and Cherlin 1991; Townsend 2004), where fatherhood is contingent on the relationship between the father and the child's mother. In this view, men attempting to father outside of the context of a marriage or a coresidential union will have difficulty staying involved with their children. On a practical level, fathers must pay additional transaction costs to retain contact with children after a coresidential or romantic partnership ends, such as planning for visitation time, traveling to the mother's house and picking up the child, and having to bargain with the custodial parent for access to the child. Never-married fathers' costs may be particularly high, since no automatic procedure exists for adjudicating conflicts between parents or granting visitation rights to unmarried fathers at the time that paternity is established or child support is assigned. Fatherhood roles are even more difficult to fulfill when fathers have competing familial obligations in the context of multiple-partner fertility. These conflicts may be especially salient for whites and Hispanics, subpopulations where there may be no ready-made set of expectations for non–nuclear family relationships (Mincy and Pouncy 2007).

Relationship quality, crowding out, and gatekeeping

Fathers' relationships with the mothers of their children become increasingly complicated when the fathers and their former partners take on new partners and have subsequent children. For fathers this may lead to a "crowding out" effect, reducing fathers' investments and involvement with any one family. Furstenberg and his colleagues suggest that fathers' priorities may shift as they move from one family to the next, taking on commitments and obligations with a new romantic partner (Furstenberg 1995; Furstenberg and Cherlin 1991; Furstenberg and Harris 1992). Indeed, fathers visit their nonresident children less frequently (Carlson and Furstenberg 2007; Manning and Smock 1999) and provide less economic support to them via formal and informal arrangements (Manning and Smock 2000) when they have children with new partners. Fathers with children in different households are also less intensively involved with their current residential children (Carlson, McLanahan, and Brooks-Gunn 2008), causing strain for couples' current relationships (Carlson and Furstenberg 2007; Classens 2007; Hill 2007). Upon starting new romantic relationships, men also become more involved in the lives of the new partners' other children who live in the household, to whom they are not biologically related, taking on the role of "social father." In turn, biological fathers often see these new male partners as competition, asserting the primacy of the biological father-child role (Edin, Tach, and Mincy 2009).

Relationship quality between parents is crucial for the intensity and quality of fathers' involvement with their children, both in the context of romantic relationships and after those relationships have ended (Carlson, McLanahan, and England 2004; Coley and Chase-Lansdale 1999; Furstenberg and Cherlin 1991; Marsiglio and Cohan 2000). In other words, "good partners make good parents" (Carlson, McLanahan, and Brooks-Gunn 2006). Cooperative coparenting—the ability of mothers and fathers to actively engage with one another to share child-rearing responsibilities (Ahrons 1981; Furstenberg and Cherlin 1991)—is relatively uncommon, but it predicts more frequent and higher-quality father-child contact (Sobelewski and King 2005). Custodial mothers play an important role as "gatekeepers," either facilitating or hindering a nonresident father's involvement (Arditti 1995; Buchanan, Maccoby, and Dornbusch 1996), and mothers are more likely to restrict access when the two have a troubled relationship, regardless of whether they are currently romantically involved (Waller and Swisher 2006).

Survey data reveal an enormous amount of complexity in the family arrangements of disadvantaged men who have children outside of marriage. This complexity creates a new web of relationships with current and former partners and their children that men must navigate to remain involved with their children. What is more, fathers often must try to maintain relationships with the mothers of their children even after their romantic bond has ended, and more research is needed to unpack how former couples establish and maintain coparenting arrangements.

Conclusions

Developing accurate policy supports for low-income men—and the unstable and complex families in which they reside—requires more knowledge of the roles men play in these families as partners and as parents. The research we have reviewed here offers a glimpse into the relationship dynamics between young disadvantaged men and their romantic partners. These relationships, many of them recent and casual, are more likely to result in pregnancies that are neither completely planned nor avoided. When this occurs, most young men do not flee but stay involved with the mother during her pregnancy. For couples who make it through these often volatile nine months and are still together at the time of the birth, fathers are optimistic about the future of their romantic relationship with the mothers and are committed to being there for their children. Yet these couples face a host of barriers to realizing this optimism, including economic disadvantage, incarceration, mistrust and conflict, and a lack of institutionalized norms to govern behavior. These forces pull couples apart during the first years after their children are born, and researchers are only just starting to understand the family dynamics that underlie these high rates of instability. The relationships fathers have with the mothers of their children do not end once they break up, however, and the quality of the relationship between the two is a crucial foundation upon which nonresidential fathers are able to remain involved with their children and coparent within complex family settings. We know little about disadvantaged men's romantic partnerships that do not involve children, however.

With our growing understanding of the presence of fathers as partners in non-marital households, policy-makers must adapt their policies to support, rather than undermine, these fragile unions. This requires an understanding of not only how policies affect targeted populations but also how such policies affect the family as a whole. For example, household-based income limits on government pro-grams—such as the Earned Income Tax Credit or food stamps—may dissuade couples from pooling resources or getting married. Sending incarcerated men to prisons far away from their families may undermine fathers' ability to remain in regular contact with their partners and children. Child support paid by disad-vantaged fathers is often garnisheed by the state if the mothers receive welfare, creating incentives for noncompliance and evasion. Viewed in this light, it is clear that contemporary policy debates must broaden the focus from disadvantaged men as individuals to disadvantaged men as fathers, as partners, and as members of fragile and complex families.

Notes

1. For exceptions to this trend, see Anderson (1990, 1999) and Furstenberg (1995).

2. As nonmarital births are concentrated among disadvantaged men and women, this survey offers a wealth of new information. Its liability is that it excludes a considerable number of men who enter into romantic partnerships but do not become fathers. Due to this limitation, we largely confine our focus to young disadvantaged men with children.

3. Qualitative data drawn from a variety of relatively large disadvantaged urban samples (including data from the Time, Love, Cash, Care, and Commitment study [TLC3], an in-depth longitudinal qualitative study of a subsample of forty-eight unmarried couples drawn from the Fragile Families and Child Wellbeing study) put the modal length of courtship prior to a conception at well under a year (a median of six to seven months). This estimate, which is remarkably consistent across several other samples, takes into account all couples, not just the lucky half whose relationships survived through the first year of the child's life (Edin and Kefalas 2005; Edin, Nelson, and Reed forthcoming; Reed 2008).

4. Though these estimates are based on complete fertility histories (including miscarriages and termina-tions), none of these studies include men who had conceived but not fathered at least one child.

5. No representative survey we know of asks men whether they denied a pregnancy, but Edin and Kefalas (2005), in their in-depth qualitative study of 165 low-income single mothers in Philadelphia,

found that paternal denial occurred in only a small fraction—9 percent—of women's most recent conceptions.

6. When limiting the sample to mothers for whom a father's interview was completed, the percentages saying there was a good or certain chance were identical.

7. The TLC3 study includes cohabitations entered into both after conception and in the first year of the child's life and finds somewhat higher rates (Reed 2008).

8. Some of the overwhelming optimism unmarried parents in the Fragile Families and Child Wellbeing study share about the future of their relationships may be a product of the study design—most parents were interviewed in the hospital shortly after the birth of their child—but in-depth interviews with a subset of couples conducted two to three months after the birth show that the level of overstatement is only slight (Gibson-Davis 2007).

9. By contrast, cohabitations among parents in Scandinavian countries (Sweden, Norway, and Finland) are nearly as stable as American marriages (Andersson 2002, table 5).

10. There is considerable debate over whether marriage itself may have an independent causal effect on men's employment and earnings and other markers of disadvantage such as health and criminal activity (see, for example, Laub, Nagin, and Sampson 1998; Sampson and Laub 1993; Sampson, Laub, and Wimer 2006).

11. Presumably, this is true for men as well, but we know of no direct evidence on this point.

References

Achatz, Mary, and Crystal A. MacAllum. 1994. *Young unwed fathers: Report from the field*. Philadelphia, PA: Public/Private Ventures.

Ahrons, Constance R. 1981. The continuing co-parental relationship between divorced parents. *American Journal of Orthopsychiatry* 51 (3): 415–28.

Amato, Paul R., and Denise Previti. 2003. People's reasons for divorcing: Gender, social class, the life course, and adjustment. *Journal of Family Issues* 24 (5): 602–26.

Amato, Paul R., and Stacy J. Rogers. 1997. A longitudinal study of marital problems and subsequent divorce. *Journal of Marriage and Family* 59 (3): 612–24.

Anderson, Elijah. 1990. *Streetwise: Race, class, and change in an urban community*. Chicago, IL: University of Chicago Press.

Anderson, Elijah. 1999. *Code of the street: Decency, violence and the moral life of the inner city*. New York, NY: Norton.

Andersson, Gunnar. 2002. Children's experience of family disruption and family formation: Evidence from 16 FFS countries. *Demographic Research* 7 (7): 343–64.

Arditti, Joyce A. 1995. Noncustodial parents: Emergent issues of diversity and process. *Marriage and Family Review* 20 (1/2): 283–304.

Arditti, Joyce A., Jennifer Lambert-Shute, and Karen Joest. 2003. Saturday morning at the jail: Implications of incarceration for families and children. *Family Relations* 52 (3): 195–204.

Arditti, Joyce A., Sara A. Smock, and Tiffaney S. Parkman. 2005. It's been hard to be a father: A qualitative exploration of incarcerated fatherhood. *Fathering* 3 (3): 267–288.

Augustine, Jennifer, Timothy Nelson, and Kathryn Edin. 2009. Why do poor men have children? Fertility intentions among low-income unmarried U.S. fathers. *The Annals of the American Academy of Political and Social Sciences* 624 (1): 99–117.

Bean, Frank D., Ruth R. Berg, and Jennifer Van Hook. 1996. Socioeconomic and cultural incorporation and marital status disruption among Mexican Americans. *Social Forces* 75 (2): 593–617.

Beck, Audrey, Carey E. Cooper, Sara McLanahan, and Jeanne Brooks-Gunn. 2009. Relationship transitions and maternal parenting. Center for Research on Child Wellbeing Working Paper 2008-12-FF, Princeton, NJ.

Bourgois, Phillippe. 1996. *In search of respect: Selling crack in El Barrio*. New York, NY: Cambridge University Press.

Brown, Susan. 2000. Union transitions among cohabitors: The significance of relationship assessments and expectations. *Journal of Marriage and Family* 62 (3): 833–46.

Buchanan, Christy M., Eleanor E. Maccoby, and Sanford M. Dornbusch. 1996. *Adolescents after divorce*. Cambridge, MA: Harvard University Press.

Bumpass, Larry L., James A. Sweet, and Andrew J. Cherlin. 1991. The role of cohabitation in declining rates of marriage. *Journal of Marriage and Family* 53 (4): 913–27.

Bzostek, Sharon. 2008. Social fathers and child wellbeing. *Journal of Marriage and Family* 70 (4): 950–61.

Carlson, Marcia J., and Frank F. Furstenberg. 2006. The prevalence and correlates of multipartnered fertility among urban U.S. parents. *Journal of Marriage and Family* 68 (3): 718–32.

Carlson, Marcia J., and Frank F. Furstenberg. 2007. The consequences of multi-partnered fertility for parental resources and relationships. Center for Research on Child Wellbeing Working Paper, Princeton University, Princeton, NJ.

Carlson, Marcia, Sara McLanahan, and Jeanne Brooks-Gunn. 2006. Do good partners make good parents? Relationship quality and parenting in two-parent families. Center for Research on Child Wellbeing Working Paper, Princeton, NJ.

Carlson, Marcia, Sara S. McLanahan, and Jeanne Brooks-Gunn. 2008. Coparenting and nonresident fathers' involvement with young children after a nonmarital birth. *Demography* 45 (2): 461–88.

Carlson, Marcia, Sara S. McLanahan, and Paula England. 2004. Union formation in fragile families. *Demography* 41 (2): 237–61.

Cavanagh, Shannon, and Aletha Huston. 2006. Family instability and children's early problem behavior. *Social Forces* 85 (1): 551–81.

Center for Research on Child Wellbeing. 2001. *New parents' attitudes towards fathers' rights and obligations*. Princeton, NJ: Bendheim Thoman Center for Child Wellbeing.

Center for Research on Child Wellbeing. 2003. *Introduction to the Fragile Families One-Year Public Use Data*. Princeton, NJ: Bendheim Thoman Center for Child Wellbeing.

Center for Research on Child Wellbeing. 2007. *Parents' relationship status five years after a non-marital birth*. Fragile Families Research Brief 39. Princeton, NJ: Princeton University.

Cherlin, Andrew J. 1992. *Marriage, divorce, remarriage*. Cambridge, MA: Harvard University Press.

Cherlin, Andrew, Tera Hurt, Linda Burton, and Diane Purvin. 2004. The influence of physical and sexual abuse on marriage and cohabitation. *American Sociological Review* 69 (6): 768–89.

Child Trends. 2002. *Charting parenthood: A statistical portrait of fathers and mothers in America*. Washington, DC: Child Trends.

Classens, Amy. 2007. Gatekeeper moms and (un)involved dads: What happens after a breakup? In *Unmarried couples with children*, eds. Paula England and Kathryn Edin, 204–27. New York, NY: Russell Sage Foundation.

Coley, Rebekah L., and Lindsay P. Chase-Lansdale. 1999. Stability and change in paternal involvement among urban African American families. *Journal of Family Psychology* 13 (3): 416–34.

Cooper, Carey E., Cynthia A. Osborne, Audrey N. Beck, and Sara McLanahan. 2008. Partnership instability and child wellbeing during the transition to elementary school. Center for Research on Child Wellbeing Working Paper 2008-08-FF, Princeton, NJ.

Craigie, Terry-Ann. 2008. Effects of paternal presence and family instability on child cognitive performance. Center for Research on Child Wellbeing Working Paper 2008-03-FF, Princeton, NJ.

Edin, Kathryn, Paula England, and Kathryn Linnenberg. 2003. Love and distrust among unmarried parents. Paper presented at National Poverty Center Conference Marriage and Family Formation among Low Income Couples: What Do We Know From Research? 4–5 September, Washington, DC.

Edin, Kathryn, Paula England, Emily Fitzgibbons Shafer, and Joanna Reed. 2007. Forming fragile families: Was the baby planned, unplanned, or in between? In *Unmarried couples with children*, eds. Paula England and Kathryn Edin, 25–54. New York, NY: Russell Sage Foundation.

Edin, Kathryn, and Maria Kefalas. 2005. *Promises I can keep: Why poor women put motherhood before marriage*. Berkeley: University of California Press.

Edin, Kathryn, Maria Kefalas, and Joanna Reed. 2004. A peek inside the black box: What marriage means for poor unmarried parents. *Journal of Marriage and Family* 66 (4): 1007–14.

Edin, Kathryn, Timothy J. Nelson, and Rechelle Paranal. 2004. Fatherhood and incarceration as potential turning points in the criminal careers of unskilled men. In *Imprisoning America: The social effects of mass incarceration*, eds. Mary Pattillo, David F. Weiman, and Bruce Western, 46–75. New York, NY: Russell Sage Foundation.

Edin, Kathryn, Timothy Nelson, and Joanna Reed. Forthcoming. Daddy, baby; momma maybe: Low income urban fathers and the "package deal" of family life. In *Families in an unequal society*, eds. Paula England and Marcia Carlson. Palo Alto, CA: Stanford University Press.

Edin, Kathryn, Laura Tach, and Ronald Mincy. 2009. Claiming fatherhood: Race and the dynamics of paternal involvement among unmarried men. *The Annals of the American Academy of Political and Social Science* 621 (1): 149–77.

Ellwood, David T., and Christopher Jencks. 2004. The uneven spread of single-parent families. In *Social inequality*, ed. Kathryn Neckerman, 3–77. New York, NY: Russell Sage Foundation.

Finer, Lawrence B., and Stanley K. Henshaw. 2006. Disparities in rates of unintended pregnancy in the United States, 1994 and 2001. *Perspectives on Sexual and Reproductive Health* 38 (2): 90–96.

Fomby, Paula, and Cynthia Osborne. 2008. The relative effects of family instability and mother/partner conflict on children's externalizing behavior. Center for Research on Child Wellbeing Working Paper WP08-07-FF, Princeton, NJ.

Furstenberg, Frank F. 1976. *Unplanned parenthood: The social consequences of teenage childbearing*. New York, NY: Free Press.

Furstenberg, Frank F. 1995. Changing roles of fathers. In *Escape from poverty: What makes a difference for children?* ed. P. Lindsay Chase-Lansdale and Jeanne Brooks-Gunn, 189–210. New York, NY: Cambridge University Press.

Furstenberg, Frank F. 2001. The fading dream: Prospects for marriage in the inner city. In *Problem of the century: Racial stratification in the United States*, eds. Elijah Anderson and Douglas S. Massey. New York, NY: Russell Sage Foundation.

Furstenberg, Frank F., and Andrew J. Cherlin. 1991. *Divided families: What happens to children when parents part*. Cambridge, MA: Harvard University Press.

Furstenberg, Frank F., and Kathleen M. Harris. 1992. The disappearing American father? Divorce and the waning significance of biological parenthood. In *The changing American family: Sociological and demographic perspectives*, eds. Scott J. South and Stewart E. Tolnay, 197–223. Boulder, CO: Westview.

Gibson-Davis, Christina M. 2007. Expectations and the economic bar to marriage among low income couples. In *Unmarried couples with children*, eds. Paula England and Kathryn Edin, 84–103. New York, NY: Russell Sage Foundation.

Gibson-Davis, Christina. 2009. Money, marriage, and children: Testing the financial expectations and family formation theory. *Journal of Marriage and Family* 71 (1): 146–60.

Gibson-Davis, Christina M., Kathryn Edin, and Sara McLanahan. 2005. High hopes but even higher expectations: The retreat from marriage among low-income couples. *Journal of Marriage and Family* 67 (5): 1301–12.

Goffman, Alice. 2009. On the run: Wanted men in a Philadelphia ghetto. *American Sociological Review* 74 (2): 339–57.

Goldstein, Jeremy R., and Catherine T. Kenney. 2001. Marriage delayed or marriage forgone? New cohort forecasts of first marriage for U.S. women. *American Sociological Review* 66 (4): 506–19.

Graefe, Deborah R., and Daniel T. Lichter. 1999. Life course transitions of American children: Parental cohabitation, marriage, and single motherhood. *Demography* 36 (2): 205–17.

Graefe, Deborah R., and Daniel T. Lichter. 2007. When unwed mothers marry: The marital and cohabiting partners of midlife women. *Journal of Family Issues* 28 (5): 595–622.

Guzzo, Karen B., and Frank F. Furstenberg. 2007a. Multipartnered fertility among American men. *Demography* 44 (3): 583–601.

Guzzo, Karen B., and Frank F. Furstenberg. 2007b. Multipartnered fertility among young women with a nonmarital first birth: Prevalence and risk factors. *Perspectives on Sexual and Reproductive Health* 39 (1): 29–38.

Hagan, John, and Ronit Dinovitzer. 1999. Collateral consequences of imprisonment for children, communities, and prisoners. *Crime and Justice* 26:121–62.

Hamer, Jennifer F. 2001. *What it means to be daddy: Fatherhood for black men living away from their children*. New York, NY: Columbia University Press.

Hannerz, Ulf. 1969. *Soulside: Inquiries into ghetto culture and community*. New York, NY: Columbia University Press.

Harknett, Kristen, and Jean Knab. 2007. More kin, less support: Multipartnered fertility and perceived support among mothers. *Journal of Marriage and Family* 69 (1): 237–53.

Harknett, Kristen, and Sara McLanahan. 2004. Racial and ethnic differences in marriage after the birth of a child. *American Sociological Review* 69 (6): 790–811.

Henshaw, Stanley K. 1998. Unintended pregnancy in the United States. *Family Planning Perspectives* 30 (1): 24–9.

Hill, Heather D. 2007. Steppin' out: Infidelity and sexual jealousy among unmarried parents. In *Unmarried couples with children*, eds. Paula England and Kathryn Edin, 104–32. New York, NY: Russell Sage Foundation.

Jarrett, Robin L. 1997. African American family and parenting strategies in impoverished neighborhoods. *Qualitative Sociology* 20 (2): 275–88.

Jarrett, Robin L., and Linda M. Burton. 1999. Dynamic dimensions of family structure in low-income African American families: Emergent themes in qualitative research. *Journal of Comparative Family Studies* 30:177–87.

Jarrett, Robin L., Kevin M. Roy, and Linda M. Burton. 2002. Fathers in the hood: Insights from qualitative research on low-income African American men. In *Handbook of father involvement: Multidisciplinary perspectives*, eds. Catherine S. Tamis-LeMonda and Natasha Cabrera, 211–48. Mahwah, NJ: Lawrence Erlbaum.

Kennedy, Sheela, and Larry Bumpass. 2007. Cohabitation and children's living arrangements: New estimates from the United States. *Demographic Research* 19 (47): 1663–92.

Kreider, Rose M., and Jason Fields. 2005. *Number, timing and duration of marriages and divorces: 2001.* Current Population Reports: P70-97. Washington, DC: U.S. Census Bureau.

Laub, John H., Daniel S. Nagin, and Robert J. Sampson. 1998. Trajectories of change in criminal offending: Good marriages and the desistance process. *American Sociological Review* 63 (1): 225–38.

Lichter, Daniel T., Felicia B. LeClere, and Diane K. McLaughlin. 1991. Local marriage markets and the marital behavior of black and white women. *American Journal of Sociology* 96 (4): 843–67.

Lichter, Daniel T., Diane K. McLaughlin, George Kephart, and David J. Landry. 1992. Race and the retreat from marriage: A shortage of marriageable men? *American Sociological Review* 57 (6): 781–99.

Liebow, Elliot. 1967. *Tally's corner: A study of Negro streetcorner men.* Boston, MA: Little, Brown.

Lloyd, Kimm M., and Scott J. South. 1996. Contextual influences on young men's transition to first marriage. *Social Forces* 74 (3): 1097–1119.

Lopoo, Leonard M., and Bruce Western. 2005. Incarceration and the formation and stability of marital unions. *Journal of Marriage and Family* 67 (3): 721–34.

Manlove, Jennifer, Cassandra Logan, Erum Ikramullah, and Emily Holcombe. 2008. Factors associated with multiple-partner fertility among fathers. *Journal of Marriage and Family* 70 (2): 536–48.

Manning, Wendy D., and Pamela J. Smock. 1995. Why marry? Race and the transition to marriage among cohabitors. *Demography* 32 (4): 509–20.

Manning, Wendy D., and Pamela J. Smock. 1999. New families and nonresident father-child visitation. *Social Forces* 78 (1): 87–116.

Manning, Wendy D., and Pamela J. Smock. 2000. "Swapping" families: Serial parenting and economic support for children. *Journal of Marriage and Family* 62 (1): 111–22.

Manning, Wendy D., and Pamela Smock. 2005. Measuring and modeling cohabitation: New perspectives from qualitative data. *Journal of Marriage and the Family* 67 (4): 989–1002.

Manning, Wendy D., Pamela J. Smock, and Debarun Majumdar. 2004. The relative stability of cohabiting and marital unions for children. *Population Research and Policy Review* 23 (2): 135–59.

Marsiglio, William, and Mark Cohan. 2000. Contextualizing father involvement and paternal influence: Sociological and qualitative themes. *Marriage & Family Review* 29 (2/3): 75–95.

Martin, Steven. 2004. Unpublished calculations. University of Maryland, College Park.

Martinez, Gladys M., Anjani Chandra, Joyce C. Abma, Jo Jones, and William D. Mosher. 2006. Fertility, contraception, and fatherhood: Data on men and women from Cycle 6 (2002) of the National Survey of Family Growth. National Center for Health Statistics. *Vital Health Statistics* 23 (26): 1–142.

McLanahan, Sara. 2004. Diverging destinies: How children are faring under the second demographic transition. *Demography* 41 (4): 607–27.

McLanahan, Sara, Irwin Garfinkel, Nancy Reichman, Julien Teitler, Marcia Carlson, and Christina Norland Audigier. 2003. *The Fragile Families and Child Wellbeing study: Baseline national report.* Princeton, NJ: Center for Child Wellbeing, Princeton University.

Mincy, Ronald B. 2002. Who should marry whom? Multiple partner fertility among new parents. Center for Research on Child Wellbeing Working Paper 02-03-FF, Princeton University, Princeton, NJ.

Mincy, Ronald B., and Hilard Pouncy. 2007. *Baby fathers and American family formation: Low-income, never-married parents in Louisiana before Katrina.* New York, NY: Institute for American Values.

Musick, Kelly. 2002. Planned and unplanned childbearing among unmarried women. *Journal of Marriage and Family* 64 (4): 915–29.

National Center for Health Statistics. 2002. Cohabitation, marriage, divorce, and remarriage in the United States. *Vital and Health Statistics* 23 (22): 1–93.

Nelson, Timothy J. 2004. Low-income fathers. *Annual Review of Sociology* 30:427–51.

Nelson, Timothy J., K. C. Torres, and Kathryn Edin. 2002. Not planned but not accidental: Low-income, non-custodial fathers' participation in childbearing decisions. Presented at the American Sociological Association Annual Meeting, 16–19 August, Chicago, IL.

Nock, Stephen. 2007. *Marital and unmarried births to men.* Hyattsville, MD: U.S. Department of Health and Human Services.

Nurse, Anne M. 2002. *Fatherhood arrested: Parenting from within the juvenile justice system.* Nashville, TN: Vanderbilt University Press.

Oppenheimer, Valerie. 2000. The continuing importance of men's economic position in marriage formation. In *The ties that bind: Perspectives on marriage and cohabitation,* ed. Linda Waite, 283–301. New York, NY: Aldine de Gruyter.

Osborne, Cynthia. 2005. Marriage following the birth of a child for cohabiting and visiting parents. *Journal of Marriage and Family* 67 (1): 14–26.

Osborne, Cynthia, Wendy D. Manning, and Pamela J. Smock. 2007. Married and cohabiting parents' relationship stability: A focus on race and ethnicity. *Journal of Marriage and Family* 69 (5): 1345–66.

Osborne, Cynthia, and Sara McLanahan. 2007. Partnership instability and child wellbeing. *Journal of Marriage and Family* 64 (4): 1065–83.

Rainwater, Lee. 1970. *Behind ghetto walls.* Chicago, IL: Aldine.

Raley, Kelly, and Elizabeth Wildsmith. 2004. Cohabitation and children's family instability. *Journal of Marriage and Family* 66 (1): 210–19.

Reed, Joanna. 2007. Anatomy of a breakup: How and why do unmarried couples with children break up? In *Unmarried couples with children,* eds. Paula England and Kathryn Edin, 133–56. New York, NY: Russell Sage Foundation.

Reed, Joanna. 2008. A closer look at unmarried parenthood: Relationship trajectories, meanings of family life, gender and culture. PhD diss., Northwestern University, Evanston, IL.

Roy, Kevin M. 2005. Transitions on the margins of work and family for low-income African American fathers. *Journal of Family and Economic Issues* 26 (1): 77–100.

Roy, Kevin M. 2008. A life course perspective on fatherhood and family policies in the United States and South Africa. *Fathering* 6 (2): 92–112.

Roy, Kevin M., and Omari L. Dyson. 2005. Gatekeeping in context: Babymama drama and the involvement of incarcerated fathers. *Fathering* 3 (3): 289–310.

Royster, Deirdre A. 2003. *Race and the invisible hand: How white networks exclude black men from blue-collar jobs.* Berkeley: University of California Press.

Sampson, Robert J., and John H. Laub. 1993. *Crime in the making: Pathways and turning points through life.* Cambridge, MA: Harvard University Press.

Sampson, Robert, John Laub, and Christopher Wimer. 2006. Does marriage reduce crime? A counterfactual approach to within-individual causal effects. *Criminology* 44 (3): 465–508.

Sassler, Sharon. 2004. The process of entering into cohabiting unions. *Journal of Marriage and Family* 66 (2): 491–505.

Sayer, Liana, Nathan Wright, and Kathryn Edin. 2003. Class differences in family values: A 30-year exploration of Americans' attitudes toward the family. Paper presented at the Annual Meeting of the Population Association of America, 1–3 May, Minneapolis, MN.

Smock, Pamela J., and Wendy D. Manning. 1997. Cohabiting partners' economic circumstances and marriage. *Demography* 34 (2): 331–41.

Smock, Pamela, Wendy Manning, and Meredith Porter. 2005. Everything's there except money: How economic factors shape the decision to marry among cohabiting couples. *Journal of Marriage and Family* 67 (3): 680–96.

Sobolewski, Juliana M., and Valerie King. 2005. The importance of the coparental relationship for nonresident fathers' ties to children. *Journal of Marriage and Family* 67 (5): 1196–1212.

Stack, Carol. 1974. *All our kin: Strategies for survival in a black community*. New York, NY: Harper & Row.

Stewart, Susan D., Wendy D. Manning, and Pamela J. Smock. 2003. Union formation among men in the U.S.: Does having prior children matter? *Journal of Marriage and Family* 65 (1): 90–104.

Sullivan, Mercer L. 1989. Absent fathers in the inner city. *The Annals of the American Academy of Political and Social Science* 501 (1): 48–58.

Sullivan, Mercer L. 1993. Young fathers and parenting in two inner-city neighborhoods. In *Young unwed fathers: Changing roles and emerging policies*, eds. Ronald Lerman and Theodora Ooms, 52–73. Philadelphia, PA: Temple University Press.

Sweeney, Megan M. 2002. Two decades of family change: The shifting economic foundations of marriage. *American Sociological Review* 67 (1): 132–47.

Swisher, Raymond, and Maureen Waller. 2008. Incarceration and paternal involvement among nonresident white, African American, and Latino fathers. *Journal of Family Issues* 29 (8): 1067–88.

Tach, Laura, Ronald Mincy, and Kathryn Edin. 2010. Parenting as a package deal: Relationships, fertility, and nonresident father involvement among unmarried parents. *Demography* 47 (1): 181–204.

Testa, Mark, Nan Astone, Marilyn Krogh, and Kathryn Neckerman. 1989. Employment and marriage among inner-city fathers. *The Annals of the American Academy of Political and Social Science* 501 (1): 79–91.

Townsend, Nicholas W. 2004. *The package deal: Marriage, work, and fatherhood in men's lives*. Philadelphia, PA: Temple University Press.

Upchurch, Dawn M., Lee A. Lillard, and Constantijn W. A. Panis. 2001. The impact of nonmarital childbearing on subsequent marital formation and dissolution. In *Out of wedlock: Causes and consequences of nonmarital fertility*, eds. Lawrence L. Wu and Barbara L. Wolfe, 344–80. New York, NY: Russell Sage Foundation.

Venkatesh, Sudhir. 2000. *American project: The rise and fall of a modern ghetto*. Cambridge, MA: Harvard University Press.

Venkatesh, Sudhir. 2006. *Off the books: The underground economy of the urban poor*. Cambridge, MA: Harvard University Press.

Waller, Maureen R. 2002. *My baby's father: Unwed parents and paternal responsibilities*. Ithaca, NY: Cornell University Press.

Waller, Maureen R. 2008. How do disadvantaged parents view tensions in their relationships? Insights for relationship longevity among at-risk couples. *Family Relations* 57 (2): 128–43.

Waller, Maureen R., and Sara S. McLanahan. 2005. His and her marriage expectations: Determinants and consequences. *Journal of Marriage and Family* 67 (1): 53–67.

Waller, Maureen R., and Raymond Swisher. 2006. Fathers' risk factors in fragile families: Implications for "healthy" relationships and father involvement. *Social Problems* 53 (3): 392–420.

Watson, Tara, and Sara McLanahan. 2009. Marriage meets the Joneses: Relative income, identity, and marital status. National Bureau of Economic Research Working Paper 14773, Cambridge, MA.

Western, Bruce, Leonard Lopoo, and Sara McLanahan. 2004. Incarceration and the bonds between parents in fragile families. In *Imprisoning America: The social effects of mass incarceration*, eds. Mary Pattillo and David F. Weiman, 21–45. New York, NY: Russell Sage Foundation.

Western, Bruce, and Sara McLanahan. 2000. Fathers behind bars: The impact of incarceration on family formation. In *Families, crime, and criminal justice: Charting the linkages, series on contemporary perspectives in family research*, vol. 2, eds. Greer Litton Fox and Michael L. Benson, 307–22. Stamford, CT: JAI.

Western, Bruce, and Christopher Wildeman. 2009. The black family and mass incarceration. *The Annals of the American Academy of Social and Political Science* 621:221–42.

Wilson, Melvin, and Jeanne Brooks-Gunn. 2001. Health status and behaviors of unwed fathers. *Children and Youth Services Review* 23 (4–5): 377–401.

Wilson, William J., and Kathryn A. Neckerman. 1986. Poverty and family structure: The widening gap between evidence and public policy issues. In *Fighting poverty: What works, and what doesn't*, eds. Sheldon H. Danziger and Daniel H. Weinberg, 232–59. Cambridge, MA: Harvard University Press.

Young, Alford. 2004. *The minds of marginalized black men: Making sense of mobility, opportunity, and future life chances*. Princeton, NJ: Princeton University Press.

Young, Alford, and Pamela Holcomb. 2007. *Voices of young fathers: The partners for fragile families demonstration projects*. Washington, DC: Urban Institute.

Low-Income Fathers' Influence on Children

By
MARCIA J. CARLSON
and
KATHERINE A. MAGNUSON

This article examines what we know about how low-income fathers matter for children. The authors first provide a theoretical background about how parents generally (and fathers more specifically) are expected to influence children's development and well-being. The authors note the importance of considering differences across children's age, gender, and race/ethnicity; and they identify key methodological challenges in this area. Then, they summarize the literature on residential fathers and child well-being, finding that greater involvement has been linked to better outcomes for children; however, much of this research has been conducted on more socioeconomically advantaged samples. For fathers who live away from their children, child support payments appear to improve children's outcomes, but the benefits of father-child interaction are much less clear and likely depend on the quality of the interaction and the characteristics of fathers. Overall, the authors conclude that low-income fathers *can* have a positive influence on children's well-being, but the evidence about the population overall is rather weak.

Keywords: low-income fathers; father involvement; child well-being

Marcia J. Carlson is an associate professor of sociology and an affiliate at the Center for Demography and Ecology and the Institute for Research on Poverty at the University of Wisconsin–Madison. Her research interests center on the links between family contexts and the well-being of children and parents, with a particular focus on unmarried families. Her current research is supported by a grant from NICHD (R01HD57894) and by core funding to the Center for Demography and Ecology (R24HD047873).

Katherine A. Magnuson is an associate professor of social work and associate director of research and training at the Institute for Research on Poverty at the University of Wisconsin–Madison. Her research focuses on the effects of poverty and socioeconomic status on children and family well-being and the effects of early childhood and family interventions. She is currently working in collaboration with colleagues at the National Forum for Early Childhood Programs and Policies (Harvard University) on a large meta-analysis of early intervention programs to identify what features of such programs improve low-income children's school readiness.

DOI: 10.1177/0002716210393853

Fathers represent an important resource for children, ideally investing the time, money, and emotional support that contribute to healthy child development. Over the past four decades, two important—and related—changes have occurred within the postindustrial family, reflecting shifts in family gender roles as well as the division of household labor and market work. First, mothers are increasingly likely to be employed outside the home; and second, fathers' roles have expanded from primarily that of "breadwinner," who provides economic support, to include that of "caregiver." As noted in the article by Berger and Langton (this volume), fathering today often includes nurturing and caregiving; engaging in leisure and play activities; providing the child's mother with emotional and practical support; providing moral guidance and discipline; ensuring the safety of the child; taking responsibility for coordinating the child's care and activities; and connecting the child to his or her extended family, community members, and other resources (Cabrera et al. 2000; Marsiglio et al. 2000; Palkovitz 2002). With the broadening of paternal roles, there has been growing attention to how fathers affect children. Early research focused on the consequences of fathers' absence for children's well-being. More recent studies have focused on how fathers' involvement may be associated with children's well-being.

While changes in the gender division of labor have occurred across all demographic groups, the shift in fathers' involvement has played out quite differently by socioeconomic status. Employed fathers in middle-income families have had the opportunity to expand their paternal roles into new areas. In contrast, fathers with limited job prospects in low-income families have been more likely to retreat from the father role altogether (Furstenberg 1988). Although unmarried or low-income fathers sometimes describe their roles in terms similar to those used by married or middle-class fathers (Furstenberg, Sherwood, and Sullivan 1992; Jarrett, Roy, and Burton 2002; Waller 2002), it is likely that a few years after the birth of the child, the former will be living away from their children (Carlson and McLanahan 2010). Once nonresident, fathers are unlikely to be actively involved in raising their children, and many have very limited contact with their children.

In this article, we review the literature about how low-income men and fathers matter for children. We first outline our conceptual framework for fathers' roles. Then, we summarize the literature about fathering and child well-being, distinguishing between resident fathers and nonresident fathers and highlighting low-income fathers in each section. We briefly discuss social fathering and children's well-being, and we conclude by discussing implications for future research and public policy.

Theoretical Perspectives

The importance of parenting for children's health, development, and well-being is well established (Baumrind 1966; Collins et al. 2000; Maccoby 2000; Maccoby and Martin 1983). Yet it is also clear that there remains much to learn about which dimensions of parenting affect children and how such dimensions

FIGURE 1
Heuristic Diagram: Parents' Contributions to Child Well-Being

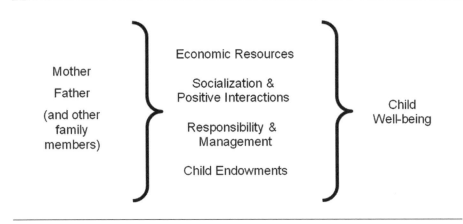

may vary across individuals and contexts (Collins et al. 2000). "Authoritative" parenting, characterized by appropriate warmth and control, has long been thought to contribute to children's healthy development (Baumrind 1966, 1986). Until recently, most theories of parenting either focused on mothering or discussed parenting generally without regard to a particular parent.

Family scholars have long recognized the interdependence of family relationships. Within a given family system, dyadic relationships affect each other (Cox and Paley 1997; Minuchin 1988) and influence individual-level change (Chase-Lansdale, Kiernan, and Friedman 2004; O'Brien 2005). For this reason, we begin our conceptual discussion of fathering by first providing a heuristic model of the family system and the broader factors that influence child development and well-being (see Figure 1). Parents and other family members, jointly, provide the active ingredients that, taken together, promote healthy development. Although clearly not exhaustive, our categorizations of parents' contributions are divided into three basic domains: *economic resources, socialization and positive interactions*, and *responsibility and management*. We also note that children's own *endowments* (i.e., inherited genes and related traits) are important, as these endowments may be attributable, at least in part, to parents and interact with aspects of the family context to influence children's outcomes (Collins et al. 2000).

A vast literature points to the importance of *economic resources* in enhancing children's outcomes. Greater economic resources enable parents to purchase the necessary material goods and services, such as medical care, higher-quality child care or schools, and books and toys, all of which improve developmental processes. Greater economic resources may also reduce parents' psychological distress, which in turn will reduce harsh parenting and thus benefit children (McLoyd 1998). Although some debate remains about the magnitude of the associations, accumulated evidence suggests that links between poverty in early childhood and persistent poverty and academic and cognitive skills are particularly pronounced (Duncan and Brooks-Gunn 1997; Magnuson and Votruba-Drzal 2009). Furthermore, recent research suggests that at least some of the effect of income on children's achievement is likely to be causal (Dahl and Lochner 2008; Milligan and Stabile 2008).

The quality of *parent-child interactions and socialization* also contributes to children's development. High-quality parent-child interactions are characterized by positive engagement and discipline; this involves not only parental warmth, such as being responsive, affectionate, and nurturing and rewarding positive behavior but also teaching children in a productive and supportive manner (Brooks-Gunn and Markman 2005). Research suggests that such positive engagement is most effective when coupled with appropriate control and discipline, so that children learn that there are consequences for misbehavior (Baumrind 1986).

The final dimension of parenting that we highlight is *responsibility and management*, which includes the supervisory tasks of making sure a child's activities are appropriately monitored as well as scheduling and completing routine child-related tasks. This domain encompasses such tasks as making sure that a young child goes to a well-baby doctor exam or that someone walks the child home from preschool, as well as making sure that an older child completes her or his homework or gets to soccer practice. Parents differ in the extent to which—and priorities by which—they manage their children's lives, and striking differences have been observed by social class. Lareau (2003) argues that middle-class parents, defined by having highly skilled jobs, engage in "concerted cultivation" by providing stimulating learning activities and social interactions; in contrast, working-class and poor parents, with less skilled jobs, view child development as unfolding "naturally" and believe they need do little more than provide for basic needs, including food, shelter, and comfort.

Whether a child's biological parents reside together or apart, these parenting tasks require collaboration and coordination—sometimes referred to as *coparenting* (McHale 1995). Thus, understanding the direct and indirect "effects" of fathering or mothering is difficult without situating it in the broader family context of interdependent roles and transactional processes (Parke 2004). Moreover, the whole may be more than the sum of individual parts, such that the overall quantity and quality of all family resources that children experience, including the extent to which such interactions are coordinated, matters the most for children (Cox and Paley 1997). Low-income families may structure the rearing of children in fundamentally different ways from their middle-class counterparts, in particular creating a greater role for nonresident and extended family members (Furstenberg 2007; Lareau 2003; Stack 1974).

During the past two decades, fatherhood scholars have developed conceptual models to identify the key components of fathers' involvement. One of the first "typologies" of father involvement, developed by Lamb and colleagues, identifies three key components—accessibility, engagement, and responsibility (Lamb et al. 1985). *Accessibility* (or *availability*) refers to time that fathers are available to children, even if they are not directly interacting; *engagement* (or *interaction*)

FIGURE 2
Conceptual Diagram: Fathers' Involvement and Child Well-Being

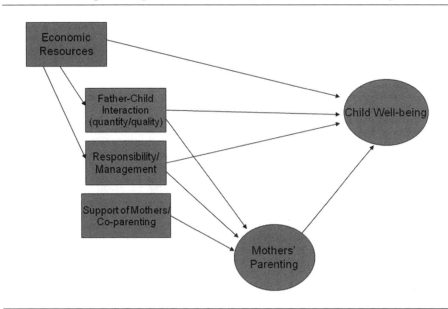

refers to time spent with children, especially doing activities together that are known to contribute to healthy development (e.g., reading); and *responsibility* refers to fathers' helping to arrange resources and activities for children.

Building on Lamb and colleagues' (1985) early work and the broader conceptualization of parenting described above, we rely on a model of fathering that highlights four key domains of fathering, each of which is expected to be important to children's well-being (see Figure 2).

First, as described above, *economic resources* enable parents to provide the food, clothing, and shelter requisite for daily living, as well as the material goods and experiences that promote positive child development. In addition, fathers' financial support may function to increase or improve their nonpecuniary involvement with their children (Nepomnyaschy 2007; Seltzer, Schaeffer, and Charng 1989). Second, father-child *interaction* provides the opportunity to demonstrate the appropriate warmth, support, control, and monitoring that are intrinsic to authoritative parenting (Baumrind 1986; Maccoby and Martin 1983). Yet time spent interacting is a necessary, but not sufficient, condition for developing close parent-child ties; both the quantity and quality of interaction are important. Third, *responsibility* captures the aspects of parenting related to managing and coordinating the activities of childhood. Although paternal responsibility is important, it is often neglected in surveys (Cabrera et al. 2000; Lamb 1986), and there is limited research evaluating its effects. As a result, we do not focus on it within this review. Finally, *coparenting*—defined as the extent to which parents can effectively work together to rear a child—is distinct from both couple relation-ship quality and parenting behavior and may have unique implications for child well-being (Hayden et al. 1998; McHale 1995; McHale et al. 2000).

Since the influence of fathering may differ across contexts, below we summa-rize three key factors that may moderate the effects of fathers' involvement on child and adolescent well-being: children's age or developmental period, gender, and race and ethnicity.

Developmental perspective

Parenting tasks and activities evolve and adapt as children grow and develop. During infancy, children are dependent on their caregivers to meet their physical, social, and emotional needs. During toddlerhood and the preschool years, chil-dren express unique personalities and acquire language and self-regulation skills, which in turn promote their greater independence and social integration, which continue to grow during childhood. During middle childhood, children continue to develop a sense of self and a range of important competencies as they engage in an increasingly wide array of activities and social relationships. During adoles-cence, youths seek even greater autonomy from their families as they establish their own identities.

Changes in children's developmental needs and tasks suggest that the effects of parenting are likely to differ, both in magnitude and nature, over the course of childhood and adolescence. For example, some scholars argue that fathering may become especially important during adolescence (Forehand and Nousiainen 1993). Studying and comparing the effects of parenting across childhood is chal-lenging because of its changing nature, and few studies have systematically inves-tigated whether the effects of fathering differ as children develop. With respect to nonresident fathers, divorced fathers with offspring in middle childhood or adolescence are most often studied, so less is known about father involvement in early childhood. Although it is important to consider developmental processes, to date the research base is too thin to make any conclusions about how fathering and its effects may differ across particular periods of childhood and adolescence.

Gender perspective

Social learning theory suggests that fathers may be more involved with and have a greater influence on sons than daughters because of the comparative advan-tage, greater internal rewards, and higher external expectations for socializing same-gender children (Harris and Morgan 1991; Rossi and Rossi 1990). Some (but not all) studies show that fathers are more involved with sons than with daughters, particularly at older ages (Anderson 1989; Cooksey and Fondell 1996; Harris and Morgan 1991). Gender differences in father involvement may depend on the type of activity, with some types of involvement being more "gendered" than others (Cooksey and Craig 1998). Of particular interest, however, is the extent to which the *effects* of father involvement differ by children's gender; the few studies that have examined this issue have found that father involvement is as beneficial for daughters as for sons (Amato and Gilbreth 1999; King, Harris, and Heard 2004). Whether this pattern of findings is equally true among low-income children is unclear.

Race and ethnicity perspective

Scholars of the family have long recognized racial, ethnic, and cultural differences in family roles and functioning, including parenting (Parke 2004; Stack 1974). The sources of such differences are complicated, including limited prospects for male employment and economic mobility (Mincy 2006); adaptation to other structural and historical factors, most notably slavery (Patterson 1999); and cultural contexts (Edin, Tach, and Mincy 2009; Furstenberg 2007; Mincy and Pouncy 2007). These differences imply that fathering may have differing effects on child well-being, depending on a family's cultural background, and that the interpretative meaning of fathering and the processes by which it affects children may vary (Livingston and McAdoo 2007; Nelson 2004). Studies have documented differences across broadly defined racial or ethnic groups in terms of patterns of fathering and father involvement (see Berger and Langton this volume; Hofferth 2003; Hofferth et al. 2007). Yet few studies have systematically considered whether and how the effects of fathering differ across racially, ethnically, or culturally defined populations, and studies that have considered subgroup differences have yielded mixed results (Coley 1998; King 1994b). As a result, variation by race/ethnicity (and by immigration status and origin) is an important avenue for future research.

Methodological Challenges

As with all nonexperimental research, the research on fathering (and parenting more generally) is largely descriptive and faces considerable challenges to establishing causal effects, even if there is strong theoretical support for such. We describe several key challenges here. The first relates to social selection, namely, that omitted variables may bias the estimates of the effects of fathers' involvement on child well-being. For example, if differences in the characteristics of nonresident fathers who pay higher levels of child support (and are more advantaged along a number of dimensions) versus those who provide less support (Berger and Langton this volume), are not fully taken into account, then studies may attribute to fathers' involvement what is really due to some other unobserved characteristic(s). Studies differ in the rigor of their efforts to reduce such omitted variable bias and often face the unenviable position of overcontrolling or undercontrolling for confounding covariates. In the absence of experimental studies, these issues are unlikely to be easily resolved, yet researchers' continued attention to ruling out alternative explanations for observed associations is an important effort in moving the field forward.

A related selection issue is how to untangle the effects of multiple dimensions of fathers' involvement on child well-being. Despite theoretical reasons for distinguishing among dimensions of fathers' involvement, such distinctions are rarely made in empirical research. Most studies characterize fathers' involvement in general terms, describing levels of involvement (e.g., high vs. low) as measured by contact, activity frequency, or father-child closeness (or some combination). Rarely do studies evaluate the unique, additive, or multiplicative effects of several aspects of fathers' involvement and explicitly consider issues of quantity versus quality.

A second key methodological issue is that most studies focus on estimating models in which fathers' involvement affects children's development, rather than modeling more complicated processes by which fathers' involvement affects children (both directly and indirectly) and child well-being also affects fathering. Family scholars have become increasingly mindful of the extent to which family relationships are reciprocal, and within the dyadic parent-child relationship, children influence parents just as parents influence children (Crouter and Booth 2003). If so-called "child effects" are prevalent, as is suggested by some recent research on nonresident fathers' involvement and adolescents (Coley and Medeiros 2007; D. Hawkins, Amato, and King 2007), then many studies may be overstating the importance of fathers' involvement in determining children's well-being. For example, if nonresident fathers become less involved *because* children are having trouble, then estimates of how fathering and child outcomes are linked reflect, at least in part, this reverse causality and should not be interpreted as evidence that fathers' involvement entirely drives child well-being.

Third, scholars have increasingly recognized the need to evaluate fathers' involvement in the context of mothers' involvement (Marsiglio et al. 2000). Within families, levels of mothers' and fathers' parenting are positively correlated (Aldous, Mulligan, and Bjarnason 1998; Harris and Ryan 2004), or, as described by Marsiglio and colleagues (2000, 1185), "fathering is often a co-constructed accomplishment." Therefore, it is important to use data and methods that enable evaluation of the direct, indirect, and conjoint influence of fathers along with mothers on child well-being. Similarly, who provides the information about the nature, content, and quality of fathers' involvement with children also matters. Fathers, especially nonresident or low-income fathers, are typically underrepresented in national surveys (Garfinkel, McLanahan, and Hanson 1998; Nelson 2004), so early studies often relied on mothers' reports about fathers. However, mothers typically report lower levels of fathers' involvement than fathers report, especially for nonresident fathers (Coley and Morris 2002). Finding modest correlations across individual reporters' perceptions about the same family relationship is more often the norm than the exception (Tein, Roosa, and Michaels 1994), so researchers would be well served by using methods that can incorporate information from multiple reporters (Marsiglio et al. 2000).

Research on Residential Fathers and Child Well-Being

Before turning to the research on particular types of father involvement, it is important to note that studies on family structure provide insight into the effects of fathers' coresidence with their children, even if such research does not identify how and why fathers matter. An extensive literature suggests that children fare better on a host of social-psychological, behavioral, and cognitive outcomes when they spend their entire childhood living with both of their biological parents (McLanahan and Sandefur 1994; Sigle-Rushton and McLanahan 2004). This research (using observational data) suffers from the concerns about social selection described above, and indeed some of the "effect" of stable family structures is certainly due to the characteristics of parents who remain in stable unions (Cherlin 1999). Yet a recent review of the literature suggests that beyond selection factors, there is also likely some (perhaps small) causal effect of living in a two-parent family (versus a single-parent family) on at least some aspects of child well-being (Sigle-Rushton and McLanahan 2004). This suggests that fathers' commitment to "being there" for children, and all that it entails, promotes children's well-being.

Not surprisingly, coresident fathers typically spend more time with their children than nonresident fathers, simply because sharing a household affords greater opportunity for contact and day-to-day interactions (Amato and Gilbreth 1999). Beyond the higher *level* of involvement typical among resident fathers, fathers' involvement in two-parent families may also yield greater benefit for children, because it reinforces mothers' parenting and thereby strengthens the cohesiveness of the family as an institution (Gable, Belsky, and Crnic 1994; Harris, Furstenberg, and Marmer 1998). On average, fathers' involvement across the domains outlined above is associated with better outcomes for children when provided by a coresidential biological father (Amato 1998; Harris, Furstenberg, and Marmer 1998; Lamb 2004; Marsiglio et al. 2000).

With respect to *economic resources*, it is difficult to evaluate specifically how coresident fathers' economic contributions benefit children, since studies cannot easily isolate the unique effects of financial resources from other aspects of coresident fathers' involvement, as fathers' education and income are strong predictors of fathers' engagement and involvement (Amato and Rivera 1999). Two-parent families do have significantly higher economic resources than single-parent families; according to U.S. census data, in 2006, average family cash income for married couples with children was $89,096, compared with only $28,865 for single-mother families with children (U.S. House of Representatives 2008). Economic resources, in turn, have been shown to account for about half of the gap in well-being between children living in two-parent versus single-parent families (McLanahan and Sandefur 1994), leading scholars to conclude that at least in the United States, fathers' economic contributions are fundamental to their children's well-being.

With respect to *father-child interactions*, an extensive literature has demonstrated the benefits of resident fathers' involvement for child well-being, although much of this work has focused on samples of middle-income, school-aged children or adolescents (Shannon et al. 2002). Greater interaction with fathers has been significantly linked to decreases in delinquency and behavioral problems and to increases in cognitive development, educational attainment, and psychological well-being (Amato and Rivera 1999; Harris, Furstenberg, and Marmer 1998;

Hofferth 2006; Marsiglio et al. 2000; Tamis-LeMonda et al. 2004). A 2000 *Journal of Marriage and Family* review of fatherhood scholarship noted that fifty-five studies in the 1990s explored the link between paternal involvement and outcomes for children ages zero to 19 in two-parent families; the authors concluded that the results "are consistent with the belief that positive father involvement is generally beneficial to children" (p. 1183), with no discernible differences by child's age or race/ethnicity (Marsiglio et al. 2000).

It is important to note that many studies are correlational in nature, do not include extensive control variables, and do not use longitudinal data with techniques that are best suited to causal inference by ruling out omitted variable bias and child "effects." Moreover, nearly all of the research on coresident fathers' involvement is based on married fathers, so we have little evidence about how children may fare in long-term cohabiting unions. However, since cohabiting unions with children in the United States are much more likely to dissolve than marital unions with children (Osborne, Manning, and Smock 2007), it is the rare child who will experience a stable cohabiting family. Still, there are good theoretical reasons to expect coresident biological fathers' involvement to positively influence children, so it is likely that the association is positive for cohabitors; more at issue is the magnitude of the association.

Coparenting

We know that mothers play an important role in shaping father-child interactions. Research on resident, and especially married, fathers has underscored that men's roles as fathers are strongly linked to men's roles as partners in the so-called "package deal" (Furstenberg and Cherlin 1991; Schoppe-Sullivan et al. 2008; Townsend 2002). Better coparenting among married parents is linked to better child development, net marital quality, and parent-child relationships (Gable, Belsky, and Crnic 1994; Schoppe, Mangelsdorf, and Frosch 2001).

Low-income fathers

Most of the literature about coresident fathers' involvement has focused on middle-income (mostly married) families, leaving uncertain whether the nature and strength of the associations may differ among low-income populations. However, several recent studies have made use of data from the Early Head Start Research and Evaluation Project to examine low-income, coresident biological fathers. Positive father-child interactions and parenting (sensitivity, positive regard, and cognitive stimulation) are linked to children's language development, cognitive functioning, and socioemotional behavior at ages two and three (Cabrera, Shannon, and Tamis-LeMonda 2007; Shannon et al. 2002; Tamis-LeMonda et al. 2004) and children's math and language abilities at age five (Martin, Ryan, and Brooks-Gunn 2007). These findings suggest that the quality of coresident fathers' parenting is likely to matter for their children's development across the economic spectrum. However, it is important to note that this research is based on a small and select sample of men who resided with their biological child and agreed to participate in the study. As the authors of this work recognize, these findings cannot be generalized to low-income coresident fathers overall (Cabrera et al. 2004).

Research on Nonresidential Fathers and Child Well-Being

After increases in divorce rates in the 1970s and 1980s, researchers began to examine the nature and consequences of fathers' involvement following a divorce. Therefore, much of the early literature on nonresident fathers focused on samples of only (or mostly) divorced fathers. Today, another common pathway into being a nonresident father is nonmarital childbearing. Due to the high dissolution rates of unmarried romantic relationships, unmarried fathers, who are disproportionately low-income, are likely to live away from a new child just a few years after the baby's birth (Carlson and McLanahan 2010). Yet this is not a new phenomenon, especially among black families. A study of children born to young (mostly disadvantaged) mothers between 1979 and 1983 found that more than half of African American children never lived with their biological fathers over their first four years of life (based on reports from annual surveys), compared with 9 percent of non-black children (Mott 1990).

Economic resources (child support)

Although family roles have changed over time, so that mothers and fathers now often share breadwinning and caregiving roles, fathers' important contributions to family economic well-being cannot be underestimated. Unmarried fathers are less likely to pay formal child support (and at lower amounts when they do pay) than previously married fathers (Seltzer 1991). Informal financial support (i.e., outside the legal child support enforcement system), especially the purchase of goods and services for the child, is quite common among unmarried fathers, especially around the time of a baby's birth (Edin and Lein 1997; Marsiglio and Day 1997; Waller 2002). In contrast, formal child support orders are rare just after a birth, in part because many unwed couples are still romantically involved and coresiding. By five years after the focal birth, 47 percent of mothers had a child support order in place (and 27 percent had received a formal payment), while 45 percent received in-kind support (and 32 percent received informal financial support) (Nepomnyaschy and Garfinkel 2007). As explained in more detail by Berger and Langton (this volume), there are several explanations for the relatively low levels of formal support and the higher prevalence of informal support among low-income fathers; and Cancian, Meyer, and Han (this volume) highlight the challenges in securing child support from nonresident fathers.

Consonant with the broader literature about how family income affects child well-being, there is evidence (though not entirely consistent) that child support income is associated with better outcomes for children. In their meta-analysis of research about nonresident fathers' involvement and child well-being, Amato and Gilbreth (1999) identified fourteen studies that examined child support and children's achievement and behavioral outcomes. The average (weighted) effect size for child support predicting children's academic success was .09, and for externalizing behavior problems it was –.08, although there was no significant link between child support and children's internalizing behavior problems. These effects did not appear to differ by child's gender. Several of the studies included in the meta-analysis indicated that an additional dollar of child support had significantly larger effects on child well-being than other sources of family income for at least some demographic groups (Argys et al. 1988; Knox and Bane 1994).

Recent studies also suggest that the amount of support that mothers receive matters. Put another way, whether fathers pay any support appears to be less important than how much they pay. Two recent studies found no association between child support receipt and a range of adolescents' outcomes (D. Hawkins, Amato, and King 2007; King and Sobolewski 2006); however, these studies used a binary indicator of whether the father generally paid support, rather than more detailed information about actual payments. An additional study of African American welfare clients and their young children found that after controlling for father's contact and the quality of his relationship with the mother, formal and informal child support predicted better child behavior, and informal child support predicted higher-quality home environments (Greene and Moore 2000). Neither formal nor informal support predicted children's school readiness. By federal law at the time, welfare recipients received a small portion of any formal child support paid ($50); thus, it is not surprising that formal child support in this study shows little evidence of improving children's well-being.

Father-child interaction

Although the literature about nonresident fathers' involvement has grown over the past two decades, the evidence on the effects of these fathers' interactions and time spent with children is more limited and less consistent than that for resident fathers (Amato and Gilbreth 1999; King 1994a; King and Sobolewski 2006). A review article by Cabrera and colleagues characterized the state of nonresident fatherhood research in this way: "Little is known about the effects of nonresident fathers' involvement on children's development" (Cabrera et al. 2000, 130).

Early studies focused on the frequency of contact or visitation by nonresident fathers (among samples of primarily divorced fathers) and found that greater father-child contact was *not* associated with child well-being regardless of the child's race or gender, mother's education, or marital status at birth (Furstenberg, Morgan, and Allison 1987; A. Hawkins and Eggebeen 1991; King 1994a, 1994b; Seltzer and Bianchi 1988). Marsiglio and colleagues' (2000) review of thirty-eight studies published in the 1990s on nonresident fathers and child well-being noted that "taken together, these studies suggest that the frequency of visitation and children's feeling about their fathers are not good predictors of children's development or adjustment" (p. 1184).

The fact that more father-child interaction is not linked to better outcomes for children of nonresident fathers may be due, at least in part, to the characteristics of men who end up living away from their children (Jaffee et al. 2001). Nonresident fathers are more likely than resident fathers to be depressed, to have problems with drugs or alcohol, to have engaged in criminal behavior, and to have been incarcerated (DeKlyen et al. 2006; Garfinkel, McLanahan, and Hanson 1998; Lerman 1993); and this is all the more true for young, low-income fathers. Time spent with fathers who display such characteristics, particularly antisocial behavior, may detract from children's healthy development (Jaffee et al. 2003).

In contrast, when nonresident fathers have the motivation, skills, and capacities to engage in positive interactions with their children, their presence may facilitate healthy outcomes for children. Thus, scholars argue that the quality of nonresident fathers' involvement may be more important than the mere quantity (Amato and Gilbreth 1999; Cabrera et al. 2000). A number of studies have suggested that positive interaction and engagement by nonresident fathers (characterized by close and supportive father-child relationships and responsive parenting) can, in fact, promote child well-being (Amato and Gilbreth 1999; Marsiglio et al. 2000), including reducing children's and adolescents' behavioral problems (Carlson 2006; Coley and Medeiros 2007; King and Sobolewski 2006), facilitating adolescents' adjustment postdivorce (Stewart 2003), improving adolescents' eating habits (Stewart and Menning 2009), and decreasing the likelihood that adolescents will start smoking or drop out of school (Menning 2006b, 2006a). At the same time, although such associations are statistically significant, they are typically substantively small. Also, there is little evidence that the benefits of fathers' positive involvement are moderated by children's age, gender, race, or socioeconomic disadvantage (Amato and Gilbreth 1999; King and Sobolewski 2006). As noted earlier, we must also be mindful that some of the positive association between nonresident fathers' involvement and children's outcomes might arise from bidirectional influences in the father-child relationship, particularly for adolescents (Coley and Medeiros 2007; D. Hawkins, Amato, and King 2007); thus, we must be cautious in interpreting the estimates as reflecting only causal effects of fathering.

Coparenting

For fathers living away from their children, mothers play an important "gatekeeping" role in encouraging or deterring fathers' access to children (Ahrons and Miller 1993; Allen and Hawkins 1999); and fathers' ability to coordinate parenting with mothers, sometimes referred to as "coparenting," is a predictor of fathers' continued involvement with their children (Carlson, McLanahan, and Brooks-Gunn 2008; Sobolewski and King 2005). To our knowledge, beyond studies of children postdivorce (e.g., Maccoby and Mnookin 1992), there is no existing research about whether or how cooperative coparenting between nonresident fathers and custodial mothers directly benefits children, although this is a fruitful topic for future research.

Low-income fathers

Although low-income fathers are included in most studies of nonresident fathers, they are typically underrepresented because they are less strongly attached to households compared with higher-income men; they are more likely to be in the military or incarcerated (Garfinkel, McLanahan, and Hanson 1998; Nelson 2004). A small but growing literature has focused specifically on low-income nonresident fathers to better understand whether greater involvement by such fathers is beneficial for children's development. A study of low-income African American families found that fathers' nurturing behavior is correlated with children's language skills at age three (Black, Dubowitz, and Starr 1999). In addition, nonresident fathers' consistent contact with their children predicted fewer behavioral problems and better cognitive outcomes among a small sample of school-age children born to teenage mothers (Howard et al. 2006). Finally, increases in nonresident-father contact and parenting responsibility led to reductions in delinquency among young adolescents (ages 10–14) living in low-income neighborhoods (Coley and Medeiros 2007). By contrast, one study of young children of welfare recipients found no association between the frequency of fathers' visitation and child well-being, although this study had limited information about fathers' involvement (Greene and Moore 2000). Also, analysis of the Fragile Families and Child Wellbeing data shows that the quantity and quality of nonresident fathers' involvement has no overall association with children's behavior problems at age five, although there are beneficial effects when involvement occurs in the context of a strong coparenting relationship with the child's mother (Carlson, McLanahan, and Brooks-Gunn 2009).

Taken together with the more general literature on nonresident fathers, this research suggests that there are circumstances under which low-income, nonresident fathers' involvement *can* have a positive influence on children's development and well-being, but, on average, it does not. Furthermore, many of these studies include only the "best" fathers who are willing to participate in surveys about fathers' roles, so estimates of the beneficial effects of fathering cannot be generalized to the larger population of low-income fathers, many of whom are much less involved with their children and may have other characteristics that limit the potential for positive influence.

Social Fathers and Child Well-Being

Biological fathers are not the only father figures in the lives of low-income children, and it is important not to overlook nonbiological father figures, or so-called "social fathers." With high rates of divorce and nonmarital union dissolution, many children are likely to live with the romantic partner of one of their biological parents at some point during childhood. About one-third of children will spend time in a (married) stepfamily before age 18 (Seltzer 1994), and recent estimates suggest that fully two-fifths of children will spend time living with their mother and a cohabiting partner by age 12 (Kennedy and Bumpass 2008). The chance of living with a nonbiological social parent is far greater for children born outside of marriage. Given the instability in coresident romantic relationships, men in low-income communities will often fulfill multiple father roles over time—biological coresident father, biological father to own children who live away, and social coresident father to the children of a romantic partner (Edin, Tach, and Mincy 2009). Yet maternal repartnering likely complicates and possibly deters the involvement of nonresident biological fathers with their children (Tach, Mincy, and Edin 2010).

Berger and Langton (this volume) provide greater detail about levels of involvement as social fathers by low-income men. The extant literature suggests that among coresident parents, married stepfathers tend to exhibit lower-quality parenting practices toward stepchildren than married biological fathers do toward biological children (Amato and Sobolewski 2004; Coleman, Ganong, and Fine 2000; Hetherington and Stanley-Hagan 1999; Nelson 2004). Married stepfathers are less likely than married biological fathers to participate in activities with resident children, as well as to express support and positive feelings toward them or to provide monitoring and supervision (Thomson, McLanahan, and Curtin 1992). In contrast, analysis of the Fragile Families and Child Wellbeing data indicate that unmarried resident social fathers are often involved with (nonbiological) young children to the same extent as are unmarried resident biological fathers (Berger et al. 2008).

Although research on how social fathers affect children's development is limited, there is some evidence that social fathers' involvement is beneficial for young children's behavior and health status (Bzostek 2008); although again, the magnitudes of the associations are typically quite small. Also, having a close relationship with a stepfather is shown to reduce adolescents' depressive symptoms and delinquent behaviors (Yuan and Hamilton 2006), including externalizing and internalizing behavior problems (White and Gilbreth 2001). Other work that differentiates the types of social fathers involved with low-income children suggests that involvement by male relatives may be more beneficial than involvement by mothers' romantic partners (Jayakody and Kalil 2002). At the same time, research on married social fathers finds that children in such stepfamilies fare no better than children in single-parent families, despite their higher incomes (McLanahan and Sandefur 1994). This suggests that either stepfamilies spend their money differently than two-biological-parent families or that stepfamily relationships do not confer the same benefits as biological family relationships (for various reasons, including the possible role of stepsiblings). Future research should consider the variation in patterns of involvement by fathers and father figures, especially as family structure changes over time, as well as the conjoint influence of involvement by biological and social fathers on children's well-being.

Conclusions

This article has summarized research about how low-income fathers matter for children. Sociological, developmental, and family system theories all point to fathering as an important influence on children, and research has found that, indeed, some measures of fathering appear to be associated with at least some measures of child and adolescent well-being. In particular, fathers' financial contributions to their children's households and the quality of father-child interactions, including authoritative parenting, appear to be linked to better outcomes for children. Focusing specifically on low-income fathers, however, the evidence base becomes quite thin. This is perhaps not surprising, given how difficult it may be to study fathering among a population of men who often have comparatively little involvement in their children's lives, experience unstable living arrangements, and have a relatively high likelihood of spending time in jail or prison.

Scholars have increasingly called for better and more research on fatherhood in general and on low-income and nonresident fathers in particular (e.g., Nelson 2004). Our review reaches the same conclusion: there is still much to learn about how fathers affect their children's lives, both directly and indirectly. We suggest that several important areas in need of research include (1) understanding how biological and social fathers (independently and jointly) matter for children, considering the full range of involvement domains and situating analyses within theoretical models; (2) evaluating how fathering processes and their effects may differ by race, ethnicity, and cultural background as well as by child's age and gender; and (3) analyzing the nature and implications of fathering in the context of contemporary, highly complex patterns of union formation and fertility among low-income populations (e.g., multipartner fertility). We also urge researchers to improve their study designs with particular attention to issues of social selection, measurement, and bidirectional and indirect effects.

With respect to implications for public policy, we are reluctant to draw strong conclusions, given the limited evidence available about low-income fathers to date. As we have described, existing research suggests that *some* low-income men and fathers can and do have a positive influence on children, with the most consistent findings about the payment of child support (by nonresident fathers). This finding suggests that increasing child support payments is a worthy policy goal. As noted by Sum and colleagues (this volume), many low-income men are unemployed and have little hope of improving their economic position through the formal labor market. Thus, child support enforcement policy should strive both to collect support from fathers who *can* afford to pay and to improve the labor market prospects of low-income men so that more men are able to pay (Cancian, Meyer, and Han this volume).

Cumulative evidence also points to the benefits of high-quality interaction and authoritative parenting. But a number of studies find that fathers' greater involvement (especially frequency of contact) has essentially no effect on children's outcomes. Thus, it is unclear whether fatherhood programs that encourage paternal involvement generally would, in fact, benefit children. Also, to the extent that unobserved heterogeneity plays a role in why high-quality fathering is shown to improve child well-being, one may worry that the fathers not currently involved—but who would be incentivized to become involved by an intervention—might differ in key characteristics that are related to both involvement and children's well-being. As a result, we conclude that interventions and programs should strive to encourage fathers' positive and engaged parenting as opposed to increasing the mere quantity of time spent parenting. We hope that future research will shed light on the most promising avenues for enhancing fathers' positive roles in family life and their contributions to children's well-being.

References

Ahrons, Constance R., and Richard B. Miller. 1993. The effect of the postdivorce relationship on paternal involvement: A longitudinal analysis. *American Journal of Orthopsychiatry* 63 (3): 441–50.

Aldous, Joan, Gail M. Mulligan, and Thoroddur Bjarnason. 1998. Fathering over time: What makes the difference? *Journal of Marriage and the Family* 60 (4): 809–20.

Allen, Sarah M., and Alan J. Hawkins. 1999. Maternal gatekeeping: Mothers' beliefs and behaviors that inhibit greater involvement in family work. *Journal of Marriage and Family* 61 (1): 199–212.

Amato, Paul. 1998. More than money? Men's contributions to their children's lives. In *Men in families: When do they get involved? What difference does it make?* eds. Alan Booth and Ann C. Crouter, 241–78. Mahwah, NJ: Lawrence Erlbaum.

Amato, Paul R., and Joan G. Gilbreth. 1999. Nonresident fathers and children's well-being: A meta-analysis. *Journal of Marriage and the Family* 61 (3): 557–73.

Amato, Paul R., and Fernando Rivera. 1999. Paternal involvement and children's behavior problems. *Journal of Marriage and the Family* 61 (2): 375–84.

Amato, Paul, and Juliana Sobolewski. 2004. The effects of divorce on fathers and children: Nonresidential fathers and stepfathers. In *The role of the father in child development*, 4th ed., ed. Michael E. Lamb, 341–67. Hoboken, NJ: Wiley.

Anderson, Elijah. 1989. Sex codes and family life among poor inner-city youths. *The Annals of the American Academy of Political and Social Science* 501 (1): 59–78.

Argys, Laura M., H. Elizabeth Peters, Jeanne Brooks-Gunn, and J. R. Smith. 1988. The impact of child support on cognitive outcomes of young children. *Demography* 35 (2): 159–73.

Baumrind, Diana. 1966. Effects of authoritative parental control on child behavior. *Child Development* 37 (4): 887–907.

Baumrind, Diana. 1986. Authoritarian versus authoritative parental control. *Adolescence* 3:255–72.

Berger, Lawrence M., Marcia J. Carlson, Sharon H. Bzostek, and Cynthia Osborne. 2008. Parenting practices of resident fathers: The role of marital and biological ties. *Journal of Marriage and Family* 70 (3): 625–39.

Black, Maureen M., Howard Dubowitz, and Raymond H. Starr Jr. 1999. African American fathers in low income, urban families: Development, behavior, and home environment of their three-year-old children. *Child Development* 70 (4): 967–78.

Brooks-Gunn, Jeanne, and Lisa B. Markman. 2005. The contribution of parenting to ethnic and racial gaps in school readiness. *The Future of Children* 15 (1): 139–68.

Bzostek, Sharon. 2008. Social fathers and child well-being. *Journal of Marriage and Family* 70 (4): 950–61.

Cabrera, Natasha J., Rebecca M. Ryan, Jacqueline D. Shannon, Cheri Vogel, Helen Raikes, Catherine Tamis-LeMonda, and Rachel Cohen. 2004. Low-income fathers' involvement in their toddlers' lives: Biological fathers from the Early Head Start Research and Evaluation Study. *Fathering* 2 (1): 5–30.

Cabrera, Natasha J., Jacqueline D. Shannon, and Catherine Tamis-LeMonda. 2007. Fathers' influence on their children's cognitive and emotional development: From toddlers to pre-K. *Applied Developmental Science* 11 (4): 208–13.

Cabrera, Natasha J., Catherine S. Tamis-LeMonda, Robert H. Bradley, Sandra L. Hofferth, and Michael E. Lamb. 2000. Fatherhood in the twenty-first century. *Child Development* 71 (1): 127–36.

Carlson, Marcia J. 2006. Family structure, father involvement, and adolescent behavioral outcomes. *Journal of Marriage and Family* 68 (1): 137–54.

Carlson, Marcia J., and Sara S. McLanahan. 2010. Fathers in fragile families. In *The role of the father in child development*, ed. Michael E. Lamb, 241–69. New York, NY: Wiley.

Carlson, Marcia J., Sara S. McLanahan, and Jeanne Brooks-Gunn. 2008. Coparenting and nonresident fathers' involvement with young children after a nonmarital birth. *Demography* 45 (2): 461–88.

Carlson, Marcia J., Sara S. McLanahan, and Jeanne Brooks-Gunn. 2009. Nonmarital fathering and the wellbeing of children. Center for Research on Child Wellbeing Working Paper, Princeton University, Princeton, NJ.

Chase-Lansdale, P. Lindsay, Kathleen Kiernan, and Ruth J. Friedman, eds. 2004. *Human development across lives and generations: The potential for change.* Cambridge: Cambridge University Press.

Cherlin, Andrew J. 1999. Going to extremes: Family structure, children's well-being, and social science. *Demography* 36 (4): 421–28.

Coleman, Marilyn, Lawrence Ganong, and Mark Fine. 2000. Reinvestigating remarriage: Another decade of progress. *Journal of Marriage and Family* 62 (4): 1288–1307.

Coley, Rebekah Levine. 1998. Children's socialization experiences and functioning in single-mother households: The importance of fathers and other men. *Child Development* 69 (1): 219–30.

Coley, Rebekah Levine, and Bethany L. Medeiros. 2007. Reciprocal longitudinal relations between nonresident father involvement and adolescent delinquency. *Child Development* 78 (1): 132–47.

Coley, Rebekah Levine, and J. E. Morris. 2002. Comparing father and mother reports of father involvement among low-income minority fathers. *Journal of Marriage and Family* 64 (4): 982–97.

Collins, W. Andrew, Eleanor Maccoby, Laurence Steinberg, E. Mavis Hetherington, and Marc H. Bornstein. 2000. Contemporary research on parenting: The case for nature and nurture. *American Psychologist* 55 (2): 218–32.

Cooksey, Elizabeth C., and Patricia H. Craig. 1998. Parenting from a distance: The effects of paternal characteristics on contact between nonresidential fathers and their children. *Demography* 35 (2): 187–200.

Cooksey, Elizabeth C., and Michelle M. Fondell. 1996. Spending time with his kids: Effects of family structure on fathers' and children's lives. *Journal of Marriage and the Family* 58 (3): 693–707.

Cox, Martha J., and Blair Paley. 1997. Families as systems. *Annual Review of Psychology* 48:243–67.

Crouter, Ann C., and Alan Booth. 2003. *Children's influence on family dynamics: The neglected side of family relationships.* Mahwah, NJ: Lawrence Erlbaum.

Dahl, Gordon B., and Lance Lochner. 2008. The impact of family income on child achievement: Evidence from the Earned Income Tax Credit. National Bureau of Economic Research Working Paper w14599, Cambridge, MA.

DeKlyen, Michelle, Jeanne Brooks-Gunn, Sara McLanahan, and Jean Knab. 2006. The mental health of married, cohabiting, and non-coresident parents with infants. *American Journal of Public Health* 96 (10): 1836–41.

Duncan, Greg J., and Jeanne Brooks-Gunn. 1997. *The consequences of growing up poor.* New York, NY: Russell Sage Foundation.

Edin, Kathryn, and Laura Lein. 1997. *Making ends meet: How single mothers survive welfare and low-wage work.* New York, NY: Russell Sage Foundation.

Edin, Kathryn, Laura Tach, and Ronald Mincy. 2009. Claiming fatherhood: Race and the dynamics of paternal involvement among unmarried men. *The Annals of the American Academy of Political and Social Science* 621 (1): 149–77.

Forehand, Rex, and Sarah Nousiainen. 1993. Maternal and paternal parenting: Critical dimensions in adolescent functioning. *Journal of Family Psychology* 7 (2): 213–21.

Furstenberg, Frank F. 1988. Good dads—bad dads: Two faces of fatherhood. In *The changing American family and public policy,* ed. Andrew J. Cherlin, 193–209. Washington, DC: Urban Institute.

Furstenberg, Frank F. 2007. The making of the black family: Race and class in qualitative studies in the twentieth century. *Annual Review of Sociology* 33:429–48.

Furstenberg, Frank F., and Andrew Cherlin. 1991. *Divided families: What happens to children when parents part.* Cambridge, MA: Harvard University Press.

Furstenberg, Frank F., Jr., S. Philip Morgan, and Paul D. Allison. 1987. Paternal participation and children's well-being after marital dissolution. *American Sociological Review* 52 (5): 695–701.

Furstenberg, Frank F., Jr., Kay E. Sherwood, and Mercer L. Sullivan. 1992. *Caring and paying: What fathers and mothers say about child support.* New York, NY: MDRC.

Gable, Sara, Jay Belsky, and Keith Crnic. 1994. Coparenting within the family system: Influences on children's development. *Family Relations* 43 (4): 380–86.

Garfinkel, Irwin, Sara S. McLanahan, and Thomas L. Hanson. 1998. A patchwork portrait of nonresident fathers. In *Fathers under fire: The revolution in child support enforcement*, eds. Irwin Garfinkel, Sara S. McLanahan, Daniel R. Meyer, and Judith A. Seltzer. New York, NY: Russell Sage Foundation.

Greene, Angela Dungee, and Kristin Anderson Moore. 2000. Nonresident father involvement and child well-being among young children in families on welfare. *Marriage & Family Review* 29 (2–3): 159–80.

Harris, Kathleen Mullan, Frank F. Furstenberg Jr., and Jeremy K. Marmer. 1998. Paternal involvement with adolescents in intact families: The influence of fathers over the life course. *Demography* 35 (2): 201–16.

Harris, Kathleen Mullan, and S. Philip Morgan. 1991. Fathers, sons and daughters: Differential paternal involvement in parenting. *Journal of Marriage and the Family* 53 (3): 531–44.

Harris, Kathleen Mullan, and Suzanne Ryan. 2004. Father involvement and the diversity of family context. In *Conceptualizing and measuring father involvement*, eds. Randal D. Day and Michael E. Lamb, 293–319. Mahwah, NJ: Lawrence Erlbaum.

Hawkins, Alan J., and David J. Eggebeen. 1991. Are fathers fungible? Patterns of coresident adult men in maritally disrupted families and young children's well-being. *Journal of Marriage and the Family* 53 (4): 958–72.

Hawkins, Daniel N., Paul R. Amato, and Valarie King. 2007. Nonresident father involvement and adolescent well-being: Father effects or child effects? *American Sociological Review* 72 (6): 990–1010.

Hayden, Lisa C., Masha Schiller, Susan Dickstein, Ronald Seifer, Steven Sameroff, Ivan Miller, Gabor Keitner, and Steven Rasmussen. 1998. Levels of family assessment: I. Family, marital, and parent-child interaction. *Journal of Family Psychology* 12 (1): 7–22.

Hetherington, E. Mavis, and M. Stanley-Hagan. 1999. Stepfamilies. In *Parenting and child development in "nontraditional" families*, ed. Michael E. Lamb, 137–59. Mahwah, NJ: Lawrence Erlbaum.

Hofferth, Sandra L. 2003. Race/ethnic differences in father involvement in two-parent families: Culture, context, or economy? *Journal of Family Issues* 24 (2): 185–216.

Hofferth, Sandra L. 2006. Residential father family type and child well-being: Investment versus selection. *Demography* 43 (1): 53–77.

Hofferth, Sandra L., Natasha Cabrera, Marcia Carlson, Rebekah Levine Coley, Randal Day, and Holly Schindler. 2007. Resident father involvement and social fathering. In *Handbook of measurement issues in family research*, eds. S. L. Hofferth and L. M. Casper, 335–74. Mahwah, NJ: Lawrence Erlbaum.

Howard, Kimberly S., Jennifer E. Burke Lefever, John G. Borkowski, and Thomas L. Whitman. 2006. Fathers' influence in the lives of children with adolescent mothers. *Journal of Family Psychology* 20 (3): 468–76.

Jaffee, Sara R., Avshalom Caspi, Terrie E. Moffitt, Alan Taylor, and Nigel Dickson. 2001. Predicting early fatherhood and whether young fathers live with their children: Prospective findings and policy recommendations. *Journal of Child Psychology and Psychiatry* 42 (6): 803–15.

Jaffee, Sara R., Terrie E. Moffitt, Avshalom Caspi, and Alan Taylor. 2003. Life with (or without) father: The benefits of living with two biological parents depend on the father's antisocial behavior. *Child Development* 74 (1): 109–26.

Jarrett, Robin L., Kevin M. Roy, and Linda M. Burton. 2002. Fathers in the "hood": Insights from qualitative research on low-income African American men. In *Handbook of father involvement: Multidisciplinary perspectives*, eds. Catherine S. Tamis-LeMonda and Natasha Cabrera, 211–48. Mahwah, NJ: Lawrence Erlbaum.

Jayakody, Rukmalie, and Ariel Kalil. 2002. Social fathering in low-income, African American families with preschool children. *Journal of Marriage and Family* 64 (2): 504–16.

Kennedy, Sheela, and Larry Bumpass. 2008. Cohabitation and children's living arrangements: New estimates from the United States. *Demographic Research* 19:1663–92.

King, Valarie. 1994a. Nonresident father involvement and child well-being: Can dads make a difference? *Journal of Family Issues* 15 (1): 78–96.

King, Valarie. 1994b. Variation in the consequences of nonresident father involvement for children's well-being. *Journal of Marriage and the Family* 56 (4): 963–72.

King, Valarie, Kathleen Mullan Harris, and Holly E. Heard. 2004. Racial and ethnic diversity in nonresident father involvement. *Journal of Marriage and Family* 66 (1): 1–21.

King, Valarie, and Juliana M. Sobolewski. 2006. Nonresident fathers' contributions to adolescent well-being. *Journal of Marriage and Family* 68 (3): 537–57.

Knox, Virginia, and Mary Jo Bane. 1994. Child support and schooling. In *Child support and child well-being*, eds. Irwin Garfinkel, Sara S. McLanahan, and Philip K. Robins, 285–310. Washington, DC: Urban Institute.

Lamb, Michael E. 1986. *The fathers' role: Applied perspectives*. New York, NY: Wiley.

Lamb, Michael E. 2004. *The role of the father in child development*. New York, NY: Wiley.

Lamb, Michael E., Joseph H. Pleck, Eric L. Charnov, and James A. Levine. 1985. Paternal behavior in humans. *American Zoologist* 25 (3): 883–94.

Lareau, Annette. 2003. *Unequal childhoods: Class, race, and family life*. Berkeley: University of California Press.

Lerman, Robert I. 1993. A national profile of young unwed fathers. In *Young unwed fathers: Changing roles and emerging policies*, eds. Robert I. Lerman and Theodora J. Ooms, 27–51. Philadelphia, PA: Temple University Press.

Livingston, Jonathan N., and John L. McAdoo. 2007. The roles of African American fathers in the socialization of their children. In *Black families*, ed. Harriette Pipes McAdoo. Thousand Oaks, CA: Sage.

Maccoby, Eleanor E. 2000. Parenting and its effects on children: On reading and misreading behavior genetics. *Annual Review of Psychology* 51:1–27.

Maccoby, Eleanor E., and John A. Martin. 1983. Socialization in the context of the family: Parent-child interaction. In *Handbook of child psychology*, vol. 4, *Socialization, personality, and social development*, ed. E. Mavis Hetherington, 1–101. New York, NY: Wiley.

Maccoby, Eleanor E., and Robert H. Mnookin. 1992. *Dividing the child: Social and legal dilemmas of custody*. Cambridge, MA: Harvard University Press.

Magnuson, Katherine, and Elizabeth Votruba-Drzal. 2009. Enduring influences of poverty. In *Changing poverty, changing policies*, eds. Maria Cancian and Sheldon Danziger. New York, NY: Russell Sage Foundation.

Marsiglio, William, Paul Amato, Randal D. Day, and Michael E. Lamb. 2000. Scholarship on fatherhood in the 1990s and beyond. *Journal of Marriage and the Family* 62 (4): 1173–91.

Marsiglio, William, and Randal Day. 1997. Social fatherhood and paternal involvement: Conceptual, data, and policymaking issues. Presented at Conference on Fathering and Male Fertility: Improving Data and Research, National Institutes of Health, 13–14 March, Bethesda, MD.

Martin, Anne, Rebecca M. Ryan, and Jeanne Brooks-Gunn. 2007. The joint influence of mother and father parenting on child cognitive outcomes at age 5. *Early Childhood Research Quarterly* 22 (4): 423–39.

McHale, James P. 1995. Coparenting and triadic interactions during infancy: The roles of marital distress and child gender. *Developmental Psychology* 31 (6): 985–96.

McHale, James P., Regina Kuersten-Hogan, Allison Lauretti, and Jeffrey L. Rasmussen. 2000. Parental reports of coparenting and observed coparenting behavior during the toddler period. *Journal of Family Psychology* 14 (2): 220–36.

McLanahan, Sara, and Gary Sandefur. 1994. *Growing up with a single parent: What hurts? What helps?* Cambridge, MA: Harvard University Press.

McLoyd, Vonnie C. 1998. Socioeconomic disadvantage and child development. *American Psychologist* 53 (2): 185–204.

Menning, Chadwick L. 2006a. Nonresident fathering and school failure. *Journal of Family Issues* 27 (10): 1356–82.

Menning, Chadwick L. 2006b. Nonresident fathers' involvement and adolescents' smoking. *Journal of Health and Social Behavior* 47 (1): 32–46.

Milligan, Kevin, and Mark Stabile. 2008. Do child tax benefits affect the wellbeing of children? Evidence from Canadian child benefit expansions. National Bureau of Economic Research Working Paper w14624, Cambridge, MA.

Mincy, Ronald B. 2006. *Black males left behind*. Washington, DC: Urban Institute Press.

Mincy, Ronald B., and Hillard Pouncy. 2007. *Baby fathers and American family formation: Low-income, never-married parents in Louisiana before Katrina*. New York, NY: Center for Marriage and Families, Institute for American Values.

Minuchin, Patricia. 1988. Relationships within the family: A systems perspective on development. In *Relationships within families: Mutual influences*, eds. Robert A. Hinde and Joan Stevenson-Hinde, 7–26. New York, NY: Oxford University Press.

Mott, Frank L. 1990. When is a father really gone? Paternal-child contact in father-absent homes. *Demography* 27 (4): 499–517.

Nelson, Timothy J. 2004. Low-income fathers. *Annual Review of Sociology* 30:427–51.

Nepomnyaschy, Lenna. 2007. Child support and father-child contact: Testing reciprocal pathways. *Demography* 44 (1): 93–112.

Nepomnyaschy, Lenna, and Irwin Garfinkel. 2007. Child support, fatherhood, and marriage: Findings from the first five years of the Fragile Families and Child Wellbeing study. *Asian Social Work and Policy Review* 1:1–20.

O'Brien, Marion. 2005. Studying individual and family development: Linking theory and research. *Journal of Marriage and Family* 67 (4): 880–90.

Osborne, Cynthia, Wendy D. Manning, and Pamela J. Smock. 2007. Married and cohabiting parents' relationship stability: A focus on race and ethnicity. *Journal of Marriage and Family* 69 (5): 1345–66.

Palkovitz, Rob. 2002. Involved fathering and child development: Advancing our understanding of good fathering. In *Handbook of father involvement*, eds. Catherine S. Tamis-LeMonda and Natasha J. Cabrera, 33–64. Mahwah, NJ: Lawrence Erlbaum.

Parke, Ross D. 2004. Development in the family. *Annual Review of Psychology* 55:365–99.

Patterson, Orlando. 1999. *Rituals of blood: The consequences of slavery in two American centuries*. New York, NY: Basic Civitas Books.

Rossi, Alice S., and Peter H. Rossi. 1990. *Of human bonding: Parent-child relations across the life course*. New York, NY: Aldine de Gruyter.

Schoppe-Sullivan, Sarah J., Geoffrey L. Brown, Elizabeth A. Cannon, Sarah C. Mangelsdorf, and Margaret Szewczyk Sokolowski. 2008. Maternal gatekeeping, coparenting quality, and fathering behavior in families with infants. *Journal of Family Psychology* 22 (3): 389–98.

Schoppe, Sarah J., Sarah C. Mangelsdorf, and Cynthia A. Frosch. 2001. Coparenting, family process, and family structure: Implications for preschoolers' externalizing behavior problems. *Journal of Family Psychology* 15 (3): 526–45.

Seltzer, Judith A. 1991. Relationships between fathers and children who live apart: The father's role after separation. *Journal of Marriage and the Family* 53 (1): 79–101.

Seltzer, Judith A. 1994. Intergenerational ties in adulthood and childhood experience. In *Stepfamilies: Who benefits? Who does not?* eds. Alan Booth and Judy Dunn, 153–66. Hillsdale, NJ: Lawrence Erlbaum.

Seltzer, Judith A., and Suzanne M. Bianchi. 1988. Children's contact with absent parents. *Journal of Marriage and the Family* 50 (3): 663–77.

Seltzer, Judith A., Nora Cate Schaeffer, and Hong-Wen Charng. 1989. Family ties after divorce: The relationship between visiting and paying child support. *Journal of Marriage and Family* 51 (4): 1013–31.

Shannon, Jacqueline D., Catherine Tamis-LeMonda, Kevin London, and Natasha Cabrera. 2002. Beyond rough and tumble: Low-income fathers' interactions and children's cognitive development at 24 months. *Parenting: Science and Practice* 2 (2): 77–104.

Sigle-Rushton, Wendy, and Sara McLanahan. 2004. Father absence and child well-being: A critical review. In *The future of the family*, eds. Daniel P. Moynihan, Timothy M. Smeeding, and Lee Rainwater, 116–55. New York, NY: Russell Sage Foundation.

Sobolewski, Juliana M., and Valarie King. 2005. The importance of the coparental relationship for non-resident fathers' ties to children. *Journal of Marriage and Family* 67 (5): 1196–1212.

Stack, Carol. 1974. *All our kin*. New York, NY: Basic Books.

Stewart, Susan D. 2003. Nonresident parenting and adolescent adjustment: The quality of nonresident father-child interaction. *Journal of Family Issues* 24 (2): 217–44.

Stewart, Susan D., and Chadwick L. Menning. 2009. Family structure, nonresident father involvement, and adolescent eating patterns. *Journal of Adolescent Health* 45 (2): 193–201.

Tach, Laura, Ronald Mincy, and Kathryn Edin. 2010. Parenting as a package deal: Relationships, fertility, and nonresident father involvement among unmarried parents. *Demography* 47 (1): 181–204.

Tamis-LeMonda, Catherine S., Jacqueline D. Shannon, Natasha J. Cabrera, and Michael E. Lamb. 2004. Fathers and mothers at play with their 2- and 3-year-olds: Contributions to language and cognitive development. *Child Development* 75 (6): 1806–20.

Tein, Jen-Yun, Mark W. Roosa, and Marcia Michaels. 1994. Agreement between parent and child reports on parental behavior. *Journal of Marriage and Family* 56 (2): 341–55.

Thomson, Elizabeth, Sara S. McLanahan, and Roberta Braun Curtin. 1992. Family structure, gender, and parental socialization. *Journal of Marriage and the Family* 54 (4): 368–78.

Townsend, Nicholas W. 2002. *The package deal: Marriage, work and fatherhood in men's lives*. Philadelphia, PA: Temple University Press.

U.S. House of Representatives. 2008. *Green Book: Background material and data on the programs within the jurisdiction of the Committee on Ways and Means*. Washington, DC: U.S. Government Printing Office.

Waller, Maureen R. 2002. *My baby's father: Unmarried parents and paternal responsibility*. Ithaca, NY: Cornell University Press.

White, Lynn, and Joan G. Gilbreth. 2001. When children have two fathers: Effects of relationships with stepfathers and noncustodial fathers on adolescent outcomes. *Journal of Marriage and Family* 63 (1): 155–67.

Yuan, Anastasia S. Vogt, and Hayley A. Hamilton. 2006. Stepfather involvement and adolescent well-being. *Journal of Family Issues* 27 (9): 1191–1213.

Keywords: low-income fatherhood; culture; identity; choice-making; behavior

Comment: Reactions from the Perspective of Culture and Low-Income Fatherhood

By
ALFORD A. YOUNG JR.

The four articles discussed here provide descriptive assessments of the state of research on low-income fatherhood in America and reflect the richness and vastness of contemporary research in this area. In particular, the articles by Lawrence Berger and Callie Langton ("Young Disadvantaged Men as Fathers"), Laura Tach and Kathryn Edin ("The Relationship Contexts of Young Disadvantaged Men"), and Marcia Carlson and Katherine Magnuson ("Low-Income Fathers' Influences on Children") convey the extent to which the choice-making and behavior of low-income fathers involve a broader arena of considerations than implied by the long-standing concern with the narrow question of whether such men are committed to being involved fathers. This classic depiction of low-income fatherhood (sometimes cast as the decent daddy versus the failed daddy distinction) did not allow researchers and concerned parties to fully apprehend the myriad ways by which these men struggle with their roles and duties as fathers nor even how they came to understand them.

However, these articles consider the multiple forms of fatherhood that operate in low-income community contexts, including social fathering, the custodial-noncustodial divisions in fathering, and the residential-nonresidential division. The expansion of such fathering categories reflects

Alford A. Young Jr. is Arthur F. Thurnau Professor of Sociology and in the Center for Afro-American and African Studies at the University of Michigan. His research focuses on the experiences of low-income African American men. His books include The Minds of Marginalized Black Men: Making Sense of Mobility, Opportunity, and Future Life Chances *(Princeton University Press 2004) and a coauthored work titled* The Souls of W. E. B. Du Bois *(Paradigm Publishers 2006).*

DOI: 10.1177/0002716210390316

how researchers have been responsive to the fluidity that is associated with father-hood in low-income family life, and this fluidity involves men cycling in and out of relationships and in and out of their children's lives. Hence, these articles compel deeper thinking about the cultural sphere in terms of what has been introduced about low-income fathering and what needs further consideration.

Before proceeding, it is essential to offer a definition of the cultural analysis of fathering. At its basic level, cultural analysis is the exploration and interpretation of the ways such men perform that social role and the views, attitudes, outlooks, and opinions that they maintain about it. In terms of assessing the culture of low-income fatherhood, then, one of the most important findings presented in the three articles mentioned above is that low-income fathers clearly hold great value for the identity of father. They also strongly desire to engage partnerships that they hope will lead to the creation and cultivation of emotionally and physically healthy families.

However, each article also explores the range of behaviors that low-income men pursue to minimize the kind of problems associated with family life in the midst of socioeconomic constraints. Of course, some of these approaches, such as withdraw-ing from a household when tension and conflict emerge, ultimately may exacerbate problems in relating to the mothers of their children as such mothers may regard these men as abandoning them and their children rather than contending with the turmoil. Indeed, each article explores how choice-making by such men, whether it be in regard to issues concerning their children, their partners, the mothers of their children (who may not be the same women), or the entire family unit, is a critical cultural domain to consider, especially because such choice-making is not effectively explained as a by-product of these men's inability to value fatherhood.

Furthermore, what is revealed more fully when the article by Andrew Sum and his colleagues ("No Country for Young Men: Deteriorating Labor Market Prospects for Low-Skilled Men in the United States") is brought into the con-versation is that the new terrain for cultural analysis must be properly informed by understandings of how the structural dimensions of the lives of low-income males—particularly around employment and schooling—have transformed in the past decade. Of course, this has great bearing on how these men do or may function as fathers. Sum and colleagues document the extent of the extreme distance that exists between low-income men and consistent employment. Implicated in the rise of this distancing are a range of conditions and outcomes, such as the effects of having a criminal record, being a member of a racial or ethnic minority group, or attaining specific kinds of educational credentials (GED, associate's degrees, etc.) that do not meet the demands of the work world. Ultimately, each of these attributes either exacerbates the employment problems that these men face or else does not significantly alleviate these prob-lems. Sum and his colleagues show that the condition that such men are in is not one of being marginal to the work world but actually increasingly distant from it. Hence, they lack access to the kind of wages that would allow them to function even as minimally consistent providers to their children. These structural factors provide critical context for the cultural dimensions of low-income fatherhood.

A key emphasis concerning culture in the other articles is how low-income fathers struggle with the range of duties, services, and obligations that are associated with modern fatherhood (and which transcend the traditional fatherly role of serving as the principal breadwinner in a family). As Berger and Langton, Tach and Edin, and Carlson and Magnuson assert, fatherhood in late-twentieth-century America no longer was wholly associated with material earnings. Instead, various kinds of involvement with children (including, but not restricted to, provision of emotional support, character development, and caretaking of younger children) now compose modern notions of responsible fatherhood.

As men have moved (or at least have been encouraged to move) toward embracing parent and family functioning that emphasizes the provision of emotional support, there remains a major question of what to make of men who have not achieved success in functioning in the traditional capacity of material provider. Put more directly, can men embrace a new vision of fatherhood if they have not met the kind of success they desire with a former vision? Essentially, a dilemma remains for low-income fathers in that they have not experienced success in achieving what has been traditionally defined as responsible fatherhood. Consequently, what degree of investment might these men prepare to make in achieving a more modern notion that is still largely associated with middle-class American men who, by virtue of their class location, have already demonstrated success at traditional fatherhood?

I further flesh out the prospects for this more thorough understanding of the culture of low-income fatherhood by exploring two dimensions of this practice: fatherhood identity and the community context in which low-income fathering unfolds. As I demonstrate below, each dimension is a site for more extensive consideration of culture, given what the article by Sum and colleagues brings to the arguments and findings delivered in the other three articles.

Identity

A major issue addressed in these articles is how fathers define and then manage their identities. By drawing distinctions between fathers who are below and those at or above the age of 25, Berger and Langton point to a crucial issue concerning what it means to be a young struggling father in comparison to one who is older and thus has maintained a longer history of functioning in that capacity. The lingering question is to what extent has the inability to function as fathers in the ways that such men might have hoped to factor into the ways in which they make choices concerning children born to them later on in life. The resulting questions include the following: Does longer-term failure to serve as a functional father lead to sustained withdrawal from the lives of one's children? Might such fathers be more willing to engage younger children better than older ones, as the younger do not bear the scars of distal or negligent fatherhood in the ways that older ones might? How might failed fathers respond to their children later in life? Finally, how do fathers who do not regard themselves as failed fathers assess themselves when others regard them as such?

Essentially, Berger and Langton's article calls for placing men's personal histories as fathers more directly into consideration in assessments of their actions, or inactions, with their children. Of course, when taking into account what Sum and his colleagues present about employment conditions, greater attention to personal history must also include the particular histories of work experiences that fathers have encountered, how those histories may shape choice-making and action at various stages of their lives, and what residual effects prior choices and actions have on later ones concerning the interaction of fathers with their children.

A second arena of interest is whether willful avoidance of children is a means by which low-income fathers shield their children from their own history of personal failings. For example, it is plausible that fathers who are ex-offenders may not care to expose their children to their troubled pasts. This does not mean that such men mindlessly avoid investing behaviorally, socially, or otherwise in their children but that withdrawal may be their notion of what is in the best interest of their children. Hence, in such cases, problematic action in regard to fatherhood emerges precisely because such men have embraced personal identities as failed fathers. Accordingly, a critical matter in advancing further understandings of the culture of low-income fathering is the challenge to incorporate more fully men's sense of their personal histories as fathers in ways that shed light on whether and how they embrace certain identities as fathers and how they consequently act in response to those identities.

The Community Context

In taking stock of the ways in which the community context affects the cultural dynamics of low-income fatherhood, there remains a challenge to grasp aspects of the social condition of low-income fatherhood that do not necessarily emerge in demographic analyses or in studies that focus on the family unit. This is precisely why the article by Sum and colleagues must be placed in direct conversation with the other three articles. Here, Sum and his colleagues also provide significant evidence as to why absentee fatherhood is so prevalent in low-income communities. Stated simply, when men are out of work or in institutions such as prison, they cannot, will not, or sometimes are asked not to maintain an effective presence in the household. What this condition produces for low-income men, especially African Americans, is the formation of absentee fatherhood as a community-level phenomenon and not just a household or family condition. Certainly, absentee fatherhood is a problem for any child who experiences it in his or her home. However, when such a circumstance is common in a residential community rather than just in a household, absentee fatherhood takes the form of a normative, rather than the exceptional, social condition.

The stake for any child who experiences this more extreme form of absentee fatherhood is severe, but for boys in particular, this condition means that they not only grow up without the consistent and successful presence of fathers in their lives, but they are also unable to witness other men serving as fathers in communities afflicted by economic constraint. Ultimately, then, such boys are reared without extensive insight into how fathers may navigate the tenuous terrain of fatherhood in low-income circumstances. Again, the articles affirm quite well that many of these men do embrace notions of responsible fatherhood and do desire to conduct themselves as such. Yet their life experiences do not involve their learning in intimate and consistent fashion how to do so because neither home nor community has provided them with models of such behavior. Hence, an emergent cultural context of fatherhood is the process of committing to the role without sufficient understanding of how the complexities and challenges of the role may be handled by such men. Furthermore, understandings of how the role should be performed are often rooted in ideas about what was not present in the lives of these young men (i.e., "a good father is simply construed as being the opposite of what my father was") rather than in a secure sense of precisely how a father struggles with the challenges of trying to effectively perform that role.

The final community context issue stimulated by these articles is the absence of social space and institutions that allow young men to pose and resolve questions, concerns, inadequacies, or fears about being fathers. It is well known that many low-income men, but especially those who are African American and Latino, live in social environments that do not foster healthy emotional or physical development. Indeed, the social spaces that such men occupy often demand that they maintain aggressive dispositions so that they can manage the challenges that these communities present to their social, emotional, and physical well-being. Think, for instance, of the kind of male bravado that unfolds on public basketball courts, in barbershops, or on street corners as men go about demonstrating their stability and comfort (actual as well as imagined or disguised) in being men and acting like men. When the needs and demands for professing bravado, intensity, and assertiveness while engaging public spaces in low-income communities remain overwhelming, there is less space for such men to express and reconcile with the kinds of doubts, anxieties, and insecurities that may come with entering into the role of father, especially from positions of extreme socioeconomic disadvantage. A part of the contemporary situation for urban-based, low-income fathers, then, is the absence of public or institutionalized spaces for constructively working out and resolving tensions, perceived inadequacies, and self-misunderstandings about being fathers (and this is a problem that may be most effectively addressed by faith-based institutions, which, by their very nature, can provide such safe spaces and opportunities).

These men often find little support in formal organizational spaces, such as child welfare agencies or the legal system, where they (wrongly or rightly) perceive their interests to be suppressed by the attention given to women and children. Hence, these men not only endure consistent social exposure to so-called "failed fathers" in their communities, but lack the means to express and resolve challenges to their capacity to serve as effective fathers because they recognize no formal or institutional outlets to do so (that is, unless they have access to social programs aimed at resolving these problems—and far too many low-income men lack such access). Taking this into account means recognizing that the community context for low-income fathering is not simply a neutral backdrop for these men, but one that houses and facilitates the conditions and circumstances that drastically increase their inability to make better sense of how to learn to function as effective fathers, even if a value for fatherhood is fully embraced by them. In the case of low-income fathers, then, the contemporary structure of the community setting is a pivotal causal factor for shaping the important cultural dimensions of fathering.

Conclusion

Taken together, these articles encourage some profound rethinking of the cultural aspects of low-income fathering. They bring closure to one long-standing issue in the cultural analysis of low-income fathers—such men do value the role of father, desire to fulfill it in healthy and successful ways, and often try to do so upon first becoming fathers. The tribulations of living in contexts where success-ful, or even struggling but committed, fatherhood is not plainly evident, coupled with how men grapple with their own personal identities as troubled (if not yet failing) fathers, is the source of the problem. Accordingly, there now exist a range of issues that must take center stage in the continued pursuit of understanding the choice-making and behavior of low-income fathers in regard to the mothers of their children and to the children more directly.

Keywords: young black men; incarceration; families

Comment: Young Disadvantaged Men: Reactions from the Perspective of Race

By
DEVAH PAGER

Despite promising reforms following the civil rights movement of the 1960s and continuing through the 1970s, the progress of black men since the early 1980s has been relatively stagnant. The black-white gaps in high school graduation, earnings, and unemployment have improved little over the past 30 years. On some indicators, black men are doing steadily worse: faced with poor employment prospects, less-educated young black men have become increasingly likely to exit the labor force altogether, with rates of labor force participation declining by 17 percent between 1979 and 2000 (Holzer, Offner, and Sorensen 2005). More troubling, roughly 60 percent of black male high school dropouts will end up in prison by the age of 30, with current rates of incarceration exceeding those of formal employment among this group (Pettit and Western 2004).

A recent and growing line of research recognizes that the poor prospects for low-income black men have consequences that extend well beyond the individuals themselves. These young men's fortunes affect the women they partner with and the children they father. Understanding the problems facing young black men today, then, is an important part of understanding problems facing the black family as a whole.

This insight is not, of course, entirely new. The controversial Moynihan report, written more

Devah Pager is an associate professor of sociology and faculty associate in the Office of Population Research at Princeton University. Her research focuses on institutions affecting racial stratification, including education, labor markets, and the criminal justice system. Her book Marked: Race, Crime, and Finding Work in an Era of Mass Incarceration *(University of Chicago 2007) investigates the racial and economic consequences of large-scale imprisonment for contemporary U.S. labor markets. Pager's research is supported by grants from NIH K01, NSF CAREER, and the W. T. Grant Scholar's Award.*

DOI: 10.1177/0002716210393322

than 40 years ago, pays significant attention to the problem of joblessness among young black men and its implications for rising rates of female-headed families (Moynihan 1965, 61–73). The Moynihan report was prescient in its analysis of the problems of disadvantaged black men and women, and yet what Moynihan could not have foreseen was the sharp dismantling of career ladders (Bernhardt et al. 2001); the replacement of steady, well-paying blue-collar jobs with casual, low-wage service work (Meisenheimer 1998); and the rise of mass incarceration (Western 2006). Each of these developments has intensified the barriers to economic self-sufficiency facing young less-educated men, with disproportionate consequences for African Americans.

The articles in this volume address the dilemmas of young disadvantaged men with these forces as their backdrop, examining the experiences of low-income men as workers, partners, and fathers. Each of these articles presents a crisp, lucid overview of the relevant literature, identifying what we know and where we need to learn more. In the following remarks, I offer comments on each of the articles with an emphasis on the specific dilemmas facing black men and their families.

"No Country for Young Men," by Andrew Sum and colleagues, provides a comprehensive overview of the economic status of young men. The article is full of clear, easy-to-interpret graphs that document the many ways that young men today are falling behind those of a previous generation and the growing inequalities across race and education groups in both economic fortunes and family outcomes. The analyses go beyond previous surveys of this kind to document the early consequences of this most recent Great Recession, which has intensified negative trends already under way.

This article took on a significant charge in providing such an extensive overview. Presumably by design, the authors take a largely descriptive approach, remaining silent on the various forces of supply and demand that may have produced the observed outcomes. Indeed, it would surely require a second article—if not an entire volume—to begin to explain the multitude of factors that have led to the deteriorating labor market outcomes of young non-college-educated men. At the same time, understanding the backdrop for these trends plays an important role in their interpretation. Race differences in the pathways toward human capital accumulation, for example, play an important role in our measurement and analysis of rising inequality. To take one specific case, one of the striking findings in this article is the extent to which high school graduates, not just high school dropouts, have lost ground over the past three decades. Table 5, for example, shows that median real annual earnings of 20- to 29-year-old men between 1979 and 2007 fell by nearly 18 percent for high school dropouts, but close to 29 percent for high school graduates. Other estimates—in labor force participation, for example—also show high school graduates falling steadily behind, with declines in employment to population ratios (15 percent) more similar to those of dropouts (17 percent) than those with some college (10 percent).

Without question, the educational premium now favors college graduates at the expense of those with less schooling. At the same time, there have been important composition shifts among those coded here as high school graduates that may affect our assessment of their relative status. In particular, these analyses count GED holders among high school graduates, thus conflating the outcomes of those who have completed traditional high school degrees with those who dropped out of high school but received an equivalency certification. The conflation of these two groups may be problematic for several reasons. First, studies of GED holders find that they are far from equivalent to high school graduates: the earnings of GED holders tend to be similar to those of dropouts, suggesting that there is little economic payoff to this particular credential (Cameron and Heckman 1993; Heckman and LaFontaine 2006). Second, the fraction of GED holders has increased over time: about 20 percent of all new high school credentials issued each year are GEDs, relative to only 2 percent in 1960 (Heckman and LaFontaine 2006; Mishel and Roy 2006). The rising prevalence of GED holders makes the comparability of this group especially relevant to assessments of trends over time. Third, the classification of high school completion is especially relevant for under- standing the economic status of young black men. Indeed, black male high school completers are twice as likely to hold a GED relative to whites with nominally similar levels of schooling. Many of these young men obtained their GED while in prison (Heckman and LaFontaine 2007; Tyler 2001).[1] Excluding GED holders, trends show that there has been little convergence in high school graduation rates between whites and minorities over the past 35 years (Heckman and LaFontaine 2007). We thus may be overstating the losses experienced by high school gradu- ates but simultaneously overstating the gains made by young black men. As an increasing number of young black men complete their formal schooling within prisons, taking account of any corresponding heterogeneity in outcomes becomes more important. To fully appreciate the extent of young black men's disconnection from the mainstream institutions of school and work, it is important to recognize the alternative pathways by which the credentialing process takes place, includ- ing prison GEDs and criminal records.[2]

The prevalence of incarceration among young less-educated black men likewise has implications for our understanding of racial disparities in employment and earnings. Typical labor force estimates, as in the current article, rely on data from the Current Population Survey (CPS). While the CPS provides some of the best labor force indicators, the sample is restricted to noninstitutionalized civilian populations. While these sampling restrictions were not of serious concern in the 1970s and 1980s, today the omission of these groups can create substantial distor- tions in our labor market estimates, especially in the case of less-educated black men. By 1999, on any given day, more than 10 percent of young white male drop- outs and more than 40 percent of young black male high school dropouts were in prison or jail (Pettit and Western 2004). The exclusion of these large populations of low-education young men has important implications for estimates of human capital development and labor market outcomes. Research by Bruce Western and his colleagues suggests that estimates of racial disparities are substantially muted by the exclusion of incarcerated populations: adjusted unemployment rates reveal a 40 percent larger black-white disparity relative to standard labor market esti- mates (Western and Beckett 1999), and adjusted wage rates for black and white workers suggest an increase in the black-white earnings gap of up to 60 percent among young men (Western and Pettit 2005).

The "invisible inequality" of excluded populations that is associated with large-scale inequality adds an important dimension to our understanding of labor market indicators, particularly those related to racial disparities. Estimates of human capital formation, employment, and earnings may be overly optimistic in light of the significant population hidden from view.

The article on low-income men as partners does a beautiful job of drawing out important trends from what is only a fairly recent line of inquiry. Tach and Edin's portrait shows young, low-income men entering into parenthood at extremely early ages and courtship patterns characterized by truncated, often haphazard, pathways leading to parenthood. Family relations are further complicated by the growing incidence of multipartner fertility (Carlson, McLanahan, and England 2004), thinly stretching resources and investments across multiple contexts and further blurring the norms around responsible partnering and parenting.

Remarkably, despite these radically new configurations, low-income men continue to express relatively traditional values about family formation. The vast majority of these men believe that marriage is the best context in which to raise children, and despite the fact that most of these men become fathers before entering official unions, the majority report a commitment to building stable relationships with the mothers of their children and aspiring to marriage with their partners once certain financial and relationship conditions have been met (Edin and Kefalas 2005).

Unfortunately, these aspirational norms are often quite dissimilar from the norms guiding everyday behavior. Tach and Edin document the high levels of instability and uncertainty that characterize these young men and their partnerships. After reviewing the multitude of individual factors that contribute to these men's unstable outcomes, the authors conclude with a discussion of some of the important unintended consequences of social policies targeting low-income men. By ignoring their role "as fathers, as partners, and as members of fragile and complex families," these policies may further undermine the precarious social order of family life: for example, household income limits on government transfers may inhibit marriage, and incarceration policies disrupt families.

The regulatory framework under which low-income men and their families operate strikes me as a particularly important focus of study. Indeed, it has now become fairly standard for family researchers to consider the disruptive effects of paternal incarceration (see Comfort 2007; Western 2006; Wildeman 2010). But moving beyond this most extreme intervention, new evidence suggests that levels of punitive surveillance are far greater than we have come to appreciate. Goffman (2009) turns our attention to those young men who have not been convicted of serious crimes, but who, because of child support arrears, court fees, or other minor violations, have warrants out for their arrest. Goffman's intensive ethnographic account documents the disruptive impact of these policies for the already tenuous social relations in poor communities. Fearing detection, "wanted" men become even less likely to show up for basic responsibilities such as the birth of a child or formal employment, avoiding regular routines or institutional environments where the police might track them down. The daily realities of getting by, staying out of jail, and staying alive complicate even the most heartfelt aspirations for traditional family life. When these are added to the burden of child support arrears and garnishment of legal pay, sometimes beyond 50 percent of legal wages (Holzer, Offner, and Sorenson 2005), the situation becomes all the more untenable. Social policies intended to discipline unruly young men can thus have perverse effects for the families and communities of which they are a part. This line of research seems especially important, as the development of effective social policies requires an appreciation not only for specific social problems but for the social systems in which those problem behaviors emerge.

In the two articles on low-income men as fathers and parents, by Berger and Langton as well as Carlson and Magnuson, the most striking picture we get is one of complexity. It has become increasingly rare for low-income children, especially African Americans, to grow up in a home with two married parents and only their biological children (Carlson and Magnuson). Parental time and resources are spread across multiple households, often characterized by frequent disruption and poorly defined norms as to how these new family configurations should best be managed.

The two articles cover a lot of ground as to the causes and consequences of father involvement. Beyond those individual attributes reliably associated with father involvement—such as age, race, education, and economic resources—Carlson and Magnuson emphasize the importance of studying families as "systems" rather than focusing on the effects of fathers in isolation. Indeed, aspects of the relationship between father and child (e.g., quantity and quality of father-child interaction and biological versus social relationship) as well as aspects of the relationship between father and mother (e.g., coparenting and gatekeeping) mediate the impact of fathers' characteristics on child well-being.

Extending the notion of families as "systems," we might also consider the local context in which the family system operates. Less attention appears to be placed on the community characteristics in which a family is located, but I wondered to what extent the prevailing expectations and experiences of fathers are in part shaped by the social demography of their neighborhoods. The urban inequality literature has well-documented wide variation in the social characteristics of neighborhoods, with the concentration of poverty, joblessness, and single-parent families exerting an independent influence on behaviors of young men and the outcomes of youth (see Sampson 1987; Wilson 1987). Add to this the intense geographic concentration of incarceration, leading to massive population removal of young black men and a churning of residents in and out of communities (Clear 2007). One study finds that high-incarceration neighborhoods in Washington, D.C., contain roughly 60 men per 100 women (Braman 2004, 86). What are the consequences of these extreme conditions for the expectations and experiences of fathers? To what extent do community norms shift as a result of changing social and demographic conditions (Harding 2007)? Tach and Edin cite several studies suggesting a responsiveness of marriage to prevailing local conditions. Might norms about fatherhood be similarly affected by variable or changing community characteristics?

The wide range of individual and relational factors that shape fathers' involvement presents a complex portrait, and one not easily distilled in a few short sound bites. Nevertheless, I found myself wondering whether it might be possible to estimate relative magnitudes for the various pathways, as a way of moving us toward more effective policy intervention. What are the expected effects of raising paternal age by five years, for example, relative to increasing education to a high school degree? What dollar amount in income would it take to compensate for the negative effects of incarceration status (ignoring for the moment that the effect of the latter often runs through the former)? Is there some level at which the quality of father-child interaction can outweigh a shortage of economic resources? Moving beyond a catalog of what matters to *how much* each matters would help us to identify where and how targeted policy interventions might maximize their impact.

Given the nascency of much of this literature, as well as limitations of the existing data, it may be unrealistic to think about generating such precise effect sizes. Nevertheless, as a programmatic goal, this would seem to be a useful exercise for considering which of these factors matter most and which might be amenable to influence through social policy (Isaacs, Sawhill, and Thomas 2009).

The complexity of contemporary family relations represents a challenge for both research and policy, as traditional ways of thinking about, measuring, and intervening into the family system become quickly outdated. At the same time, the accumulation of research in this field has provided certain clear insights that, given sufficient political will, could be the target of effective policy intervention. The primacy of men's economic resources, in particular, emerges in this literature as a central predictor of entry into marriage, involvement with children, and child well-being. Though solving the employment problems of young less-educated men is no simple matter, any cost-benefit analysis of possible interventions should take into account the positive spillover effects for families and children. In considering the specific dilemmas facing low-income black men, the imposing presence of the criminal justice system cannot be overstated. To be sure, poor families and communities have been disproportionately victimized by crime and violence, suggesting that police and court interventions play a much-needed role in restoring and maintaining order. Nevertheless, as research accumulates as to the harmful collateral consequences of our punitive crime policies—for ex-offenders, their families, their children, and their communities—greater attention to possible alternatives is warranted. Particularly in the case of nonviolent drug offenders, who make up a large and growing fraction of the black men admitted to prison each year, evidence suggests that community-based treatment programs represent a far more effective strategy for dealing with the problems of addiction and reducing future recidivism. Given the substantial financial and social costs of incarceration, investments in less expensive and more effective prevention and treatment efforts are worth serious exploration.

Amid the growing flexibility and complexity of the contemporary family, fathers continue to play an integral role. Recognizing the barriers facing young low-income men with respect to achieving stability in employment, marriage, and their relationships with their children represents an important goal for social policy. The articles in this volume represent an admirable step in this direction.

Notes

1. According to Heckman and LaFontaine (2007, Web appendix), prison GED recipients now account for more than 10 percent of all GED certificates issued in the United States each year. Among blacks, 21 percent of all GEDs issued in 2005 were obtained in prison.

2. Pager (2007) discusses the ways in which criminal records can be viewed as "negative credentials." The credential of a criminal record, like educational or professional credentials, constitutes a formal and enduring classification of social status, which can be used to regulate access and opportunity across numerous social, economic, and political domains (see pp. 32–37).

References

Bernhardt, Annette, Martina Morris, Mark Handcock, and Marc Scott. 2001. *Divergent paths: Economic mobility in the new American labor market*. New York, NY: Russell Sage Foundation.

Braman, Donald. 2004. *Doing time on the outside: Incarceration and family life in urban America*. Ann Arbor: University of Michigan Press.

Cameron, Stephen V., and James J. Heckman. 1993. The nonequivalence of high school equivalents. *Journal of Labor Economics* 11 (1): 1–47.

Carlson, Marcia, Sara McLanahan, and Paula England. 2004. Union formation in fragile families. *Demography* 41 (2): 237–61.

Clear, Todd. 2007. *Imprisoning communities: How mass incarceration makes disadvantaged neighborhoods worse*. New York, NY: Oxford University Press.

Comfort, Megan. 2007. *Doing time together: Love and family in the shadow of the prison*. Chicago, IL: University of Chicago Press.

Edin, Kathryn, and Maria Kefalas. 2005. *Promises I can keep: Why poor women put motherhood before marriage*. Berkeley: University of California Press.

Goffman, Alice. 2009. On the run: Wanted men in a Philadelphia ghetto. *American Sociological Review* 74 (3): 339–57.

Harding, David. 2007. Cultural context, sexual behavior, and romantic relationships in disadvantaged neighborhoods. *American Sociological Review* 72 (3): 341–64.

Heckman, James, and Paul LaFontaine. 2006. Bias corrected estimates of GED returns. *Journal of Labor Economics* 24 (3): 661–700.

Heckman, James, and Paul LaFontaine. 2007. The American high school graduation rate: Trends and levels. IZA Working Paper #3216, Institute for the Study of Labor (IZA), Bonn, Germany.

Holzer, Harry, Paul Offner, and Elaine Sorensen. 2005. What explains the continuing decline in labor force activity among young black men? *Labor History* 46 (1): 37–55, n. 3.

Isaacs, Julia, Isabel Sawhill, and Adam Thomas. 2009. *Mapping the social genome: A project proposal*. Washington, DC: Brookings Institution.

Meisenheimer, Joseph R., II. 1998. The services industry in the "good" versus "bad" jobs debate. *Monthly Labor Review* 121 (2): 22–47.

Mishel, Lawrence, and Joydeep Roy. 2006. *Rethinking high school graduation rates and trends*. Washington, DC: Economic Policy Institute.

Moynihan, Daniel Patrick. 1965. *The Negro family: A case for national action*. Washington, DC: Office of Policy Planning and Research, U.S. Department of Labor. (Reprinted in Lee Rainwater and William L. Yancey, *The Moynihan Report and the politics of controversy*, Cambridge, MA: MIT Press, 1967.)

Pager, Devah. 2007. *Marked: Race, crime, and finding work in an era of mass incarceration*. Chicago, IL: University of Chicago Press.

Pettit, Becky, and Bruce Western. 2004. Mass imprisonment and the life course: Race and class inequality in U.S. incarceration. *American Sociological Review* 69 (2): 151–69.

Sampson, Robert J. 1987. Urban black violence: The effect of male joblessness and family disruption. *American Journal of Sociology* 93:348–82.

Tyler, John. 2001. What do we know about the economic benefits of the GED? A synthesis of the evidence from recent research. Available from www.brown.edu/Departments/Education/resources/what_do_we _know.pdf.

Western, Bruce. 2006. *Punishment and inequality in America*. New York, NY: Russell Sage Foundation.

Western, Bruce, and Katherine Beckett. 1999. How unregulated is the U.S. labor market? The penal system as a labor market institution. *American Journal of Sociology* 104 (4): 1030–60.

Western, Bruce, and Becky Pettit. 2005. Black-white wage inequality, employment rates, and incarceration. *American Journal of Sociology* 111 (2): 553–78.

Wildeman, Christopher. 2010. Paternal incarceration and children's physically aggressive behaviors: Evidence from the Fragile Families and Child Wellbeing Study. *Social Forces* 89 (1): 285–309.

Wilson, William Julius. 1987. *The truly disadvantaged: The inner city, the underclass, and public policy*. Chicago, IL: University of Chicago Press.

Keywords: low-income fathers; family processes; child well-being

Comment: How Do Low-Income Men and Fathers Matter for Children and Family Life?

By
FRANK F. FURSTENBERG JR.

Twenty-five years ago, hardly anyone thought about men's involvement in the family. Research on fatherhood was still a novelty when Andy Cherlin asked me to write a piece on the topic for a small conference on the family (Furstenberg 1988). Believe it or not, it was still possible to fit most of what was known in a single paper. Although I have remained reasonably in touch with this area, I was nonetheless astounded at the quantity of literature reviewed in the quartet of articles on which I was asked to comment. The list of unexplored issues and questions is still long, as the authors duly demonstrate at the end of their articles, but we now know much more than we did a quarter century ago.

The first part of my comments attempts to distill what we have learned during the past several decades, particularly about the role of men in family formation and child rearing. I then turn to the consequences of paternal involvement in its myriad forms. These consequences have only become more varied and

Frank F. Furstenberg Jr. is a professor of sociology and a research associate in the Population Studies Center at the University of Pennsylvania. He is current chair of the MacArthur Foundation Research Network on Transitions to Adulthood and senior research fellow at the University of Bocconi, Milan, Italy. His interest in the American family began at Columbia University, where he received his PhD in 1967. His recent books include Destinies of the Disadvantaged: The Politics of Teen Childbearing *(Russell Sage Foundation 2007);* On the Frontier of Adulthood: Theory, Research, and Public Policy, *with Richard A. Settersten Jr. and Ruben G. Rumbaut (University of Chicago Press 2005); and* Managing to Make It: Urban Families in High-Risk Neighborhoods, *with Thomas Cook, Jacquelynne Eccles, Glen Elder, and Arnold Sameroff (University of Chicago Press 1999).*

DOI: 10.1177/0002716210390430

complex over time as family production has become de-standardized. At the micro level, the consequences, explored in the Carlson and Magnuson article, are vital to the well-being of children. Yet the micro-level effects, important as they are, pale in comparison to the macro-level impacts that changing marriage and kinship practices are having on stratification in American society. My principal aim is to think about these impacts as they might be addressed by public policy, both to prevent bad outcomes for children and to ameliorate those that do occur. I will say in advance that the prospects of doing so are challenging, to say the least, and have become more so with the passage of time.

A Tale of Gender: Changing Fortunes of Men and Women

Why has the production of marriage among lower-income families been so feeble over the past several decades? The article by Sum and colleagues documents two glaring facts: (1) males with less than a college degree are falling ever further behind because of structural changes in the labor market and episodic recessions; and (2) marriage rates have declined as the returns from unskilled and semiskilled labor have diminished. Given the understandable preference of low-income women for partners with stable earning potential that Tach and Edin document, it seems highly plausible that these two trends—losing ground in a higher-skilled market and declining marriage rates—are causally connected (Sweeney 2002).

Sum and colleagues hint at this connection when they show that marriage rates rise steadily with income for all men and in particular for African American men. It would be useful to see how this pattern compares with trends in earlier periods, but it is likely that the salience of education and income as a signal of marriageability for both men and women has grown during the past several decades. Couples no longer rush into marriage as they once did, propelled by sexual initiation and impending parenthood. Instead, they have become more wary about marrying today without the means to support a family. This has driven up the age of marriage and, accordingly, increased the risk of nonmarital childbearing. Although contraceptive use before marriage has increased, improvements in methods and use have not been great enough to offset the delay of marriage. This is clearly an issue to which policy-makers might, indeed must, pay more attention in the future.

Sum and colleagues provide other clues to the slowdown in both the timing and prevalence of marriage among low-income couples. Women's education and income have increased both absolutely and relatively to men's. Females have effectively replaced the less talented and less motivated males in the higher ranks of the labor market. These high-achieving females tend to marry males of similar status, leaving low-status couples to fend for themselves in what amounts to a secondary marriage market, in which couples face precarious conditions in forming stable unions. Therefore, a growing number of women with poor earning prospects must choose partners from a pool of men with similarly poor earnings possibilities.

Tach and Edin's article nicely sums up the relatively sparse literature on how these couples form and maintain relationships: more women have come to doubt whether they will be better off if they marry the fathers of their children. Confidence and trust are in short supply, and living together provides little reassurance to assuage their apprehensions. In short, cohabitation after parenthood has become the functional alternative to the early marriages of yesteryear. Like shotgun marriages, many cohabitations precipitated by pregnancy end in separation.

Behind the grim statistics that Sum and colleagues present is a tale of gender: men and women accommodating to the new realities of the marketplace and the home. Lower-status men are worse off than they once were, while the circumstances of lower-status women have improved. But men are having a difficult time adjusting to the collapse of the advantages they once held, and women are frequently emboldened to demand more in the way of cooperation and collaboration at home. This creates turmoil about the old and the new rules in relationships. No doubt the same turmoil occurs among more privileged couples; however, better-educated males have come to cede more power to their partners, at least in theory, or they are more willing to outsource many domestic chores. In any event, we see little evidence that marriage has either declined or become less stable among the well educated and affluent.

New Forces Also Affect Parenting and Childhood

The articles by Berger and Langton and by Carlson and Magnuson review how these broad economic and cultural changes also affect parenting and the welfare of children. There is little good news here. Parents are committed to their children, but fragile romantic relationships undermine those commitments, at least for men. When men exit the household, their contributions to child support and child rearing almost inevitably depart as well. It is hard to parent across households, especially when new partners enter the scene. And it is not easy to substitute a social father for a biological one or coordinate parenting as the number of actors grows. Although alternate arrangements can work out, they are generally less efficient and may be less effective than is a simpler household form. Children benefit from stability and predictability in parenting, but overall volatility in unions has steadily increased over time (Cherlin 2009).

Clearly, the high percentage of nonmarital pregnancies and births testifies to the fact that many women are willing to run the risk of getting pregnant by men who offer little in the way of long-term security; however, it is easy to forget that almost all of these pregnancies are unplanned if not always unwanted. Women who are unwilling or unable to seek an abortion nonetheless resist marriage, at least in the short term. Research on early and out-of-wedlock childbearing reveals that many women (and men) are unduly optimistic about their prospects of marriage to the father of the child (Furstenberg 2007; Edin and Kefalas 2005). They quickly become disillusioned and often seek refuge in another partnership, which frequently results in a second or third child. More effective family planning and reproductive health services could go a long way toward reducing the number of fragile families.

Returning to the macro level, it must be said that the making of "good" dads, men who play an active, consistent, and nurturing role in their children's lives, has become scarce in the bottom strata. This contributes to a sharp divergence from the pattern at the top, as Sara McLanahan (2004) observed several years ago. Again, it would be wrong to chalk this up merely to economic conditions. Changing gender relationships and the continuing high rate of unplanned parenthood are important parts of why the situation of children born to poor and near-poor parents has worsened with time.

The very different opportunity system that disadvantaged and well-off children are exposed to is nothing new. The family has always generated and reproduced inequality. But the gap has grown, producing a widening chasm in the family life of the affluent and the disadvantaged. Even those families in the middle now can no longer assume reasonable prospects for their children. Family conditions have become more dissimilar as the bottom two-thirds of the population face greater volatility and fewer resources than those at the top. It is difficult to imagine how these circumstances will not result in lower rates of social mobility in the next generation.

I have been examining the demands being placed on parents in different social strata as the timetable for growing up has lengthened (Furstenberg 2010). The parenting contract has been extended into the 20s, creating a dilemma for lower-income parents, who often lack the means to sustain their children's lengthier and more demanding transition to adulthood. Young adults of limited means often cannot find work to support themselves in school or out, and their parents are less and less able to help them out. The parents, themselves, are facing a crunch between saving for their retirements and helping their young adult children. Ultimately, lower-income parents, as Sum and colleagues note, will have to pick up the slack by working more years (as they have recently begun to do), thus further crowding out younger workers from the labor market.

Policies to Target the Forces Producing Today's Families

Social scientists concerned with the quantity and quality of parental investment in children in American society need to think more systemically about how families and parents are produced—the production side of the process—which determines to a great extent the stratification of families. This process is governed by educational opportunities, the labor market, taxes and redistribution, gender relations, assortative mating (that is, partners with advantages seeking mates with similar or comparable advantages), and fertility practices, which in turn lead to sharply divergent patterns of family formation. It is quite feasible, given the data now available, to develop formal models of this production process. In effect, we can develop an accounting scheme that reveals the production of "good" dads and "bad" dads.

This brings me to the challenge of constructing public policy that can alter this production process. Where do we begin? The Sum et al. article points to the importance of macroeconomic policies that stimulate employment and earnings as a critical ingredient in narrowing inequalities. We saw, for example, a sharp, albeit temporary, decline in early single parenthood during the 1990s, when the economy generated more jobs and higher earnings for low-income males and the changes in the Earned Income Tax Credit provided more resources to low-income families. Perhaps it was too brief a trend to affect union formation and stability, but I suspect that it takes something like an extended period of economic growth to shift the production process to create more "good" dads.

To achieve such a growth spurt, policy-makers must give greater attention, as the current administration appears to be doing, to improving education opportunities for low-income children. The family system cannot be changed, I believe, without increasing educational mobility for children born into low- and moderate-income families. Policies that provide more and better preschool, after-school programs, summer programs, and greater assistance to students making the transition to higher education are urgently needed. The current administration is committed to such programs, but the changes in the offing are far less dramatic than are required to offset the decline in economic fortunes of low- and middle-income families over the past 35 years. We have more lower-income students entering college than in earlier decades, but the rate of college graduation has barely budged.

Beyond conditions of high economic growth, intense compensatory education, and greater support for higher education, important changes in the production of "good" dads could be achieved by placing far greater emphasis on reducing unintended pregnancies and births. Low-income couples are poorly prepared to use contraception effectively. Were contraception practices as great as typically occur among low-income couples in Canada or Europe, we would see significant declines in the rate of nonmarital births in this country. We do a poor job of providing reproductive health information and services to low-income youth and young adults.

After dropping significantly in the 1990s, the rate of sexually active students having protected sex has declined slightly in the current decade—a trend that may be at least partially linked to the "abstinence-only" policies of the Bush administration. This has resulted in a reversal of a long period of decline in the rate of pregnancy and childbearing among teens and young adults. This decline can and must be reversed by a renewal of sex education programs that provide contraception information and an expansion of reproductive health services in underserved communities coupled with programs that give young adolescent women and men a vision of a future that does not involve childbearing at a very early age. I am less sanguine about programs specifically designed to help expectant parents, fathers especially, to become more responsible and nurturing parents once they have children. Census data indicate that there has been a slight increase during the past 15 years in the number of days that nonresidential fathers see their children. However, the increase, while encouraging, is not large enough to produce any effects on the welfare of children, even if we believed that paternal contact necessarily has a beneficial impact.

For a host of reasons, reducing the level of incarceration among nonviolent offenders may ease some of the problems that lower-income males face in education and employment, if only because they will reduce the stigma faced by those with a prison record. However, unless males who would have otherwise spent time in prisons are able to use that time to gain schooling and employment experience, the benefits of reducing incarceration are likely to be limited.

The two articles by Carlson and Magnuson and by Berger and Langton on the consequences of fathers' participation on children's welfare provide scant evidence that we can alter current practices of involvement significantly enough to improve the welfare of children or their ultimate prospects of social mobility. Programs designed to increase fathers' awareness of their responsibilities, build parental skills, and increase collaboration between parents are well-intentioned. However, I am not persuaded by any existing evidence that these programs have much impact on children's well-being, and I doubt that they represent a cost-effective approach to strengthening low-income families. This does not mean we should be indifferent to the problems created by changing gender roles. There is a role for parent education and counseling in the schools and community. Yet there is little reason to expect immediate returns for children on the basis of existing evidence.

Summing Up

It is important—as Sum and colleagues' title, "No Country for Young Men," suggests—to consider the macro-level processes that are shaping families in the bottom strata of American society. Doing so requires intensive attention to improving education among disadvantaged children while improving the employment prospects of their parents and the material benefits attached to work. Reducing the population of young men imprisoned for minor infractions can also lead to a greater production of "good" dads, especially if those men are afforded a way of entering the labor force and attaining stable employment. We also can affect the supply of "good" dads by helping individuals and couples avoid unintended pregnancies by providing greater assistance and access to contraception for young couples who frequently enter parenthood before they are prepared to form families. Fewer unintended pregnancies early in life will provide more life space for men and women from low- and moderate-income families to gain education and work experience. Without increasing the human capital of prospective parents, delaying childbearing alone will do little to counteract the haphazard process of family formation that is typical of the disadvantaged.

We are currently producing many more vulnerable unions than can be treated by counseling and remedial services, even if we knew how to make these services work well and be cost-effective. However difficult it is to increase human capital and reduce unplanned parenthood among disadvantaged children and youth, it is far more feasible to implement these policies than the alternative approach of altering parenting practices within fragile families.

References

Cherlin, Andrew. 2009. *The marriage-go-round: The state of marriage and the family in America today*. New York, NY: Knopf.

Edin, Kathryn, and Maria Kefalas. 2005. *Promises I can keep: Why poor women put motherhood before marriage*. Berkeley, CA: University of California Press.

Furstenberg, Frank F. 1988. Good dads-bad dads: The two faces of fatherhood. In *The changing American family and public policy*, ed. Andrew J. Cherlin, 193–218. Washington, DC: Urban Institute Press.

Furstenberg, Frank F. 2007. *Destinies of the disadvantaged: The politics of teen childbearing*. New York, NY: Russell Sage Foundation.

Furstenberg, Frank F. 2010. On a new schedule: Transitions to adulthood and family change. *The Future of Children* 20 (1): 67–87.

McLanahan, Sara. 2004. Diverging destinies: How children are faring under the second demographic transition. *Demography* 41 (4): 607–27.

Sweeney, Megan M. 2002. Two decades of family change: The shifting economic foundations of marriage. *American Sociological Review* 67 (1): 132–47.

Policy Papers

Child Support: Responsible Fatherhood and the Quid Pro Quo

Over time, public policy changes have strengthened the private child support system while reducing access to public support—welfare. Given the especially limited availability of public support, nonresident fathers' economic contributions through child support can play an important role in helping children to avoid poverty. In this article, the authors review evidence on nonresident fathers' ability to pay support, provide an overview of the way child support policies affect disadvantaged fathers, and propose new directions for child support policy. The authors argue that the current work-focused safety net, which aims to require and help to enable disadvantaged mothers to work, creates a context in which government should similarly require and help to enable all fathers, even those who are disadvantaged, to work and pay child support. However, reforms are needed to make this a realistic expectation, given many fathers' limited employment options and complex families.

Keywords: fatherhood; child support; single-parent families; poverty

BY
MARIA CANCIAN,
DANIEL R. MEYER,
and
EUNHEE HAN

Both legal and social expectations regarding fathers' responsibility for their children have varied tremendously over time. In the contemporary United States, married parents living together with their children share their parental rights and responsibilities without any explicit legal distinction between mothers' and fathers' roles. However, when parents do not live together, children most often live with their mothers (Grall 2009). This raises a complex set of questions about the relative rights and responsibilities of nonresident fathers and resident mothers and the role of government in regulating, or substituting for, parents' contributions to their children's support.

NOTE: This article was originally prepared for the IRP Working Conference on "Young Disadvantaged Men: Fathers, Families, Poverty and Policy," September 14–15, 2009. The authors thank Yoonsook Ha, Jennifer Noyes, and David Pate for their helpful comments and contributions to related analysis.

DOI: 10.1177/0002716210393640

ANNALS, *AAPSS*, 635, May 2011

These issues are particularly pressing as most children in the United States will spend some portion of their childhood living apart from at least one of their parents. This occurs both because of high divorce rates and an increasing proportion of births to unmarried parents.[1] Children in single-parent (usually single-mother) families are a focus of public policy concern, in part due to their high rates of poverty and public program participation.

Two systems address the potential negative economic consequences for children living apart from their fathers. The formal child support system, largely regulated by family law, articulates the expectations for the private financial support expected of nonresident fathers.[2] Income support programs, especially welfare (Temporary Assistance for Needy Families [TANF]), provide cash assistance, in-kind supports, and tax credits to poor children, primarily those living in single-mother homes. To a large extent "private" and "public" child support have been substitutes, rather than complements; for example, in most states, any child support that a nonresident parent pays reduces, dollar-for-dollar, welfare benefit payments (Cancian, Meyer, and Caspar 2008).

Over time, public policy changes have strengthened the private child support system (Garfinkel, Meyer, and McLanahan 1998; Pirog and Ziol-Guest 2006) while reducing access to public support—welfare. In particular, the entitlement to cash assistance has been replaced with time-limited, work-based welfare programs (TANF and the Earned Income Tax Credit [EITC]), available to working low-income resident parents. These changes reflect the increasing emphasis of policy on reducing dependence and promoting self-sufficiency and a related shift in the burden of responsibility for children's costs from the government to individual mothers and fathers.

The current work-focused safety net aims to require and help to enable disadvantaged mothers to work. Given this approach, we argue that government

Maria Cancian is a professor of public affairs and social work, an affiliate of the Institute for Research on Poverty at the University of Wisconsin–Madison, and a W. T. Grant Distinguished Fellow in residence at the Wisconsin Department of Children and Families during 2010–2011. Her research considers changes in women's employment and implications for income and family structure; multiple-partner fertility; and the interactions of welfare, child support, and child welfare policies.

Daniel R. Meyer is the Mary C. Jacoby Professor of Social Work and a research affiliate of the Institute for Research on Poverty at the University of Wisconsin–Madison. From 2001 to 2008, he was the director of the School of Social Work. His current research interests include effects of child support and welfare reforms, international approaches to family policy, multiple-partner fertility, and how much individuals know about the social policies that affect them. He is coprincipal investigator, with Maria Cancian, of a research agreement between the Institute for Research on Poverty and the Wisconsin Department of Children and Families.

Eunhee Han is a doctoral student in social welfare at the University of Wisconsin–Madison. Her research interests include impacts of welfare reform and child support enforcement, measurement of income and poverty, and comparative family policy. She is currently involved in projects investigating income growth of nonresident fathers, dynamics of multiple program participation, and Wisconsin poverty measurement.

should similarly require and help to enable all fathers, even those who are disadvantaged, to work and pay child support. However, because many fathers have limited employment options, and because many fathers face the need to support children in multiple families, we argue that reforms are needed to make the payment of child support a realistic expectation.

Should We Expect Disadvantaged Nonresident Fathers to Support Their Children?

In determining reasonable expectations regarding fathers' child support contributions, a key issue is fathers' financial resources—both relative to their own needs and relative to the resources and needs of their child(ren)'s mother(s). Much has been written about the declining economic fortunes of young men, especially men without college degrees or men of color (e.g., Holzer and Offner 2006; Danziger and Ratner 2010; Blank 2009). Over the past three decades, the average earnings of less-educated young men have declined significantly. For example, Danziger and Ratner (2010) find that the median earnings of employed young men ages 25 to 34 years old with only a high school diploma fell by 17 percent for whites, 18 percent for blacks, and 21 percent for Hispanics between 1975 and 2007. Over the same period, the median earnings of employed young women with comparable education fell 2 percent among blacks, but rose by 33 percent and 14 percent for whites and Hispanics, respectively. Although the trends favor low-educated women, their earnings are still lower than men's. In 2007, the median earnings for employed high school graduates were about $33,000[3] for white men and $27,000 for black and Hispanic men, compared to $21,000 for white and Hispanic women and $19,000 for black women. Thus, based on gender alone, we would expect that on average fathers with low education would have an advantage over similarly educated mothers in providing financial support.

These trends highlight the importance of examining estimates of fathers' ability to pay child support. Several studies since 1995 have examined the incomes of all nonresident fathers (Garfinkel, McLanahan, and Hanson 1998; Meyer 1998; Sorensen 1997), while others have focused on groups more likely to be disadvantaged, including unmarried nonresident fathers (Garfinkel et al. 2009; Rich 2001; Rich, Garfinkel, and Gao 2007; Sinkewicz and Garfinkel 2009); nonresident fathers of children on welfare (Cancian and Meyer 2004; Rich, Garfinkel, and Gao 2007); or those not paying child support (Garfinkel, McLanahan, and Hanson 1998; Mincy and Sorensen 1998; Sorensen and Zibman 2001). Not surprisingly, unmarried nonresident fathers have less income on average than divorced nonresident fathers, with estimates as low as $17,000 in earnings at the time of their child's birth (Garfinkel et al. 2009); however, their earnings increase over time to an average of more than $23,000 by the time their children are three years old (Garfinkel et al. 2009). Fathers of children on welfare have even lower incomes (Cancian and Meyer 2004; Rich, Garfinkel, and Gao 2007); their poverty rates have been estimated at 34 to 43 percent (Cancian and Meyer 2004).

Although some fathers have very limited resources, there is some evidence that on average, nonresident fathers are better off than resident mothers and their children. Considering all nonresident fathers and mothers, 15 to 26 percent of all nonresident fathers are estimated to have income below the poverty line, compared with 27 to 46 percent of all resident mothers (Garfinkel, McLanahan, and Hanson 1998; Grall 2009; Meyer 1998; Sorensen 1997; Sorensen and Zibman 2001). It is difficult to draw definitive conclusions from these estimates, however, as measures of mothers' and fathers' incomes often come from different data sources or from specialized samples. For example, studies that rely on a sample of resident mothers receiving welfare necessarily include only mothers with very low incomes. Thus, it may not be surprising that the associated fathers have, on average, higher incomes. Relatively few data sources provide income information for both the mother and the father for a broad sample of parents.

Moreover, the most appropriate comparison for relative economic status is posttax, posttransfer income, adjusted for family size. Resident-parent families have access to a much larger EITC than is available to those not living with children, and, in contrast to nonresident parents, resident parents have access to TANF. On the other hand, resident parents have to provide both income and care for their children. A full comparison of posttax, posttransfer income of matched pairs of nonresident fathers and resident mothers using recent data and a broad sample is not available. Recent estimates using Wisconsin administrative data and income adjusted for family size on a sample of couples with new child support orders in 2000 suggest that accounting for public benefits (including the EITC) has a substantial effect but does not eliminate fathers' relative income advantage. For example, when income is known, 68 percent of fathers have higher market income than mothers. After adding benefits and subtracting taxes paid, only 61 percent of fathers have higher income than mothers; if child support is added to mothers' incomes and subtracted from fathers', 47 percent of fathers have higher incomes, 17 percent have similar incomes, and 36 percent of mothers have higher incomes. While data are limited, and more research is needed, we believe the available evidence supports our conclusion that both parents should generally be expected to provide for their children.

Disadvantaged men, the focus of this volume of *The Annals*, often father children with disadvantaged women.[4] Disadvantaged resident mothers generally face the dual challenges of working in the paid labor market and being the primary parent and child caretaker. Especially given the extremely limited availability of public support, nonresident fathers' economic contributions through child support play an important role in helping children to avoid poverty. But there are a number of difficult challenges and contentious trade-offs that must be faced in designing a child support system to balance the needs of vulnerable children and the constraints that disadvantaged fathers and mothers face. Broader public policy has a fundamental role in shaping the context within which the child support system works. For example, the lack of public income support for children and parents and the limited work opportunities available to many disadvantaged parents, while outside the child support system, are key determinants of the need for child support. In the next section, we largely take that context as given and focus on child support policy and how it functions, and fails to function, for disadvantaged fathers and their families.

Current Child Support Policy and Disadvantaged Fathers

What is the purpose of child support?

The Child Support Enforcement (CSE) or IV-D (Title IV-D of Social Security Act) program was established in 1974 to collect child support on behalf of children receiving welfare. The original focus on welfare participants reveals that a primary purpose of child support was cost recovery—that is, much of the reason for collecting child support was to limit public expenditures in the welfare system. Although providing child support across the income spectrum was seen as important, assistance was originally provided to nonwelfare families only on request and as a temporary service. Enforcement activities on behalf of nonwelfare families were not made a permanent part of the child support agency's mission until 1980.

Current policy statements often suggest that the purpose of the child support enforcement system is to improve the economic well-being of children, but some features of policy continue to reveal a focus on cost recovery. For example, mothers applying for welfare must cooperate with the child support agency in establishing paternity, locating nonresident parents, establishing orders, and collecting support unless they have a "good cause" exemption—in general, disadvantaged mothers are required to pursue child support, regardless of whether they think it is in their best interest. Furthermore, welfare participants assign their rights to any child support that is collected to the state, a requirement not made of other resident parents. Finally, when child support is collected on behalf of current welfare participants, in most states it is used exclusively to offset welfare costs; nothing goes to the family. A related policy is that in some states the child support agency tries to recoup from nonresident fathers the costs of any nonmarital births paid for by Medicaid. This focus on cost recovery has been found to be counterproductive; when Wisconsin experimented with a plan to let welfare participants keep all the child support paid on their behalf, more fathers paid support, and the policy actually showed no net costs to the government (Cancian, Meyer, and Caspar 2008).

How much child support does the current system expect from disadvantaged fathers?

The 1984 federal reforms to the child support system required states to establish advisory guidelines for child support, providing a numeric formula for determining the amount of child support orders; in 1988, these guidelines were made presumptive (that is, to be used unless a specific finding was made that the amount resulting from the guidelines would be inappropriate). Although each state may develop its own formula, federal requirements specify that all of the income of nonresident fathers must be taken into consideration (U.S. Department of Health and Human Services, Office of Child Support Enforcement 2008). Two formula types are most prevalent: the percentage-of-income formula and the income-shares formula. Both types rely on a "continuity of expenditure" approach (Garrison 1999), in which the amount ordered in child support combined with the amount spent on the child by the resident parent should approximate the amount that would have been spent on the child had the parents been together. Wisconsin's formula is a typical example of the percentage-of-income model. Nonresident parents are ordered to pay 17 percent of their gross income for one child, and 25 percent, 29 percent, 31 percent, and 34 percent for two, three, four, or five or more children, respectively. Resident parents are assumed to spend an equivalent percentage of their income on the children, but this does not enter the formula directly. The income-shares formula estimates the amount spent on children by multiplying the combined income of both parents by a percentage that varies with income; responsibility for providing this amount to be spent on the children is then distributed between the two parents based on their share of total income. This approach can yield similar orders to the percentage-of-income approach in most income ranges (Garfinkel and Melli 1990).

In some states, the guidelines have explicit instructions for adjustments that are to be made for low-income or high-income cases. The adjustments for higher-income cases generally result in lower orders. But for low-income fathers, there is no consensus on whether orders should be a higher or lower percentage of income than they would be for middle- or higher-income fathers.

In Figure 1, we illustrate three different states' guidelines to show different approaches to how orders for disadvantaged fathers vary with income. In each case, we assume that there are two children and that the father and mother have the same income. Wisconsin (WI) requires a smaller percentage of income from low-income fathers; more specifically, those with the lowest incomes would have an order of 16.37 percent of income, with order amounts gradually increasing until the full 25 percent of income is due for those with monthly incomes of $1,050.

Another approach, used in about half the states, is to have a minimum order. Figure 1 shows orders for Minnesota (MN)—a state that uses a minimum order and an income-shares formula. If the father's gross income is less than 120 percent of the poverty line, there is a minimum basic support amount of $50 per month that is then split between the parents based on their relative incomes. Because

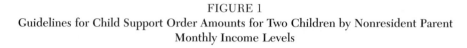

FIGURE 1

Guidelines for Child Support Order Amounts for Two Children by Nonresident Parent Monthly Income Levels

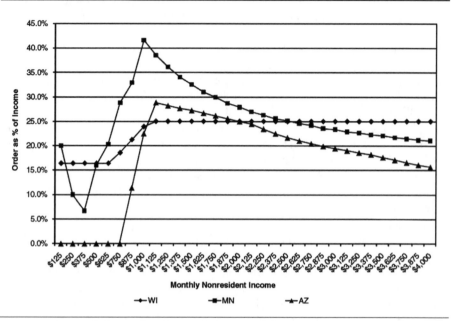

NOTE: Authors' calculations based on each state's guidelines. Figure assumes equal incomes for resident and nonresident parents. For simplicity, Arizona's calculations assume gross and adjusted gross incomes are identical.

the minimum order is for a flat amount, it is a higher percentage of income for those with the lowest incomes. In the first range, as income increases, the order does not change, so the percentage of income owed decreases. Once income is more than $350 per month, the adjustment for the lowest-income cases is no longer in effect, and orders rise as a percentage of income until income is about $1,000 per month, then gradually decline.

A third approach, required in twenty states, uses a self-support reserve, which ensures that parents have an income sufficient to provide at least a subsistence level of living before they owe support (Venohr and Griffith 2005). Figure 1 also shows orders in Arizona (AZ), a state with an explicit self-support reserve. If the nonresident parent's adjusted gross income is at or below the self-support reserve of $775 per month (in 2009), he is assumed to be unable to pay child support. As income increases beyond $775, orders increase until income reaches about $1,125 per month, at which point the low-income adjustment is no longer in effect.

Thus, Figure 1 illustrates the implications of some of the alternative approaches to setting child support orders for low-income nonresident parents. Minimum orders result in orders that are an extremely high percentage of income for very low-income parents—higher percentages of income than we require of moderate-income fathers. Moreover, if the figure were expanded to show a broader income range, it could be seen that higher-income fathers are asked to pay a smaller percentage of income than moderate-income fathers in all three states. This regressivity, in which higher-income fathers sometimes pay the lowest percentages of their income, results because it is thought that beyond a certain absolute level of expenditures higher-income parents spend a lower percentage of their income on their children.

In theory, child support order amounts, largely based on nonresident fathers' incomes, should not exceed most fathers' ability to pay. In practice, however, child support orders vary substantially even across fathers with similar incomes, and sometimes substantially exceed the amounts defined by the guidelines as appropriate. One study analyzing administrative data in eight sites between 1998 and 2000 suggests that nonresident fathers with the lowest income levels were given child support orders requiring between 21 and 61 percent of monthly earnings, whereas order amounts for higher earners ranged from 8 to 21 percent of their monthly earnings (Pearson et al. 2003). Studies in Washington (Stirling and Aldrich 2008) and Wisconsin (Meyer, Ha, and Hu 2008) also show that low-income fathers owe higher, sometimes substantially higher, percentages of their income in child support.[5]

In addition to explicit modifications of the guidelines for low-income nonresident parents, orders also vary due to administrative procedures and implementation challenges. A limitation of either the self-support reserve or low-income adjustment approaches is the administrative difficulty associated with frequent adjustments for fathers with unstable employment and earnings. Evaluated at a given point in time, orders may call for an inappropriate proportion of income if income changes and orders do not respond (Ha, Cancian, and Meyer 2009). Another related reason for deviation from the guidelines for low-income fathers is income imputations. If a nonresident father fails to appear in court or provide income information, or if he is unemployed or considered underemployed, income imputation is allowed in some states (U.S. Department of Health and Human Services, Office of Inspector General 2000b). Imputed earnings, generally calculated by multiplying the minimum wage by 40 hours per week, may exceed (or be less than) actual earnings. If they exceed actual earnings, the order that is based on imputed income is likely to exceed the amount called for in the guidelines.

What are child support enforcement strategies?

Generally, establishing and enforcing a child support obligation involves three steps: establishing a legal child support order, determining the child support amount, and collecting the payments. For marital cases, a child support order is established as a part of divorce or legal separation process. For nonmarital cases, to establish a child support order, paternity first has to be established.

Historically, establishing paternity has been the purview of family courts, and rates of establishing paternity were fairly low, in part because the courts rely on an adversarial process. More recently, states have developed voluntary paternity acknowledgment programs, and since 1993, in-hospital paternity acknowledgment programs have been required in each state. Recent research shows that nearly 70 percent of nonmarital births have paternity established within a child's first year, and in a majority of these cases, paternity was voluntarily acknowledged in the hospital (Mincy, Garfinkel, and Nepomnyaschy 2005).[6] If paternity is not voluntarily acknowledged, court proceedings are used and genetic tests are nearly always ordered; a legal finding of paternity will then be made if genetic testing confirms paternity. In-hospital paternity establishment and the availability of genetic testing have been found to contribute to increased rates of establishing paternity (see Pirog and Ziol-Guest 2006).[7]

Two components of current policy result in paternity establishment working differently for disadvantaged fathers than for other fathers. First, public program participation (TANF in every state and, in some states, food stamps) requires an applicant to cooperate with the child support enforcement agency as a condition of receiving benefits. Thus, when low-income resident parents apply for benefits, paternity establishment proceedings may result, whereas paternity establishment is more voluntary for those not applying for benefits. Moreover, because the child support agency has a cost recovery goal, the agency has a direct financial incentive in establishing paternity (and, further, in establishing a child support order and collecting that order) when the family is receiving assistance.

Second, some states allow for default paternity establishment (U.S. Department of Health and Human Services, Office of Inspector General 2000a). This can occur if putative fathers do not come to a court hearing; qualitative research has shown that some disadvantaged nonresident fathers have substantial distrust of courts and the child support agency (see Pate 2006) and may not understand the consequences of ignoring a subpoena to attend a paternity hearing (e.g., legal paternity may result, with the financial repercussions of a child support order). Other fathers are excited about establishing paternity but are unaware that this may lead to financial obligations (see Pate 2002).

Collecting child support is, in principle, equivalent to a form of income tax withholding. If a child support order is established and a nonresident father is employed at that time, an automatic wage withholding order is issued. The employer sends the amount withheld to a child support agency, which forwards the money to the resident mother.[8] (If the nonresident father changes jobs, the child support agency will eventually be informed, as employers must report new hires to a centralized database that is then matched with whether these new employees owe support.) If children and single mothers are receiving governmental cash assistance, the child support is distributed according to the disregard and pass-through rules—which determine what portion of support paid goes to the resident parent and what portion goes to offset welfare costs—for that state. If a nonresident father fails to pay child support, penalties for noncompliance can be quite severe. For instance, the father's tax refund may be intercepted, his driver's license may be suspended, or liens may be imposed on his personal property. Nonresident parents may also be incarcerated for failure to pay child support.

Empirical evidence suggests that child support receipts have improved with a variety of enforcement policies, including immediate income withholding (Beller and Graham 1993; Case, Lin, and McLanahan 2003; Garfinkel and Klawitter 1990; Sorensen and Hill 2004), presumptive guidelines (Case, Lin, and McLanahan 2003; Sorensen and Hill 2004), income tax intercepts (Sorensen and Hill 2004), in-hospital paternity establishment (Sorensen and Hill 2004), and implementation of the Directory of New Hires (Cassetty, Cancian, and Meyer 2002; Sorensen and Hill 2004). Experimental evidence also suggests that a full disregard and pass-through speeds paternity establishment and increases child support payments of fathers with children on welfare (Cancian, Meyer, and Caspar 2008). Some researchers emphasize that policies are effective only when they are effectively implemented (Freeman and Waldfogel 1998; Huang and Edwards 2009) and understood by parents (Meyer, Cancian, and Nam 2007).

Many child support enforcement strategies are less effective, and potentially less appropriate, in cases involving disadvantaged nonresident fathers. For example, automatic income withholding is most effective for nonresident fathers with consistent employment in the formal economy. Moreover, there are substantial concerns that some child support enforcement efforts may be counterproductive. For example, driver's license suspension may reduce fathers' employability, which may ultimately make them less likely to pay child support (Hatcher and Lieberman 2003). Especially for less stable relationships involving disadvantaged fathers, the child support system may also disrupt fragile family bonds (Waller 2002; Pate 2002).

How much do fathers pay and how much debt remains?

Despite child support enforcement innovations, a significant number of children eligible for support do not receive any payments from their fathers (Case, Lin, and McLanahan 2003; Grall 2009; Meyer, Ha, and Hu 2008; Sorensen and Hill 2004). Estimates of child support payment rates vary over time and across datasets and samples but do not generally show increases in the proportion who make payments, despite the policy changes over the past 30 years. Some of the reasons for the lack of progress have included increases in nonmarital births, inflation, unilateral divorce, and a decrease in men's earnings. Data from the Current Population Survey–Child Support Supplement (CPS-CSS) from 1993 to 2007 show little improvement: 39 percent of mothers reported receiving payments in 1993, compared with 37 percent in 2007 (Grall 2009). Among those who were due support, the figures are much higher, though still relatively flat, varying from 76 percent to 78 percent over the same period (Grall 2009). There is some improvement in the overall compliance rate over time: among those due support, the proportion receiving the full amount increased from 37 percent in 1993 to 47 percent in 2007. Among those due something, the average amount received has not increased much over this period, from an average of about $3,500 in 1993 to $4,000 in 2005 but back to $3,500 in 2007 (all in 2008 dollars).

Because of the difficulty in getting information from nonresident fathers, most of the survey data on child support reflect mothers' reports of child support received, rather than fathers' reports of formal child support paid. Fathers report paying more child support than mothers report receiving (U.S. Census Bureau 2005); in part this is because fathers may be more likely to include informal support as well as formal. Moreover, not all of what fathers pay is received by mothers (some is for fees, and for mothers who receive TANF or who had a nonmarital birth paid for by Medicaid, a portion or all of the payment can be retained by the state to recoup these expenditures).[9] National data do not provide much information on compliance from the perspective of fathers. However, information is available using administrative data from some states. Among those with newly established orders in Wisconsin in 2000, around half pay the full amount in each of the first six years of the order, and in each year, in only 14 to 17 percent of the cases were there no payments (Ha et al. 2008).

Payments are strongly tied to fathers' economic status: poor fathers and those with low education or low earnings are less likely to pay any support and less likely to pay the full amount due. In the national data, only about 10 percent of young nonresident fathers who have personal or family incomes below the poverty threshold paid support in 1990, compared with about half of those above poverty (Mincy and Sorensen 1998). Among fathers who pay, those with less than a high school diploma pay less than half of what those with college degrees pay (U.S. Census Bureau 2005). Similarly, in the Wisconsin data on fathers with new orders in 2000, fathers earning less than $10,000 in the third year of the order paid formal support that averaged $1,155, while those earning $40,000 or more paid $8,218 (Meyer, Ha, and Hu 2008).

When orders are not paid, or not paid in full, interest is charged on the balance due. Consistent lack of payment combined with interest charges can result in high child support arrears. Overall, the child support agency reported that $105 billion was owed as of 2008 (U.S. Department of Health and Human Services, Office of Child Support Enforcement 2009). Although $8 billion was collected toward these arrears, the amount past due is growing rapidly. Arrears are disproportionately owed by fathers with low or no reported earnings, with orders that were a high proportion of earnings, and by fathers who owed support to more than one family (Sorensen, Sousa, and Schaner 2007). High arrears are also a concern because they may discourage fathers from working in the formal labor market, further reducing the resources available to children and their parents (Cancian, Heinrich, and Chung 2009).

In summary, most studies suggest that of the fathers who owe support, at least three-quarters pay something, but half fail to pay the full amount. Not surprisingly, a greater proportion of disadvantaged fathers fail to pay the full amount due; all of the nonpayers and partial payers are accumulating child support arrears, and these arrears are substantial.

Barriers to paying support: Incarceration

Issues related to incarceration deserve special mention. The United States has the highest incarceration rate of any developed country, and among some populations, including black men with less than a high school diploma, incarceration is almost normative. Of particular relevance to our discussion is the impact of incarceration on fathers' ability to pay child support and the appropriate design and administration of the child support system.

Available statistics suggest that a substantial proportion of incarcerated men are fathers, and many have child support obligations. According to the Bureau of Justice Statistics, 744,200 inmates, or 49 percent of the total inmates in the nation's prisons in 2007, were fathers to 1,706,600 children under the age of 18 (Glaze and Maruschak 2008). Among those fathers held in state prisons in 2007, half reported living with their minor children prior to incarceration or reported that they had provided the primary financial support for their minor children (Glaze and Maruschak 2008). Not only are many incarcerated men fathers, a substantial portion of disadvantaged fathers are, or have been, incarcerated. According to analysis of the Fragile Families and Child Wellbeing study, 27 percent of men or their partners reported that the fathers had been incarcerated (Western 2006). Some local data also provide estimates; for example, of all the nonresident parents with active child support orders in Maryland in September 2004, 13 percent of them were incarcerated at that time or had been incarcerated in the past (Ovwigho, Saunders, and Born 2005).

Incarceration limits nonresident fathers' ability to pay child support in several ways. First, it is almost impossible for incarcerated fathers to meet their child support obligations since they have virtually no income. For example, incarcerated nonresident parents in Massachusetts paid only 5 percent of what they owed in 2001 and in 2003 (Griswold et al. 2004). Second, unless a child support order is suspended or adjusted to a minimum level, nonresident fathers accumulate high child support arrears while in prison. In many states, incarceration is assumed to be a form of voluntary unemployment, which means that incarceration cannot be considered an appropriate reason for order modification (Pearson 2004). Even in states where incarceration may be a sufficient reason for adjustment, child support orders are not automatically adjusted when nonresident fathers become incarcerated; all states require a request for order modification from either parent.[10] Accordingly, incarceration often results in the accumulation of high child support arrears for currently and previously incarcerated fathers (Pearson and Davis 2003; Cancian et al. 2007). Third, as discussed by Raphael (this volume) and others (for example, Lewis, Garfinkel, and Gao 2007), limited skills along with a record of incarceration make finding employment difficult, which may also contribute to recidivism. Finally, nonpayment of child support may contribute to rearrest and reincarceration for these fathers (Travis, Solomon, and Waul 2001; Pate 2006).

Acknowledging issues of child support encountered by incarcerated and reentering fathers, some states have implemented policies and programs designed to help to reduce incarcerated fathers' payment obligations or increase fathers' ability to pay (Bloom 2006; U.S. Department of Health and Human Services, Office of Child Support Enforcement 2006; Levingston and Turetsky 2007; Noyes 2006; Cancian et al. 2007). Suggested reforms include better integration of the corrections system and child support enforcement system by, for example, identifying debt and financial obligations as part of the prison intake process; offering debt management and repayment assistance to fathers after release; and giving higher priority to the payment of reasonable child support obligations than to other obligations, such as the recovery of state judicial system costs (Levingston and Turetsky 2007).

Barriers to paying support: Complex family obligations

Many, if not most, disadvantaged fathers have had children with more than one partner and therefore are at risk for owing child support to multiple households. While a number of data limitations make it difficult to estimate levels of family complexity among disadvantaged fathers, there is growing evidence that multiple-partner fertility is far from uncommon. For example, analyzing a cohort of first-born-to-mother nonmarital children in Wisconsin, Cancian, Meyer, and Cook (forthcoming) found that more than 40 percent of the fathers had obligations to a child of another mother within 10 years.

Fathers facing obligations to support children across multiple households inevitably face additional economic strains. Using data on unwed fathers, Sinkewicz and Garfinkel (2009) conclude that past research on the potential ability of fathers to pay child support resulted in substantial overestimates of how much could be collected because fathers' obligations across multiple households were not taken into account. Difficulties resulting from these multiple obligations may be exacerbated by a child support enforcement system that is not well designed to handle the situations of complex families. The most common approaches to complex families call for fathers to meet each obligation with relatively modest adjustments to account for the demands associated with other families (Brito 2005; Venohr and Griffith 2005). This results in much higher orders than would be the case if the fathers had the same number of children with only one woman. In Wisconsin, for example, the guidelines call for a father who has three children with the same mother to pay 29 percent of his income in child support. In contrast, if he has three children with three different mothers, the guidelines call for him to pay 17 percent of his income for the first child, 17 percent of the income remaining after the first order is paid for the second child, and 17 percent of the income remaining after the first two orders are paid for the third child, for a total of about 43 percent of his income.

Developing appropriate guidelines for complex families is very challenging. From a conceptual standpoint, the appropriate standard is not clear. If child support is to provide "continuity of expenditures" (holding a child harmless when his or her parents choose not to live together), it is not clear how to apply this principle to a situation where all parents (i.e., the father and the mothers of all his children) living together is generally never observed. Even if an expenditure level from a simple family is used, it is difficult, if not impossible, to develop a system that meets key criteria from the perspectives of fathers, mothers, and children. The difficulties arise in part because some (but not all) fathers with multiple partners have had children with mothers who also have multiple partners and, therefore, multiple sources of support (Cancian and Meyer 2006).

Does child support make a difference? Child support and the income packages of disadvantaged fathers and mothers

Adequate child support has the potential to play an important role in reducing child poverty in single-parent households by directly and immediately increasing the income available to children. Several studies using different data sources, samples, and time periods have estimated that child support reduced the poverty rate among female-headed families by approximately 6 to 10 percentage points (Bartfeld 2000; Cancian, Meyer, and Park 2003; Meyer and Hu 1999). However, the percentage of families that were poor before child support was counted that are lifted out of poverty by child support varies substantially across states: 15 to 23 percent poverty reduction in Wisconsin, compared with 6 to 8 percent in other states (Cancian, Meyer, and Park 2003). Even when child support is not sufficient to bring families out of poverty, it may reduce the poverty gap—the gap between the poverty line and family income. For example, child support decreased the poverty gap by 13 to 23 percent for poor families in the National Survey of America's Families (NSAF) (see Cancian, Meyer, and Park 2003).[11] The figures reviewed above suggest a fairly modest impact of child support in large part because in a given year, a majority of poor families do not receive any payments. Antipoverty effects are larger among the pre-child-support poor who received child support (Meyer and Hu 1999; Cancian, Meyer, and Park 2003), and estimates of the full potential (all single parents have orders set according to the guidelines and these orders are full paid) suggest substantial effects (Bartfeld 2000).

Paying child support inevitably impoverishes some fathers, though most estimates suggest that the effect is smaller than the poverty-reducing potential for resident parents receiving support. Estimates across data sources and samples suggest an increase in the poverty rate due to paying child support of 2 to 3 percentage points (Bartfeld 2000; Cancian and Meyer 2004; Meyer 1998). Although a relatively small number of nonpoor fathers became poor as a result of paying child support, poor fathers became poorer after paying child support. For example, among poor nonresident fathers of children on welfare in Wisconsin, the average poverty gap increased from $6,902 before paying child support to $7,362 after paying in 1998 and from $5,708 to $6,379 in 1999 (Cancian and Meyer 2004).

Although the estimates vary, it is clear that paying child support impoverishes some low-income nonresident fathers even as it has the potential to be an important income source for low-income families in recipient households. In good part because of data limitations, there is a scarcity of research that simultaneously considers the effect of child support on both resident parent and nonresident parent poverty. However, the available evidence suggests that potential child support would do more to reduce poverty among poor single-mother families than to increase poverty among nonresident fathers (Bartfeld 2000; Cancian and Meyer 2004; Meyer 1998; Stirling and Aldrich 2008).

That most disadvantaged fathers are no less able to support their children than most disadvantaged mothers does not address the key issues: what can, and should, be done to increase fathers' ability to support both themselves and their children—to help to lift themselves and their children out of poverty? These issues are largely unrelated to the child support system. However, the interaction of child support enforcement with other systems raises an important set of questions, which we address in our concluding section.

Toward a System That Allows Disadvantaged Fathers to Support Their Children

Our reviews suggest that several policy and administrative issues will need to be reconsidered if the child support enforcement system is to reach its potential; issues range from interest charges on arrears to the way child support guidelines account for disadvantaged nonresident parents to the complications faced by parents who have had children with multiple partners. Here we highlight two overarching core issues, not because the other issues are unimportant, but because we believe these issues are central to efforts to improve the child support system for low-income families: (1) the need for child support policies to be redesigned with a clear focus on supporting vulnerable children, rather than reducing public expenditures, and (2) the need to complement enforcing nonresident fathers' obligation to support their children with programs and policies that improve disadvantaged fathers' ability to meet those obligations.

Child well-being over cost recovery

Redesigning the child support system to focus on improving the economic well-being of children, rather than cost recovery, requires several changes. In some cases, the required policy change is straightforward and is already part of pending legislative proposals. In other instances, the issues are more complex. In particular, we would

- *Allow TANF families to keep all child support paid on their behalf.* Federal policy should require states to pass through all child support to TANF families and disregard at least as much as is disregarded for resident parents' earnings. The Deficit Reduction Act of 2005 (DRA) allowed states to choose to increase the amount passed through, and some research suggests such changes are cost-neutral overall. However, especially in times of tight state budgets, there are barriers to states increasing the pass-through.

- *Eliminate the requirement that TANF applicants assign past-due support to the state.* Federal policy recently required states to discontinue assignment of past-due support for former TANF participants; past-due child support can be used to offset government costs only if collected while the family is receiving assistance. Because TANF is a time-limited program, with most participants receiving cash benefits for a short period (U.S. Department of Health and Human Services, Office of Family Assistance 2009), eliminating assignment of past-due support would simplify the system and align it with a focus on child well-being over cost recovery, without substantially more revenue loss.

- *Eliminate attempts to collect Medicaid birthing costs from nonresident fathers.* Some states attempt to recoup the medical expenses associated with a nonmarital birth from nonresident fathers, often even when the parents would qualify for Medicaid were they married and both parents' incomes considered for eligibility. In contrast, no state attempts to recoup Medicaid coverage for marital births. Eliminating efforts to recoup these public costs primarily from disadvantaged fathers would be another step toward child support being focused on supporting children rather than repaying the state.

Variations of all these proposals are part of the Responsible Fatherhood and Healthy Families Act cosponsored by then-Senator Obama. If these recommendations were implemented, no new case would have debt owed to the state, as all child support would go to families. In the short term, there would be a need for procedures for reviewing and reducing debt owed to the state under previous policy. Such debt reduction would put some fathers back into paying status, and consistency across cases would simplify administrative issues.

These reforms are necessary if the child support system is to focus on improving the economic well-being of families. That said, it is important to recognize that they would also eliminate an important source of revenue for child support enforcement agencies, as well as potentially undercutting support for child support enforcement from those who are primarily concerned with cost recovery. The National Governors Association (2009) recently noted, "While governors recognize that the ideal goal of the child support program may be to improve a family's economic security, making drastic changes to the child support system without considering the financial stability of the program will not lead to better outcomes for the families and children served." The reforms we advocate will eliminate an important source of revenue for the CSE system. However, we believe that it is not feasible for a well-designed system to be self-financing. Enforcing policy and law with regard to parents' obligations to their children is a general social responsibility and should be funded from general revenues, not by diverting money meant for children.

Enforcing and supporting disadvantaged
fathers' obligation to support their children

In judging the fairness of the child support system, a fundamental question concerns the point of comparison. In a context in which the alternative to private child support is public support, we may ask whether a low-income father's resources are large enough that he should be expected to offset public welfare costs. This was the context when low-income single mothers were entitled to cash assistance and when child support paid on behalf of children receiving assistance went to offset welfare costs, rather than support families. In that context, the appropriate point of comparison for low-income fathers was the government (or the general taxpayer). In the absence of an effective public safety net, however, the primary point of comparison is the resident-parent family. Thus, especially for disadvantaged fathers who have had children with mothers who also face limited opportunities, we must ask whether a nonresident father's resources and opportunities are so much more constrained than those available to the resident mother that the mother should be expected to be both the primary caretaker and the source of income, while a father can be exempted from being a source of income.

The evidence reviewed above suggests to us that in most cases, disadvantaged fathers should not be exempt from the obligation to support their children. However, for the expectation of financial support to be reasonable and enforceable, we must address the barriers to self-sufficiency that disadvantaged men face. Not surprisingly, low income and problems with unemployment are the most important factors for explaining nonpayment of child support (Ha et al. 2008). In contrast to the popular image of nonresident fathers as "deadbeat dads," research highlights nonresident fathers' multiple barriers to employment. For example, estimates from the NSAF suggest that 43 percent of poor noninstitutionalized nonresident fathers who did not pay child support were high school dropouts, 39 percent had health problems, 57 percent were not working at the time of the survey, and 32 percent had not worked during the three years prior to the survey (Sorensen and Zibman 2001).

In the United States, poor children and their resident parents are generally no longer entitled to cash assistance. The traditional welfare system has been replaced by a work-focused system that provides resident parents, usually mothers, with limited training and work experiences. Some states approach the possibility of providing a "job of last resort," but by far, most assistance is provided as "work supports"—an EITC to supplement low earnings, subsidized child care and health care, and food stamps substantially increase the total resources available to disadvantaged resident mothers who are working low-wage jobs and caring for their children.

Child support can and should be an important part of the income package for most of these families. However, for nonresident parents, usually fathers, to pay a reasonable amount of support on a regular basis they, too, need supports. We have a child support enforcement system that is extremely effective when non-resident parents have steady employment (Ha et al. 2008). But many nonresident fathers fail to meet their child support obligations because they are not able, or not willing, to find and sustain a job. Like resident mothers, nonresident fathers should be expected to work to support themselves and their children. If they cannot find employment, we envision services comparable to those available to resident families in some TANF programs, that is, job placement services, case management, and training in occupational skills. If fathers are still unable to find employment, we propose transitional jobs (that is, temporary, subsidized jobs with integrated skill development) be made available to fathers (and also to mothers). When fathers work, they should benefit from work supports, including subsidized health insurance and an EITC. This could be accomplished by expanding the childless worker EITC, or by expanding the EITC for nonresident parents who are paying their child support obligations.[12]

That said, many programs and policies—including the EITC—are largely limited to parents who are supporting their children. Benefits made available to nonresident parents (but not to childless adults) should be contingent on nonresident parents meeting their child support obligations—even if the nonresident parent has a very low income. Our goal is to make the supports for resident and nonresident parents more parallel, as long as the nonresident parents are demonstrating serious efforts toward fulfilling their obligations.

Contemporary American social policy emphasizes the responsibility of parents to provide for their children. With only very limited public cash assistance available, child support is a critical component of efforts to improve the economic conditions of children born to disadvantaged parents. Disadvantaged resident mothers cannot be expected to both parent and support their children financially with no assistance. Disadvantaged fathers cannot be expected to pay support if they do not have opportunities to earn an income. Work supports must be strengthened for resident parents, and expanded to nonresident parents, so that both parents can reasonably be expected to contribute; and when nonresident parents pay support, their contributions should fully benefit their children.

Notes

1. Some nonmarital births occur for cohabiting parents. While these children are initially living with both their parents, these relationships are relatively unstable, and many of these children will live with only one parent during their childhood (Osborne, Manning, and Smock 2007; Raley and Wildsmith 2004).

2. In this article, we focus on formal support. Many fathers also make informal in-kind or cash contributions (for quantitative research, see, for example, Garasky et al. 2007; Nepomnyaschy 2007).

3. All dollar amounts in this article are in 2008 dollars.

4. The findings of Sinkewicz and Garfinkel (2009) suggest that even among nonmarried couples, the characteristics of mothers and fathers are closely related to each other.

5. The negative relationship between the burden of child support orders and income levels also holds when fathers' incomes are estimated based on mothers' characteristics (Huang, Mincy, and Garfinkel 2005).

6. If these voluntary paternity acknowledgments are not contested within 60 days, they become a legal finding of paternity; for more information, see Roberts (2006).

7. If mothers do not know where fathers live, state child support agencies may use the Federal Parent Locator Service (FPLS), which matches data from the National Directory of New Hires (NDNH). The NDNH includes information on new jobs, claims for unemployment insurance benefits, and quarterly wage reports. The FPLS can also access other databases such as those of the Social Security Administration and the IRS to locate nonresident parents.

8. Self-employed parents may send their payments to the agency. If the resident-parent family is not receiving assistance, the parents may decide not to use the central collection agency but to enter into a private pay arrangement.

9. Note also that even when the amount should be comparable, amounts reported by fathers and mothers differ; some research suggests that mothers' reports more closely match administrative records, so they are thought to be more accurate (Schaeffer, Seltzer, and Klawitter 1991).

10. Sometimes, fathers are reluctant to seek aid to modify a child support order. They may have limited access to and understanding of the child support system and opportunities for modification (Nam, Cancian, and Meyer 2009; Pate 2006; Cancian et al. 2007). Furthermore, some scholars have suggested that "men [do] not want to talk about child support because they [do] not want to seem like deadbeat dads and [are] ashamed to reveal how much money they [owe]" (Kotloff 2005, 26).

11. International evidence confirms the potential importance of child support in the income packages of low-income families across developed countries (Bradshaw 2006; Skinner and Meyer 2006; Skinner, Bradshaw, and Davidson 2007).

12. Within the current system, most proposals to provide an EITC to nonresident parents would create a marriage penalty—both parents would qualify for an EITC if they lived apart but often not if they lived together. For a discussion of the incentives, and costs, associated with alternative proposals to expand the EITC for childless workers, see Carasso et al. (2008). We understand that limiting eligibility to those who have paid full child support limits participation; our argument is based on seeing the expanded EITC as providing support to those who are supporting children.

References

Bartfeld, Judi. 2000. Child support and the postdivorce economic well-being of mothers, fathers, and children. *Demography* 37 (2): 203–13.

Beller, Andrea H., and John W. Graham. 1993. *Small change: The economics of child support*. New Haven, CT: Yale University Press.

Blank, Rebecca. 2009. Economic change and the structure of opportunity for less-skilled workers. In *Changing poverty*, eds. Maria Cancian and Sheldon Danziger. New York, NY: Russell Sage Foundation.

Bloom, Dan. 2006. *Employment-focused programs for ex-prisoners: What have we learned, what are we learning, and where should we go from here?* New York, NY: MDRC.

Bradshaw, Jonathan. 2006. Child support and child poverty. *Benefits* 14 (3): 199–208.

Brito, Tonya. 2005. *Child support guidelines and complicated families: An analysis of cross-state variation in legal treatment of multiple-partner fertility*. Madison: Institute for Research on Poverty, University of Wisconsin–Madison.

Cancian Maria, Carolyn Heinrich, and Yiyoon Chung. 2009. Does debt discourage employment and payment of child support? Evidence from a natural experiment. Institute for Research on Poverty Discussion Paper 1366-09, Madison, WI.

Cancian, Maria, and Daniel R. Meyer. 2004. Fathers of children receiving welfare: Can they provide more child support? *Social Service Review* 78 (2): 179–206.

Cancian, Maria, and Daniel R. Meyer. 2006. *Alternative approaches to child support policy in the context of multiple-partner fertility*. Madison: Institute for Research on Poverty, University of Wisconsin–Madison.

Cancian, Maria, Daniel R. Meyer, and Emma Caspar. 2008. Welfare and child support: Complements, not substitutes. *Journal of Public Policy and Management* 27 (2): 354–75.

Cancian, Maria, Daniel R. Meyer, and Steven Cook. Forthcoming. Evolution of family complexity from the perspective of children. *Demography*.

Cancian, Maria, Daniel R. Meyer, and Hwa-Ok Park. 2003. *The importance of child support for low-income families.* Madison: Institute for Research on Poverty, University of Wisconsin–Madison.

Cancian, Maria, Jennifer Noyes, Yiyoon Chung, and Katherine Thornton. 2007. *Holding child support orders of incarcerated payers in abeyance: Implementation of a policy change in Milwaukee County and plans for evaluation.* Madison: Institute for Research on Poverty, University of Wisconsin–Madison.

Carasso, Adam, Harry J. Holzer, Elaine Maag, and C. Eugene Steuerle. 2008. The next stage for social policy: Encouraging work and family formation among low-income men. Urban Institute Discussion Paper 28, Washington, DC.

Case, Anne C., I. Fen Lin, and Sara S. McLanahan. 2003. Explaining trends in child support: Economic, demographic, and policy effects. *Demography* 40 (1): 171–89.

Cassetty, Judith, Maria Cancian, and Daniel R. Meyer. 2002. Child support disregard policies and program outcomes: An analysis of data from the OCSE. In *W-2 child support demonstration evaluation. Report on nonexperimental analyses*, vol. III, *Quantitative nonexperimental analyses, Background reports*, eds. Daniel R. Meyer and Maria Cancian, 1–26. Madison: Institute for Research on Poverty, University of Wisconsin–Madison.

Danziger, Sheldon H., and David Ratner. 2010. Labor market outcomes and the transition to adulthood. *The Future of Children* 20 (1): 133–58.

Freeman, Richard B., and Jane Waldfogel. 1998. Does child support enforcement policy affect male labor supply? In *Fathers under fire: The revolution in child support enforcement*, eds. Irwin Garfinkel, Sara S. McLanahan, Daniel R. Meyer, and Judith A. Seltzer, 94–127. New York, NY: Russell Sage Foundation.

Garasky, Steven, Susan D. Stewart, Craig Gundersen, and Brenda J. Lohman. 2007. Toward a fuller understanding of nonresident father involvement: A joint examination of child support and in-kind support receipt. National Poverty Center Working Paper Series 07-12, University of Michigan, Ann Arbor.

Garfinkel, Irwin, and Marieka M. Klawitter. 1990. The effect of routine income withholding of child support collections. *Journal of Policy Analysis and Management* 9 (2): 155–77.

Garfinkel, Irwin, Sara S. McLanahan, and Thomas L. Hanson. 1998. A patchwork portrait of nonresident fathers. In *Fathers under fire: The revolution in child support enforcement*, eds. Irwin Garfinkel, Sara S. McLanahan, Daniel R. Meyer, and Judith A. Seltzer, 31–60. New York, NY: Russell Sage Foundation.

Garfinkel, Irwin, Sara S. McLanahan, Sarah O. Meadows, and Ronald Mincy. 2009. Unmarried fathers' earnings trajectories: Does partnership status matter? Center for Research on Child Wellbeing Working Paper 09-02, Princeton, NJ.

Garfinkel, Irwin, and Marygold S. Melli. 1990. Use of normative standards in family law decisions: Developing mathematical standards for child support. *Family Law Quarterly* 24 (2): 157–78.

Garfinkel, Irwin, Daniel R. Meyer, and Sara S. McLanahan. 1998. A brief history of child support policies in the United States. In *Fathers under fire: The revolution in child support enforcement*, eds. Irwin Garfinkel, Sara S. McLanahan, Daniel R. Meyer, and Judith A. Seltzer, 14–30. New York, NY: Russell Sage Foundation.

Garrison, Marsha. 1999. Child support policy: Guidelines and goals. *Family Law Quarterly* 33 (1): 157–89.

Glaze, Lauren E., and Laura M. Maruschak. 2008. *Parents in prison and their minor children.* Washington, DC: U.S. Department of Justice, Bureau of Justice Statistics.

Grall, Timothy S. 2009. *Custodial mothers and fathers and their child support: 2007.* Washington, DC: U.S. Census Bureau.

Griswold, Esther, Jessica Pearson, Nancy Thoennes, and Lanae Davis. 2004. *Fathers in the criminal justice system.* Denver, CO: Center for Policy Research.

Ha, Yoonsook, Maria Cancian, and Daniel R. Meyer. 2009. *Unchanging child support orders in the face of unstable earnings.* Madison: Institute for Research on Poverty, University of Wisconsin–Madison.

Ha, Yoonsook, Maria Cancian, Daniel R. Meyer, and Eunhee Han. 2008. *Factors associated with nonpayment of child support.* Madison: Institute for Research on Poverty, University of Wisconsin–Madison.

Hatcher, Daniel L., and Hannah Lieberman. 2003. Breaking the cycle of defeat for "deadbroke" non-custodial parents through advocacy on child support issues. *Journal of Poverty Law and Policy* 37 (1–2): 5–22.

Holzer, Harry J., and Paul Offner. 2006. Trends in employment outcomes of young black men, 1979–2000. In *Black males left behind*, ed. Ronald B. Mincy. Washington, DC: Urban Institute Press.

Huang, Chein-Chung, and Richard L. Edwards. 2009. The relationship between state efforts and child support performance. *Children and Youth Services Review* 31 (2): 243–48.

Huang, Chien-Chung, Ronald B. Mincy, and Irwin Garfinkel. 2005. Child support obligations and low-income fathers. *Journal of Marriage and Family* 67 (5): 1213–25.

Kotloff, Lauren J. 2005. *Leaving the street: Young fathers move from hustling to legitimate work*. Philadelphia, PA: Public/Private Ventures.

Levingston, Kristen D., and Vicki Turetsky. 2007. Debtors' prison: Prisoners' accumulation of debt as a barrier to reentry. *Journal of Law and Public Policy Clearinghouse Review* 41 (3–4): 187–97.

Lewis, Charles E., Irwin Garfinkel, and Qin Gao. 2007. Incarceration and unwed fathers in fragile families. *Journal of Sociology and Social Welfare* 34 (3): 77–94.

Meyer, Daniel R. 1998. The effect of child support on the economic status of nonresident fathers. In *Fathers under fire: The revolution in child support enforcement*, eds. Irwin Garfinkel, Sara S. McLanahan, Daniel R. Meyer, and Judith A. Seltzer, 67–93. New York, NY: Russell Sage Foundation.

Meyer, Daniel R., Maria Cancian, and Kisun Nam. 2007. Welfare and child support program knowledge gaps reduce program effectiveness. *Journal of Policy Analysis and Management* 26 (3): 575–97.

Meyer, Daniel R., Yoonsook Ha, and Mei-Chen Hu. 2008. Do high child support orders discourage child support payments? *Social Service Review* 82 (1): 93–118.

Meyer, Daniel R., and Mei-Chen Hu. 1999. A note on the antipoverty effectiveness of child support among mother-only families. *Journal of Human Resources* 34 (1): 225–34.

Mincy, Ronald, Irwin Garfinkel, and Lenna Nepomnyaschy. 2005. In-hospital paternity establishment and father involvement in fragile families. *Journal of Marriage and Family* 67 (3): 611–26.

Mincy, Ronald B., and Elaine J. Sorensen. 1998. Deadbeats and turnips in child support reform. *Journal of Policy Analysis and Management* 17 (1): 44–51.

Nam, Kisun, Maria Cancian, and Daniel R. Meyer. 2009. How program participants learn program rules: Implications for implementation and evaluation. *Social Service Review* 83 (1): 53–78.

National Governors Association. 2009. Child support enforcement. National Governors Association Policy Position HHS-08, Washington, DC. Available from www.nga.org/ (accessed 27 July 2009).

Nepomnyaschy, Lenna. 2007. Child support and father-child contact: Testing reciprocal pathways. *Demography* 44 (1): 93–112.

Noyes, Jennifer. 2006. *Review of child support policies for incarcerated payers*. Madison: Institute for Research on Poverty, University of Wisconsin–Madison.

Osborne, Cynthia, Wendy D. Manning, and Pamela J. Smock. 2007. Married and cohabiting parents' relationship stability: A focus on race and ethnicity. *Journal of Marriage and Family* 69 (5): 1345–66.

Ovwigho, Pamela Caudill, Correne Saunders, and Catherine E. Born. 2005. *The intersection of incarceration & child support: A snapshot of Maryland's caseload*. Baltimore: Family Welfare Research and Training Group, University of Maryland.

Pate, David. 2002. An ethnographic inquiry into the life experiences of African American fathers with children on W-2. In *W-2 child support demonstration evaluation. Report on nonexperimental analyses*, vol. II, *Fathers of children in W-2 families*, eds. Daniel R. Meyer and Maria Cancian. Madison: Institute for Research on Poverty, University of Wisconsin–Madison.

Pate, David. 2006. *Welfare and child support policy knowledge among parents of children on W-2 in Dane County*. Madison: Institute for Research on Poverty, University of Wisconsin–Madison.

Pearson, Jessica. 2004. Building debt while doing time: Child support and incarceration. *Judges' Journal* 43 (1): 5–12.

Pearson, Jessica, and Lanae Davis. 2003. Serving fathers who leave prison. *Family Court Review* 41 (3): 307–20.

Pearson, Jessica, Nancy Thoennes, Lanae Davis, Jane C. Venohr, David A. Price, and Tracy Griffith. 2003. *OCSE responsible fatherhood programs: Client characteristics and program outcomes*. Denver, CO: Center for Policy Research and Policy Studies Inc. Available from www.policy-studies.com/Portals/0/docs/Publications/Fatherhood/OCSE-Responsible-Fatherhood-Client-Char-and-Prog-Outcomes.pdf (accessed 9 November 2010).

Pirog, Maureen A., and Kathleen M. Ziol-Guest. 2006. Child support enforcement: Programs and policies, impacts and questions. *Journal of Policy Analysis and Management* 25 (4): 943–90.

Raley, R. Kelly, and Elizabeth Wildsmith. 2004. Cohabitation and children's family instability. *Journal of Marriage and Family* 66 (1): 210–19.

Rich, Lauren M. 2001. Regular and irregular earnings of unwed fathers: Implications for child support practices. *Children and Youth Services Review* 23 (4–5): 353–76.

Rich, Lauren M., Irwin Garfinkel, and Qin Gao. 2007. Child support enforcement policy and unmarried fathers' employment in the underground and regular economies. *Journal of Policy Analysis and Management* 26 (4): 791–810.

Roberts, Paula. 2006. *Voluntary paternity acknowledgment: An update of state law.* Washington, DC: Center for Law and Social Policy.

Schaeffer, Nora Cate, Judith A. Seltzer, and Marieka M. Klawitter. 1991. Estimating nonresponse and response bias: Resident and nonresident parents' reports about child support. *Sociological Methods and Research* 20 (1): 30–59.

Sinkewicz, Marilyn, and Irwin Garfinkel. 2009. Unwed fathers' ability to pay child support: New estimates accounting for multiple-partner fertility. *Demography* 46 (2): 247–63.

Skinner, Christine, Jonathan Bradshaw, and Jacqueline Davidson. 2007. *Child support policy: An international perspective.* London: U.K. Department for Work and Pensions.

Skinner, Christine, and Daniel R. Meyer. 2006. After all the policy reform, is child support actually helping low-income mothers? *Benefits* 14 (3): 209–22.

Sorensen, Elaine. 1997. A national profile of nonresident fathers and their ability to pay child support. *Journal of Marriage and Family* 59 (4): 765–97.

Sorensen, Elaine, and Ariel Hill. 2004. Single mothers and their child-support receipt: How well is child-support enforcement doing? *Journal of Human Resources* 39 (1): 135–54.

Sorensen, Elaine, Liliana Sousa, and Simon Schaner. 2007. *Assessing child support arrears in nine large states and the nation.* Washington, DC: Urban Institute.

Sorensen, Elaine, and Chava Zibman. 2001. Getting to know poor fathers who do not pay child support. *Social Service Review* 75 (3): 420–34.

Stirling, Kate, and Tom Aldrich. 2008. Child support: Who bears the burden? *Family Relations* 57 (3): 376–89.

Travis, Jeremy, Amy L. Solomon, and Michelle Waul. 2001. *From prison to home: The dimensions and consequences of prisoner reentry.* Washington, DC: Urban Institute.

U.S. Census Bureau. 2005. Amounts of support provided on behalf of children under 21 years old living in another household by selected characteristics of provider: 2005. In *Support Providers: 2005.* Washington, DC: U.S. Government Printing Office. Available from www.census.gov/hhes/www/childsupport/providers2005.html.

U.S. Department of Health and Human Services, Office of Child Support Enforcement. 2006. *Working with incarcerated and released parents: Lessons from OCSE grants and state programs.* Washington, DC: U.S. Government Printing Office.

U.S. Department of Health and Human Services, Office of Child Support Enforcement. 2008. Guidelines for setting child support awards. Washington, DC: U.S. Government Printing Office. Available from http://edocket.access.gpo.gov/cfr_2008/octqtr/45cfr302.56.htm.

U.S. Department of Health and Human Services, Office of Child Support Enforcement. 2009. *Office of Child Support Enforcement FY 2008 preliminary report.* Washington, DC: U.S. Government Printing Office. Available from www.acf.hhs.gov/programs/cse/pubs/2009/reports/preliminary_report_fy2008/.

U.S. Department of Health and Human Services, Office of Family Assistance. 2009. *Temporary Assistance to Needy Families Program (TANF). Eighth annual report to Congress.* Washington, DC: U.S. Government Printing Office.

U.S. Department of Health and Human Services, Office of Inspector General. 2000a. *Paternity establishment: Administrative and judicial methods.* Washington, DC: U.S. Government Printing Office. Available from http://oig.hhs.gov/oei/reports/oei-06-98-00050.pdf.

U.S. Department of Health and Human Services, Office of Inspector General. 2000b. *State policies used to establish child support orders for low income non-custodial parents.* Washington, DC: U.S. Government Printing Office. Available from http://oig.hhs.gov/oei/reports/oei-05-99-00391.pdf.

Venohr, Jane C., and Tracy E. Griffith. 2005. Child support guideline: Issues and reviews. *Family Court Review* 43 (3): 415–28.

Waller, Maureen R. 2002. *My baby's father: Unmarried parents and parental responsibility*. Ithaca, NY: Cornell University Press.

Western, Bruce. 2006. Incarceration, marriage, and family life. With Leonard Lopoo. In *Punishment and inequality in America*, 131–67. New York, NY: Russell Sage Foundation.

Improving Education and Employment for Disadvantaged Young Men: Proven and Promising Strategies

By
CAROLYN J. HEINRICH
and
HARRY J. HOLZER

Low high school graduation rates and sharply declining employment rates among disadvantaged youth have led to an increasing number of youths who are disconnected from both school and work. What programs and policies might prevent these disconnections and improve educational and employment outcomes, particularly among young men? The authors review the evidence base on *youth development* policies for adolescents and young teens; programs seeking to improve educational attainment and employment for *in-school* youths; and programs that try to "reconnect" those who are *out of school* and frequently out of work, including public employment programs. The authors identify a number of programmatic strategies that are promising or even proven, based on rigorous evaluations, for disadvantaged youths with different circumstances and conclude that policy efforts need to promote a range of approaches to engage and reconnect youths, along with ongoing evaluation efforts to improve our understanding of what works, including which program components, for whom.

Keywords: youth development; training; employment; interventions; effectiveness

It is increasingly well known that employment rates among less-educated young men, especially young African American men, have declined sharply in recent years. Sum et al. (2008) point out that there was no net gain in employment for U.S. teens and young adults between 2000 and 2007, and they have been the largest net losers of jobs in the labor market downturn that began in 2007. At the same time that their labor force participation rates have dwindled, incarceration rates among young men have risen dramatically. At any point in time, a large number of these young men are "disconnected" from both school and work (Edelman, Holzer, and Offner 2006).

What programs and policies might be undertaken that could prevent this disconnection from occurring and improve the educational and employment outcomes of these young men? Some experts (e.g., Heckman 2008) have grown extremely skeptical about the cost-effectiveness

DOI: 10.1177/0002716210391968

of educational and workforce development policies for disadvantaged youths as well as for adults. Indeed, while some youth advocates claim that we have a strong knowledge base on what "works" for disadvantaged youths (e.g., Bowles and Brand 2009), the evidence from rigorous evaluation efforts has been much less positive. For example, the evaluation of the Job Training Partnership Act (JTPA) in the 1990s showed positive impacts for adult men and women, while those for youths generally ranged from zero to negative (Holzer 2009), and the tendency of short-term positive effects in the Job Corps and other studies to fade with time has become increasingly clear (Schochet, Burghardt, and McConnell 2008; Bloom 2009).

On the other hand, a careful review of the evidence in a range of areas indicates somewhat more positive impacts, at least in the short run, than have widely been recognized. And many programs that are not yet *proven*—in terms of rigorous evaluation evidence—seem at least to be quite *promising*, on the basis of their positive outcomes for participants, while achieving at least some substantial level of scale.[1] Given the enormous social costs associated with low employment and high incarceration for this population, it is very important that we identify and then invest in cost-effective strategies to improve youths' outcomes.

In this article, we review what we know to date about programs to improve educational and employment outcomes for disadvantaged youths. In particular, we review *youth development* policies aimed at adolescents and young teens, efforts aimed at improving educational attainment and employment for at-risk youth *in school* (high school or community college), and programs that try to "reconnect" those who are *out of school* and frequently out of work. We also briefly consider public employment programs for youths. We focus the discussion most heavily on efforts proven to be effective (or ineffective) through rigorous evaluation, while also highlighting some promising programs that still require more evaluation.

Carolyn J. Heinrich is director of the La Follette School of Public Affairs; professor of public affairs and affiliated professor of economics, Regina Loughlin Scholar; and affiliate of the Institute for Research on Poverty at the University of Wisconsin–Madison. Her research focuses on social welfare policy, public management, and social-program evaluation. She works directly in her research with governments at all levels, including with the federal government on evaluating workforce development programs, the state of Wisconsin on child-support programs, school districts in evaluating supplemental educational services, and other governments on their poverty reduction programs. Other ongoing projects include the study of labor market intermediaries and labor market outcomes for low-skilled and disadvantaged workers.

Harry J. Holzer is a professor of public policy at the Georgetown Public Policy Institute and a faculty director of the new Georgetown Center on Poverty, Inequality and Public Policy. He is also an institute fellow at the Urban Institute, senior affiliate of the National Poverty Center at the University of Michigan, national fellow of the Program on Inequality and Social Policy at Harvard University, nonresident senior fellow at the Brookings Institution, and affiliate of the Institute for Research on Poverty at the University of Wisconsin–Madison. His research focuses primarily on the low-wage labor market, particularly the problems of minority workers in urban areas. He has worked on the quality of jobs; workers in the labor market; and how job quality affects the employment prospects of the disadvantaged, worker inequality, and insecurity. He has also written extensively about the employment problems of disadvantaged men, advancement prospects for the working poor, and workforce policy more broadly.

After reviewing the evidence, we consider some practical proposals for implementing effective programs for youths, despite our imperfect base of knowledge about what works. A variety of important issues—such as the scale at which these efforts should be administered, the level of government that would be responsible for implementation, and how to ensure accountability and performance incentives—are considered here. We conclude with a summary of what we have learned in this investigation and what we recommend going forward.

A Review of the Current Evidence Base on Youth Development, In-School, and Out-of-School Youth Programs

A key objective of this research was to undertake a comprehensive review of programs that target disadvantaged youths, particularly males at risk of dropping out of school or already out of school and without a job, and to identify programs or aspects of these interventions that suggest promise for improving the educational and employment trajectories and longer-term labor market outcomes of young men. In this review, we distinguish four types of programs aimed at improving the chances of stable employment for young men:

- youth/adolescent development programs, including mentoring, holistic education/services, and afterschool programs;
- programs targeting in-school youth that emphasize dropout prevention, work-based learning, and strategies to promote access to higher education;
- programs targeting out-of-school youth or young men that focus on dropout recovery, education and training, and service employment; and
- public employment programs for youths.

The appendix to this article lists many of the most promising or proven programs in each of these areas (in our view), for which at least some outcome or impact analysis has been done. Across and within program types, these diverse interventions share some common goals and mechanisms by which they expect to improve opportunities and outcomes for young men, but there are also important differences in their approaches and emphases.

Youth development programs

Youth development programs, such as Big Brothers Big Sisters, Boys and Girls Clubs of America, and Harlem Children's Zone (HCZ), typically place emphasis on the following primary components: mentoring through supportive relationships with adults and older peers; case management and individual assessments, with referrals to outside services as necessary; tutoring and homework assistance; engagement in daily club activities, arts and drama, and sports; and in a few programs, health education and health care utilization efforts. In Big Brothers Big Sisters, for example, the matching of a youth with an adult or older youth mentor who will serve as a positive role model and the cultivation of a relationship between the pair through regular meetings and participation in activities are the core components around which other facets of the program (e.g., social and cultural enrichment, homework help and tutoring, and recreation) are built. Community service projects are an additional element of Boys and Girls Clubs, although games, arts and crafts, and recreation are the primary activities of youths in these clubs.

In other examples, these approaches are part of broader and more comprehensive strategies involving local schools and neighborhoods as well as family members. For instance, HCZ, which aims to reach children as early in their lives as possible and create a "critical mass of adults" to guide them through a holistic system of education (e.g., preschool, charter schools, and afterschool activities), and to provide social services based in the community and job training and college preparation programs in their later years, is among the most comprehensive of these programs. And an array of efforts generally referred to as "expanded learning opportunities" (ELOs) provide a range of academic and social services to youths in the afterschool and weekend and summertime periods (Bowles and Brand 2009).

Program evaluations and related literature correspondingly explore the effects of youth development programs in a wide range of areas, including behavioral and social outcomes, such as social engagement, school attendance or absences and delinquent behavior, sexual knowledge and activity, and alcohol and drug use, in addition to examining academic outcomes and impacts such as student grades or grade point averages, effort, and schoolwork quality and completion. Rhodes and DuBois (2008) report that recent meta-analyses of mentoring program evaluations find effects of participation in social/psychological, behavioral, and academic areas. Of this type of program, the Big Brothers Big Sisters programs have been among the most rigorously evaluated, and multiple experimental studies report effects in increasing academic performance and college expectations, reducing school infractions and unexcused absences, and other positive social effects. In general, the meta-analyses and experimental evaluations suggest that, while statistically significant, the magnitude of the youth development program impacts are typically small and often do not persist. In contrast, recent evidence from HCZ (Dobbie and Fryer 2009) suggests large effects on student test scores, which persist at least through graduation from middle school. Of course, since this program combines intensive classroom instruction with a variety of family and community-oriented services, it is hard to tell exactly which components of the intervention generated the impacts and whether some or all are really needed for these effects.[2] And whether HCZ can be replicated on a broader scale remains to be seen as well, with the Obama administration proposing to generate ten to twenty "Promise Neighborhoods" around the country as part of a replication effort.

Two key features of youth development programs that appear to increase program effectiveness are the frequency and intensity with which these programs engage youth in activities (academic and nonacademic), particularly in their relationships with mentors. Although the experimental evaluations do not allow for the identification of specific components that contribute to the academic and behavioral/social impacts, the quality and length of relationships that youths develop with their mentors is cited as an important factor in studies of Big Brothers Big Sisters, the Boys and Girls Clubs of America, and Children's Aid Society/Carrera programs, as well as in the meta-analyses of mentoring programs (Rhodes and DuBois 2008; Herrera et al. 2007; Anderson-Butcher, Newsome, and Ferrari 2003). Theoretical models of mentoring in youth programs (Rhodes 2005) describe the strong bonds that youths forge with their mentors—based on trust, empathy, and shared experiences that come with regular time spent together—as the critical mechanism through which social-emotional and cognitive effects are achieved. Youths in the Big Brothers Big Sisters programs who had mentoring relationships that lasted at least a year and grew stronger (or more structured) over time were more likely to realize social and academic benefits from participating (Herrera et al. 2007). Unfortunately, high attrition in the second year diluted the average academic impacts for participants.

A probable factor limiting the effectiveness of this and other youth development programs, such as those offering afterschool tutoring and remediation services outside of the regular school day, is a lack of engagement and regular participation. A meta-analysis by Lauer et al. (2006) of thirty-five peer-reviewed studies of out-of-school-time programs that used control or comparison groups to estimate effect sizes (specifically, gains in academic achievement test scores) explored the relationship of program focus, duration, time frame, student grouping, and grade level to program outcomes. They found that these programs can have a positive effect on student achievement, with effect sizes larger for programs of longer duration (more than 45 hours), although diminishing returns set in for the longest. In a random assignment study of a national afterschool program, Dynarski et al. (2004) found no effects on reading test scores or grades for elementary or middle school students, and a follow-up study using these same data by Vandell et al. (2005) reported positive effects on test scores only for elementary school students highly active in high-quality programs. Perhaps the stronger effects of HCZ on test scores reflect the consistency and continuity of the intervention over several years as well as its comprehensiveness.

In-school youth programs

The programs that target in-school youth—especially those who are at risk of dropping out and engaging in other problematic behaviors—are quite diverse in their goals. Generally, they aim to

- improve cognitive achievement,
- reduce high school dropout rates,
- raise postsecondary attendance and completion, and
- improve postschool employment and earnings.

Some programs focus primarily on one of these goals, while others aim to generate improvements on some or all of these dimensions. For instance, the Multiple Pathways to Graduation (MPG) programs of New York City primarily focus on improving achievement and reducing dropout rates. Achievement via Individual Determination (AVID), Gear Up, and Upward Bound target high school students and seek to raise their awareness of and prepare them for post-secondary education, while Opening Doors (OD) is a multisite demonstration project at community colleges that tests a number of different interventions— including financial assistance, small "learning communities," and various support and remediation efforts—to improve attendance and completion of low-income students.[3] In contrast, Career Academies (CA), which number more than two thousand nationwide, are a form of career and technical education (CTE) in which a sector-specific "academy" exists within a broader high school, with students taking courses in both areas and supplementing their classroom education with summer and year-round employment. Other forms of CTE include Tech-Prep, which combines the last two years of high school and two years of community college, as well as various apprenticeship models (Lerman 2007).

Despite the wide range of goals and interventions that appear in these programs, some commonalities are also evident. Mentoring and individualized attention and counseling are important elements of in-school and out-of-school youth interventions, although these activities may be more likely to take place in the context of (or in combination with) more formal activities, such as developing an individual education plan and providing career counseling and case management to assess individual, supportive service needs. A primary focus of the in-school youth programs is on helping youths to stay engaged in and complete high school, which they aim to accomplish through varying approaches, some involving broader school-level efforts and others more individually targeted. Earlier identification of youths at risk for dropping out is an increasingly common feature; once identified, programs typically take multipronged approaches to increase students' chances of graduation (New York City Department of Education 2006). Some programs, such as MPG and Quantum Opportunities programs (QOP), emphasize supplemental education activities and accelerated learning or time to credentialing, including afterschool programming; virtual, evening, and summer schooling; and other approaches to compressing time to earn a diploma. Another approach that MPG, CA, OD, and other programs have adopted is to create smaller "learning communities" within schools that aim to engender a more supportive, personalized learning environment, where students may take blocks of classes with the same peers and receive more customized instructional support and academic advising that is intended to foster stronger interpersonal and peer support.

Other important goals of in-school youth interventions are to increase youths' awareness of career, college, and postsecondary training opportunities and to more closely tie the knowledge and skills they gain in high school to work and study options available to them after graduating. Many of the well-known or widely adopted program models—MPG, CA, OD, and QOP, for example—include work-based learning components, such as curricula tightly linked with work/skills training or career themes and partnerships with employers to facilitate job shadowing, on-the-job training, and summer jobs. Additional features in programs such as CAs include career fairs, guest speakers, and career guidance; while programs such as AVID, Gear Up, and Upward Bound emphasize college-readiness counseling, precollege course taking, college field trips, and parent education about access to higher education opportunities. A number of these programs also incorporate financial incentives for youths to reach behavioral, learning, and other education or career milestones. Among the most far-reaching of these incentives was the combination of stipends, accrual account deposits, and bonuses developed in the QOP to encourage youths' attendance and participation in program activities; their attainment of a high school diploma or GED; and enrollment in college, a certified apprenticeship program, an accredited vocational or technical training program, or the armed forces. The scholarship incentives that the Louisiana site of the OD program offered, on the other hand, more explicitly encouraged college attendance and progression by rewarding college course grades and completion.

The primary or most prevalent features of in-school youth interventions described above do not represent the full inventory of program elements and innovations that have been implemented and investigated in the growing literature on the effectiveness of promising programs for in-school youth.[4] Yet it is clear that a majority of these programs employ a comprehensive approach to addressing youths' needs, which also complicates efforts to understand which program features contribute to youths' outcomes. Focusing on the CA, OD, Upward Bound, and QOP that have been experimentally evaluated, one finds that each of these programs sought to increase high school graduation rates, with QOPs having a modest impact on graduating with a diploma for the entire treatment group (increasing the likelihood by 7 percentage points).[5] And the evaluations of OD, Upward Bound, and QOP all reported positive effects on youths' continuing (post–high school) education; of these, OD (Louisiana) and Upward Bound, both of which were more strongly oriented toward encouraging college attendance, and significantly increased college attendance (by approximately 6 percentage points), course credits earned, and performance in college coursework.

The results from OD and the other programs suggest, more broadly, the important potential role of community colleges in our efforts to improve education and employment outcomes for disadvantaged youths. Econometric results consistently show strong returns for low-income youths or adults who complete at least a year of community college, if not an associate's degree (Lerman 2007). Jacobson and Mokher (2009) also find strong returns for low-income youths who can complete certificate programs in high-demand occupations and sectors, especially if they involve at least some technical training.

Pell grants are the primary vehicle through which the federal government encourages low-income youths and adults to attend community college. To date, the empirical evidence suggests Pell grants are more successful at encouraging attendance for adults than for youths (Turner 2007), although reforms to simplify the Pell grant application process and improve funding will likely help in this regard (Dynarski and Scott-Clayton 2007; Haskins, Holzer, and Lerman 2009). Furthermore, a broad range of programs are being piloted and even administered on a larger scale in community colleges across the country to improve access for disadvantaged young people through financial assistance, support, and counseling about opportunities. The Achieving the Dream program funded by several foundations in a variety of states is one such example; the various Career Pathway programs at the state and local levels, which seek to establish well-designed combinations of classroom curricula and work experience that place individuals in high-paying jobs, are another.[6] Of course, not all disadvantaged youths are ready for successful program completion at community college and instead enter remedial courses at community colleges from which they never emerge to take coursework for credit. Reforms in this process might include better integration of remedial and occupational training, as is now done in the I-BEST (Integrated Basic Education Skills Training) program in the state of Washington with promising results.[7]

As success at community college is more likely for those who successfully complete high school, more attention must be paid to what works at the high school level as well. In this regard, the CAs clearly emerge as the most effective intervention for at-risk youths, especially young men, to date. An eight-year evaluation of CAs reported no significant effects on high school completion for the overall sample of participants, but they generated notable reductions in dropping out for at-risk youths. Furthermore, participants (primarily males) self-reported significantly higher monthly earnings, months worked, hours worked per week, and hourly wages than control youths (Kemple and Willner 2008). In the eight years that these youths were tracked following their scheduled high school graduation, they realized an 11 percent increase in monthly earnings over the control (non-CA) group, or an additional $2,088 in earnings per year (in 2006 dollars); for males, the increase was 17 percent. It is plausible that the differing emphases on career awareness and work-based learning versus college and postsecondary education opportunities in these programs explains their varying impacts on continuing education versus labor market outcomes, but it is not possible to assert this with confidence based on the currently available evidence. What is important is that CAs did not produce results through "tracking" students into nonacademic paths; the tendency of youth to attend postsecondary schools was no lower for students in the CAs than in the control groups.[8]

Other efforts show some successes in specific locations, though efforts to replicate them and bring them to scale have not succeeded. The report on the QOP short-term impacts (Maxfield, Schirm, and Rodriguez-Planas 2003) compared its features to those of other youth programs that the U.S. Department of Labor or Department of Education supported in an effort to better understand why QOP generated impacts in some areas but not others, despite the intensity of services offered and relatively high per-enrollee costs ($25,000 on average). These reports argue that QOP was more comprehensive than most other federal youth programs: it includes attention to physical and mental health; nutrition; substance abuse; conflict resolution; gang membership and delinquent behavior; dysfunctional, abusive, or unsupportive family situations; and personal finances, in addition to its academic, basic education, and work/career skills components. They also suggest that it likely enrolled less motivated youths than most programs because QOP did not limit participation and explicitly targeted youths with lower grades than other programs, and accordingly, it placed greater emphasis on mentoring than did other federal youth programs. Unfortunately, while impacts at a few early sites were quite positive, those of the broader replication effort were by and large disappointing, with no effects on in-school academic performance or risky/delinquent behaviors and only small impacts on high school graduation and enrollment in postsecondary education or training. Once again, a lack of youths' engagement and regular participation in program activities were cited as important limiting factors, with enrollees coming up far short of annual hour goals and average time spent in activities declining steadily over time.

We note a few other categories of programs that have generated at least some successful impacts in at least moderately rigorous evaluations. First, the Youth Incentive Entitlement Pilot Project (YIEPP) of the late 1970s guaranteed summer and year-round minimum wage employment to low-income and mostly minority students in urban areas as long as they did not drop out of high school. Experimental evaluations of YIEPP showed enormous impacts on short-term employment; indeed, white-minority gaps in employment disappeared almost completely in these sites. There were also positive impacts on postschool earnings for at least a year.[9] These results, along with those of CA and other forms of CTE, suggest the potential of stipends and paid employment to attract and engage young people in a range of programmatic efforts.

In addition, a variety of "whole school reforms," including the Talent Development High Schools, High Schools That Work, and the Early College High School Initiative, might be promising at large urban schools with high dropout rates. The first two of these rely on small learning communities and other curricular and governance changes in these schools; the latter combines the late high school and community college years into programs on community college campuses. Thus far, the Talent Development model has generated some positive impacts in rigorous evaluations (Kemple, Herlihy, and Smith 2005), though more evidence on all of these is clearly needed.[10]

Finally, another set of efforts target entire low-income communities, and both in-school and out-of-school youths within these communities, for a comprehensive set of educational and employment interventions. One such effort was the Youth Opportunity Program, which provided grants to thirty-six low-income communities through a competitive process in 2000.[11] Statistical evidence comparing outcomes at these sites relative to similar sites showed improvements in school enrollments and in overall employment and wage rates, especially among minorities and teens, although full-time employment declined as school enrollments rose (Decision Information Resources 2008).

Out-of-school youth programs

Out-of-school youth programs, which typically target youths who are not working or enrolled in high school, college, or other postsecondary education or training and who may or may not have completed high school, tend to be more work-oriented than in-school youth interventions, and many also include a more intensive focus on vocational and on-the-job training. Employer involvement in designing training and arranging job placements is common. Job Corps, for example, has developed vocational curricula in more than seventy-five trades with the input of business and labor organizations.

As deficiencies in cognitive and noncognitive skills are often greater among those who have already failed at school, more intensive remedies might be needed before these young men can complete secondary school, attain postsecondary education, and succeed in the labor market. The types of supportive services offered must also recognize the differential needs of an older youth population that is attempting to move toward self-sufficiency, such as assistance with housing, referrals for substance abuse treatment and other health/mental health issues, and "life-coping" skills. Two prominent programs, Job Corps and the National Guard ChalleNGe, include residential components, in which youths reside at a center where intensive vocational/job and other life skills training are provided. In Job Corps and the Center for Employment Training programs, the training offered is frequently individualized, self-paced, and competency-based to prepare youth to work in a specific trade. Most out-of-school youth programs also offer those who dropped out of high school the opportunity to earn a GED. An alternative model, stressing service employment and efforts to improve education as well as civic values and leadership skills, is most prominently represented by YouthBuild and the Conservation and Youth Service Corps (Edelman, Holzer, and Offner 2006).

In a recent review of out-of-school youth programs, Bloom (2009) points out that the distinctions between in-school and out-of-school youth interventions are fading, as school districts have expanded the range of options they offer to keep youths in school and progressing toward graduating with a diploma. The CAs, for example, establish partnerships with local employers to provide work-based learning opportunities for high school students, and central goals of the program include improving students' preparation for the labor market and promoting successful school-to-work transitions as well as college attendance. At the same time, out-of-school youth programs such as YouthBuild and the Conservation and Youth Service Corps are focusing more on opening youth pathways to postsecondary education, which have been shown to generate payoffs for those holding a GED as well as for those with a high school diploma if they complete the program of study (Tyler and Lofstrom 2009).[12]

We focus on reviewing the results from experimental evaluations and studies of larger publicly funded programs, including Job Corps, the Center for Employment Training, and National Guard ChalleNGe; other employment programs, such as the Job Training Apprenticeship program and YouthBuild, have not undergone serious evaluation to date. A Government Accountability Office (GAO; 2007) report on studies of YouthBuild and its program performance concluded that, although a number of smaller-scale evaluations suggested findings of increased employment, wages, and educational attainment and reduced delinquent behavior or recidivism for those with correctional system involvement, these studies did not have sufficient follow-up data or adequate comparisons (with other programs or nonparticipants) to merit confidence in the results.[13] The report also stated, in a comment that applies to nearly all of the youth programs discussed in this article, that it is difficult to generalize results from a specific program evaluation to the universe of programs of the same type (given heterogeneity in implementation) or to rigorously identify which elements of a particular intervention are contributing to observed outcomes or impacts.[14]

Illustrating both of these points, the early (in the 1990s) success of the San Jose, California, Center for Employment Training (CET) in generating statistically significant and unprecedented earnings impacts over 30- and 60-month follow-up periods (totaling $2,062 per enrollee in the first 30 months and subsequently averaging close to $100 per month) led to a twelve-site, U.S. Department of Labor–funded replication and experimental evaluation of the program's impacts (Miller et al. 2005). The core CET feature was the opportunity to participate in employment and training services (e.g., occupational, basic skills, and full-time and competency-based training on an open-entry and open-exit basis) that mirrored the workplace, with the close involvement of industry in both program design and operation. The final twelve-site evaluation presented disappointing findings, however; aggregating across all sites, the program had no effect on youths' employment and earnings. The study uncovered difficulties in a majority of the sites in implementing the San Jose CET approach (particularly the job development component) and concluded that only four sites replicated the original model with high fidelity. An analysis of just the four high-fidelity sites showed some early impacts on time spent in education and training activities and receipt of training credentials, although these impacts faded substantially by the end of the follow-up period.[15] Once again, low intensity of participation was a factor in more poorly performing sites, where many students failed to attend regularly or dropped out before completing competencies and receiving job placement assistance.

Still, some successes can be found and some generalizations drawn. Job Corps is the largest publicly funded program providing academic and vocational education and training to economically disadvantaged out-of-school youths, serving approximately sixty thousand new participants each year at a per-participant cost of approximately $24,000.[16] The most recent experimental evaluation completed by Mathematica Policy Research, Inc. (Schochet, Burghardt, and McConnell 2008), involving more than fifteen thousand youths in 1994 and 1995 and using four years of survey data and nine years of administrative records on earnings (after Job Corps exits), showed that Job Corps was successful in substantially increasing education and training among participants, with the impact equal to approximately one high school year and reflected in significant increases in receipt of GED and vocational certificates (21 and 31 percentage points, respectively). The evaluation design also allowed for subgroup impact estimation, and these analyses showed larger, statistically significant earning impacts ($4,500 in total earnings over 1998–2003) for older youths, ages 20 to 24 (vs. those 16–19 years old). The study's authors noted that these older youths participated for 1.3 months longer on average and were "more highly motivated and well behaved" as reported by program staff. The program also significantly reduced arrest and conviction rates as well as time spent incarcerated for participants.

One might view many of the above reported Job Corps impacts as encouraging, although a corresponding cost-benefit analysis suggested that the benefits of the program faded after four years, so that program costs exceeded benefits for the full evaluation sample. Still, the benefits did exceed costs for the most engaged participants (older youth), and the earning impacts of this subgroup persisted longer. Early experimental evaluation results of the National Guard ChalleNGe program likewise report promising trajectories for participating youths, with short-term (nine-month) impacts on earning a high school diploma or GED, full-time work, self-rated health and reductions in obesity and arrests, and convictions and time incarcerated (Bloom, Gardenhire-Crooks, and Mandsager 2009). The Job Corps experience, with fading longer-term impacts, however, suggests that a longer follow-up period will be essential before drawing firm conclusions about a program's effectiveness, which the National Guard ChalleNGe study's authors acknowledge as well. Few studies conduct a full accounting and comparison of costs and benefits, as in the Job Corps evaluation or the earlier National Supported Work Demonstration. Another overarching criticism of the evidence base is that because youth program evaluations are for the most part compartmentalized and relatively few include a longer-term follow-up, we do not see studies that track youths as they enter different interventions at different stages of their progression from youths to young men (or women). Further information that would enable us to compare costs and benefits *across* different types of youth interventions and over time is necessary to offer more specific policy advice on how public resources should be invested to maximize the benefits realized for youths.

The above discussion also raises another question: are youths not fully engaging in and participating in these programs long enough because the interventions do not offer what they need or want, or is this problem fundamentally one of lack of motivation or other individual barriers to participation that even the most supportive and comprehensive interventions are not able to address? For some programs, such as HCZ, which attempts to reach children early in preschool and to provide holistic services through their early adulthood, we do not yet have enough information to answer this question, although early reports of youths' outcomes look promising. The ongoing evaluation of CAs includes a plan to compile data across programs in the effort to identify specific program components that appear to be working most effectively in engaging youths and contributing to program impacts. Clearly, this is an area where additional research would be beneficial, along with a careful examination of the costs of different components of these interventions, so that cost-benefit analyses might speak not only to the value of whole programs but also to any specific parts that might be driving positive outcomes.

Public "jobs of last resort" for youths

Some young people with a range of barriers to employment—such as poor skills and work experience, physical or emotional disabilities, and criminal records—are part of a group known as the "hard-to-employ," for whom getting or retaining private-sector employment at even the minimum wage is quite difficult (Loprest and Martinson 2008). For these individuals, another possibility remains: publicly funded "jobs of last resort" in the public or private not-for-profit sectors. Danziger and Gottschalk (1995) endorsed such jobs, in which individuals would obtain time-limited community service jobs.

Public "jobs of last resort" would differ significantly from those described above, such as YIEPP, YouthBuild, and the Conservation and Youth Service Corps, as these three programs are really employment-based *training* programs, whose postprogram impacts on participant earnings are judged relative to costs like any other training program. Another employment-based training approach is the "transitional job" (or TJ) for ex-offenders, where individuals get several months of paid employment plus supportive services to help them to transition into private-sector jobs. Evaluation evidence for those with criminal records suggests little impact on postprogram earnings but reductions in recidivism for some subsamples of these men.[17]

In contrast, efforts to create "jobs of last resort" would not necessarily be judged by their postprogram impacts but rather by their ability to generate net new employment (plus public services) while they are in place. As such, they are work-based "safety net" programs rather than training programs. Furthermore, an ongoing program of public employment would differ from the publicly funded job creation efforts of the American Recovery and Reconstruction Act (ARRA), which are temporary countercyclical measures designed to provide employment only during a period of severe recession.[18]

Gottschalk (1997) and Ellwood and Welty (2000) review the U.S. experience with public employment programs for the disadvantaged. Some programs they review have successfully created *net* new employment for the disadvantaged by carefully targeting those who are unsuccessful in gaining such employment in the private sector or elsewhere in the public sector; some have also generated services that the public actually values.

However, even when successful, such programs are extremely expensive. For instance, a minimum-wage job at 30 hours per week for a year (plus administrative expenses) would likely cost about $15,000; creating one million of these jobs would therefore cost $15 billion per year. And allowing for at least some displacement of private employment or "fiscal substitution" in the public sector would reduce the net amount of employment generated with these funds. Given the extremely tight federal and state budgetary environments of the coming years, such expenditures would be very difficult to sell politically. Cheaper efforts that provide some income or employment support, like those outlined by Loprest and Martinson (2008), seem more plausible in this fiscal environment.

How to Move Forward with the Most Promising and Proven Interventions

In light of the above findings on promising programs for cost-effectively improving educational attainment and employment outcomes for disadvantaged youths, what policies for youths seem most appropriate, and by how much would optimal policies differ from the status quo? Without being overly prescriptive in terms of exactly which programmatic models to implement, it seems as though our policy efforts should encourage more of the promising or proven approaches described above, along with continuing evaluation efforts. At-risk high school students, as well as dropouts, should be able to consider a range of "pathways" to high school completion, postsecondary education, and good middle-skill careers. Different opportunities should be available to those at different levels of risk of failure and with different underlying skills and track records. Secondary schools, community colleges, and local employers should be more engaged in local youth "systems" that integrate educational and employment opportunities for them, with fewer "silos" separating the relevant youth populations, institutions, and policies.

Unfortunately, our current policies fall well short of these goals. Programs that the U.S. Departments of Education and Labor fund and administer operate in almost complete isolation from one another. A jointly administered program to encourage more integration of these youth programs in the 1990s, known as the School-to-Work Opportunities Act, provided very modest (and not well-targeted) seed money to school districts around the country but ultimately was not reauthorized. The Department of Education funds CTE through the Perkins Act, though states and localities fund most such efforts. Dropout prevention efforts receive some funding from the Elementary and Secondary Education Act (ESEA), while Pell grants and other services for those in college are funded through the Higher Education Act (HEA) independently of local workforce development efforts.

The Department of Labor funds youth services through the Workforce Investment Act (WIA), with funds disbursed through local Workforce Investment Boards (WIBs) and their Youth Councils. But representation by the leaders of local educational agencies on these councils is usually quite limited, except in a few well-known cases (such as the Philadelphia Youth Network and the San Francisco Youth Council); links between "One-Stop" career centers and community colleges are quite limited, too (Edelman, Greenberg, and Holzer 2009). Little is currently known about how WIA youth funds are spent and how effective they are, as there has been no national evaluation since the JTPA effort two decades ago; and the performance measures used by WIA for youth or adults, such as employment placement rates, likely lead to "cream-skimming" and other manipulative efforts by program operators (Barnow and Smith 2004).

Funding remains extremely limited as well. Youth services under WIA receive less than $1 billion per year in general funds, in addition to dedicated funds for Job Corps ($1.2 billion) and YouthBuild ($60 million) (Holzer 2009). Given that roughly one million young students drop out of high school every year (Heckman and LaFontaine 2007), and given the costs per participant of programs identified above (from $5,000 in YO to about $15,000 for National Guard ChalleNGe and YouthBuild or $20,000 for Job Corps), it is clear that few of these young people can be reached with this level of funding. For instance, it would require $5 billion annually to provide moderately intensive services to half of the nation's dropouts each year—if it were, in fact, possible to engage them on such a large scale.[19]

These deficiencies could at least potentially be corrected through some changes in federal youth policy that have been outlined elsewhere (Edelman, Greenberg, and Holzer 2009). A new youth title of WIA, or perhaps a separate piece of youth legislation, could create a program administered jointly by the Departments of Education and Labor. Formula funding to localities would provide greater support for paid work experience and work-based learning through high-quality CTE efforts such as CAs. High schools and community colleges, along with employer associations, would face incentives to develop new career pathways for both in-school youths and also for those currently out of school who might be "reconnected" with community colleges. Funding would also be available for intensive academic remediation and other services that prepare youths to finish high school and obtain postsecondary education down the road. Some existing strands of federal policy, similar to the current youth funding under WIA as well as the Perkins Act and ESEA, could be brought together under this approach and made more effective. The Obama administration's new community college initiative, which provides competitive grants to states to invest more in these systems, could be part of this effort as well.

What is more, any new legislation in this area should strongly incentivize more comprehensive and integrated youth "systems" to be built at the local level. Of course, it is hard to make such systems work, given the differing vested interests and incentives that local agency officials often face in their frequently conflicting jurisdictions. The new incentives might include a much greater reliance on bonus payments to localities that achieve these goals operationally, as well as competitive grants (like the Youth Opportunity Program) to those that convincingly propose to do so. The competitive grants might include some matching funds to encourage states and localities to leverage other resources (public and private) in their youth efforts.[20] Renewal of these competitive grants would be contingent on having achieved some significant scale in these efforts, as well as on performance measures (described below). States would also play a role in the use of both formula and competitive funds, by building systems in smaller towns and rural areas, analyzing data on trends in local labor demand (to identify the occupations and sectors with greatest growth potential), and setting policies for their educational institutions and workforce boards to follow at the local level.

Performance measurement and accountability in the formula-funded programs should also be revamped. One option is to rely on population-wide measures of education and employment outcomes, rather than those of program participants, to diminish incentives to "cream-skim," but this might require new data collection at the local level and would likely reflect economic and demographic trends in states that are beyond policy-makers' control. Alternatively, data on participants could be used to track *changes* rather than levels in education and labor market certifications over time, as well as improvements in work experience and earnings, with significant adjustments for participants who enter programs with documented personal barriers that put them at higher risk of failure. Such analyses could also explore how type and intensity of services relate to measured outcomes and potentially identify how program differences, or differential responses by youth with varying characteristics, influence outcomes.

And given how little we know in terms of what actually works for different kinds of youth, an exceptionally strong evaluation component for both formula and competitive funds would be critically important. At least ideally, the structure of the formula and competitive grants in the future would be updated to reflect what is learned through this evaluation process.

Even if such comprehensive youth legislation is not achieved, the various pieces of youth policy under WIA, the Perkins Act, and other vehicles might create better incentives for such coordination and evaluation. Indeed, some recent proposals for new youth legislation all involve competitive grants to states and localities to fund some of the services as well as the systems that are described above.[21]

Conclusion

On the basis of the programs and evidence reviewed above, what can we say about policies and programs to reduce disconnection and improve education and employment outcomes of disadvantaged youths? While the results in every category of programs are mixed, and the exact mechanisms that generate success in some cases are not well understood, some positive findings do emerge. Investments in youth development and mentoring efforts for adolescents can be quite cost-effective, even though the impacts are modest and tend to fade over time. Paid work experience, especially when combined with high-quality career and technical education, can be quite successful for at-risk students in high school, both by effectively engaging them in the short term and giving them valuable skills and labor market experience that can improve their earnings over time. The CAs, in particular, are an immensely effective means of improving skills and earnings as well as high school graduation rates among at-risk young men. Other programs that allow for individual monitoring and case management that identify at-risk youths fairly early and provide them with intensive academic and personal services seem promising as well, as do other programs that create small learning communities.

Disadvantaged youths who finish a GED or high school can also do quite well in the labor market if they can obtain an associate's degree or at least a certificate in a high-demand occupation or sector. Programs to improve attendance and completion of community college in the OD example show the potential impacts of efforts to improve financial aid (conditional on meeting performance standards) as well as a range of supports and services. Programs that combine the last few years of high school with community college, such as Tech-Prep and the Early College High School Initiative models, are promising, as are efforts to reconnect high school dropouts to alternative education efforts on these campuses.

Identifying successful programs for high school dropouts and other "disconnected" youth is somewhat more challenging. But even here, some modest successes appear. Intensive residential programs such as Job Corps and National Guard ChalleNGe provide important benefits in the short term, while service employment programs such as YouthBuild and the Conservation and Youth Service Corps have shown some positive outcomes and are, thus, promising as well. Comprehensive, community-based efforts such as the Youth Opportunity programs look successful, as does HCZ for a younger population. Publicly funded "jobs of last resort" for the hardest-to-employ might also generate net benefits for young men, particularly if they are well-targeted, although because such programs are expensive, they are less likely to garner essential political support. Clearly, different programmatic strategies are promising or even proven for different populations of disadvantaged youths with different circumstances, suggesting that policy efforts should seek to promote a range of approaches for youths, along with ongoing evaluation efforts to improve our understanding of what works, and specifically, which program components, for whom.

To be successful, such efforts will inevitably require more public resources than they get right now. At the same time, incentives for leveraging private resources and for generating coherent systems that break down institutional "silos" and effectively combine education and labor market services are important, as are revamping performance standards for individual program participants. Competitive grants to states and localities can also play an important role in such efforts.

Appendix
Summary of Youth Development, In-School, and Out-of-School Youth Interventions

Program	Study Description	Authors (Study Year)	Program Mechanism	Outcomes Examined
Youth/adolescent development programs				
Big Brothers Big Sisters	Two random assignment impact evaluations and qualitative and quantitative studies observing the intervention, analyzing program variations, and examining recruitment and screening procedures	Herrera et al. (2007); Rhodes, Grossman, and Resch 2000; Tierney, Grossman, and Resch (1995)	Mentoring through supportive relationships with adults and older peers; academic and nonacademic activities, and supervision and training to support relationship development	Overall academic performance,[a] assignments completed,[a] coursework quality,[a] GPA,[a] scholastic efficacy,[a] skipping school,[a] unexcused absences,[a] serious school infractions,[a] classroom effort,[a] teacher-student relationship quality, academic self-esteem, college expectations,[a] substance use, misconduct, prosocial behavior and acceptance,[a] emotional support from peers, self-worth, assertiveness, relationship with parents/family/peers
Boys and Girls Clubs of America	Nonexperimental studies examining participation, motivation for attendance, attrition, quality of support, drug problems and prevention, and impacts on academic achievement, school engagement, and substance use	Anderson-Butcher, Newsome, and Ferrari (2003); Arbreton and McClanahan (2002)	Individualized case management (relationship with supportive adults), mobilization of community resources (e.g., referrals for drug treatment, job training, educational services), daily club activities, drug use prevention	Gang involvement, contact with criminal justice system, delinquent behaviors (stealing, drug use), use of leisure time, social relationships, and school attendance and grades
Children's Aid Society/Carrera	Random assignment study, including surveys and interviews, to assess the effects of program participation on current sexual activity, contraceptive use, pregnancy, and health care access	Philliber et al. (2002)	Job club; tutoring; individual assessment; test preparation; assistance with college applications; family/sexuality education; reproductive health counseling; art, drama, and writing workshops; individual sports engagement; mental health care, medical care	Sexual activity/pregnancy,[a] contraceptive use[a] (impacts on females only), receipt of health care,[a] age-appropriate sexual knowledge,[a] pregnancy[a]

(continued)

Appendix (continued)

Program	Study Description	Authors (Study Year)	Program Mechanism	Outcomes Examined
Harlem Children's Zone	Nonexperimental studies with preintervention and postintervention measures of health, contraceptive use, school absences, and student achievement test scores	Dobbie and Fryer (2009); Spielman et al. (2006)	Holistic system of education (preschool, charter schools, afterschool activities), community-based social services, job training and college preparation programs, home visits, and health care programs	Educational/cognitive achievement, school absences, social/emotional and life skills, behavioral problems, engagement in risky behaviors, physical and mental health, preventive health care, contraceptive use
Supplemental educational services/ afterschool tutoring	Random assignment study of a national afterschool program, nonexperimental studies of supplemental educational services, and meta-analyses of out-of-school programs using comparison or control groups to assess impacts on student achievement	Dynarski et al. (2004); Vandell et al. (2005); Chicago Public Schools (2007); Rickles and Barnhart (2007); Zimmer et al. (2007); Heinrich, Meyer, and Whitten (forthcoming)	Additional (out-of-school) academic instruction to supplement in-school instruction and strengthen skill sets in key areas of reading and mathematics and contribute to improved learning and higher scores on state academic achievement assessments	Academic achievement (test scores), grades
In-school youth interventions				
Early Indicators	A nonexperimental, longitudinal study of 13,000 students to assess the effectiveness of an early identification and intervention system for middle-grade schools to combat student disengagement and increase graduation rate	Balfanz, Neild, and Herzog (2007)	School district data, including test scores, report card grades, behavior marks, attendance records, special education status, English language learner status, and demographic categories, are examined to empirically identify early signals of students at risk of disengaging and dropping out of school	Four indicators reflecting poor attendance, misbehavior, and course failures in sixth grade can be used to identify 60 percent of the students who will not graduate from high school: a final grade of F in mathematics, a final grade of F in English, attendance below 80 percent for the year, and a final "unsatisfactory" behavior mark in at least one class

(continued)

Appendix (continued)

Program	Study Description	Authors (Study Year)	Program Mechanism	Outcomes Examined
Multiple Pathways/ Alternative Pathways	Primarily qualitative and process studies on profiles of the target population, the challenges of identifying effective options and alternative pathways, and analyses of educational outcomes, including graduation and dropout rates	New York City Department of Education (2006); Neild and Balfanz (2006); Consortium on Chicago School Research (2007); Harris and Ganzglass (2008)	Early identification, credit recovery, accelerated learning and time to credential, curriculum linked to work/skills training, reenrollment in alternative education/multiple pathways programs (GED, small/transfer schools, learning to work), work-based learning, wrap-around supportive services, tangible rewards (including pay) for learning	Four-year graduation and dropout rates
Career Academies	Random assignment study with 1,400 students in nine high schools across the United States, including medium-size and large school districts and schools confronting educational challenges found in low-income urban settings, with an eight-year follow-up period	Kemple and Willner (2008)	Small learning communities to create supportive, personalized learning environment, academic/career/technical curricula around career themes to enrich teaching and learning, interpersonal and peer supports, partnerships with local employers to provide career awareness and work-based learning opportunities (e.g., job shadowing, work-based learning activities, career fairs, guest speakers, and career-related guidance)	Staying in school through twelfth grade, attendance, credits earned toward graduation, standardized test scores, average monthly earnings,[a] months employed during follow-up period,[a] hours worked per week,[a] hourly wages,[a] high school completion, postsecondary program enrollment, marital status,[a] parenting status,[a] living arrangements,[a] public assistance receipt, access to health insurance, voter registration, involvement with the criminal justice system
Job Training Apprenticeship	Nonexperimental studies on the use of apprenticeships to train workers, federal and state resources used in administering apprenticeship programs, representation of minorities and women in programs, and program retention and attrition	Berik and Bilginsoy (2000); Bilginsoy (2003)	On-the-job training and formal instruction to teach practical and theoretical aspects of a skilled occupation; mentoring by a fully trained worker (journey worker)	Retention rate, completion rate

(continued)

Appendix (continued)

Program	Study Description	Authors (Study Year)	Program Mechanism	Outcomes Examined
Quantum Opportunity	Two random assignment impact evaluations, three-year follow-up periods in five sites and five-year follow-up period in seven sites, including a cost-benefit analysis	Maxfield, Schirm, and Rodriguez-Planas (2003); Hahn (1994)	After-school programming, intensive case management, mentoring, supplemental education/tutoring, developmental and community service activities, supportive services (referrals to community health/mental health services, summer jobs programs, housing, food, income support, child care), financial incentives (stipends, accrual accounts, and enrollee and staff bonuses)	High school grades, achievement test scores, risky behaviors (substance abuse, gang activity, crime, sexual activity, and teen parenting), high school graduation (with diploma),[a] GED, enrollment in postsecondary education or training[a]
Opening Doors	Random assignment impact study of effects of supplemental financial aid with incentives	Richburg-Hayes et al. (2009)	Financial support, including scholarships up to $2,000 (in incentive monies), curricular and instructional innovations (e.g., "learning communities," customized instructional support, academic instruction, enhanced orientation courses, and student services)	College registration,[a] college credits attempted and accumulated,[a] grades in college courses (GPA),[a] degree attainment, transfer to four-year college, course withdrawal, cumulative academic achievement over seven semesters,[a] student-reported effort (number of hours studying, percentage of classes attended), self-reported optimism, goal engagement, life engagement, self-esteem, sense of self,[a] general social support, political engagement,[a] mental/physical health
Advancement via Individual Determination (AVID)	Nonexperimental, longitudinal (pre and post), and mixed-methods studies of AVID effects on high school performance and educational aspirations	Cunningham, Redmond, and Merisotis (2003); Watt, Yanez, and Cossio (2002); Guthrie and Guthrie (2001)	Rigorous curriculum with extra academic support, tutoring, college preparation, motivational activities, parent education and advising services, participation in at least one AVID class every day,	College attendance rates,[a] retention rates and college completion, high school dropout rates

(continued)

Appendix (continued)

Program	Study Description	Authors (Study Year)	Program Mechanism	Outcomes Examined
(AVID cont.)			partnerships and close working relationships cultivated with postsecondary institutions	
Gear Up—Gaining Early Awareness and Readiness for Undergraduate Programs	Nonexperimental studies using survey and longitudinal data (pre- and post-measures) and a matched comparison group in one study to assess academic performance, attendance and dropout, college readiness, and student behavior	Standing et al. (2008); Van Kannel-Ray, Lacefield, and Zeller (2008); New Jersey Commission on Higher Education (2005); Finch and Cowley (2003)	Tutoring, mentoring, college field trips, career awareness, college-readiness counseling, classes, meetings, parent education about access to higher education, curriculum reform, and teacher training	Interim outcomes include increased knowledge, improved behavior, increased expectations; GEAR UP students had not yet completed high school, so longer-term outcomes of increased postsecondary enrollment and completion could not be measured
Upward Bound	National, random assignment impact evaluation involving 67 projects and 2,800 students and a meta-analysis	U.S. Department of Education (2004); Myers and Schirm (1999)	Counseling, academic enrichment support, personal enrichment/social integration, mentoring, precollege courses and activities and six-week intensive academic program, financial assistance and scholarships	Total credits,[a] AP and honors credits,[a] GPA, high school status (graduation, GED, dropout), postsecondary school status,[a] four-year college attendance,[a] credits earned at postsecondary schools[a] (two-year, four-year, vocational schools), worked for pay and hours
Talent Development high schools	Random assignment evaluation of impacts on academic achievement of ninth-grade students in seven Philadelphia inner-city high schools	Kemple, Herlihy, and Smith (2005)	Small learning communities within high schools, accelerated math and English homework, intensive remediation for students, staff development, parental involvement	Attendance,[a] test scores, courses completed and credits earned,[a] algebra pass rate,[a] and promotion rates of ninth-grade students to tenth grade[a]
Youth Opportunity Grant Initiative	Nonexperimental analysis of education and employment outcomes for youth in thirty-six grantee neighborhoods compared to a set of low-income neighborhoods	Jackson et al. (2007)	Comprehensive services provided to both in-school and out-of-school youth (ages 14–21) to encourage schooling and employment	School enrollment, full-time and part-time employment, wages

(continued)

Appendix (continued)

Program	Study Description	Authors (Study Year)	Program Mechanism	Outcomes Examined
Out-of-school youth interventions				
Job Corps	Random assignment study of over 15,000 youth in 1994–1995, including four years of survey data and nine years of administrative records on earnings; nonexperimental analysis of data on 15,386 participants	Schochet, Burghardt, and McConnell (2008)	Intensive vocational/job and life skills training through residential component, vocational curricula with business and labor organization input to prepare youth for work in a specific trade, basic skills training to earn a GED, assistance with housing, referrals for substance abuse treatment and other health/mental health issues	Enrollment in education and training programs (increases in receipt of GED and vocational certificates[a]), wages, earnings (older youth[a] and younger youth), occupation, and crime/arrest rates
American Conservation and Youth Service Corps	Random assignment impact evaluation and cost-benefit analysis of national and community service programs of American Conservation and Youth Service Corps, including eight programs and 2,382 participants over 15 months	Yastrzab et al. (1996)	Full-time, team-based residential program for men and women ages 18–24; team-based national and community service in partnership with nonprofit, state and local, faith-based, and other community organizations; training in CPR, first aid, public safety, and other skills	Participants more likely to have worked for pay and worked more hours. Not significant results: participants less likely to be arrested and earn a technical degree (Corps was a substitute for enrollment)
National Guard ChalleNGe	Random assignment impact evaluation of 3,000 participants in ten programs and program annual reports of outcomes for cadets (graduation rates, academic achievement, and job placements)	Bloom (2009); National Guard Bureau (2005)	Seventeen-month program: two-week Pre-ChalleNGe orientation and assessment, 20-week Residential Phase, one-year Post-residential Phase; Residential Phase curriculum with core components on leadership, citizenship, community service, life-coping skills, fitness/health/hygiene, job skills, and academic excellence; post-residential placements in employment, education, and military service	Earned high school diploma or GED;[a] working full time;[a] in high school or GED prep; enrolled in college courses;[a] enrolled in job training;[a] arrested, convicted,[a] in jail, prison, or detention center;[a] self-rating of health, BMI (overweight, obese[a]), self-efficacy

(continued)

185

Appendix (continued)

Program	Authors (Study Year)	Study Description	Program Mechanism	Outcomes Examined
Center for Employment Training	Miller et al. (2005); Walsh et al. (2000)	Random assignment impact evaluation with 1,136 participants and 30- and 54-month follow-up, and study of implementation experiences in twelve sites	Employment and training services that mirror the workplace (trainings include occupational, basic skills, full-time, self-paced, and competency-based, and operated on an open-entry, open-exit basis); close involvement of industry in program design and operation	Ever worked during follow-up period[a] (positive for women), number of months worked in six-month intervals, average annual earnings, average wage at most recent job,[a] hours worked at most recent job,[a] household structure/living arrangements/size/status, child care/Head Start,[a] alcohol use,[a] marijuana use,[a] arrests
YouthBuild	GAO (2007)	Nonexperimental studies including a review of literature on YouthBuild programs, comparisons with other youth programs, an examination of the Department of Housing and Urban Development records, site visits to twenty YouthBuild grantees, and cost-effectiveness analyses	Alternative school with small classes for work toward GED or high school diplomas; job training and preapprenticeship program, including training in construction skills; leadership development and civic engagement; community service through construction of affordable housing; personal counseling, life planning processes and YouthBuild Alumni Association	Percentage of youth in employment (including the military) or enrolled in postsecondary education or advanced training or occupational skills training; percentage of participants who attain a diploma, GED, or certificate; percentage of youth who increase their basic educational functioning level in literacy or numeracy; average cost per participant

a. Experimental impact.

Notes

1. "Scale" refers to program size.

2. This study used a lottery to generate random admissions to HCZ charter school, as well as instrumental variable methods to measure HCZ's impact.

3. The four sites in the OD example include one in Kingsborough (Brooklyn) that created small learning communities; another in Louisiana that primarily focused on financial supplements of $2,000 per year, along with Pell grants; two in Ohio that provided supplemental services and a very modest ($300 per year) stipend; and two programs in Southern California that provided remedial services for those on probation. While all sites generated at least some modest short-term impacts on enrollments and credits earned, the largest and most lasting impacts seem to be generated by the financial supplements in Louisiana and mandatory participation in remedial programs for probation students in California.

4. See, for example, the Youth Development Institute (2008) for a broader list of programs—including Dare to Dream, First Things First, I Have a Dream, and Project Grad—that rely on many of the same approaches described in this section. Most of these have not been rigorously evaluated or scaled up in any major way.

5. Some smaller programs that use these strategies and have been evaluated, such as Check and Connect, have generated impacts on dropout rates as well (Tyler and Lofstrom 2009).

6. Achieving the Dream is setting up programs in eighty-three community colleges in fifteen states. These programs focus heavily on advising and counseling for low-income students, curricular changes, and other institutional reforms. Career Pathway programs now operate statewide in at least a half dozen states.

7. I-BEST fully integrates remedial and occupational training by coassigning teachers for each to every course taken by students. An econometric analysis by Jenkins, Zeidenberg, and Kienzl (2009) suggests positive impacts on test scores and credits earned for enrollees.

8. A recent econometric analysis of Tech-Prep also indicates that it reduces dropping out and improves enrollments in two-year colleges but has modest negative impacts on enrollments in four-year colleges (Lerman 2007).

9. The YIEPP was canceled in 1981 before there was a chance to see whether impacts on employment or earnings would persist over time. See Bloom (2009).

10. The Talent Development High Schools evaluation focused on seven low-income high schools in Philadelphia. In addition to small learning communities, this program emphasizes a heavy focus on English and math classes, intensive remediation, staff development, and parental involvement. Positive impacts on attendance, credits attained, promotions to tenth grade, and algebra pass rates were observed there.

11. The evaluation compared outcomes of *all* youths living in these thirty-six neighborhoods to those residing in comparable low-income neighborhoods not participating in the program. The fact that outcomes are measured for all residents rather than only program participants directly reflects the fact that the program was designed to "saturate" a neighborhood with services and thus change local behavior and norms regarding schooling and employment.

12. A range of local efforts to reconnect high school dropouts to schools and employment are described in Martin and Halperin (2006). Another promising effort is the Gateways Program, which began at Portland Community College and attempts to "reconnect" high school dropouts to high school completion efforts on community college campuses, with the hope that some might seamlessly enroll in community college courses once they achieve their high school diplomas.

13. Cohen and Piquero (2008) provide some econometric evidence of significant positive impacts on educational attainment as well as reduced recidivism for a small sample enrolled in a special YouthBuild program for ex-offenders.

14. Jastrzab et al. (1996) report impressive 15-month impacts on employment and reduced behavioral problems from a random assignment evaluation of a small number of Conservation and Youth Service Corps sites. A larger random assignment evaluation focusing on more sites and longer term impacts is now under way.

15. Community college attendance at the "high-fidelity" sites in California was unusually high for control group members, which likely generates a negative bias in impact estimates.

16. Cost figure is for 2007; see www.whitehouse.gov/omb/expectmore/detail/10002372.2007.html.

17. See Redcross et al. (2009), who present evaluation evidence on the Center for Employment Opportunities in New York City. These findings are fairly consistent with those on the National Supported Work (NSW) program. While the early evaluation evidence suggested no impacts, Uggen's (2000) reanalysis of the data shows that the program reduced recidivism for men in their late 20s and older.

18. As of this writing, another emergency jobs bill has passed in the U.S. House of Representatives but not yet in the Senate.

19. These calculations assume that we would provide relatively intensive services (averaging $15,000 per year) to some students and less intensive ones (averaging $5,000) to an equal number of others.

20. For a proposal of a competitive grant program for states to build systematic "advancement" systems for disadvantaged adults and youths alike, see Holzer (2007).

21. Other recent proposals in Congress to create competitive grant programs for education and training of disadvantaged youths include the Graduation Promise Act, which would provide grants to states for dropout prevention, and Promoting Innovations to 21st Century Careers for grants to states to build partnerships between employers and community colleges that generate more career pathways.

References

Anderson-Butcher, Dawn, W. Sean Newsome, and Theresa M. Ferrari. 2003. Participation in Boys and Girls Clubs and relationships to youth outcomes. *Journal of Community Psychology* 31 (1): 39–55.

Arbreton, Amy J. A., and Wendy S. McClanahan. 2002. *Targeted outreach: Boys & Girls Clubs of America's approach to gang prevention and intervention*. Philadelphia, PA: Public/Private Ventures.

Balfanz, Robert, Ruth Curran Neild, and Liza Herzog. 2007. An early warning system. *Educational Leadership* 65 (2): 28–33.

Barnow, Burt, and Jeffrey Smith. 2004. Performance management of U.S. job training programs. In *Job training policy in the United States*, eds. Christopher J. O'Leary, Robert O. Straits, and Stephen A. Wandner, 21–56. Kalamazoo, MI: W. E. Upjohn Institute for Employment Research.

Berik, Gunseli, and Cihan Bilginsoy. 2000. Do unions help or hinder women in training? Apprenticeship programs in the United States. *Industrial Relations* 39 (4): 600–624.

Bilginsoy, Cihan. 2003. The hazards of training: Attrition and retention in construction industry apprenticeship programs. *Industrial and Labor Relations Review* 57 (1): 54–67.

Bloom, Dan. 2009. Out-of-school youth and the transition to adulthood. MDRC Working Paper, New York, NY.

Bloom, Dan, Alissa Gardenhire-Crooks, and Conrad Mandsager. 2009. *Reengaging high school dropouts: Early results of the National Guard ChalleNGe Program evaluation*. New York, NY: MDRC.

Bowles, Anne, and Betsy Brand. 2009. *Learning around the clock: Benefits of expanded learning opportunities for older youth*. Washington, DC: American Youth Policy Forum.

Chicago Public Schools. 2007. *The 2007 Supplemental Educational Services Program: Year 4 summative evaluation*. Chicago, IL: Chicago Public Schools Office of Extended Learning Opportunities, Research, Evaluation and Accountability.

Cohen, Mark, and Alex Piquero. 2008. *Costs and benefits of a targeted intervention program for youthful offenders: The YouthBuild USA Youthful Offender Project*. Nashville, TN: Vanderbilt University.

Consortium on Chicago School Research. 2007. *What matters for staying on-track and graduating in Chicago public high schools: A close look at course grades, failures, and attendance in the freshman year*. Chicago, IL: Consortium on Chicago School Research.

Cunningham, Alisa, Christina Redmond, and Jamie Merisotis. 2003. *Investing early: Intervention programs in selected U.S. states*. Montreal: Canada Millennium Scholarship Foundation.

Danziger, Sheldon, and Peter Gottschalk. 1995. *America unequal*. New York, NY: Russell Sage Foundation.

Decision Information Resources, Inc. 2008. *Executive summary. Youth Opportunity Grant Initiative: Impact and synthesis report*. Houston, TX: Decision Information Resources, Inc. Available from http://wdr.doleta.gov/research/FullText_Documents/YO%20Impact%20and%20Synthesis%20Report.pdf.

Dobbie, Will, and Roland Fryer. 2009. *Are high-quality schools enough to close the achievement gap? Evidence from a bold social experiment in Harlem*. Cambridge, MA: Harvard University.

Dynarski, Mark, Susanne James-Burdumy, Mary Moore, Linda Rosenberg, John Deke, and Wendy Mansfield. 2004. *When schools stay open late: The national evaluation of the 21st Century Community Learning Centers Program: New findings*. Washington, DC: U.S. Government Printing Office.

Dynarski, Susan, and Judith Scott-Clayton. 2007. *College grants on a postcard: A proposal for simple and predictable federal student aid*. Washington, DC: Brookings Institution.

Edelman, Peter, Mark Greenberg, and Harry Holzer. 2009. *The administration and Congress should adopt a comprehensive approach to youth education, employment and connection*. Washington, DC: Georgetown Center on Poverty, Inequality and Public Policy, Georgetown University.

Edelman, Peter, Harry Holzer, and Paul Offner. 2006. *Reconnecting disadvantaged young men*. Washington, DC: Urban Institute Press.

Ellwood, David, and Elisabeth Welty. 2000. Public service employment and mandatory work: A policy whose time has come and gone and come again? In *Finding jobs: Work and welfare reform*, eds. David E. Card and Rebecca M. Blank. New York, NY: Russell Sage Foundation.

Finch, Nicole L., and Kimberley S. Cowley. 2003. *Fairmont State College GEAR UP Project: Year 4 baseline seventh-grade survey and tenth-grade follow-up survey*. Charleston, WV: AEL, Inc.

Gottschalk, Peter. 1997. The impact of changes in public employment on low-wage labor markets. In *Generating jobs: How to increase demand for less-skilled workers*, eds. Richard B. Freeman and Peter Gottschalk. New York, NY: Russell Sage Foundation.

Government Accountability Office (GAO). 2007. *YouthBuild: Analysis of outcome data needed to determine long-term benefits*. GAO-07-82. Washington, DC: GAO.

Guthrie, Larry F., and Grace Pung Guthrie. 2001. *Longitudinal research on AVID, 1999–2000: Final report*. Burlingame, CA: Center for Research, Evaluation and Training in Education.

Hahn, Andrew. 1994. *Evaluation of the Quantum Opportunities Program (QOP). Did the program work? A report on the post-secondary outcomes and cost-effectiveness of the QOP Program (1989–1993)*. Waltham, MA: Center for Human Resources, Brandeis University.

Harris, Linda, and Evelyn Ganzglass. 2008. *Creating post-secondary pathways to good jobs for young school dropouts: The possibilities and the challenges*. Washington, DC: Center for American Progress.

Haskins, Ron, Harry Holzer, and Robert Lerman. 2009. *Promoting economic mobility by increasing post-secondary education*. Washington, DC: Economic Mobility Project, Pew Charitable Trusts.

Heckman, James. 2008. Schools, skills and synapses. National Bureau of Economic Research Working Paper 14064, Cambridge, MA.

Heckman, James, and Paul LaFontaine. 2007. The American high school graduation rate: Trends and levels. National Bureau of Economic Research Working Paper 13670, Cambridge, MA.

Heinrich, Carolyn J., Robert H. Meyer, and Greg Whitten. 2010. Supplemental education services under No Child Left Behind: Who signs up, and what do they gain? *Educational Evaluation and Policy Analysis* 32 (2): 273 [1/n] 98.

Herrera, Carla, Jean Baldwin Grossman, Tina J. Kauh, Amy F. Feldman, Jennifer McMaken, and Linda Z. Jucovy. 2007. *Making a difference in schools: The Big Brothers Big Sisters school-based mentoring impact study*. Philadelphia, PA: Public/Private Ventures.

Holzer, Harry. 2007. *Better workers for better jobs: Improving worker advancement in the low-wage labor market*. Washington, DC: The Hamilton Project, Brookings Institution.

Holzer, Harry. 2009. Workforce development as an antipoverty strategy: What do we know? What should we do? In *Changing poverty, changing policies*, eds. Maria Cancian and Sheldon Danziger. New York, NY: Russell Sage Foundation.

Jackson, Russell H., R. Malené Dixon, Ann McCoy, Carol Pistorino, Paul Zador, Cynthia Thomas, John Lopdell, Juanita Lucas-McLean, Frank Bennici, Andy Sum, et al. 2007. *Youth Opportunity Grant Initiative: Impact and synthesis report*. Houston, TX: Decision Information Resources, Inc.

Jacobson, Louis, and Christine Mokher. 2009. *Pathways to boosting the earnings of low-income students by increasing their educational attainment*. Washington, DC: Hudson Institute and Center for Naval Analysis.

Jastrzab, JoAnn, Julie Masker, John Blomquist, and Larry Orr. 1996. *Evaluation of national and community service programs. Impacts of service: Final report on the evaluation of American Conservation and Youth Service Corps*. Washington, DC: Abt Associates.

Jenkins, Davis, Matthew Zeidenberg, and Greg Kienzl. 2009. *Educational outcomes of I-BEST, Washington state community and technical college system's Integrated Basic Education and Skills Training program: Findings from a multivariate analysis*. New York, NY: Community College Research Center.

Kemple, James, Corinne Herlihy, and Thomas Smith. 2005. *Making progress toward graduation. Evidence from the Talent Development High School model*. New York, NY: MDRC.

Kemple, James J., and Cynthia J. Willner. 2008. *Career academies: Long-term impacts on labor market outcomes, educational attainment, and transitions to adulthood*. New York, NY: MDRC.

Lauer, Patricia A., Motoko Akiba, Stephanie B. Wilkerson, Helen S. Athorp, David Snow, and Mya L. Martin-Glenn. 2006. Out-of-school-time programs: A meta-analysis of effects for at-risk students. *Review of Educational Research* 76 (2): 275–313.

Lerman, Robert. 2007. Career-focused education and training for youth. In *Reshaping the American workforce in a changing economy*, eds. Harry J. Holzer and Demetra Smith Nightingale. Washington, DC: Urban Institute Press.

Loprest, Pamela J., and Karin Martinson. 2008. *Supporting work for low-income people with significant challenges*. Washington, DC: The Urban Institute.

Martin, Nancy, and Samuel Halperin. 2006. *Whatever it takes: How twelve communities are reconnecting out-of-school youth*. Washington, DC: American Youth Policy Forum.

Maxfield, Myles, Allen L. Schirm, and Nuria Rodriguez-Planas. 2003. The Quantum Opportunity Program demonstration. U.S. Department of Labor, Employment and Training Administration Occasional Paper, 2003-05, Washington, DC.

Miller, Cynthia, Johannes M. Bos, Kristin E. Porter, Fannie M. Tseng, and Yasuyo Abe. 2005. *The challenge of repeating success in a changing world: Final report on the Center for Employment Training Replication Sites*. New York, NY: MDRC.

Myers, David, and Allen Schirm. 1999. *The impacts of regular Upward Bound: Results from the third follow-up data collection*. Washington, DC: Mathematica Policy Research, Inc.

National Guard Bureau. 2005. *National Guard Youth ChalleNGe program: 2005 performance and accountability highlights*. Chantilly, VA: AOC Solutions, Inc.

Neild, Ruth Curran, and Robert Balfanz. 2006. *Unfulfilled promise: The dimension and characteristics of Philadelphia's dropout crisis, 2000–2005*. Philadelphia, PA: Philadelphia Youth Network, Johns Hopkins University, and University of Pennsylvania.

New Jersey Commission on Higher Education. 2005. *Preparing New Jersey students for college and careers: Evaluation of New Jersey GEAR UP*. Trenton: New Jersey Commission on Higher Education.

New York City Department of Education. 2006. *Multiple pathways research and development: Summary findings and strategic solutions for over-age under-credited youth*. New York, NY: Office of Multiple Pathways to Graduation.

Philliber, Susan, Jacqueline Williams Kaye, Scott Herrling, and Emily West. 2002. Preventing pregnancy and improving health care access among teenagers: An evaluation of the Children's Aid Society-Carrera Program. *Perspectives on Sexual and Reproductive Health* 34 (5): 244–51.

Redcross, Cindy, Dan Bloom, Gilda Azurdia, Janine Zweig, and Nancy Pindus. 2009. *Transitional jobs for ex-prisoners: Implementation, two-year impacts, and costs of the Center for Employment Opportunities (CEO) Prisoner Reentry Program*. New York, NY: MDRC.

Rhodes, Jean E. 2005. A model of youth mentoring. In *Handbook of youth mentoring*, eds. David L. DuBois and Michael J. Karcher, 30–43. Thousand Oaks, CA: Sage.

Rhodes, Jean E., and David L. DuBois. 2008. Mentoring relationships and programs for youth. *Current Directions in Psychological Science* 17 (4): 254–58.

Rhodes, Jean E., Jean Baldwin Grossman, and Nancy L. Resch. 2000. Agents of change: Pathways through which mentoring relationships influence adolescents' academic adjustment. *Child Development* 71 (6): 1662–71.

Richburg-Hayes, Lashawn, Thomas Brock, Allen LeBlanc, Christina Paxson, Cecilia Elena Rouse, and Lisa Barrow. 2009. *Rewarding persistence: Effects of a performance based scholarship program for low income parents*. New York, NY: MDRC.

Rickles, Jordan H., and Melissa K. Barnhart. 2007. *The impact of supplemental educational services participation on student achievement: 2005–06*. Los Angeles, CA: Los Angeles Unified School District Program Evaluation and Research Branch, Planning, Assessment and Research Division Publication No. 352.

Schochet, Peter Z., John Burghardt, and Sheena McConnell. 2008. Does Job Corps work? Impact findings from the National Job Corps Study. *American Economic Review* 98 (5): 1864–86.

Spielman, Seth E., Cynthia A. Golembeski, Mary E. Northridge, Roger D. Vaughan, Rachel Swaner, Betina Jean-Louis, Katherine Shoemaker, Sandra Klihr-Beall, Eric Polley, Linda F. Cushman, et al. 2006. Interdisciplinary planning for healthier communities: Findings from the Harlem Children's Zone Asthma Initiative. *Journal of the American Institute of Planners* 72 (1): 100–108.

Standing, Kim, David Judkins, Brad Keller, and Amy Shimshak. 2008. *Early outcomes of the GEAR UP Program*. Washington, DC: U.S. Department of Education.

Sum, Andrew, Joseph McLaughlin, Sheila Palma, Jacqui Motroni, and Ishwar Khatiwada. 2008. Out with the young and in with the old: U.S. labor markets 2000–2008 and the case for an immediate jobs creation program for teens and young adults. Working Paper, Northeastern University, Boston, MA.

Tierney, Joseph P., Jean Baldwin Grossman, and Nancy L. Resch. 1995. *Making a difference: An impact study of Big Brothers Big Sisters*. Philadelphia, PA: Public/Private Ventures.

Turner, Sarah. 2007. Higher education policies generating the 21st century workforce. In *Reshaping the American workforce in a changing economy*, eds. H. Holzer and D. Nightingale. Washington, DC: Urban Institute Press.

Tyler, John H., and Magnus Lofstrom. 2009. Finishing high school: Alternative pathways and dropout recovery. *The Future of Children* 19 (1): 77–103.

Uggen, Christopher. 2000. Work as a turning point in the life course of criminals: A duration model of age, employment and recidivism. *American Journal of Sociology* 65 (4): 529–46.

U.S. Department of Education. 2004. *The impacts of regular Upward Bound: Results from the third follow-up data collection*. Washington, DC: Policy and Program Studies Service.

Vandell, Deborah L., Elizabeth R. Reisner, B. Bradford Brown, Kimberly Dadisman, Kim M. Pierce, Dale Lee, and Ellen M. Pechman. 2005. *The study of promising after-school programs: Examination of intermediate outcomes in Year 2*. Madison: Wisconsin Center for Education Research.

Van Kannel-Ray, Nancy, Warren E. Lacefield, and Pamela J. Zeller. 2008. Academic case managers: Evaluating a middle school intervention for children at risk. *Journal of MultiDisciplinary Evaluation* 5 (10): 21–29.

Walsh, Stephen, Deana Goldsmith, Yasuyo Abe, and Andrea Cann. 2000. *Evaluation of the Center for Employment Training Replication Sites: Interim report*. Washington, DC: Office of Policy Research, U.S. Department of Labor, Employment, and Training Administration.

Watt, Karen M., Darlene Yanez, and Griselda Cossio. 2002. AVID: A comprehensive school reform model for Texas. *National Forum of Educational Administration and Supervision Journal* 19 (3): 43–59.

Yastrzab, JoAnn, Julie Masker, John Blomquist, and Larry Orr. 1996. *Evaluation of national and community service programs. Impacts of service: Final report on the evaluation of American Conservation and Youth Service Corps*. Cambridge, MA: Abt Associates, Inc.

Youth Development Institute. 2008. *What works for young adult learners*. New York, NY: Youth Development Institute.

Zimmer, Ron, Brian Gill, Paula Razquin, Kevin Booker, and J. R. Lockwood III. 2007. *State and local implementation of the No Child Left Behind Act: Volume I—Title I School Choice, supplemental educational services, and student achievement*. Washington, DC: Evaluation and Policy Development, U.S. Department of Education.

Incarceration and Prisoner Reentry in the United States

By
STEVEN RAPHAEL

This article addresses the reentry challenges faced by low-skilled men released from U.S. prisons. The author empirically characterizes the increases in incarceration occurring since 1970 and assesses the degree to which these changes result from changes in policy as opposed to changes in criminal behavior. The author discusses what is known about the children of inmates and the likelihood that a child in the United States has an incarcerated parent. The article then addresses the employment barriers that former prison inmates face, with a particular emphasis on how employers view criminal records in screening job applicants. Finally, the author discusses a number of alternative models for aiding the reentry of former inmates. Transitional cash assistance, the use of reentry plans, traditional workforce development efforts, and transitional jobs for former inmates all are among the tools used across the United States. The author reviews the existing evaluation literature on the effectiveness of these programmatic interventions.

Keywords: prisoner reentry; incarceration; workforce development

Over the past 30 years in the United States, state governments and the federal government have increased the frequency with which incarceration is used to sanction criminal activity as well as the length of the sentences imposed and ultimate time served for specific offenses. Through myriad sentencing policy changes and changes in postrelease supervision, the nation's incarceration rate has increased to unprecedented levels and now exceeds that of every other country. For lesser-educated men, and especially less-educated minority men, the likelihood of serving prison time is high (many are more likely to serve time than not). Moreover, among certain subgroups of noninstitutionalized men, large proportions have served prison time in the past.

Steven Raphael is a professor of public policy at the University of California, Berkeley. His research focuses on the economics of low-wage labor markets, housing, crime, and corrections.

DOI: 10.1177/0002716210393321

The challenges that former inmates face when attempting to reenter noninstitutionalized society are vast. Many have tenuous housing arrangements. Prison time weakens social connections to families and friends. Most former inmates have poor job skills and face stigma associated with their criminal records. Many of these reentrants fail and are sent back to prison, often for violating the conditions of their supervised release but sometimes for the commission of new felony offenses. Such failures are costly, as admitting someone anew to prison costs more than supervision in the community, and new victimizations are clearly a social cost.

Moreover, the adverse effects of incarceration and failed reentry extend beyond the inmates themselves. In 2007, roughly 52 percent of state prisoners and 63 percent of prisoners in federal penitentiaries had children under the age of 18 (Glaze and Maruschak 2009). Many of these inmates lived with their children prior to their incarceration. In total, 2.3 percent of children in the United States had a parent in prison in 2007. The proportion with parents who have ever done time in prison is certainly higher.

In this article, I discuss the reentry challenges faced by increasing numbers of low-skilled men released from prison each year. I begin with an empirical description of the magnitude of the issue. Since the mid-1970s, the U.S. incarceration rate has increased more than fourfold largely due to policy choices pertaining to sentencing and the postrelease monitoring of parolees. This increase has disproportionately affected less-educated black men and has greatly increased the lifetime risk of serving time. I document these changes and describe what is known about who currently serves and who will eventually serve time. I discuss what is known about the children of inmates and the likelihood that a child in the United States has an incarcerated parent.

Former inmates face a number of challenges upon leaving prison that greatly impede their employment prospects. Low formal levels of schooling, low levels of accumulated labor market experience, and employer reluctance to hire former inmates are among these barriers. I empirically document these challenges. I also review the research pertaining to how employers view criminal records in screening job applicants.

Finally, I discuss a number of alternative models for aiding the reentry transition of former inmates. Transitional cash assistance, the use of reentry plans, traditional workforce development efforts, and transitional jobs for former inmates are among the tools used across the United States. I review the existing evaluation literature on these programmatic interventions with regard to their impacts on postrelease employment and recidivism and highlight potential fruitful policy options.

Why Are So Many Americans in Prison?

The United States currently incarcerates its residents at a very high rate. Combining state and federal prisoners and local jail inmates, there were 765 inmates per 100,000 U.S. residents in 2007.[1] This compares with a world average of

FIGURE 1
Prisoners in State or Federal Prison per 100,000 U.S. Residents, 1925–2007

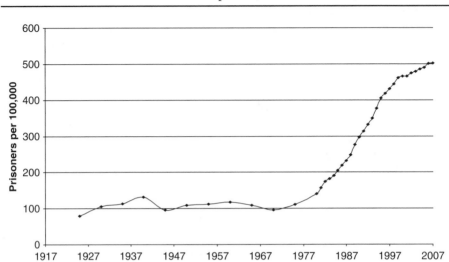

SOURCE: National Prisoner Statistics, various years.

166 per 100,000 and an average among European Union member states of 135 (International Centre for Prison Studies 2007). Of the approximately 2.3 million U.S. residents incarcerated in 2007, roughly 66 percent were inmates in state and federal prisons, while the remaining 34 percent resided in local jails.

Current U.S. incarceration rates are also unusually high relative to historical figures for the United States. Figure 1 displays historical data on state and federal prison inmates per 100,000 U.S. residents. Prior to the mid-1970s, the incarceration rate was stable, hovering in a narrow band around 110 inmates per 100,000 people. Thereafter, however, the incarceration rate increased precipitously. Between 1975 and 2007, the prison incarceration rate more than quadrupled, from 111 to 502 per 100,000. The annual incarceration rate increased by an average of 15.7 inmates per 100,000 per year during the 1980s, 16.8 inmates per year during the 1990s, and 5 inmates per year during the first 7 years of the new century.

Behind this steady increase in the incarceration rate are large flows of inmates into and out of the nation's prisons. While there are certainly many prisoners who are serving very long sentences in the nation's penitentiaries, there are many more U.S. residents who serve relatively short spells in prison or who cycle in and out of correctional institutions serving sequential short spells over substantial portions of their adult lives. As demonstrated by Travis (2005), nearly all inmates are eventually released from prison, most within five years of admission. Most tellingly, annual admissions to U.S. prisons have consistently hovered around one-half the size of the prison population, while slightly less than half of all inmates are released in any given year.

Changes in incarceration rates are driven by three broad categories of factors that likely exert reciprocal influences on one another. First, the incarceration rate depends on crime rates. Second, the incarceration rate will be higher the greater the likelihood that someone who commits a crime is sent to prison. Finally, the longer the amount of time that an individual committed to prison can expect to serve, the higher the incarceration rate. These three factors can be measured by the crime rate, the number of prison commitments per crime committed, and the expected time served conditional on being sent to prison.

Table 1 presents estimates of these values for 1984 and 2002 from my research with Michael Stoll (Raphael and Stoll 2009), using National Corrections Reporting Program (NCRP) data for various years as well as data from the Uniform Crime Reports.[2] There are sizable increases in the expected time served within all crime categories. In other words, conditional on being sent to prison, and conditional on the crime committed, felons admitted in 2002 faced much longer prison spells than offenders admitted in 1984.

For the nation as a whole, prison admissions per 100,000 U.S. residents increased considerably between 1984 and 2002 (from 98.41 to 223.12). This large overall increase was driven primarily by increases in prison admissions for drug offenses and parole violations. In Raphael and Stoll (2009), we found very little evidence of an increase in arrest rates for specific crimes. Thus, the increased admission rates reflect entirely an increase in the propensity to punish apprehended offenders with a spell in prison. While it is impossible to assess whether reoffending among parolees has increased, it is worth noting that over the time period covered in Table 1, the annual parole failure rate increased appreciably.

Finally, comparing crime rates in 1984 and 2002 reveals sizable declines in crime, especially property crime. While there is a notable increase in drug crime, it should be kept in mind that drug crimes are measured by arrests in Table 1. Hence, this surely reflects changes in policy regarding drug enforcement as well as possible changes in offending levels.

If one were willing to assume that, holding "offense" constant, those being admitted in the latter year are comparable to those admitted in the earlier year, then a natural interpretation of the patterns described in Table 1 is that sentencing and parole policy have become much tougher. The table indicates that there is a small role for crime trends.

Of course, current crime rates are certainly lower today as a result of the massive increases in incarceration rates. Higher incarceration rates incapacitate a larger proportion of the population (i.e., an adult behind bars cannot commit crime in noninstitutionalized society), and the higher incarceration risk may deter some would-be offenders. Even accounting for this fact, however, increases in crime cannot explain a substantial portion of incarceration growth.

The column in Table 1 labeled "2002 Counterfactual" provides our best guess of what crime rates would have been had sentencing practices in the United States not changed since 1984.[3] Crime would certainly have been higher in the absence of sentencing changes due to less incapacitation and deterrence, and

TABLE 1
Comparison of Expected Time Served, Prison
Admission Rates, Incarceration Risk per Crime, and Crime Rates
for the United States by Type of Criminal Offense, 1984 and 2002

	Expected Time Served in Years		Prison Admissions per 100,000 U.S. residents		Crime Rate per 100,000			Prison Admissions per Crime Committed	
							2002		
	1984	2002	1984	2002	1984	2002	Counterfactual	1984	2002
Murder	6.49	8.13	5.47	4.98	7.92	5.63	6.95	0.69	0.89
Rape	2.98	5.30	4.35	7.70	35.71	33.11	42.01	0.12	0.23
Robbery	3.13	3.80	12.51	9.97	205.44	146.12	207.38	0.06	0.07
Assault	2.01	2.86	5.00	12.03	290.23	309.54	309.50	0.02	0.04
Other violent	2.30	3.47	1.72	3.53	21.34[a]	35.65[a]	44.45[c]	0.06[e]	0.10[e]
Burglary	1.99	2.48	19.08	14.21	1263.70	747.22	1,034.25	0.02	0.02
Larceny	1.44	2.17	13.93	17.83	2791.30	2,450.72	2,915.05	0.00	0.01
Motor vehicle	1.42	1.87	0.99	2.79	437.11	432.91	564.38	0.00	0.01
Other property	1.52	2.49	3.01	4.98	828.26[a]	725.46[a]	904.65[c]	0.00[f]	0.01[f]
Drugs	1.63	2.11	8.73	43.93	264.31[b]	469.68[b]	469.68[d]	0.03	0.09
Other	2.92	2.27	12.45	20.26	138.37[a]	184.18[a]	229.67[c]	0.06[g]	0.07[g]
Parole violators	1.27	1.44	20.48	80.75	—	—		—	—

NOTE: Time served estimates come from Raphael and Stoll (2009). Each value is rescaled so that the expected value of time served is equal to the value implied by the national prison release rate for the year described. Prison admissions rates are estimated by applying the distribution of admissions by offense category estimated from the 1984 and 2002 National Corrections Reporting Program files to the overall national admissions rates. Crime rates are based on the Uniform Crime Reports unless otherwise noted. Counterfactual crime rates are estimated using crime-specific incapacitation and deterrence effect estimates of incarceration on crime taken from Johnson and Raphael (2007).
a. Crime rate estimates based on imputed admissions per crime and the observed admissions rates.
b. Crime rates for drug crimes are equal to the number of adult arrests for drug crimes per 100,000 U.S. residents.
c. Assumes a 25 percent increase in offending above the 2002 level (equal to the 2002 admissions weighted sum of the predicted increase above 2002 for the seven Part 1 offenses).
d. Set equal to the arrest rate for 2002.
e. Based on average admissions per crime committed for nonhomicide violent crimes by year.
f. Based on average admissions per crime committed for nonburglary property crimes by year.
g. Based on the weighted average admissions per crime for all crimes by year.

hence the incarceration rate would have increased. However, we tabulate that the incarceration rate would have increased by no more than 17 percent of the actual increase experienced over this time period, leaving the remaining 83 percent attributable to changes in policy. Moreover, even this 17 percent is likely to be an overestimate, as this tabulation attributes the entire increase in drug arrests to changes in behavior rather than changes in drug enforcement policy.[4] Hence, our

TABLE 2

Proportion Institutionalized among U.S. Adult Men, Ages 18 to 55, by Race/Ethnicity, Educational Attainment, and Age, 2007

	All	Non-Hispanic White	Non-Hispanic Black	Non-Hispanic Asian	Hispanic
All	.024	.014	.080	.006	.028
Less than high school					
All ages	.066	.049	.190	.023	.041
18 to 25	.080	.053	.181	.041	.061
26 to 35	.078	.064	.280	.048	.043
36 to 45	.060	.052	.200	.016	.033
46 to 55	.039	.029	.115	.010	.023
High school grad/GED					
All ages	.029	.019	.081	.010	.027
18 to 25	.025	.016	.065	.010	.024
26 to 35	.041	.026	.118	.017	.029
36 to 45	.032	.022	.085	.006	.030
46 to 55	.020	.013	.057	.006	.023
Some college					
All ages	.013	.008	.039	.006	.015
18 to 25	.007	.004	.015	.004	.012
26 to 35	.017	.011	.048	.012	.018
36 to 45	.017	.011	.051	.008	.018
46 to 55	.012	.007	.042	.003	.012
College graduate					
All ages	.002	.002	.011	.000	.004
18 to 25	.001	.001	.004	.001	.006
26 to 35	.002	.001	.011	.000	.002
36 to 45	.003	.002	.013	.000	.003
46 to 55	.003	.002	.011	.001	.007

SOURCE: American Community Survey (2007).

decomposition suggests behavior, in terms of variation in crime rates, is a big player in the story.[5] On the other hand, policy changes, in particular a large increase in the severity of punishment, is of first-order importance.

Who Served Time in the United States?

The impacts of changes in sentencing policy have not been borne equally across demographic groups. Those who are male, relatively less educated, and minority have experienced the largest increases in incarceration. Table 2 presents tabulations from the 2007 American Community Survey (ACS), demonstrating the proportion of various groups that were incarcerated in either prison or jail on a given day. The first notable pattern concerns the enormous racial disparities in

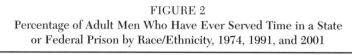

FIGURE 2
Percentage of Adult Men Who Have Ever Served Time in a State
or Federal Prison by Race/Ethnicity, 1974, 1991, and 2001

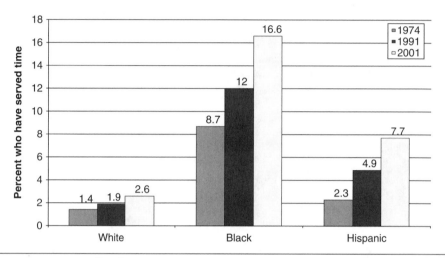

SOURCE: Bonczar (2003).

incarceration rates. While 1.4 percent of non-Hispanic whites and 0.6 percent of non-Hispanic Asians were incarcerated on any given day in 2007, 8 percent of African American men were in either jail or prison. The Hispanic male incarceration rate (2.8 percent), while lower than that for African Americans, is double that of white males.

There are even larger disparities among subpopulations defined by educational attainment and age. For all groups, the least educated have the highest incarceration rates. However, these rates are particularly high for black high school dropouts (19 percent compared with 5 percent for white male high school dropouts and 4.1 percent for Hispanic male high school dropouts). Among all race-education groups, the highest incarceration rates are observed for men ages 26 to 35. Again, the highest rates are observed for black men, with nearly 30 percent of black high school dropouts in this age range in prison or jail on any given day.

To be sure, the proportion of men who have ever served time is certainly higher. Most inmates eventually return to noninstitutionalized society and live the remainder of their lives outside of institutions, but usually after several failed attempts at reentry. Thus, increases in incarceration rates tend to leave in their wake increases in the population of former inmates.

Figure 2 presents estimates from the Bureau of Justice Statistics (BJS) of the percentage of adult men who have ever served time in a state or federal prison by race/ethnicity in 1974, 1991, and 2001. For African American men, this percentage increases from 8.7 percent to 16.6 percent between 1974 and 2001. We

FIGURE 3
Percentage of Adult Men Who Have Ever Served Time
in a State or Federal Prison by Race/Ethnicity and Age, 2001

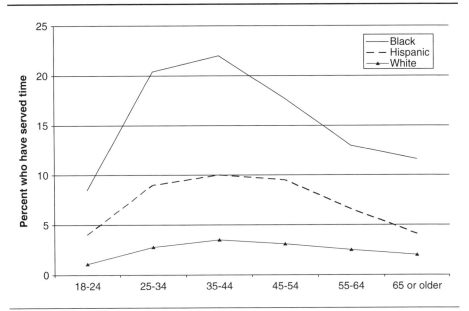

SOURCE: Bonczar (2003).

also observe increases for white and Hispanic men, though these are small by comparison. Figure 3 presents a further disaggregation of the 2001 estimates for specific age groups. Not surprisingly, the percentage that have ever served time is the highest for the age groups with the highest incarceration rates, with more than 20 percent of African American men between 25 and 44 years of age having served time at some point in their lives.

While the BJS does not present estimates of having ever served time by level of educational attainment, several researchers have investigated this question using longitudinal survey data as well as administrative prison records. In an analysis of administrative records from the California Department of Corrections, I have estimated that at the close of the 1990s, more than 90 percent of black male high school dropouts and 10 to 15 percent of black male high school graduates have served prison time in the state (Raphael 2005). Pettit and Western (2004) estimate that for all African American men born between 1965 and 1969, the proportion who have been to prison by 1999 was 20.5 percent for all black men, 30.2 percent for black men without a college degree, and 58.9 percent for black men without a high school degree.

A final summary measure of changes in the incidence of incarceration is the lifetime likelihood of serving time by year of birth. The BJS has published this projection for men by race and ethnicity, using incarceration rates and prison

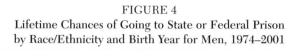

FIGURE 4
Lifetime Chances of Going to State or Federal Prison
by Race/Ethnicity and Birth Year for Men, 1974–2001

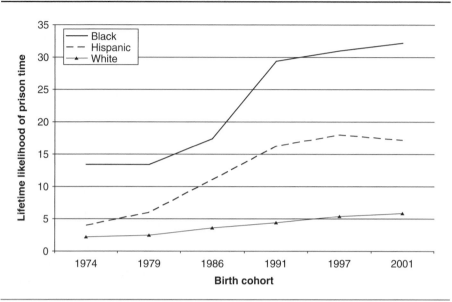

SOURCE: Bonczar (2003).

entry probabilities to forecast the likelihood that a child born in a specific year
will serve time. Figure 4 presents these projections for several years between
1974 and 2001. The lifetime likelihood of serving prison time for a black male
child born in 2001 stood at 32 percent. This compares with a lifetime risk of
13 percent for a black male child born in 1974. For Hispanic males, the lifetime
risk increases from 4 to 17.2 percent, while white males experience a more modest increase from 2 to 6 percent.

Thus, the U.S. incarceration rate has increased considerably. Moreover, given
the fluidity of prison populations, the population of noninstitutionalized former
inmates has grown continuously and now constitutes sizable minorities, and in
some instances majorities, of certain subgroups of U.S. men. The increase in
incarceration has been borne disproportionately by less-educated minority men.
Moreover, this increase is largely the result of policy choices pertaining to sentencing and parole policy rather than changes in criminal behavior.

The Children of the Incarcerated

While the likelihood of engaging in criminal activity increases during one's teen
years and peaks between the ages of 18 and 20, the likelihood of incarceration is

TABLE 3
Proportion of State and Federal Prison Inmates Who
Are the Parents of Minor Children by Gender and Age, 2004

	State Prison Inmates			Federal Prison Inmates		
	Total	Male	Female	Total	Male	Female
All inmates	.519	.512	.617	.629	.634	.559
24 or younger	.441	.435	.554	.458	.457	.475
25 to 34	.644	.633	.807	.741	.741	.745
35 to 44	.589	.583	.657	.719	.721	.682
45 to 54	.310	.314	.258	.470	.483	.312
55 or older	.126	.129	—	.238	.253	—

SOURCE: Glaze and Maruschak (2009; see Table 5).
NOTE: Missing data are due to insufficient observations in the underlying survey data.

highest for men between the ages of 25 and 34. This delay likely reflects the time difference between apprehension and sentencing, the impact of sentence length on the age distribution of inmates, and the apprehension of the criminally active during a period that is likely to represent the waning years of the most criminally active portions of their lives.

This age profile, however, also corresponds with periods of high fertility, meaning that many of the men and women behind bars are parents of minor children. Moreover, the large increases in incarceration rates experienced in the past few decades must correspond with large increases in the number and proportion of children who experience a parental incarceration.

Table 3 presents tabulations from Glaze and Maruschak (2009), showing the proportion of prison inmates with minor children by age, gender, and whether inmates are in state or federal prisons. Slightly more than half of male state prison inmates and 60 percent of female state prison inmates are the parents of children younger than 18 years of age. Among the age groups composing the bulk of the prison population (25–34 and 35–44), the proportion that are parents is considerably higher, with the figure reaching 80 percent among female state prisoners between 25 and 34. The patterns for federal prisoners are similar, although in federal prisons, male inmates are generally more likely to have minor children than are female inmates.

All in all, Glaze and Maruschak (2009) estimate that approximately 800,000 of the 1.5 million state and federal prisoners in the United States were the parents of 1.7 million minor children. Moreover, given the relatively high incarceration rates experienced by minority men, the incidence of parental incarceration differs greatly across racial groups. Figure 5 presents estimates from Glaze and Maruschak of the proportion of minor children in 2007 with a parent in either state or federal prison. Overall, 2.3 percent of minor children in 2007 had a parent in prison. The rate for white children was considerably below the national average (0.9 percent). The rate for black and Hispanic children was considerably

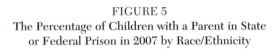

FIGURE 5
The Percentage of Children with a Parent in State
or Federal Prison in 2007 by Race/Ethnicity

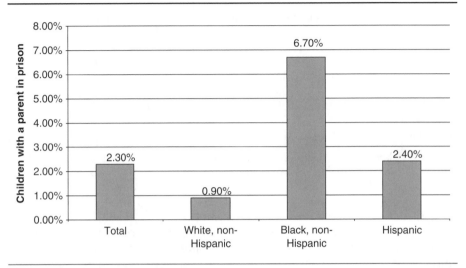

SOURCE: Glaze and Maruschak (2009).

above that for whites, with 6.7 percent of black children (7.4 times the rate for white children) and 2.4 percent of Hispanic children (2.6 times the rate for white children) having a parent incarcerated in 2007.

Little is known about the cumulative risks of experiencing a parental incarceration—that is, the proportion of children with at least one parent ever experiencing a prison spell or the proportion of children who will eventually experience a parental incarceration. Nonetheless, we know that the proportion of men who have ever been to prison is more than double the proportion of men incarcerated on any given day. Hence, one ballpark estimate of the proportion of children experiencing a parental incarceration would be double the rates presented in Figure 5.

Fortunately, we do have existing estimates of the cumulative risk of a paternal incarceration among children who reside at some point with their fathers. In an analysis of longitudinal data from the Panel Study of Income Dynamics (PSID), Johnson (2009) estimates the likelihood that PSID children born between 1968 and 2005 whose fathers lived with them at least one year during the study period experienced their fathers serving time in prison or jail. To be sure, these figures are likely to be biased estimates of the cumulative risk of paternal incarceration in prison due to a number of factors. First, many of these children were growing up during time periods when the incarceration risk was appreciably lower than today. Moreover, the sample selection criteria that the children must reside with their father for at least one year excludes all fathers who never live with their children (a group of men who are perhaps at higher risk of serving a prison spell). Both of

TABLE 4
Cumulative Risk of Paternal Incarceration among PSID Children
Born between 1968 and 2005 Who Lived with Their Fathers at Least One
Year between Birth and the Final Analysis Year by Race and Father's Education

		Father's Educational Attainment			
	All Children	HS Dropout	HS Grad/ GED	High School or Less	Greater than High School
Black children	18.66	32.20	19.51	22.91	9.89
White children	10.10	23.06	11.57	14.33	5.26

SOURCE: PSID data in Johnson (2009).
NOTE: The figures in Johnson (2009) present the proportion of children in this birth cohort, ever observed residing with their fathers, who experience a paternal incarceration at some point. Note that the figures do not include paternal incarceration among children who never reside with their fathers.

these considerations suggest that these estimates from the PSID were lower bound. Biasing in the other direction, measuring incarceration spells in prison or jail will capture many spells for relatively minor offenses and will certainly yield higher rates than one would find if the analysis focused on prisons specifically.

Table 4 presents Johnson's (2009) estimates of the proportion of children whose fathers serve a prison term. The table provides estimates for black and white children and by the father's level of education. Roughly 19 percent of black children in this cohort experience a paternal incarceration compared with 10 percent of white children in the sample. The incidence is highest among the children of the least educated men, with fully one-third of the children of black high school dropouts experiencing a paternal incarceration. Thus, the one estimate of cumulative risk of parental incarceration suggests that this rate is considerably higher than the point-in-time estimate of the proportion of children with an incarcerated parent on a specific day.

The impact of a parental incarceration on childhood outcomes is an important topic that is relatively understudied. It is quite easy to demonstrate that the children of the incarcerated have relatively poor outcomes in behavioral, educational, and criminal justice domains. It is harder, however, to disentangle the separate effects of parental incarceration from the impact on childhood outcomes of all of the other factors correlated with a parental incarceration (such as parental education, household poverty, neighborhood of residence, race/ethnicity, etc.). This debate regarding causality aside, it is hard to deny that a parental incarceration interrupts the lives of children and is likely to impose material hardships on the children and their families.

While I cannot sort out the issues surrounding causality in this brief discussion, I can discuss some of the key factors that may be affected by the incarceration of a parent. Perhaps the most immediate domain affected is the living arrangements of the children left behind. Glaze and Maruschak (2009) use a

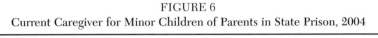

FIGURE 6
Current Caregiver for Minor Children of Parents in State Prison, 2004

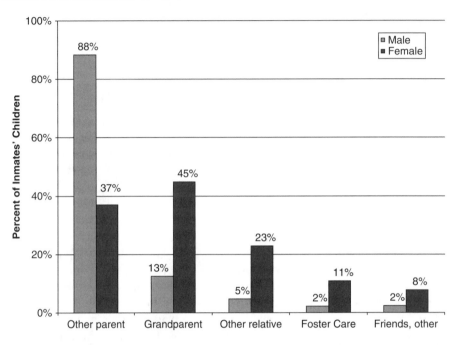

SOURCE: Glaze and Maruschak (2009).
NOTE: Details sum to more than 100 percent, as some prisoners had multiple minor children living with multiple caregivers.

2004 survey of inmates to assess who are the caregivers for the children of the incarcerated. Figure 6 reproduces their results. For male inmates who are parents, the overwhelming majority of their children are residing with the other parent (88 percent), although a nontrivial proportion of these children are also receiving care from their grandparents (13 percent) and other relatives (5 percent). A relatively small proportion of the children of male inmates are in the foster care system (2 percent). The picture is quite different, however, for the children of female prison inmates. Only 37 percent of the children of female inmates are being cared for by their fathers, while 45 percent and 23 percent are being cared for by a grandparent or another relative, respectively. Roughly 11 percent of these children are in the foster care system.

Of course, the high propensity of children of prison inmates to be living with adults other than their parents may not be entirely due to prison. It is possible that many of these incarcerated parents were not living with their children prior to incarceration for various reasons. While this is true to some extent, the data do indeed indicate that more than half of incarcerated parents were residing with their

TABLE 5
Child Family Income and Poverty Rates among Children Born between
1985 and 2000 in the PSID before, during, and after a Paternal Incarceration

	Child's Family Income (1997$)	In Poverty (%)
Year before father's incarceration	$38,960	22.34
Average during incarceration	$30,234	30.87
Year after father's release	$33,100	24.40
Difference (During – Before)	–$8,726	8.53

SOURCE: PSID data in Johnson (2009).
NOTE: Figures in Johnson (2009) are for children born between 1985 and 2000 whose fathers are residing with them prior to the paternal incarceration.

children prior to their most recent prison spell.[6] Hence, the incarceration of a parent is certainly likely to disrupt the living arrangements of their minor children.

An additional domain that I can characterize with available data concerns the impact of a paternal incarceration on the material well-being of households. Johnson (2009) analyzes how the household incomes and poverty rates of children born between 1985 and 2000 were affected by the incarceration of their fathers. The results of this analysis are reproduced in Table 5. In the year prior to a father's incarceration, average annual household income in 1997 dollars stood at $38,960. During the period of incarceration, average annual household income dropped by nearly $9,000. Concurrently, the proportion of these children living in households below the poverty line was 22 percent prior to the father's incarceration. During the father's incarceration, this poverty rate increased to nearly 31 percent.

Thus, many children are affected by the incarceration of their parents, with the impact being disproportionately felt by African American children. While I have not done justice to the many possible ways that a parental incarceration affects the lives of children (and certainly have not addressed the thorny issue of causal inference), it is undoubtedly the case that the children of the incarcerated are more likely to reside with adults who are not their parents and that parental incarceration coincides with a decline in household income and an increase in child poverty.

How Does Serving Time Affect One's Employment Prospects?

Former inmates reentering noninstitutionalized society face a number of challenges in procuring and maintaining stable employment. To start, former inmates tend to have low levels of educational attainment, little formal work experience, and other characteristics associated with poor employment prospects. To illustrate, Table 6 presents tabulations from the releases file of the 2003 NCRP data. These data present micro-level information on all inmates leaving prison during

TABLE 6
Characteristics of State Prisoners Released in 2003

	All Inmates	White	Black	Hispanic
Demographics				
Male	0.897	0.876	0.907	0.934
White	0.464	1.000	0.000	0.888
Black	0.519	0.000	1.000	0.097
Hispanic	0.202	0.069	0.007	1.000
Educational attainment				
8th grade or less	0.114	0.124	0.085	0.261
9th grade	0.114	0.111	0.112	0.146
10th grade	0.151	0.130	0.175	0.126
11th grade	0.157	0.116	0.203	0.106
12th/GED	0.386	0.432	0.351	0.328
Some college	0.060	0.065	0.061	0.024
College grad	0.009	0.011	0.010	0.005
Special ed.	0.007	0.010	0.005	0.004
Age percentiles				
25th	24.7	25.3	24.3	24.3
50th	32.0	33.0	31.7	30.1
75th	39.9	40.5	39.9	37.8
Time served percentiles[a] (months)				
25th	11.3	10.6	10.9	14.9
50th	20.8	19.6	21.3	24.0
75th	39.9	36.1	42.0	43.5
Conditionally released	0.739	0.732	0.702	0.856
Prior felony incarceration	0.327	0.292	0.410	0.203
Offense				
Murder/homicide	0.025	0.022	0.026	0.029
Rape/sexual assault	0.043	0.058	0.028	0.046
Robbery	0.073	0.046	0.097	0.074
Assault	0.081	0.075	0.078	0.105
Other violent	0.022	0.027	0.017	0.027
Burglary	0.116	0.142	0.097	0.105
Larceny	0.128	0.150	0.120	0.079
Motor vehicle theft	0.024	0.025	0.016	0.041
Other property	0.037	0.046	0.030	0.030
Drugs	0.321	0.249	0.391	0.343
Other	0.128	0.159	0.100	0.121

SOURCE: NCRP database (2003).
a. Refers to time served for release offense.

the calendar year for the thirty-five participating states. I provide tabulations for all reentering inmates as well as inmates by race/ethnicity. The data show that prison releases are overwhelmingly male (.897) and are disproportionately minority (52 percent black and 20 percent Hispanic). Roughly 54 percent of reentering inmates have not completed a high school degree, with a slightly higher figure for blacks and higher still for Hispanic releases. The median reentering inmate is 32 years old and has finished a 21-month spell in prison. However, many of these inmates have served prior time, with fully 33 percent indicating that they have a prior felony incarceration (prior to the current spell). Certainly, many have also served time in local jails awaiting the adjudication of the charges leading to the current spell. Nearly three-quarters of released inmates are conditionally released, meaning that they are under the active supervision of the state's community corrections system.

The human capital deficits of former inmates are likely to limit their employment prospects after release from prison. However, the experience of incarceration may further limit one's employment opportunities. What causal pathways may link changes in incarceration rates to the employment outcomes of low-skilled men? First, there is a simple contemporaneous mechanical incapacitation effect of incarceration, in that institutionalized men cannot be employed in a conventional manner. While labor force attachment among the criminally active is relatively low, there is evidence indicating that a substantial proportion of prison inmates were gainfully employed at the time of their arrest. Hence, incarceration certainly prevents some from working who would otherwise be employed.[7]

Beyond this contemporaneous effect, incarceration is also likely to have a lagged impact on the employment prospects of former inmates as well as a contemporaneous impact on the employment outcomes of men who have not been to prison yet come from demographic subgroups with high incarceration rates. On the positive side, a spell in prison may straighten some men out, instilling a desire to avoid future prison spells and to live a conventional, law-abiding life. Such a positive impact is akin to what criminologists refer to as a specific deterrent effect of incarceration and may ultimately increase the employability of former inmates.

On the negative side, inmates fail to accumulate human capital while incarcerated and may experience an erosion of prosocial tendencies and perhaps the enhancement of antisocial attitudes and a propensity toward violence. Moreover, the stigmatizing effect (sometimes exacerbated by state and federal policy) associated with a prior felony conviction and incarceration faced by all former inmates is certainly an obstacle while searching for a job. There is a further avenue, other than the mechanical, by which incarceration may contemporaneously affect the employment prospects of low-skilled minority men. Employers may statistically discriminate against men from high-incarceration demographic groups in an attempt to avoid hiring ex-offenders. All of these pathways are likely to suppress the current and future employment and earnings of men from demographic groups with high incarceration rates. This impact adversely affects the material well-being of those men directly as well as of those intimates and children whose welfare is determined interdependently.

Incarceration and the accumulation of work experience

Serving time interrupts one's work career. The extent of this interruption depends on both the expected amount of time served on a typical term and the likelihood of serving subsequent prison terms. The average prisoner admitted on a new offense faces a maximum sentence of three years and a minimum of one year (with many serving time closer to the minimum) (Raphael and Stoll 2005). If this were the only time served for most, then the interruption from prison would not be that substantial.

However, many people serve multiple terms in prison, either because they commit new felonies or violate parole conditions postrelease. A large body of criminological research consistently finds that nearly two-thirds of ex-inmates are rearrested within a few years of release from prison (Petersilia 2003). Moreover, a sizable majority of the rearrested will serve subsequent prison terms. Thus, for many offenders, the typical experience between the ages of 18 and 30 is characterized by multiple short prison spells with intermittent, and relatively short, spells outside of prison.

In prior longitudinal research on young offenders entering the California state prison system, I documented the degree to which prison interrupts the early potential work careers of young men. I followed a cohort of young men entering the state prison system in 1990 and gauged the amount of time served over the subsequent decade (Raphael 2005). The median inmate served 2.8 years during the 1990s, with the median white inmate (3.09 years) and median black inmate (3.53 years) serving more time and the median Hispanic inmate (2.23 years) serving less time. Roughly 25 percent served at least five years during the 1990s, while another 25 percent served less than 1.5 years.

However, as a gauge of the extent of the temporal interruption, these figures are misleading. Cumulative time served does not account for the short periods of time between prison spells where inmates may find employment yet are not able to solidify the employment match with any measurable amount of job tenure. A more appropriate measure of the degree to which incarceration impedes experience accumulation would be the time between the date of admission to prison for the first term served and the date of release from the last term.

I found that five years elapse between the first date of admission and the last date of release for the median inmate. For median white, black, and Hispanic inmates, the comparable figures are 6.2, 6.5, and 3.2 years, respectively. For approximately one-quarter of inmates, nine years pass between their initial commission to prison and their last release. In other words, one-quarter of these inmates spent almost the entire decade cycling in and out of prison.

Spending five years of one's early life (6.5 years for the median black offender) cycling in and out of institutions must affect one's earning prospects. Clearly, being behind bars and the short spans of time outside of prison prohibit the accumulation of job experiences during a period of one's life when the returns from experience are the greatest.

Does having been in prison stigmatize ex-offenders?

The potential impact of serving time on future labor market prospects extends beyond the failure to accumulate work experience. Employers are averse to hiring former prison inmates and often use formal and informal screening tools to weed ex-offenders out of the applicant pool. Given the high proportion of low-skilled men with prison time on their criminal records, such employer sentiments and screening practices represent an increasingly important employment barrier, especially for low-skilled African American men.

Employers consider criminal records when screening job applicants for a number of reasons. For starters, certain occupations are closed to felons under local, state, and in some instances federal law (Hahn 1991). In many states, employers can be held liable for the criminal actions of their employees. Under the theory of negligent hiring, employers can be required to pay punitive damages as well as damages for loss, pain, and suffering for acts committed by an employee on the job (Craig 1987). Finally, employers looking to fill jobs where employee monitoring is imperfect may place a premium on trustworthiness and screen accordingly.

In all known employer surveys where employers are asked about their willingness to hire ex-offenders, employer responses reveal a strong aversion to hiring applicants with criminal records (Holzer, Raphael, and Stoll 2006, 2007; Pager 2003). For example, more than 60 percent of employers surveyed in the Multi-City Study of Urban Inequality (MCSUI) indicated that they would "probably not" or "definitely not" hire applicants with criminal records, with "probably not" being the modal response. By contrast, only 8 percent responded similarly when queried about their willingness to hire current and former welfare recipients.

The ability of employers to act on an aversion to ex-offenders, and the nature of the action in terms of hiring and screening behavior, will depend on employer accessibility to criminal record information. If an employer can and does access criminal records, the employer may simply screen out applicants based on their actual arrest and conviction records. In the absence of a formal background check, employers may act on their aversion to hiring ex-offenders by using perceived correlates of previous incarceration, such as age, race, or level of educational attainment, to attempt to screen out those with criminal histories. In other words, employers may statistically profile applicants and avoid hiring those from demographic groups with high rates of involvement in the criminal justice system.

Such propensity to statistically discriminate is evident in the interaction effect of employers' stated preferences regarding their willingness to hire ex-offenders, their screening behavior on this dimension, and their propensity to hire workers from high incarceration rate groups. This relationship is illustrated in Figure 7, which reproduces some of the key findings in Holzer, Raphael, and Stoll (2006). The figure presents tabulations of employer survey data collected in 1993 and 1994 pertaining to the proportion of employers whose most recent hire was a black male. The table stratifies employers by their self-reported willingness to hire ex-offenders and by their self-report regarding whether they use criminal history background checks in screening their potential employees. Among employers who indicate that they are willing to hire ex-offenders, there is no statistically discernable difference in the proportion of recent hires who are black men between those who check and those who do not check criminal backgrounds. Among

FIGURE 7

The Proportion of Employers Whose Most Recent Hire Was a Black
Male by Their Self-Stated Willingness to Hire Ex-Offenders and
by Whether They Check Criminal Background in Screening Applicants

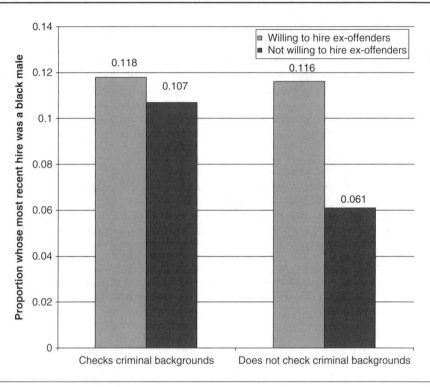

SOURCE: Holzer, Raphael, and Stoll (2006).

employers who indicate that they are unwilling to hire ex-offenders, however, checking criminal background is associated with a 5.5 percentage point increase in the likelihood that the most recent hire is a black male. Thus, among those most averse to hiring former inmates, checking backgrounds actually increases the likelihood that the firm hires black males. This pattern indicates that in the absence of such objective screening methods, employers use more informal screening tools (such as not hiring black males) to weed out potential former inmates. Holzer, Raphael, and Stoll (2006) find similar patterns with regard to employer willingness to hire other stigmatized groups, such as those with large unaccounted for gaps in their employment histories.

With regard to the direct effect of stigma on former inmates, the audit study by Pager (2003) offers perhaps the clearest evidence of employer aversion to ex-offenders and the stigma associated with having served time in prison. The study uses male auditors matched on observable characteristics, including age, education, general appearance, demeanor, and race/ethnicity, to assess the effects of prior prison experience on the likelihood that each auditor is called back for an interview. The author finds consistently sizable negative effects of prior prison experience on the likelihood of being called back by the employer, with callback rates for the auditor with prior prison time one-half that of the matched coauditor.

Discussion: What Can Be Done to Ease the Reentry of Former Prison Inmates?

Former prisoners reentering noninstitutionalized society face many challenges. More than seven hundred thousand inmates are released each year from the nation's state and federal prisons. Many will fail and be returned to prison for technical parole violations or new felony offenses. Many more will live in abject poverty and face hurdles in attempting to secure employment and reintegrate into everyday life. What can be done to aid this transition and maximize the likelihood of successful reentry?

To start, the scale of the reentry challenge would be considerably more manageable if we could reduce the annual inflow of new prison admissions. As was already discussed, nearly all men admitted to prison are eventually released, and thus reform and intervention that stems the front-end inflow would also reduce the annual outflow from the nation's penitentiaries. We have seen that much of the increase in incarceration over the past few decades has been driven by changes in sentencing policy, with the increased use of incarceration and the increases in time served for specific offenses being the principal culprits. It is high time that the states and the federal government review and rationalize sentencing practices with an eye on reducing the prison population while maintaining public safety. In research with Rucker Johnson (Johnson and Raphael 2007), I found that the crime-abating impact of increases in incarceration have declined considerably in recent years as we are increasingly incarcerating less criminally active individuals. In other words, we are preventing very few crimes by incarcerating many inmates whom we would not have incarcerated in the past. Moreover, the crimes that we are preventing by incarcerating these marginal inmates tend to be less serious forms of property crime or low-level drug offenses. Given the large monetary and social costs of incarceration, we need to reevaluate whether we are overusing incarceration in punishing nonviolent offenders.

Sentencing reform aside, there is quite strong evidence that human capital accumulation appears to reduce criminal activity and the likelihood of serving time. Lochner and Moretti (2004) present convincing research results indicating that marginal increases in formal educational attainment considerably reduce the likelihood of incarceration among those on the margin between dropping out and not dropping out of high school. In addition, many early childhood interventions appear to reduce criminal activity later in life (see Donohue 2009). To the extent that we can reduce criminal activity and incarceration through educational and developmental programs, we should.

Interestingly, several experimental evaluations find that programs such as Job Corps (Schochet, Burghardt, and Glazerman 2001), Jobstart (Cave et al. 1993), as well as the workforce development programs studied in the national Job Training Partnership Act (JTPA) evaluation (H. Bloom et al. 1994) significantly increased the formal educational attainment of program participants. The Job Corps program raised formal schooling levels among members by nearly a full year. The Job Corps evaluation also found significant and substantial impacts on arrest rates, convictions, and incarceration. Researchers and policy-makers should be exploring and evaluating the use of programs designed to increase high school graduation rates. Conditional cash transfer programs or any other intervention that provides the incentive to complete secondary schooling should be conceived of as possible tools in addressing the nation's reentry challenges, as reductions in criminal activity and front-end admissions will transmit directly to lower levels of releases.

With regard to those individuals being released from the nation's prisons, a number of prototypical models have been employed to guide reentry. As most inmates are conditionally released from prison, usually to the authority of the state's community corrections system, the primary intervention experienced by the majority of releases concerns the conditional supervision and compliance requirements of parole. Parole requires regular meetings with a parole officer, having to report any changes in residence, confinement to one's county of release, work requirements, and often the prohibition of drug and alcohol abuse. While parole officers can and often do refer parolees to service providers, their main function is to monitor the activities of recent releases and to punish violators.

Aside from postrelease surveillance, several alternative models have been used to ease the reentry process and foster reintegration. One of the most pressing issues for recently released inmates concerns having the needed resources when leaving prison to feed, clothe, and house themselves in the days following release. Most states provide released prisoners with a small amount of "gate money," usually no more than $200 (Wilson 2007), as well as clothes and transportation back to their county of commitment. Some inmates also accumulate a small amount of savings through in-prison work assignments. However, the release period is often quite difficult, with many inmates quickly violating parole, experiencing a spell of homelessness, and also experiencing unusually high mortality rates in the weeks and months following release (National Research Council 2008).

There have been several experimental evaluations of transitional cash assistance programs (Mallar and Thornton 1978; Rossi, Berk, and Lenihan 1980), with one finding substantial effects of providing transitional cash assistance on recidivism and one finding little impact. The latter evaluation also found a large negative effect of the transitional cash assistance on the labor supply of released inmates. In fact, the authors speculate that the lack of an overall impact on recidivism reflected the offsetting effects of the reduction in recidivism due to the cash assistance and the increased criminal activity associated with being idle (Rossi,

Berk, and Lenihan 1980). These experiments were implemented during a time when the incarceration rate was considerably lower (and the average prisoner considerably more criminally inclined relative to today) and involved cash assistance programs that had benefit-reduction rates of 100 percent against legitimate labor market earnings. Certainly, one could create a conditional cash transfer program that did not provide such strong disincentives to work. Moreover, the high parole failure and return-to-custody rates shown in the recent report of the National Research Council (2008) suggest that this immediate transition period is particularly crucial and that transitional cash assistance beyond the meager gate-money allowance might help tremendously.

There have also been several high-quality evaluations of the impact of providing transitional employment to former inmates. The National Supported Work (NSW) Program (recently reanalyzed by Uggen 2000) and the New York Center for Employment Opportunities (CEO) evaluated by Manpower Demonstration Research Corporation (D. Bloom et al. 2007) find some evidence that providing prison releases with transitional employment forestalls recidivism for two years postrelease. However, these programs found considerable heterogeneity in program impact, with the NSW finding significant effects for older releases and the CEO evaluation reporting significant effects for those most recently released from prison. Truth be told, we still have much to learn about the relationship between employment, recidivism, and incarceration for reentering offenders. In particular, researchers need to explore more fully which former prisoners appear to be most responsive to such interventions.

More recent models of service delivery have been built around the idea that successfully reintegrating former inmates requires wraparound services that begin while the individual is still incarcerated and that continue well into the parole terms of the releasee and, if needed, beyond. The programs funded under the Serious and Violent Offender Reentry Initiative (SVORI) serve as examples (Lattimore, Visher, and Steffey 2008). SVORI is a multiagency federal initiative that gives grants to localities to provide holistic, complete, and coordinated reentry services that begin prerelease and continue through the parole terms of releasees. While each locality is permitted the leeway to design its own programs, the grants are conditional on certain service elements, including prerelease assessment, the use of reentry plans, the use of transition teams that coordinate release and reentry, efforts to connect reentering men to community resources, and the use of graduated levels of supervision and sanctions. Although the impact evaluation of this effort is still in progress, many believe that this coordinated, continuous process of service delivery, commencing prior to release, is the key to avoiding quick reentry failures.

We are in need of more rigorous evaluations of what works for those released from prison, with an eye on flushing out the differential responsiveness of different types of former prisoners to the interventions and incentives created by these programs. The scale of the problem continues to increase with the continually rising—albeit at a slower rate than in years past—prison population. Given the social and budgetary costs of crime and incarceration, programs that have even modest effects are likely to pass cost-benefit tests.

Notes

1. Figures are from the Bureau of Justice Statistics, *Facts at a Glance*, www.ojp.usdoj.gov/bjs/glance/tables/incrttab.htm (accessed 27 July 2009).

2. See Raphael and Stoll (2009) for details behind these tabulations.

3. These counterfactual crime trends are based on estimates of the joint contemporary incapacitation and deterrence effects presented in Johnson and Raphael (2007).

4. Certainly the large increase in drug arrests does not entirely reflect changes in offending behavior. We make this assumption, however, to rule out the possibility that our decomposition results are biased by unobserved changes in drug offending.

5. Several demographic changes over this time period would have militated toward lower offending, including aging of the population, increases in educational attainment, and the increase in the proportion foreign-born.

6. Glaze and Maruschak (2009) report that 47 percent of male inmates and 64 percent of female inmates were residing with their children immediately before the arrest leading to their current incarceration spell.

7. Roughly one-third to two-thirds of inmates are employed at the time of the arrest leading to their current incarceration (see Kling 2006; Pettit and Lyons 2007; Tyler and Kling 2007; Sabol 2007).

References

Bonczar, Thomas P. 2003. *Prevalence of imprisonment in the U.S. population, 1974–2001*. Special Report, NCJ 197976. Washington, DC: Bureau of Justice Statistics.

Bloom, Dan, Cindy Redcross, Janine Zweig, and Gilda Azurdia. 2007. *Transitional jobs for ex-prisoners: Early impacts from a random assignment evaluation of the Center for Employment Opportunities Prisoner Reentry Program*. New York, NY: MDRC.

Bloom, Howard S., Larry L. Orr, George Cave, Stephen H. Bell, Fred Doolittle, and Winston Lin. 1994. *The National JTPA Study, overview: Impacts, benefits, and costs of Title II-A*. Bethesda, MD: Abt Associates.

Cave, George, Hans Bos, Fred Doolittle, and Cyril Toussaint. 1993. *JOBSTART: Final report on a program for school dropouts*. New York, NY: MDRC.

Craig, Scott R. 1987. Negligent hiring: Guilt by association. *Personnel Administration*, October, 32–34.

Donohue, John J., III. 2009. Assessing the relative benefits of incarceration: Overall changes and the benefits on the margin. In *Do prisons make us safer? The benefits and costs of the prison boom*, eds. Steven Raphael and Michael Stoll, 269–342. New York, NY: Russell Sage Foundation.

Glaze, Lauren E., and Laura M. Maruschak. 2009. *Parents in prison and their minor children*. Special Report, NCJ 222984. Washington, DC: Bureau of Justice Statistics.

Hahn, John M. 1991. Pre-employment information services: Employers beware. *Employee Relations Law Journal* 17 (1): 45–69.

Holzer, Harry J., Steven Raphael, and Michael A. Stoll. 2006. Perceived criminality, criminal background checks and the racial hiring practices of employers. *Journal of Law and Economics* 49 (2): 451–80.

Holzer, Harry J., Steven Raphael, and Michael A. Stoll. 2007. The effect of an applicant's criminal history on employer hiring decisions and screening practices: Evidence from Los Angeles. In *Barriers to reentry? The labor market for released prisoners in post-industrial America*, eds. Shawn Bushway, Michael Stoll, and David Weiman, 117–50. New York, NY: Russell Sage Foundation.

International Centre for Prison Studies. 2007. *World prison brief*. Available from www.prisonstudies.org/ (accessed 1 January 2007).

Johnson, Rucker. 2009. Ever-increasing levels of parental incarceration and the consequences for children. In *Do prisons make us safer? The benefits and costs of the prison boom*, eds. Steven Raphael and Michael Stoll, 177–206. New York, NY: Russell Sage Foundation.

Johnson, Rucker, and Steven Raphael. 2007. How much crime reduction does the marginal prisoner buy? Working Paper, University of California, Berkeley.

Kling, Jeffrey R. 2006. Incarceration length, employment, and earnings. *American Economic Review* 96 (3): 863–76.

Lattimore, Pamela K., Christy A. Visher, and Danielle M. Steffey. 2008. *Pre-release characteristics and service receipt among adult male participants in the SVORI Multi-Site Evaluation*. Washington, DC: Urban Institute.

Lochner, Lance, and Enrico Moretti. 2004. The effect of education on criminal activity: Evidence from prison inmates, arrest, and self reports. *American Economic Review* 94 (1): 155–89.

Mallar, Charles D., and Craig V. D. Thornton. 1978. Transitional aid for released prisoners: Evidence from the life experiment. *Journal of Human Resources* 13 (2): 208–36.

National Research Council. 2008. *Parole desistance from crime and community integration*. Washington, DC: National Academy Press.

Pager, Devah. 2003. The mark of a criminal record. *American Journal of Sociology* 108 (5): 937–75.

Petersilia, Joan. 2003. *When prisoners come home*. Oxford: Oxford University Press.

Pettit, Becky, and Christopher Lyons. 2007. Status and the stigma of incarceration: The labor market effects of incarceration by race, class, and criminal involvement. In *Barriers to reentry? The labor market for released prisoners in post-industrial America*, eds. Shawn Bushway, Michael Stoll, and David Weiman, 206–26. New York, NY: Russell Sage Foundation.

Pettit, Becky, and Bruce Western. 2004. Mass imprisonment and the life course: Race and class inequality in U.S. incarceration. *American Sociological Review* 69 (2): 151–69.

Raphael, Steven. 2005. The socioeconomic status of black males: The increasing importance of incarceration. In *Poverty, the distribution of income, and public policy*, eds. Alan Auerbach, David Card, and John Quigley, 319–58. New York, NY: Russell Sage Foundation.

Raphael, Steven, and Michael Stoll. 2005. The effect of prison releases on regional crime rates. In *The Brookings-Wharton papers on urban economic affairs*, vol. 5, eds. William G. Gale and Janet Rothenberg Pack, 207–55. Washington, DC: Brookings Institution.

Raphael, Steven, and Michael Stoll. 2009. Why are so many Americans in prison? In *Do prisons make us safer? The benefits and costs of the prison boom*, eds. Steven Raphael and Michael Stoll, 27–72. New York, NY: Russell Sage Foundation.

Rossi, Peter, Richard A. Berk, and Kenneth J. Lenihan. 1980. *Money, work, and crime: Experimental evidence*. New York, NY: Academic Press.

Sabol, William J. 2007. Local labor-market conditions and post-prison employment experiences of offenders released from Ohio state prisons. In *Barriers to reentry? The labor market for released prisoners in post-industrial America*, eds. Shawn Bushway, Michael Stoll, and David Weiman, 257–303. New York, NY: Russell Sage Foundation.

Schochet, Peter Z., John Burghardt, and Steven Glazerman. 2001. *National Job Corps Study: The impact of Job Corps on participants' employment and related outcomes*. Princeton, NJ: Mathematica Policy Research, Inc.

Travis, Jeremy. 2005. *But they all come back: Facing the challenges of prisoner reentry*. Washington, DC: Urban Institute Press.

Tyler, John H., and Jeffrey R. Kling. 2007. Prison-based education and reentry into the mainstream labor market. In *Barriers to reentry? The labor market for released prisoners in post-industrial America*, eds. Shawn Bushway, Michael Stoll, and David Weiman, 227–56. New York, NY: Russell Sage Foundation.

Uggen, Christopher. 2000. Work as a turning point in the life course of criminals: A duration model of age, employment, and recidivism. *American Sociological Review* 65 (4): 529–46.

Wilson, Kate J. 2007. State policies and procedures regarding "gate money." Center for Public Policy Research Working Paper, University of California, Davis.

Policies That Strengthen Fatherhood and Family Relationships: What Do We Know and What Do We Need to Know?

By
VIRGINIA KNOX,
PHILIP A. COWAN,
CAROLYN PAPE COWAN,
and
ELANA BILDNER

As described in earlier articles, children whose parents have higher incomes and education levels are more likely to grow up in stable two-parent households than their economically disadvantaged counterparts. The widening gaps in fathers' involvement in parenting and in the quality and stability of parents' relationships may reinforce disparities in outcomes for the next generation. This article reviews evidence about the effectiveness of two strategies to strengthen fathers' involvement and family relationships—fatherhood programs aimed at disadvantaged noncustodial fathers and relationship skills programs for parents who are together. Fatherhood programs have shown some efficacy in increasing child support payments, while some relationship skills approaches have shown benefits for the couples' relationship quality, coparenting skills, fathers' engagement in parenting, and children's well-being. The research suggests that parents' relationship with each other should be a fundamental consideration in future programs aimed at increasing low-income fathers' involvement with their children.

Keywords: responsible fatherhood; marriage education; fatherhood programs; evaluation

Introduction and Policy Context

Men in the United States who grow up with different racial, ethnic, and socioeconomic backgrounds experience enormous disparities in their young adult outcomes, not only in the realms of education and employment but also in their likelihood of forming stable relationships with the mothers of their children and with the children (Berger and Langton this volume). Given considerable evidence that fathers' parenting support—both financial and emotional—is an important foundation for child well-being (Carlson and Magnuson this volume), increasing the number of children who grow up either in stable two-parent families or at least with the support of both parents is an important goal of public policy.

DOI: 10.1177/0002716210394769

One set of policies and programs that might ultimately affect fathers' capacity as partners and parents are those that target the educational and economic outcomes of young fathers. A complementary set of interventions targets family relationships and includes responsible fatherhood programs for low-income noncustodial fathers and marriage education or relationship skills programs for low-income parents who are in a relationship together. Both types of family relationship interventions aim to increase fathers' likelihood of playing a positive long-term role in their children's lives, either by increasing the quality and stability of the couple's relationship if parents are together or by helping fathers stay engaged with their children if the couple's relationship has ended. This article will provide an overview of the efforts to strengthen family relationships, what we have learned from evaluations to date about their effectiveness, and areas that research suggests should be priorities for future program development and evaluation. Based on rigorous evidence to date, there are grounds for optimism with respect to each of these approaches, but there are also considerable challenges that require additional program development and research.

In the past two decades, both the federal and state governments have funded programs to encourage noncustodial fathers' involvement with their children and to strengthen two-parent families. The early 1990s saw the advent of responsible fatherhood programs aimed at bolstering the capacity of low-income noncustodial fathers to pay child support. These were one element of welfare reform efforts to recalibrate the "social contract" balancing government-provided financial support for low-income children, on one hand, with contributions from parents via their own earnings, on the other. In 1996, when the Temporary Assistance for Needy Families (TANF) program was established with passage of the Personal Responsibility and Work Opportunity Reconciliation Act (PRWORA), one of its four goals was to "encourage the formation and maintenance of two-parent families" (PRWORA 1996, 8), in recognition that on average, two parents have

Virginia Knox is director of Families and Children at MDRC and principal investigator for Supporting Healthy Marriage, a random assignment study of relationship skills programs for low-income couples. Among her publications are the book chapter "Designing a Marriage Education Demonstration and Evaluation for Low-Income Married Couples" (with David Fein) (Columbia University Press 2009) and the report Parenting and Providing: The Impact of Parents' Fair Share on Paternal Involvement *(with Cindy Redcross) (MDRC 2000).*

Philip A. Cowan is a professor of psychology, emeritus, at the University of California, Berkeley, author of Piaget with Feeling: Cognitive Social and Emotional Dimensions *(Holt, Rinehart, and Winston 1978), coauthor of* When Partners Become Parents: The Big Life Change for Couples *(Lawrence Erlbaum 2000), and coeditor of* The Family Context of Parenting in the Child's Adaptation to School *(Routledge 2005).*

Carolyn Pape Cowan is a professor of psychology, emerita at the University of California, Berkeley, codirector of three longitudinal preventive intervention projects, coauthor of When Partners Become Parents: The Big Life Change for Couples *(Lawrence Erlbaum 2000), and coeditor of* Fatherhood Today: Men's Changing Role in the Family *(Wiley 1988).*

Elana Bildner is a research assistant in MDRC's Families and Children policy area, helping to coordinate implementation research and technical assistance efforts on two national demonstrations.

greater capacity than one to provide children with economic and parenting support. A decade later, Congress authorized $150 million per year for five years for healthy marriage and responsible fatherhood funding within the Deficit Reduction Act of 2005 that reauthorized the TANF program. These funds have been used by the Administration for Children and Families (ACF) of the U.S. Department of Health and Human Services to support the 2006 Healthy Marriage and Responsible Fatherhood Grants to state, local, and community-based service providers. Grantees offer voluntary programs that help individuals and couples to build skills and knowledge that research has found to be associated with stable, healthy relationships and marriages. Some states have also allocated some of their own TANF funds to programs targeting marriage and relationship skills and fatherhood, resulting in significant funding levels for these programs in Ohio, Oklahoma, Texas, and Utah. In addition, Florida, Georgia, Maryland, Minnesota, Oklahoma, Tennessee, and Texas waive marriage license fees for couples who take a premarital skills course.

One question of importance to practitioners is whether future federal and state efforts will reduce long-standing divides between proponents of funding in three related domains: programs for noncustodial fathers, for strengthened relationships or healthy marriages between parents, and for the prevention of domestic violence. Throughout the history described above, shifts in funding among these three priorities at the federal level resulted in a "swinging pendulum" effect, creating uncertainties that undermined efforts of community-based nonprofits and other providers of direct services to build high-quality, research-based programs (Martinson and Nightingale 2008). Reducing the influence of the swinging pendulum would provide an important foundation for building evidence-based services for families.

Two recent developments indicate that responsible fatherhood and couples' relationship quality are closely linked rather than opposing priorities. First, qualitative, longitudinal, and now intervention research findings indicate that a man's capacity to fulfill his role(s) as father is often embedded in his relationship with the child's mother. For couples who live together, the quality of their relationship is associated with their ability to "coparent" (or parent cooperatively) and the father's level of engagement with his child (Coley and Chase-Lansdale 1999; Egeland and Carlson 2004). In turn, programs that are effective at *strengthening* the relationship between parents who live together have been found to increase fathers' involvement in parenting (P. Cowan et al. 2009). For parents who are no longer together, there is an even stronger link between the parents' ability to cooperate and the father's level of involvement with the child, because custodial parents (usually mothers) have considerable control over noncustodial parents' access to their young children, and ongoing conflict between parents about visitation is likely to lead to fathers' withdrawal. It therefore makes sense that responsible fatherhood programs, which have historically worked with noncustodial fathers but not the custodial parents, have found it difficult to change fathers' involvement with their children other than their child support payments (Miller and Knox 2001). In short, these basic research and intervention findings suggest that engaged fatherhood and collaborative couple relationships are closely linked.

Second, in recent years, some local service providers have expended considerable effort to find common ground on behalf of the families they serve in responsible fatherhood and marriage and relationship skills programs (Ooms et al. 2006). Partly in recognition of the research evidence mentioned above, the grants that ACF funded in 2006 allowed responsible fatherhood grantees, not only healthy marriage grantees, to provide relationship skills programs to *couples* as part of their mandate to strengthen fathers' involvement with children (U.S. Department of Health and Human Services n.d.-b). Supported by these policies, some providers of responsible fatherhood programs have added to their service menus relationship skills programs for unmarried or married couples. In addition, some family service centers that previously served primarily mothers and children but now work with couples report a better understanding of how to be supportive of fathers, a potentially important development in the community service landscape. Both responsible fatherhood and couple relationship service providers have worked closely with domestic violence partners in their communities to serve families safely and appropriately. Thus, on the ground, service offerings are beginning to reflect the evidence in research that services related to fatherhood and to couple relationships might be connected, rather than alternatives to one another.

What Do We Know from Intervention Research about Strengthening Fatherhood and Families?

This section summarizes current evidence about "what works" from research conducted on responsible fatherhood programs and relationship skills programs targeting couples. These fields currently have different levels of evidence to support evidence-based policy-making. Marriage and relationship skills programs have been the subject of randomized trials, in part because a number of interventions were originally developed by researchers who were interested in applying basic research to find effective strategies to strengthen relationships. Fatherhood programs, in contrast, grew out of government officials' interest in increasing disadvantaged fathers' capacity to pay child support and have been the subject of many more implementation studies than random assignment studies. Nevertheless, there is much to learn from the body of evidence available for each of these program types.

Two program models: Responsible fatherhood and relationship skills programs for couples

Before discussing the results of particular intervention studies, it is worth understanding some basic differences between the most common models for responsible fatherhood programs and couple-oriented relationship skills programs. As shown in the top half of Figure 1, fatherhood programs targeting low-income noncustodial fathers have typically consisted of multiple components aimed at increasing capacity

FIGURE 1
Strengthening Fatherhood and Family Relationships: Two Models

RESPONSIBLE FATHERHOOD PROGRAMS

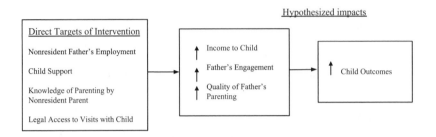

COUPLEORIENTED RELATIONSHIP SKILLS PROGRAMS

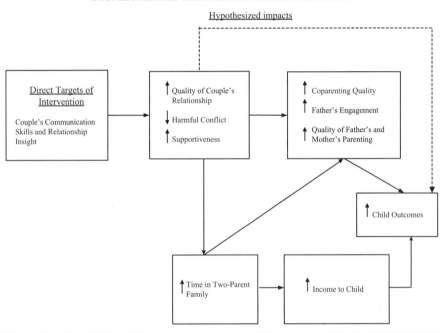

to support children financially and emotionally. These programs often provide a combination of employment services, group-based curricula aimed at helping fathers to develop a vision of their role as fathers, and, sometimes, links to the child support enforcement system. To varying degrees, they have also worked with fathers on parenting skills and relationship skills that would be helpful in coparenting with a former partner. The theory is that these programs can increase the income going to the child and improve the father-child relationship. In turn, these are expected to improve outcomes for children.

In contrast, relationship skills programs typically work with both members of a couple when they are still in a relationship together. Like responsible fatherhood programs, these programs could ultimately increase fathers' long-term engagement with their children, income available to the child, and child well-being, but as shown in Figure 1, they aim to do so through a different set of mechanisms designed to bolster the relationship quality for an existing couple by improving specific skills such as handling of conflict and supportive behaviors toward one another. Changes in the couple's relationship could improve children's emotional security and social-emotional development through (1) improved coparenting (by which we mean cooperative parenting), (2) the child witnessing less mismanaged parental conflict, (3) increased willingness of the father to become engaged in family life, (4) increased engagement by the father with parenting the child, or (5) improvements in the quality of parenting by mother or father (due to improvement in the overall climate of the home or parents' generalization of their new relationship skills to their relationships with the child). Thus, improvements in the couple's relationship may ultimately increase the quality or quantity of fathers' engagement with children, whether they increase the amount of time they actually live with their children, the amount of time they spend together if they do not live together, or the quality of the father-child relationship whenever they are together (P. Cowan et al. 2008).

What have we learned from evaluations of responsible fatherhood programs?

The Family Support Act of 1988 instituted new requirements for participation in work-related activities for custodial parents of children receiving Aid to Families with Dependent Children (AFDC). Growing in parallel was an expectation that if earnings from mothers were to contribute more to the support of children receiving AFDC, so should child support payments from noncustodial parents. As shown in Figure 2, an initial programmatic effort in this direction was the Young Unwed Fathers Project, which operated in six sites from 1991 to 1993 and targeted noncustodial fathers under age 25 (Achatz and MacAllum 1994). Services were provided on a voluntary basis for up to 18 months. These included education and training to increase the fathers' earning capacity, assistance establishing paternity and paying formal child support, and fatherhood development activities to encourage parental values and behavior using a curriculum that later evolved into two curricula still used today, Responsible Fatherhood and Fatherhood Development.

Parents' Fair Share (PFS): A random assignment demonstration program for noncustodial parents. PFS, tested experimentally from 1994 to 1996, is the only large-scale experiment to date of a multicomponent fatherhood program. Authorized by the Family Support Act, PFS was conceptualized as a test of whether employment and training services, which had been shown to work for mothers on welfare, would be similarly effective for low-income, noncustodial fathers (Miller and Knox 2001; Knox and Redcross 2000).[1] PFS recognized that to increase fathers' financial support of their children through child support would

FIGURE 2
Intervention Studies Informing Future Initiatives for Fathers and Families

FATHERHOOD PROGRAMS

**RELATIONSHIP / MARRIAGE SKILLS
WORKSHOPS FOR COUPLES**

Programs targeting disadvantaged
noncustodial fathers (1991–2003)

❖ Young Unwed Fathers
❖ Parents' Fair Share (experiment)
❖ Welfare-to-Work grant
❖ Responsible Fatherhood

Preventive programs targeting middle-class couples
(some experiments)

❖ Group Workshops on communication
  / conflict resolution

Programs targeting disadvantage
dunmarried fathers early in the child's life
(2000–2003)

❖ Partners for Fragile Families

Preventive programs targeting middle-class
couples who are parents (experiments)

❖ Schoolchildren and their Families
❖ Becoming a Family
❖ Bringing Baby Home

Current programs targeting fathers, either individually or as part of a couple

❖ Healthy Marriageand Responsible Fatherhoodgrants (2005
  Deficit Reduction Act); Programs fundedby individual states

Current random assignment studies of programs for couples or fathers:

❖ Building Strong Families (unmarried couples with newborn)

❖ Supporting Healthy Marriage (marriedcouples)

❖ Supporting Father Involvement (couples or fathers-only)

❖ Fathers, Relationships, and Marriage Education (couples,
  mothers-only, or fathers-only)

❖ Promoting Strong Families (couples)

---

also require new responsiveness by the child support system toward the men's individual circumstances and attention to their nonfinancial involvement with their children.

Over the course of the demonstration, PFS randomly assigned more than fifty-five hundred noncustodial fathers—the vast majority of whom were African American—to either a mandatory program group or a control group at one of seven sites across the country. Implemented jointly by the child support agency, employment and training providers, and local social service agencies, PFS consisted of four main components. After meeting with case managers, participants took part in *peer support* sessions led by trained facilitators and based on the Responsible Fatherhood curriculum. These sessions, held two to three times per week for six to eight weeks, focused on personal and professional skill-building. Upon completing a certain number of sessions (or concurrently), fathers participated in *employment and training*, typically implemented as job search assistance due to constraints in these fathers' access to skills training. Throughout their participation in PFS, fathers were also intended to benefit from *enhanced child support enforcement*, including temporarily lowered orders. Finally, fathers were offered the option of participating in *voluntary mediation services* with the child's mother.

Foremost among PFS's implementation challenges was creating collaboration and teamwork among agencies that typically do not work together, despite their working with the same client population. This affected recruitment and service delivery, and many sites fell short of their enrollment goals. In addition, the men who enrolled in PFS (average age 31) were significantly disadvantaged: 67 percent had been arrested at some point, only half had a high school diploma, most did not have stable housing, and 76 percent had not worked within the six months prior to entering the program. With fathers targeted for the program in part because of child support arrears, over half the men in PFS owed more than $2,000 at the time they entered the program. Fathers cited their substantial arrears as a discouragement to formal employment, which, although it might offer more stable or higher-paying jobs than the informal sector, could also result in garnisheed wages.

PFS painted a portrait of father involvement that ran counter to stereotypes of disadvantaged noncustodial fathers. These were not fathers of newborns; the average age of their youngest child was six years old. Still, nearly one-third of control group fathers saw their children at least once a week during the six months prior to the follow-up survey. Another 40 percent of the control group fathers saw their children at least once during those six months. The remaining 30 percent of fathers did not see their children at all in the six months leading up to the follow-up survey. Meanwhile, only 34 percent of control group mothers reported that their relationship with the father during this same time period was friendly (though 46 percent of fathers did), and 13 percent of control group mothers and 6 percent of fathers reported aggressive conflict. In the six months prior to the follow-up survey, 6 percent of control group mothers had had a restraining order against the fathers.

The main impact of PFS was to increase the amount of child support paid, mainly as a result of the men's closer involvement with the child support system. PFS's other impacts were limited, in some ways, to participants on the "worst-off" end of the spectrum: employment rates and earnings increased only for program group men with the most severe employment barriers, and the level of involvement with their children increased modestly for those who were least involved initially. Still, PFS gave valuable insight into the tremendous challenges faced by the men it served and suggested new approaches for working with this group. PFS's findings are consistent with other research suggesting that programs working to strengthen low-income men's relationships with their children should contain a substantive employment and earnings component, combining immediate income with longer-term skill-building and job retention. PFS also offered evidence that when working with noncustodial fathers, custodial mothers must be brought into the picture. While fathers' participation in peer support and parenting education reflected their desire for involvement with their children, their efforts were often frustrated by the children's mothers—especially if the families had lived apart for several years. PFS suggested that programs might get further if they directly address mothers' concerns, offer them some type of incentive to participate in some redesigned aspects of the program, and, when possible, help parents to develop common expectations about the father's role with the child.

Ultimately, the PFS demonstration's modest impacts suggested the value of striking while the iron is hot, that is, helping parents to map out their financial and emotional roles while parents are still together and the child is expected or very young. What is more, the PFS qualitative study revealed considerable differences in how younger and older participants viewed their goals and their challenges. The younger men (primarily in their 20s) almost all saw themselves as marrying some-day, perhaps the mother of their child, but often described themselves as too young to "settle down." The older men in the program often had more stable lives and jobs but faced substantial struggles when they tried to reconnect with their children after years of living apart (Johnson, Levine, and Doolittle 1999). Consistent with these reports, program operators often indicate that, despite the conceptual appeal of targeting younger couples or fathers, extremely disadvantaged young men can be particularly challenging to engage in responsible fatherhood programs (Martinson and Nightingale 2008).

The Responsible Fatherhood Program, Welfare-to-Work Grants, and Partners for Fragile Families. While the Responsible Fatherhood Program and Welfare-to-Work Grants worked with populations that were quite similar to PFS, Partners for Fragile Families moved the field in a new direction. Based on challenges that earlier fatherhood programs had faced in increasing fathers' engagement with older children—and consistent with then-emerging findings from the Fragile Families and Child Wellbeing study that the vast majority of unmarried parents were in a romantic relationship at the time their baby was born—Partners for Fragile Families aimed to work with fathers ages 16 to 25 before they had established paternity or had experience with the child support system and while they might still have a positive relationship with their child's mother. Nevertheless, Partners for Fragile Families still worked primarily with fathers rather than couples and experienced many of the same implementation and recruitment challenges as earlier fatherhood programs (Martinson et al. 2007).

One clear finding across demonstration programs for low-income noncustodial fathers has been that men who have previously been incarcerated face particularly acute challenges in meeting their child support obligations and in maintaining relationships with their partners and children. Interventions that are aimed at supporting fathers during incarceration and the process of reentry are the subject of the current National Evaluation of the Responsible Fatherhood, Marriage, and

Family Strengthening Grants for Incarcerated and Re-entering Fathers and their Partners (McKay et al. 2009). The study has begun to provide implementation lessons and will conduct a quasi-experimental impact evaluation for five of the twelve grantees.

What have we learned from evaluations of marriage and relationship skills programs for couples?

Whereas programs labeled "responsible fatherhood programs" have until recently typically targeted one group—disadvantaged noncustodial parents—marriage and relationship skills programs have targeted individuals or couples, married or unmarried, parents or not. Marriage education was developed as a preventive approach to help couples to learn skills that might prevent declines in relationship satisfaction, in contrast to marital therapy, which has historically worked with couples trying to repair relationships already in distress. Conducted initially as part of university-based research programs, and more recently funded on a larger scale by ACF grants, marriage and relationship skills are typically taught in group workshops, classes, or small groups facilitated by one to two people (often male-female pairs), using structured curricula.

Many of the recent grant-funded programs focus on low-income families in particular, because although such families are disproportionately affected by family breakup, they have had limited access to services that could help to strengthen their relationships and marriages. Early evaluations of such services found promising evidence of program effects, although they primarily included white, middle-income engaged or married couples who paid a fee for the services. Meta-analyses over the past two decades suggest that preventive psychoeducationally oriented programs can produce moderate positive effects on relationship satisfaction and communication (Hawkins et al. 2008; Butler and Wampler 1999; Carroll and Doherty 2003; Giblin, Sprenkle, and Sheehan 1985; Blanchard et al. 2009; Reardon-Anderson et al. 2005). However, even studies that used random assignment were limited in that many had small samples, suffered from attrition of study members, and measured a limited set of outcomes rather than longer-term marital stability or outcomes for children (Carroll and Doherty 2003; Reardon-Anderson et al. 2005). Some, but not all, reviews and meta-analyses have reported reduced impacts over time after the intervention ends (Halford et al. 2003; Reardon-Anderson et al. 2005; Hawkins et al. 2008; Blanchard et al. 2009).

Recently published random assignment studies have begun to address the limitations of these earlier studies, seeking to increase the likelihood of long-term benefits by designing programs to last for several months and by conducting studies with somewhat larger samples, more careful designs, longer follow-up, and broader outcomes of interest. What is more, at around the same time that responsible fatherhood programs were becoming increasingly interested in working with parents early in a child's life, couples-oriented relationship skills programs seized on the value of working with couples at transition points that could precede declines in marital satisfaction, such as the birth of a baby. Programs such as

Bringing Baby Home and Becoming a Family, which focused on supporting relationships during the transition to new parenthood, have found a range of positive effects, including in couple relationship quality (but not stability); parenting, coparenting, and father-infant attachment; and infants' language and emotional development (C. Cowan and Cowan 2000; Shapiro and Gottman 2005). The Schoolchildren and Their Families study, targeting parents with children entering school, has reported improved adaptation to high school for children 10 years after the intervention (C. Cowan and Cowan 2006).

Current evaluations are beginning to shed light on whether, and how, relationships skills programs work for low-income families specifically. Each of the three studies discussed below is assessing the potential for interventions to increase the engagement of low-income fathers with their children and improve outcomes for children, by strengthening the couple's relationship. While current ACF healthy marriage grantees are expected to provide at least eight hours of group workshops, all three of the programs described below use a format in which groups meet weekly for a total of 24 to 42 hours, depending on the program, and have some capacity to link couples to additional supports. Thus, they are not representative of grantees currently operating marriage and relationships skills programs. Their results will indicate what can be achieved by real-world community-based organizations that use research-based curricula, provide modest incentives for participation, and receive close monitoring and technical assistance along the way.

The Supporting Healthy Marriage (SHM) project: An intervention for low-income parents who are married. Funded by ACF, the SHM project is the first large-scale, multisite, multiyear, rigorous test of marriage education programs for low-income married couples with children. A ten-year project that began in 2003, SHM is currently operating in ten locations and will be evaluated in both an implementation study and impact study.[2]

The SHM model consists of three mutually enforcing components operating from a strengths-based, couple-oriented perspective. At the core of the program is a 24- to 30-hour marriage-education workshop series. The group meetings are facilitated in a relaxed group setting and use four structured curricula with core materials that have been field tested over many years and have been recently adapted for low-income couples. While the curricula being used vary in content, target population, and format (for example, some are intended for parents with newborns; some focus more on group discussion than others), all address six broad content areas identified in prior research as potential influences on the quality of relationships for low-income couples: understanding marriage, managing conflict, promoting positive connections between spouses, strengthening relationships beyond the couple, coping with circumstances outside the couple relationship such as financial stress, and parenting.

Groups begin soon after enrollment and last nine to 15 weeks (depending on the local program). They are complemented by supplemental marriage education activities—social and educational events that aim to reinforce curricular concepts and build community. Meanwhile, the third component of the model, family support services, pairs each SHM couple with a family support coordinator who promotes consistent engagement by maintaining direct contact with the couple for 12 months, refers the couple to community resources as needed, and reinforces the skills and themes of the core workshops.

SHM is a voluntary program. Couples must be married, have children under 18, and understand the language in which the program is offered (either English or Spanish). Each local program—with the help of a local domestic violence advocate—has also created a way to assess domestic violence at intake and throughout program participation. Program data indicate that the average age of wives in the SHM sample is 30.5 and the average age of husbands is 33 (though parents are younger in the two sites targeting families with newborns). The average length of marriage is 7.1 years. Almost three-quarters of the couples have incomes less than or equal to 200 percent of the federal poverty guidelines (and almost half have annual family incomes below $30,000). Participants are roughly 50 percent Hispanic, about 30 percent white non-Hispanic, and about 15 percent African American. SHM couples also have an average of two children.

There are no impact results available yet, but we know that couples have enrolled in large numbers and tend to keep coming once they have attended a group workshop. More than 80 percent of early SHM couples attended at least one workshop together in the first six months after enrolling. On average, SHM couples who initiated attendance have attended 20 hours of workshops in the first six months. Participation in family support has been similarly strong, with 85 percent of couples in this early sample attending at least one meeting with a family support coordinator.[3]

The fact that both spouses nearly always participate together in SHM services is a promising trend that may in part result from the programs' deliberate efforts to appeal to men. For example, program offices use gender-neutral décor, and workshops are facilitated by a male-female pair to demonstrate that both perspectives are equally valued and to model supportive interaction. Programs have intentionally hired male staff and culturally sensitive staff. Many programs have also created supplemental marriage activities (such as workshops on being an involved dad) and family support services (such as job referrals) designed to appeal to men.

The SHM impact analysis, with 12-month follow-up due in 2012, is designed to comprehensively assess effects on multiple domains, including the quality of the couple's relationship and its stability; the mental health of each parent; quality of coparenting; fathers' engagement with their children; quality of parenting by each parent; employment and income; and developmental outcomes for children, including emotional security, behavior problems, and positive behaviors.

The Building Strong Families (BSF) project: An intervention for unmarried parents of newborns. Also begun as a part of the federal Healthy Marriage initiative, the BSF project is programmatically similar to SHM but targeted to unmarried parents of newborns or of babies up to three months old. With eight programs across the country, BSF is a ten-year demonstration project that will culminate in an impact analysis of effects on the quality and status of couples' relationships, family outcomes, and children's well-being.

As in SHM, the core component of BSF has been a series of relationship skills workshops, supplemented by a family coordinator who encouraged program participation, reinforced curricular skills, and provided resource referrals. Most sites also held social events for participants, and some held ongoing educational activities to supplement the core curriculum. BSF used different curricula than those in SHM and included topics tailored to unmarried couples and parents of newborns. BSF-eligible couples were also screened for domestic violence.

The implementation study found substantial variation in the duration, length, format, and content of services.[4] Once enrolled, couples participated in their 30- to 42-hour core workshop series, which generally ranged from 10 weeks to six months. Group size also varied from six to fifteen couples. Participants typically received incentives to participate such as cash, modest gifts, or gift certificates. Once a couple completed their workshop, some sites no longer offered family support services, while others expected couples to meet with their family coordinators quarterly for up to three years. Sites also took fairly different approaches to the content of family support services.

BSF parents were generally young: in more than 40 percent of the couples, at least one member was less than 21 years old. In the majority of the couples (52 percent), both partners were African American, 20 percent were both Hispanic, and 12 percent were both white non-Hispanic. While in 37 percent of couples both partners had a high school degree, their average combined annual earnings were $20,475. Multipartner fertility was common: in 47 percent of the couples, one partner had a child from a previous relationship. In 57 percent of the couples, both partners reported that they were cohabiting "all of the time" at the time of enrollment. Another 7 percent were married (eligible for BSF because they were unmarried at the time their child was conceived).[5]

BSF gave high priority to engaging both members of the couple. However, some program operators struggled to maintain consistently strong participation levels, with participation varying considerably across sites. On average, BSF couples reported attending 12 more hours of relationship skills education groups than control-group couples. Sites reported a much higher likelihood of couple engagement if an initial contact was made with both members of the couple, and to further solidify couples' commitment to the program, many sites experimented with male-female recruiter teams.

Implementation lessons from BSF include the challenges of integrating a novel model into existing service delivery pathways, as well as the difficulties—given unpredictable schedules and many competing demands for time—of helping low-income couples maintain consistent participation in a long-term program. Still, BSF offers encouragement that relatively young, disadvantaged, unmarried parents have an interest in participating together in programs designed to improve their relationships and outcomes for their children.

A preliminary impact report for the BSF evaluation was released in May 2010, with assessments 15 months after couples entered the study. On average across all eight sites, the intervention had no overall effect on couples' status, relationship quality, ability to manage conflict, coparenting quality, or fathers' involvement. The subgroup and site-specific results, however, suggest that the effects of this type of program may depend on how it is implemented or on the specific population being served, or both. Across the eight sites combined, the intervention produced positive effects on relationship quality for couples in which both partners were African American, but there were no positive impacts for couples in which at least one member was not African American. One of the eight sites, Oklahoma, showed significant positive effects on several measures of relationship quality and stability; perhaps importantly, the Oklahoma program had substantially higher participation rates than the remaining BSF programs. Couples at that site reported attending group relationship workshops for 19 more hours than control-group couples did, whereas across all BSF sites couples reported spending only 12 hours more than control-group couples. In contrast, the BSF site in Baltimore had a pattern of negative effects; this program served a population of couples who, on average, had more tenuous relationships with one another at the outset of the program and who attended relationship skills groups for only six more hours than control-group parents.[6] Additional analyses are being conducted to further understand the effects of BSF summarized here. A 36-month follow-up report will provide information about longer-term relationship impacts as well as effects on child well-being.

Given that neither SHM nor BSF was designed to work with couples who are experiencing domestic violence, a set of questions remain about how to appropriately work with couples who may be experiencing what is referred to by some family violence researchers and practitioners as situational domestic violence. We will learn more about this issue through a study that ACF is currently funding, conducted by the Relationship Research Institute (RRI). In this study, RRI is assessing the effectiveness of the marriage-education curriculum titled Couples Together against Violence in reducing low-level situational violence, strengthening marriage/relationships, and increasing fathers' involvement. The evaluation is designed to identify not only the impact of the program but also the mechanisms responsible for decreases in domestic violence (U.S. Department of Health and Human Services n.d.-a).

The Supporting Father Involvement (SFI) study: An intervention for low-income fathers and couples. Impact results are available from the SFI study, which provided relationship skills workshops for primarily low-income Hispanic two-parent families (unmarried or married).[7] SFI was designed as a side-by-side evaluation of preventive father-focused and couple-focused approaches to fostering fathers' positive engagement and strengthening family functioning.

Like SHM and BSF, SFI was a voluntary program, operated by four family resource centers in agricultural California counties from 2003 to 2009. (Data from a fifth urban site are forthcoming.) Two-thirds of participants were of Mexican descent. Couples did not have to fit specific cohabitation, marriage, or income criteria, but they did have to be biological parents of their youngest child. In addition, if either parent suffered severe mental illness or substance abuse issues that interfered with daily functioning, or had had an instance of domestic violence or child abuse within a year prior to enrollment, the family was referred for other services. Median annual family income of $29,700 reflected that more than two-thirds of participating families fell below 200 percent of the poverty line. Ninety-four percent of participants lived together, and 72 percent of participants were married upon entering the program.

The SFI model assigned couples to a couples group, fathers group, or comparison group (all held in either English or Spanish). Couples were not given incentives for participation in the groups but were compensated for completing each of three assessments. Both fathers and couples groups met for two hours each week for 16 weeks and were facilitated by a male-female pair of mental health professionals, with an identical curriculum. Men in the fathers groups attended alone, with mothers coming for two of the 16 weeks to meet with the female coleader, while fathers and mothers attended the couples groups together for all 16 weeks. Comparison group couples (who attended together) received a single-session, three-hour dosage of a condensed version of the curriculum, taught by the same facilitators. For all sessions, child care and food were provided. Families in all three study conditions were also assigned to a case manager responsible for promoting program engagement and providing resource referrals.

The SFI curriculum was a hybrid between a therapy-group approach and the more structured psychoeducational classes offered in BSF and SHM. Based on a family risk model of factors associated with father's positive involvement, couple relationship quality, and children's well-being, the curriculum covered parenting and coparenting, couple communication, three-generational family patterns, stressors and supports, and participants' self-conception and personal goals. Although the curriculum was previously used with middle-income couples, the researchers made few modifications other than adding material on financial stressors, de-emphasizing written materials, and emphasizing interactivity. The fact that group meetings always included an open-ended check-in allowed the participants to make sure that the curriculum directly addressed their needs. Four sessions focused on the couple's relationship and four focused on parenting; each remaining topic was covered in two sessions.

Over the course of the study, programs noticed that median attendance was significantly higher (75 percent for fathers, 80 percent for mothers) in couples groups than in fathers groups (65 percent), although overall attendance was high. Men in fathers groups tended initially to offer more positive reinforcement to one another and speak more openly to their peers than those in couples groups. Partners in the couples groups tended to spend more time discussing couples' communication and conflict resolution. In addition, programs reported a "ripple effect" of SFI in terms of their broader agencies' increased attention to fathers' needs and increased father-friendliness.

Current SFI impact data are based on a sample of 289 couples, with follow-up assessments at nine and 18 months. SFI produced positive results across a number of domains (though not, interestingly, on parenting attitudes). Fathers group participants showed increased involvement with their children and stability of children's behavior problems over two years (compared with increases in problem behaviors in the comparison group). The couples group showed even larger gains in terms of increased involvement of fathers in the day-to-day lives of their young children and stable levels of children's problem behaviors. Furthermore, in the couples group only, parenting stress declined (compared with stable scores for the comparison and fathers groups), and the quality of the couple's relationship remained stable according to both fathers and mothers, whereas parents in both the comparison and fathers groups showed declining relationship quality over two years. SFI found that the positive results held across ethnic groups, income level, and marital status.

Given the lack of positive pre-post changes and the occurrence of negative changes for the comparison group, the SFI study concluded that single-dosage efforts are unlikely to benefit fathers, couples, or their children. SFI also concluded, as noted in the impact report, that "the question is not whether to intervene with fathers or with couples, but in either approach, how to involve both parents in the intervention program" (P. Cowan et al. 2009, 677).

The Fathers, Relationships, and Marriage Education (FRAME) project. We will learn more about the relative effectiveness of working with individual parents and working with couples through another multigroup randomized study currently under way, the FRAME project (Markman et al. 2009). This study, conducted by a team at the University of Denver with funding from ACF, targets parents who live together in a committed relationship and whose family income is below 200 percent of the poverty line. Couples are randomly assigned to a control group or one of three treatments—a workshop attended by couples, a workshop attended by male partners only, or a workshop attended by female partners only. All three workshops use FRAME, a 14-hour variant of the 24-hour Within Our Reach curriculum created by the Prevention and Relationship Enhancement Program (PREP) for the SHM project. Relative to Within Our Reach, FRAME is designed with increased focus on the role of fathers, parenting, and coping with economic stress. The evaluation will assess whether the efficacy of this intervention depends on whether couples, fathers, or mothers participate.

Given resource constraints, it is important to gain information about how program effectiveness varies with its mode of delivery and its intensity. Promoting Strong Families, a study by the University of Georgia of a relatively short family intervention, combines modules from two curricula that were found to be effective in prior randomized studies. A five-year demonstration sponsored by ACF, Promoting Strong Families consists of six educational sessions based on PREP, which has shown efficacy at improving couples' relationship quality, and on the Strong African American Families program, which worked primarily with mothers and their early adolescent children and had positive impacts on parenting skills and parent-reported child behavior (Brody et al. 2004). Of the 460 couples enrolled in the study, half will receive the Promoting Strong Families curriculum through in-home sessions facilitated by trained presenters, while the other half will review written materials independently (University of Georgia n.d.).

Future Directions

Responsible fatherhood programs

It is clear that we have a larger body of evidence about how to help committed couples to improve the quality of their relationships, and about the effects of those efforts, than about how to facilitate the quantity and quality of father-child engagement for disadvantaged men who are already living away from their children. There have been few impact evaluations of responsible fatherhood programs, and implementation studies of these programs have consistently highlighted the significant challenges of changing the employment and family relationship patterns for low-income noncustodial fathers (Martinson and Nightingale 2008). We offer some suggestions for ingredients of the next generation of multicomponent responsible fatherhood programs based on what has been learned to date.

- Many disadvantaged fathers highly value assistance with getting good jobs and care deeply about better relationships with their children. On the other hand, they are skeptical that the child support system will treat them fairly.
- Particularly in voluntary programs, but even in mandatory programs linked to child support mandates, it has been difficult to recruit fathers and to achieve consistent participation over time. Given both participation challenges and disadvantaged fathers' lack of access to public assistance and their need to support themselves and their children, programs for fathers that focus solely on these men will likely benefit from building in stipends, paychecks, or other financial incentives for participation.
- It will take innovative approaches in training and job ladders to substantially improve labor market prospects for very disadvantaged men.
- Responsible fatherhood programs that do not explicitly work with mothers have found it difficult to make headway in improving fathers' relationships with their children. However, it is challenging to improve adult relationships once partners are deeply estranged, suggesting that coparenting or relationship skills programs will gain more traction when offered while parents are still in a relationship together. Programs offered later are likely to need to work with some mothers and fathers outside of group workshops, and sometimes separately from one another, to create plans for fathers' involvement.
- The child support system has an important role to play in getting incentives in the right place for custodial and noncustodial parents to collaborate on parenting issues and for fathers to participate in employment-related activities.

It will be difficult to create more effective programs for young noncustodial fathers without innovation in each of these areas: child support, employment, and family relationships. To make headway, responsible fatherhood programs could be integrated with the innovative policy ideas for child support and employment that are outlined in other articles in this volume. Below, we focus on the third leg of a comprehensive responsible fatherhood strategy: interventions directly aimed at strengthening family relationships.

One area that would benefit from new attention is to develop and carefully test methods to engage custodial parents (mostly mothers) in achieving the goals of these programs. This may be important not only as a means to increase fathers' engagement with their children but because of recent evidence that low-income nonresident fathers' engagement with their children is associated positively with young children's well-being only in the context of high-quality coparenting relationships (Carlson, McLanahan, and Brooks-Gunn 2009). Involving custodial parents in fatherhood efforts does not necessarily mean that mothers would be physically present at fatherhood programs as often as noncustodial fathers; in some cases, it may make sense for them to be active participants, and in others, it may not. It is possible that such efforts could draw on some of the concepts used in coparenting programs for parents who are married, cohabiting, or divorcing that have shown some efficacy in randomized studies (Cookston et al. 2007). In addition, efforts should be informed by recent qualitative research that has uncovered issues that matter to low-income unmarried parents and about which fathers and mothers sometimes have substantially different perspectives, such as: Must a responsible and successful parent be a breadwinner? A disciplinarian? Do conflict and distrust between parents affect children and how parents relate to them? In what ways do new partners affect both parents' relationships with their children? (Waller 1997; Furstenberg 2007; Young and Holcomb 2007; England and Edin 2007; Hamer 2001). While coparenting support interventions would likely be designed quite differently for parents who are still together and those who are not, in either case, they could help fathers and mothers to clarify their own perspectives on these challenging issues, to understand their partners' or former partners' perspectives, and to agree upon joint expectations for parenting the child they have in common.

Another area for careful consideration is the content and format of peer support groups within fatherhood programs that have typically been aimed at basic "fatherhood development." For example, given what we now know, will these workshops be most effective at changing outcomes for the family if attended by noncustodial fathers alone, or with their current partners, or some of both? Should they focus on a broad range of fatherhood topics, as is currently usually the case, or cover a few topics in greater depth? Although these workshops often offer material on parenting or couple relationship skills, this tends to be covered briefly rather than in the kind of multisession format that has been found effective at building these skills (Barth 2009). Moreover, there are critical emerging issues, such as the challenges facing parents who have children with multiple partners or the role of social fathers who often play important roles in children's lives, which have not yet been the subject of extensive curriculum development. Ultimately, to treat critical topics in some depth, and to acknowledge the differing needs of different families, responsible fatherhood programs may find it useful to move away from "one-size-fits-all" curricula for group workshops and toward a more flexible approach that includes both an individual support component and a menu of group workshops that would vary depending on fathers' individual circumstances. Individualized services, in turn, require thoughtful design of tools for initial screening and assessment related to domestic violence, family composition, and other issues that will influence how services are tailored.

Finally, we should not forget that research on how fathers affect child well-being consistently finds that it is not the quantity of fathers' involvement that matters, but the quality (Carlson and Magnuson this volume). This suggests that we should clarify the basic goals of responsible fatherhood programs to ensure that they go beyond the collection of child support and the father's level of access to his children to include actively ensuring that the interaction that does occur is as supportive of child well-being as possible. For many children, greater involvement by a low-income nonresident father is likely to be unambiguously helpful; for others, for example in relationships marked by domestic violence, substance abuse, or severe mental illness, increased involvement is likely to be unwelcome and unhelpful; and for others, greater involvement may improve some domains of child well-being and undermine others. We clearly need to understand more about the dynamics of these complex relationships—how the quality, not just the quantity, of low-income nonresident fathers' involvement affects children and how public policy can balance the well-being of children with the rights and responsibilities of each parent.

To continue to improve policies and programs, both responsible fatherhood and couples-based family strengthening programs should be embedded in a rigorous research agenda that addresses outstanding questions for various types of families. Research should be focused on understanding the effectiveness of specific program components, different curriculum approaches, different levels of staff training, and what works best for different subgroups of families, as well as assessing the total effects of comprehensive programs, since individual components may have synergistic effects. In addition, given the relative paucity of research on the dynamics of low-income nonresident fathers, their children, and former or current partners, high-quality basic research on these families and their perspectives on emerging intervention strategies is critical. Given the complexity of these policies, it is important to understand their short- and long-run implications for the well-being of fathers, mothers, family relationships, children, and government budgets.

Strengthening relationships of low-income couples: Two paths for progress

Given the complexities of family behavior, no single policy or program is likely to reach all families. As we develop more understanding of what works best for whom, it might be most efficient to combine preventive strategies that are targeted to a broad population with somewhat more intensive interventions for families who face immediate challenges. Thus, "research and development" toward relationship skills programs could proceed on two tracks. One track would continue to fund local community-based service providers to offer stand-alone relationship skills programs for low-income couples, adapting the program models and targeting strategies as new research results become available. In recent years, the U.S. Department of Health and Human Services has encouraged both participation in relationship skills programs and involvement of fathers with their children through existing programs for parents such as Head Start or Early Head Start programs. However, these particular programs are largely limited to families below the poverty level, so a substantial proportion of their clients are single-parent families. To also provide existing two-parent families with access to relationship skills programs would likely require recruitment from additional venues such as health clinics, obstetricians' or pediatricians' offices, child care centers, preschools, hospital- or neighborhood-based childbirth classes, and Medicaid or Women, Infants, and Children (WIC) programs.

A second approach that could be pursued systematically could be dubbed the "developmental" approach to strengthening family relationships. The goal here would be to strive for every young person to leave high school with a basic understanding of the relationship skills that he or she will need to sustain employment, a satisfying long-term relationship with a partner, and effective parenting as an adult. These skills might include, for example, effective communication, problem-solving strategies, regulating one's emotions in difficult conversations, and understanding the perspective of another. Identifying the "active ingredients" of strong relationship skills and introducing them into *existing* educational settings at a number of developmental stages could reach a much larger number of people than stand-alone programs for which adult participants must take steps to volunteer and attend consistently over time. Even if fully implemented, this type of preventive approach would not negate the need for relationship-strengthening opportunities for couples with children or noncustodial fathers, but it would provide a foundation for these skills earlier in life. For an example of this type of layered approach, see the Triple P parenting program, which is designed with multiple tiers of increasing intensity, from support for universal parenting skills that all community members should possess to more intensive programs for those who need additional support (Prinz et al. 2009).

The foundations of this developmental approach are already beginning to emerge. Parents' capacities to nurture babies' earliest social and emotional development are being supported through Early Head Start or other programs for new parents such as those described in this article. As children enter child care, preschool, Head Start, or pre-kindergarten, evaluations are under way to understand how teachers can best support their socioemotional development and handle behavioral issues in the classroom (MDRC n.d.). Many elementary, middle, and high schools are undertaking efforts to integrate violence prevention, peer-to-peer communication, and conflict resolution training into their curricula (Aber, Brown, and Jones 2003). Comprehensive teen pregnancy prevention and youth development programs often include some attention to relationship skills, whether geared toward peer relationships, healthy dating decisions, or relationships with supervisors in a workplace. Once the young person has become a partner or spouse, strengthening that adult-couple relationship by building attention to it into existing service settings—whether in employment programs for fathers, in home visiting programs for parents of newborns, or in place-based approaches such as Baby College of the Harlem Children's Zone—could be a logical continuation of this more universal, integrated approach to strengthening family relationships.

Ultimately, it is possible that attending to partner relationships in existing programs for adults would bring benefits not only for fathers' engagement and couple relationships but also for the programs into which they are integrated, since there is evidence that attending to the couple's relationship can bolster the effects of other interventions. For example, for children with behavior problems, two different studies of parenting interventions (of the Incredible Years and Triple P) have found that when couples were in distressed relationships, adding curriculum content that focused on the couple's relationship led to an increase in the intervention's effects on parenting (Webster-Stratton and Taylor 2001). Similarly, a head-to-head test of two substance abuse treatment models found that treatment was more effective when the spouse of the substance abuser was trained to be supportive in the treatment process (O'Farrell and Fals-Stewart 2000).

We recognize that our urging of agencies to bring relationship skills more centrally into responsible fatherhood or other programs may engender some resistance. Ooms et al. (2006) describe how representatives of fatherhood, couples' relationship, and domestic violence programs each have some fear that the other approaches are missing essential ingredients or may compromise the intended goals of their own programmatic approach. Our intention here is not to replace existing programs with a new couple-focused model, but rather to take seriously the evidence that a family-relationship perspective addresses some of the key risk factors that affect both family functioning in diverse types of families and children's development. A wide range of programs—from those aimed at parents' employment or asset-building to those targeting children's early development—could find that they benefit from synergies that are created as we learn more about how to support couples in planning together for their families' well-being.

Notes

1. Though random assignment was open to all noncustodial parents who fit the eligibility criteria, more than 95 percent of the parents in the demonstration were men.

2. Information about the SHM model, implementation, and early participation rates is drawn from Gaubert et al. (2010) as well as from Knox and Fein (2009).

3. The SHM demographic information is taken from Gaubert et al. (2010).

4. This description of BSF implementation draws from Dion et al. (2008), with additional information taken from the project website at www.buildingstrongfamilies.info.

5. This description of BSF couple demographics draws from Wood et al. (2010).

6. This discussion of BSF impacts draws from Wood et al. (2010).

7. This discussion of implementation and intervention results is based on P. Cowan et al. (2009) and C. Cowan et al. (2007). Some details were taken from the project Web site at www.supportingfatherinvolvement.org.

References

Aber, J. Lawrence, Joshua L. Brown, and Stephanie M. Jones. 2003. Developmental trajectories toward violence in middle childhood: Course, demographic differences, and response to school-based intervention. *Developmental Psychology* 39 (2): 324–48.

Achatz, Mary, and Crystal A. MacAllum. 1994. *Young unwed fathers: Report from the field*. Philadelphia, PA: Public/Private Ventures.

Barth, Richard. 2009. Preventing child abuse and neglect with parent training: Evidence and opportunities. *The Future of Children* 19 (2): 95–118.

Blanchard, Victoria L., Alan Hawkins, Scott Baldwin, and Elizabeth Fawcett. 2009. Investigating the effects of marriage and relationship education on couples' communication skills: A meta-analytic study. *Journal of Family Psychology* 23 (2): 203–14.

Brody, Gene H., Velma McBride Murry, Meg Gerrard, Frederick X. Gibbons, Virginia Molgaard, Lily McNair, Anita C. Brown, Thomas A. Wills, Richard L. Spoth, Zupei Luo, et al. 2004. The Strong African-American Families Program: Translating research into prevention planning. *Child Development* 75 (3): 900–917.

Butler, Mark H., and Karen Wampler. 1999. A meta-analytic update of research on the Couple Communication Program. *American Journal of Family Therapy* 27 (3): 223–37.

Carlson, Marcia J., Sara S. McLanahan, and Jeanne Brooks-Gunn. 2009. Nonmarital fathering and the wellbeing of children. Center for Research on Child Wellbeing Working Paper, Princeton University, Princeton, NJ.

Carroll, Jason S., and William Doherty. 2003. Evaluating the effectiveness of premarital education programs: A meta-analytic review. *Family Relations* 52 (3): 105–18.

Coley, Rebekah L., and Lindsay P. Chase-Lansdale. 1999. Stability and change in paternal involvement among urban African American fathers. *Journal of Family Psychology* 13 (3): 416–35.

Cookston, Jeffrey T., Sanford Braver, William Griffin, Stephanie deLusé, and Jonathan Miles. 2007. Effects of the Dads for Life intervention on interparental conflict and co-parenting in the two years after divorce. *Family Processes* 46 (1): 123–37.

Cowan, Carolyn Pape, and Philip Cowan. 2000. *When partners become parents: The big life change for couples*. Mahwah, NJ: Lawrence Erlbaum.

Cowan, Carolyn Pape, and Philip Cowan. 2006. The case for preventive intervention to strengthen couple relationships: Good for couples, good for children. Presentation at the Evolving Families Conference, Marriage and Family: Complexities and Perspectives, 7 April, Cornell University, Ithaca, NY.

Cowan, Carolyn Pape, Philip Cowan, Marsha Pruett, and Kyle Pruett. 2007. An approach to preventing coparenting conflict and divorce in low-income families: Strengthening couple relationships and fostering fathers' involvement. *Family Process* 46 (1): 109–21.

Cowan, Philip A., Carolyn Pape Cowan, Marsha Pruett, Kyle Pruett, and Jessie Wong. 2009. Promoting fathers' engagement with children: Preventive interventions for low-income families. *Journal of Marriage and Family* 71 (3): 663–79.

Dion, M. Robin, Alan Hershey, Heather Zaveri, Sarah Avellar, Debra Strong, Timothy Silman, and Ravaris Moore. 2008. Implementation of the Building Strong Families Program. Washington, DC: Mathematica Policy Research Inc. Available from www.mathematica-mpr.com.

Egeland, Byron, and Elizabeth Carlson. 2004. Attachment and psychopathology. In *Clinical applications of attachment*, ed. Leslie Atkinson, 27–48. Mahwah, NJ: Lawrence Erlbaum.

England, Paula, and Kathryn Edin, eds. 2007. *Unmarried couples with children*. New York, NY: Russell Sage Foundation.

Furstenberg, Frank F. 2007. *Destinies of the disadvantaged: Teenage childbearing and public policy*. New York, NY: Russell Sage Foundation.

Gaubert, Jennifer Miller, Virginia Knox, Desiree Principe Alderson, Christopher Dalton, Kate Fletcher, and Meghan McCormick. 2010. *Early lessons from the implementation of a relationship and marriage skills program for low-income married couples*. New York, NY: MDRC.

Giblin, Paul, Douglas Sprenkle, and Robert Sheehan. 1985. Enrichment outcome research: A meta-analysis of premarital, marital and family interventions. *Journal of Marital and Family Therapy* 11 (3): 257–71.

Halford, W. Kim, Howard Markman, Galena Kline, and Scott Stanley. 2003. Best practice in couple rela-tionship education. *Journal of Marital and Family Therapy* 29 (3): 385–406.

Hamer, Jennifer. 2001. *What it means to be daddy: Fatherhood for black men living away from their chil-dren.* New York, NY: Columbia University Press.

Hawkins, Alan J., Victoria Blanchard, Scott Baldwin, and Elizabeth Fawcett. 2008. Does marriage and relation-ship education work? A meta-analytic study. *Journal of Consulting and Clinical Psychology* 76 (5): 723–34.

Johnson, Earl, Ann Levine, and Fred Doolittle. 1999. *Fathers' fair share: Helping poor men manage child support and fatherhood.* New York, NY: Russell Sage Foundation.

Knox, Virginia W., and David Fein. 2009. Designing a marriage education demonstration and evaluation for low-income married couples. In *Marriage and family: Complexities and perspectives*, eds. H. Elizabeth Peters and Claire M. Kamp Dush, 247–80. New York, NY: Columbia University Press.

Knox, Virginia W., and Cindy Redcross. 2000. *Parenting and providing: The impact of Parents' Fair Share on paternal involvement.* New York, NY: MDRC.

Markman, Howard, Shauna Rienks, Martha Wadsworth, Mathew Markman, Lindsey Einhorn, Erica Moran, Nicole Mead Glojek, Marcie Pregulman, and Lea Gentry. 2009. Adaptation: Fatherhood, individual, and Islamic versions of PREP. In *What works in relationship education: Lessons from academics and service deliverers in the United States and Europe*, eds. Harry Benson and Samantha Callan, 67–74. Doha, Qatar: Doha International Institute for Family Studies and Development.

Martinson, Karin, and Demetra S. Nightingale. 2008. *Ten key findings from responsible fatherhood pro-grams.* Washington, DC: Urban Institute Press.

Martinson, Karin, John Trutko, Demetra S. Nightingale, Pamela Holcomb, and Burt Barnow. 2007. *The implementation of the Partners for Fragile Families demonstration projects.* Washington, DC: Urban Institute Press.

McKay, Tasseli, Anupa Bir, Christine Lindquist, Elise Corwin, Mindy Herman Stahl, and Hope Smiley McDonald. 2009. *Bringing partners into the picture: Family-strengthening programming for incarcer-ated fathers.* ASPE Research Brief. Available from www.aspe.hhs.gov.

MDRC. n.d. Head Start CARES project. Available from www.mdrc.org/project_11_89.html.

Miller, Cynthia, and Virginia W. Knox. 2001. *The challenge of helping low-income fathers support their children: Final lessons from Parents' Fair Share.* New York, NY: MDRC.

O'Farrell, Timothy J., and William Fals-Stewart. 2000. Behavioral couples therapy for alcoholism and drug abuse. *Journal of Substance Abuse Treatment* 18 (1): 51–54.

Ooms, Theodora, Jacqueline Boggess, Anne Menard, Mary Myrick, Paula Roberts, Jack Tweedie, and Pamela Wilson. 2006. Building bridges between healthy marriage, responsible fatherhood, and domestic violence programs: A preliminary guide. Washington, DC: Center for Law and Social Policy. Available from www.clasp.org.

Personal Responsibility and Work Opportunity Reconciliation Act of 1996, Public Law 104-193. TANF Legislation, Part A, Section 401(a)(4) (1996).

Prinz, Ronald J., Matthew Sanders, Cheri Shapiro, Daniel Whitaker, and John Lutzker. 2009. Population-based prevention of child maltreatment: The U.S. Triple P System Population Trial. *Prevention Science* 10 (1): 1–12.

Reardon-Anderson, Jane, Matthew Stagner, Jennifer Ehrle Macomber, and Julie Murray. 2005. *Systematic review of the impact of marriage and relationship programs.* Washington, DC: U.S. Department of Health and Human Services, Administration for Children and Families. Available from www.acf.hhs.gov.

Shapiro, Alyson F., and John Gottman. 2005. Effects on marriage of a psycho-education intervention with couples undergoing the transition to parenthood, evaluation at 1-year post-intervention. *Journal of Family Communication* 5 (1): 1–24.

University of Georgia, Institute for Behavioral Research, Center for Family Research. n.d. Promoting Strong Families study. Available from www.uga.edu/prosaaf.

U.S. Department of Health and Human Services, Administration for Children and Families n.d.-a. ACF responsible fatherhood initiatives and healthy marriage initiative. Available from www.acf.hhs.gov.

U.S. Department of Health and Human Services, Administration for Children and Families n.d.-b. OFA 2005 healthy marriage and promoting responsible fatherhood initiatives. Available from www.acf.hhs .gov/programs/ofa/hmabstracts/summary.htm.

Waller, Maureen R. 1997. Redefining fatherhood: Paternal involvement, masculinity, and responsibility in the "Other America." PhD diss., Princeton University, Princeton, NJ.

Webster-Stratton, Carolyn, and Ted Taylor. 2001. Nipping early risk factors in the bud: Preventing substance abuse, delinquency, and violence in adolescence through interventions targeted at young children (0–8 years). *Prevention Science* 2 (3): 165–92.

Wood, Robert G., Sheena McConnell, Quinn Moore, Andrew Clarkwest, and JoAnn Hsueh. 2010. *Strengthening unmarried parents' relationships: The early impacts of Building Strong Families*. Princeton, NJ: Mathematica Policy Research.

Young, Alford, Jr., and Pamela Holcomb. 2007. Voices of young fathers: The Partners for Fragile Families evaluation. Washington, DC: Urban Institute. Available from http://aspe.hhs.gov/hsp/07/PFF/voices.

Income Support Policies for Low-Income Men and Noncustodial Fathers: Tax and Transfer Programs

By
RONALD B. MINCY,
SERENA KLEMPIN,
and
HEATHER SCHMIDT

Both wages and labor force participation have been declining for young, less-educated men since the mid-1970s. The purpose of this article is to examine how key income-security policy areas—including unemployment insurance, payroll taxes and the Earned Income Tax Credit, and child support enforcement—affect these men. The article concludes with policy recommendations to improve the impact of work-based subsidies on poverty among low-income men. Subsidized jobs in transitional job programs could play a critical role in helping these men to access these subsidies.

Keywords: low-income men; noncustodial fathers; payroll taxes; Earned Income Tax Credit; unemployment insurance; child support enforcement; subsidized jobs

That it may take as much as a year from the end of the Great Recession, as Sum and colleagues (2009) describe, before the employment-population ratios of young, less-educated men rise is alarming. Indeed, the employment-to-population ratio of black teenagers is now 14 percent, with a 49 percent unemployment

Ronald B. Mincy is the Maurice V. Russell Professor of Social Welfare Policy and Practice at Columbia University's School of Social Work and director of the Center for Research on Fathers, Children and Family Well-Being. He has devoted more than 30 years to researching the needs of low-income families, particularly black fathers. He is the editor of Black Males Left Behind *(Urban Institute Press 2006).*

Serena Klempin is a research assistant at the Center for Research on Fathers, Children and Family Well-Being within Columbia University's School of Social Work. She holds a master's degree in social work.

Heather Schmidt holds a master's degree in social work and received her juris doctorate from Rutgers School of Law–Newark. She was previously an intern at the Center for Research on Fathers, Children and Family Well-Being.

NOTE: The research for this article was supported by the Annie E. Casey Foundation, Charles Stewart Mott Foundation, the Ford Foundation, and the Open Society Institute's Campaign for Black Male Achievement (CBMA).

DOI: 10.1177/0002716210393869

rate (Baker 2009). Of greater concern is the decline in both real wages and labor force participation for this subgroup since the mid-1970s. Even during the economic boom of the 1990s—the longest economic expansion the United States has ever seen—labor force participation and wages for young, less-educated men showed little improvement (Berlin 2007; Holzer and Offner 2006).

The purpose of this article is to highlight key income-security policy areas where changes are needed to meet this challenge. These include unemployment insurance, payroll taxes and the Earned Income Tax Credit (EITC), and child support enforcement. Working together, these policies have contributed to increases in employment for young, less-educated women and reductions in child poverty, but rarely have their joint implications for less-educated men been considered (Berlin 2007; Edelman, Holzer, and Offner 2006; Scholz 2007).

Before discussing these policy areas, we note that each is predicated upon work. Therefore, we begin with a brief discussion of the provisions of the American Recovery and Reinvestment Act (ARRA) (U.S. Congress 2009b), which attempts to relieve some of the financial pressures of the Great Recession on states and workers.[1] Finally, we indicate responses needed not only by government, but also by the independent sector, through targeted philanthropy for related research and programming, especially in relation to transitional jobs programs. These critical actors' engagement will be necessary to make any policy reforms work.

Unemployment Insurance and ARRA Funds for Workforce Development

The federal government's aggressive buildup of unemployment insurance (UI) benefits under ARRA is one important indicator of the severity of the Great Recession (Shelton, Romig, and Whittaker 2009). First, ARRA provides a $25 per week increase in benefits for workers receiving UI benefits under any one of several UI funds. Second, it extends the period during which qualified unemployed workers can claim UI benefits and does not require states to share in the additional costs. As a result of these extensions, qualifying workers can now collect unemployment benefits for up to 99 weeks (the normal limit is 26 weeks). Third, ARRA includes $7 billion to fund provisions of the UI Modernization Act (UIMA), which encourages states to extend unemployment benefits to the part-time, part-year, and low-wage workers and those experiencing long-term unemployment (Bradley and Lordeman 2009). Fourth, the federal government is directly assuming a larger share of other costs of UI benefits. States are receiving $500 million to administer UI programs, and they do not repay or accrue interest when they borrow to replenish their UI trust funds. Additionally, workers do not have to pay income taxes on the first $2,400 of the UI benefits they receive in 2009.

While these changes will relieve pressure on states and older workers, financial pressures on younger unemployed workers will remain. Younger workers are overrepresented among part-time and part-year and low-wage workers, so they are less likely than older workers to meet the minimum work or earnings requirements for UI benefits, and they are more likely to quit or be dismissed for misconduct, which also make workers ineligible for UI benefits. Wandner and Stettner (2000), who conducted the most recent analysis of the age distribution of UI claims, argued that misunderstanding eligibility requirements was one reason why during the 1991 to 1992 recession only 53.4 percent of *unexperienced* unemployed males between 20 and 25 years old applied for UI benefits, while 67.9 percent of *experienced* unemployed males 25 years or older applied. Older experienced unemployed males (55.6 percent) were also more likely to receive UI benefits than their younger counterparts (36.4 percent).

The Great Recession has taken its biggest toll on young men, many of whom are childless or noncustodial parents (NCPs) (Sum et al. 2009). Many young, less-educated women who are ineligible for UI benefits are single mothers, so they can fall back on Temporary Assistance for Needy Families (TANF). Without TANF or much relief from UI benefits, young men who are childless or NCPs desperately need placement assistance, education and training, or subsidized jobs. Since broadening access to the nation's workforce development system in 1998, when it replaced the Job Training Partnership Act (JTPA) (U.S. Congress 1982) with the Workforce Investment Act (WIA) (U.S. Congress 1998), Congress has consistently reduced funding for WIA below JTPA levels (Nightingale and Sorensen 2006). ARRA provides $4 billion in new spending for job training under WIA (Bradley and Lordeman 2009). However, the legislation sunsets in September 2010, and with the unemployment rate still at 9.6 percent as of October 2010 (U.S. Department of Labor 2010), displaced workers are much more likely than young, less-educated men to be the beneficiaries of this funding (Cooper 2010). If the stimulus package holds little hope for young, disadvantaged men, what can they expect from long-standing income security policies?

Payroll Taxes and the EITC

Given downward trends in the earnings of less-educated young men, payroll tax relief for this subgroup is long overdue (Berlin 2007; Holzer and Offner 2006). Workers pay a percentage (7.65 percent) of earnings toward federal payroll taxes, which provide revenue for Social Security, Medicare, unemployment insurance, and other social insurance programs; however, annual earnings above $106,800 are exempt from the percentage of federal taxes that fund Old Age, Survivor, and Disability Insurance (OASDI) (Griffin 1999; Sammartino, Toder, and Maag 2002). Therefore, payroll taxes are regressive with respect to income, in contrast to income taxes, which are progressive (Burman and Leiserson 2007; Griffin 1999; Kobes and Magg 2003). In 2006, 94 percent of wage earners who made less than $100,000 per year paid more in payroll taxes than they did in income taxes (Burman and Leiserson 2007).

For most low-income individuals who have children, various tax credits and programs decrease their tax burden to zero, or a negative amount, which is then reimbursed. The most important of these credits for low-wage workers is the

EITC, which is the nation's largest antipoverty program (Holt 2006). In 2007, the EITC provided $49 billion to nearly 2.5 million American households (Internal Revenue Service [IRS] 2009b). Initially proposed by Senator Russell Long (D-LA) in 1975 as an antipoverty program targeted toward low-income workers with children, the credit offsets payroll taxes for low-income workers and refunds the difference, if any (Holt 2006). Since then the EITC has expanded broadly for low-income working families; by 1998 it had surpassed the amount of aid provided by other child poverty programs. However, it has expanded far more slowly for workers without custody of children. It was not until 1993 that an EITC was even established for these workers (Holt 2006). The most recent expansion to the credit, enacted under ARRA, created an additional credit for families with three or more children. This additional credit was intended to provide temporary support during the recession and thus only applied to the 2009 and 2010 tax years (IRS 2009a). However, both President Obama's 2010 and 2011 budgets contained a proposal to make this expansion permanent[2] (U.S. Department of Treasury 2009, 2010).

The EITC schedule is defined using three distinct ranges: a phase-in, or subsidy range, in which each additional dollar of earned income[3] increases the credit until a maximum credit is reached; a flat range, at which the credit remains constant as the worker's earnings increase; and a phase-out range over which the credit declines until workers' earnings makes them no longer eligible for the credit. The schedule for each of these three ranges differs according to marital status and number of children (zero, one, two, and three or more).

For example, in the 2009 tax year, the credit for a single tax filer with two children rose in the phase-in range by 40 cents for each additional dollar earned. The maximum credit for such a tax filer was $5,028 when earnings were between $12,570 and $16,420, which was between 88 and 115 percent of the earnings of a full-time, full-year (fully employed) minimum wage worker. Workers with higher earnings were in the phase-out range where the credit declined by 21 cents for each additional dollar of earned income, and the credit completely phased out when earnings reached $40,295, which was 282 percent of the earnings of a fully employed minimum wage worker. Corresponding amounts for a single parent with one child were as follows: an increase of 34 cents for each additional dollar of earned income during the phase-in range; a maximum credit of $3,043 for those who earned between $8,950 and $16,420; and a decrease of 15.98 cents for each additional dollar of earned income during the phase-out range, with the credit completely phasing out when earnings reached $35,463. By comparison, childless workers receive far less from the EITC. The credit rises by a mere 7.65 cents for each dollar of additional earned income during the phase-in range and phases out at the same rate. The maximum credit is just $457 for workers with earnings between $5,970 and $7,470, which is between 42 and 52 percent of the earnings of a fully employed minimum wage worker. The credit completely phases out when earnings reach $13,440, which is 94 percent of these earnings (Scott 2008).

Not surprisingly, given the structure of the EITC, single mothers have been the largest group of recipients (Holt 2006). During the 1990s' economic boom, welfare reform efforts increased the proportion of EITC recipients who were single mothers, while childless, less-educated workers, particularly men, saw only modest employment gains during those years (Blank and Schmidt 2001; Holzer and Offner 2006). In addition to a lack of employment gains, several other reasons help to explain why less-educated men receive fewer benefits from the EITC than do single mothers. First, some are employed in the informal economy, so only the formal part of their earnings can be subsidized through the tax system (Rich, Garfinkel, and Gao 2007). Second, many income-eligible young men are either unaware of the credit, uninformed about how to file for the credit, or do not file tax returns (Mincy, Jethwani-Keyser, and Klempin n.d.). Finally, some are prohibited from applying, because they are younger than 25, the minimum age requirement for the credit.

Ranging in cost from $3 billion to roughly $34 billion, several legislative proposals address barriers to participation in the EITC, including those that young, less-educated men are most likely to face. These proposals include increasing the childless worker credit, establishing a special credit for noncustodial parents (NCP/EITC), and reducing the minimum age requirement.

Expansion of the childless worker EITC

Childless workers are the only taxpayers in the United States who owe federal income tax when their income is below the poverty level (Aron-Dine and Sherman 2007). The EITC offsets only half of the earnings deducted for payroll taxes for childless workers (Gitterman, Gorham, and Dorrance 2007). To avoid taxing childless workers into poverty and to provide work incentives for workers with low wages, a number of bills have been introduced in the past few years to expand the childless worker EITC.

However, even if the childless worker credit were increased to avoid taxation-induced poverty, childless workers would still gain little or nothing from the EITC under current law. As early as 2007, a bill proposed by Representative Charles Rangel (HR 3970) (U.S. Congress 2007b) warned that minimum wage increases would result in nominal credits for childless workers fully employed at the minimum wage and render such workers ineligible for the EITC by 2009 (Aron-Dine and Sherman 2007). In 2008, fully employed, but childless, minimum wage workers earned $12,812,[4] and the EITC for childless workers phased out completely at $12,880 (IRS 2009a; Scott 2008). The resulting credit for such workers was approximately $50 (see Figure 1). By 2010, the annual earnings of fully employed minimum wage workers reached $15,080,[5] well in excess of the income level ($13,460) at which the childless EITC phases out completely (see Table 1).

To prevent workers with poverty-level wages from owing federal income tax and to improve work incentives, Representative Rangel proposed an expansion of the credit in 2007[6] (HR 3970). HR 3970 would (1) extend the credit's phase-out period (increasing the starting point to $10,900 and the ending point to $16,620), (2) increase the credit rate for workers earning less than $5,720 from

TABLE 1
EITC for Single Childless Workers

Current Law by Tax Year	Income Range for Maximum Credit and Respective Maximum Credit		Annual Minimum Wage Earnings[a] and Respective Credit[b]		Income Where EITC = 0
2008	$5,720–$7,160	$438	$12,812	$48	$12,880
2009	$5,970–$7,470	$457	$14,268	$0	$13,440
2010	$5,980–$7,480	$457	$15,080	$0	$13,460

SOURCE: Scott (2008).
a. We calculated annual minimum wage based on the maximum number of possible working hours (52 weeks × 40 hours a week = 2,080), rather than the 2,000 formula.
b. Based on our own calculations.

FIGURE 1
EITC for Single Childless Workers

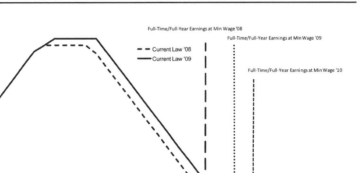

7.65 percent to 15.3 percent of earnings, and (3) increase the maximum credit to $875. The estimated cost of this proposal was $3 billion per year (Aron-Dine and Sherman 2007).

In 2009, Representative Henry Waxman included an even more ambitious approach to expanding the childless worker EITC in the American Clean Energy and Security Act (U.S. Congress 2009a). This proposal would expand the childless credit by increasing both the phase-in and the phase-out rates from 7.65 to 15.3 percent and by increasing the beginning of the phase-out range to $11,640. The expansion would be effective starting in 2012 and would double the maximum credit for childless workers from $457 to $914. Although these increases would cover fully employed minimum wage workers, these workers would still earn too much to receive the maximum credit (Edelman et al. 2009).

Noncustodial parents and the EITC

NCPs, even while required to provide financial support to their nonresident children, are ineligible to claim their nonresident children for tax purposes. Instead, they are eligible for the same EITC as childless workers with no such additional financial obligations. Of the many legislators to propose expansions of the childless worker EITC, Senator Evan Bayh and then-Senator Barack Obama were the first to propose an additional federal EITC targeting NCPs (S 1626) (U.S. Congress 2007a), which Senator Bayh reintroduced in summer 2009 (S 1309) (U.S. Congress 2009d). This proposal, modeled on the Noncustodial Parent Earned Income Tax Credit (NCP/EITC) in New York State and Washington, D.C., applied the same income requirements for NCPs as for all childless workers but doubled the credit that NCPs received by increasing the credit's phase-in and phase-out rates from 7.65 to 15.3 percent. The proposal also increases the phase-out income threshold by basing the threshold on a percentage of annual minimum wage income (defined as the federal minimum wage effective on January 1 of that year multiplied by 2,000[7]). For the 2010 tax year, the phase-out threshold would be 70 percent of annual minimum wage income, and it would gradually rise to 100 percent of annual minimum wage income by 2014. From 2015 onward the threshold would be indexed for inflation (Solomon-Fears, Falk, and Pettit 2009). To qualify for the additional benefit, however, NCPs would have to pay their child support in full for the current tax year. Therefore, to fully understand the implications of this proposal, we consider the size of the credit not only in the context of minimum wage earnings but also in the context of earnings and child support compliance.

Because the childless worker credit in Senator Bayh's proposal is half the NCP's credit, fully employed, but childless, minimum wage workers in 2010 would be barely eligible, but similarly employed NCPs would still receive about $250, about $125 more than the cost of tax preparation services (see Figure 2). In comparison, a single mother with two children pays about $350 for tax preparation services and receives an EITC of more than $5,000, or about $1,700 for each member of her household. The maximum NCP credit in 2010 under S 1309 would be less than $1,000, but this credit is available only to NCPs with earnings between $5,900 and $10,150, roughly 40 to 70 percent of the earnings of a fully employed minimum wage worker. Only NCPs who were unemployed for a substantial portion of the year or were part-time/part-year workers would be income eligible for the maximum value of the NCP/EITC.

However, unemployed and underemployed NCPs are those most likely to have defaulted on their child support orders. As much as 70 percent of total child support arrears in the United States are owed by NCPs earning less than $10,000 a year (Sorensen, Sousa, and Schaner 2007). Therefore, those most likely to be income eligible for the maximum value of the NCP/EITC are also those most

FIGURE 2
S 1309 Childless Worker and NCP EITC

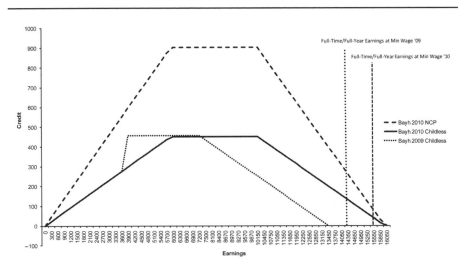

likely to be ineligible for the credit due to child support noncompliance. Thus, proposals that condition eligibility for the childless worker credit or NCP/EITC on full compliance during the year are, at best, feeble attempts to offset payroll taxes for low-income NCPs and feeble attempts to provide them with incentives to work and comply with their child support obligations. Indeed, Wheaton and Sorensen (2009) estimate that only 5 percent of all NCPs would benefit from the S 1626, NCP/EITC proposal. Preliminary estimates, based on the Fragile Families and Child Wellbeing study, show that only 9 percent of the income-eligible NCPs of children born just two years after the 1996 amendments to Title IV-D would benefit from this proposal (Mincy and Miller forthcoming).

Despite the difficulties posed by the full child support compliance requirement in S 1309, we believe that the proposal's use of the minimum wage as the basis of the phase-out threshold is crucial for the EITC to have a significant impact on low-income childless workers and NCPs. As illustrated in Figure 2, the childless worker credit phased out at such a low income threshold in 2008 that many low-wage childless workers barely qualified, and fully employed minimum wage workers became ineligible for the credit in 2009 after scheduled minimum wage increases. Nonetheless, it is important to recognize that the proposal's increases occur gradually over a span of five years, so that fully employed minimum wage workers would not receive the maximum credit until 2014.

To avoid the complications of the child support compliance requirement described above, several other EITC expansion proposals do not include a specific NCP/EITC, but instead address the needs of NCPs through their childless worker proposals. For example, supporters of HR 3970 see all childless workers as either future NCPs or future parents. This proposal also ties the increase for childless workers to Representative Rangel's desire to lower the minimum age at which a person becomes eligible for the credit. If these changes occur, NCPs and childless workers, as future parents, will have stronger labor force attachments earlier and will be better able to provide for all potential children. Representative Davis also follows this approach of reaching NCPs through the childless worker credit in HR 2979 (U.S. Congress 2009c). The increased credit for childless workers in this proposal would be equal to 20 percent of earnings up to a maximum earnings amount (Solomon-Fears, Falk, and Pettit 2009). Additionally, proposals from several policy analysts agree that expansion of the childless worker credit is sufficient to address the needs of NCPs (Greenberg, Dutta-Gupta, and Minoff 2007; Edelman, Holzer, and Offner 2006; Carasso et al. 2008; NYC Department of Consumer Affairs 2008).

By contrast, Wendell Primus (2006), now senior policy advisor on budget and health issues to former House Speaker Nancy Pelosi, offers a radically different proposal that is specifically targeted at the children and families of NCPs. It would provide benefits for up to one-half of the EITC for families of NCPs who pay at least half of their child support order, with the amount varying by the percentage of support paid. This proposal is aimed at the fact that fathers behind on their child support are the exact people who could benefit and be aided in the payment of that support with the supplement of the EITC. Few others support this proposal because it poses even more administrative complexities than the NCP/EITC proposals.

The minimum age requirement

Workers must be at least 25 years old to receive the EITC. A primary motive for this criterion is to deny the credit to full-time students. Unfortunately, this criterion denies the credit to many less-educated young men who are otherwise eligible, including NCPs. Among 24 million poor adults, about 60 percent either have no children or are NCPs (Greenberg, Dutta-Gupta, and Minoff 2007, 27). Using data from the Fragile Families and Child Wellbeing study, which is representative of unmarried births in large cities (Reichman et al. 2001), we calculated that at the birth of the child, the median age of unmarried nonresident fathers was 25 years old and that only 3 percent of fathers were students. Denying these less-educated young NCPs (and their children) access to the EITC to prevent full-time students, who also work, from receiving the EITC seems an odd compromise.

If policy-makers are committed to denying the credit to full-time students who are younger than 25 years old, the IRS could try excluding those under 25 whose parents claim them as dependents. Whether the credits accruing to income-eligible workers, who are full-time students and financially independent of their parents, outweighs the potential benefits to young low-wage workers who are not full-time students is an empirical question. Support for lowering the minimum age requirement appears to be growing, however, as evidenced by Representative Rangel's proposal, HR 3970, and others (Greenberg, Dutta-Gupta, and Minoff

2007; NYC Department of Consumer Affairs 2008; Scholz 2007). Additionally, although neither S 1309 nor HR 2979 proposes lowering the age requirement, they both call for a study examining the effect of the age eligibility restriction on young NCPs' (1) ability to pay child support, (2) child support compliance, and (3) relationship with their children.

Child support enforcement

Welfare and child support. Besides proposing the original EITC, Senator Russell Long also sponsored Title IV-D of the Social Security Act, which created the Federal Office of Child Support Enforcement (OCSE) (Garfinkel 1992). Reimbursing taxpayers for the cost of welfare benefits was an important motive for Title IV-D, which allowed states to collect child support from fathers of children receiving welfare.[8] Welfare policy continued to provide an important link between the EITC and child support enforcement during the welfare reform efforts of the 1990s. An important rationale for the major increase in the EITC in 1993 was an effort to "make work pay," so that single mothers leaving welfare for work would be better off than those who remained on welfare (Ellwood 1988).

Policy-makers also hoped to reduce welfare recidivism by increasing child support payments to mothers leaving welfare for work. OCSE had long required local child support agencies to open a welfare-related child support case, once a custodial mother started receiving welfare benefits. Doing so became increasingly difficult, however, because much of the growth of welfare caseloads after the early 1980s was due to the growth in nonmarital births. In the case of nonmarital births, paternity must be established before a child support order can be established. Therefore, universal paternity establishment became a centerpiece of the 1990s welfare reform.

In-hospital paternity programs were established by executive order in 1992, and shortly thereafter paternity establishment rates began to rise (Legler 1996). In addition, several provisions of the 1996 amendments to Title IV-D have further extended the paternity establishment rate growth (Mincy, Garfinkel, and Nepomnyaschy 2005; Pirog and Ziol-Guest 2006). These amendments allow states to increase sanctions against mothers receiving TANF benefits who fail to cooperate with the state in identifying the father (with exceptions for cases of rape and incest). In cases in which OCSE identifies fathers, they have the option to voluntarily acknowledge paternity. Without a voluntary acknowledgment, courts can conduct genetic testing of the mother, child, and putative father so that a judge can rule on an order of paternity[9] and then establish a child support order.

Child support compliance, arrears and the EITC. OCSE estimates that more than $105 billion in child support arrears have accumulated over the past 20 years (OCSE 2007). Noncustodial fathers who do not have (and most likely will not soon have) the financial resources to pay either their current child support or the accumulated arrears are held accountable for a substantial amount of these arrears (Office of Inspector General 2000; Sorensen, Sousa, and Schaner 2007). Low-income NCPs who do not pay their child support orders tend to be younger, have lower levels of work experience, be poorly educated, and have more problems with drugs and alcohol (Mincy and Sorensen 1998). Many spend a substantial part of their time in prisons, where child support orders accumulate even though market earnings are forbidden. These factors lead to less stable employment, thereby making these fathers less likely to be in compliance with their child support orders.

While there is little evidence that the child support burdens of low-income fathers reduce their employment or labor force participation rates (Freeman and Waldfogel 2001; Holzer, Offner, and Sorensen 2005), there is preliminary evidence that when arrears are high relative to fathers' income, formal labor force participation declines (Miller and Mincy 2009). Individuals with the most debt have the highest average monthly child support orders and are expected to pay a considerably higher percentage of their income toward support than those with little or no arrears (Sorenson, Sousa, and Schaner 2007). Indeed, up to 65 percent of earned income can be garnished by OCSE in most states if the father is behind in his child support payments[10] (Holzer, Offner, and Sorenson 2005).

Several studies have also found that low-income NCPs are obligated to pay a higher proportion of their income in child support than middle- and high-income NCPs, which results in lower levels of compliance among low-income NCPs (Huang, Mincy, and Garfinkel 2005; Meyer, Ha, and Hu 2008). Waller and Plotnick (2001) found that low-income NCPs felt overwhelmed by child support orders that were too high and that this may have led them to avoid market earnings or formal child support and thus pay nothing. Although these fathers may still be making informal contributions to the mothers or guardians of their children, the extent of informal support is difficult to measure. While few studies have specifically studied the amount of informal support provided by NCPs, Nepomnyaschy (2007) found that informal child support payments by never-married NCPs were (imperfect) substitutes for formal child support payments. If an NCP has a child support order, but pays informally, his arrears continue to grow because informal support does not count toward compliance with child support.

In addition to having troubling implications for formal labor force participation, the child support enforcement system may operate in ways that impede the effectiveness of the EITC. As previously mentioned, many current proposals to expand the EITC for NCPs require full compliance with child support orders during the current year. Additionally, states are entitled to collect any past-due child support owed to the state from federal tax refunds.[11] The law allows states to offset arrears by taking a portion or all the EITC, as long as the amount of support owed is at least $500. This is of particular concern, because low-income NCPs are the most likely group of NCPs to have accumulated child support arrearages.

Several factors can contribute to the growth of arrears for low-income NCPs. For example, child support orders are often calculated using an "imputed income" rather than actual income when the NCP is not present for court on the day that the order is being determined or if the NCP is unemployed or underemployed

(Office of Inspector General 2000). In some states, imputed income is based on the minimum wage, while in other states is it based on the TANF standard of need for a child (Sorensen 2004). Some states also charge the father for welfare payments received by the mother prior to the establishment of the child support order or include the Medicaid costs for the birth of the child in the support order (Lerman and Sorensen 2003). When these factors are included in computing child support, they can become prohibitively high.

The difficulty and cost associated with modifying a child support order further contribute to noncompliance and the growth of arrears. Federal law states that a modification can only be granted after the NCP demonstrates that his circumstances have changed in such a way that the current child support order is "unconscionable," a difficult standard to meet (Baron 1999). Additionally, changes in circumstances cannot be voluntary, and courts will not grant petitions for modifications if the NCP has temporarily quit his job, even to pursue further education. Twenty-one states consider incarceration "voluntary unemployment" and therefore not a justification for modifications (Pearson 2004). Some states require a percentage change or a minimum dollar change in the NCP's income. Other states determine whether a modification is appropriate based on the schedule that the state used to decide original child support orders—if the amount will change based on the schedule, then a modification may be granted. Even if an NCP qualifies for a modification of the order, however, it is rarely pursued because the court process is difficult, expensive, and time-consuming.

Interest charges are the primary factor contributing to the growth in arrears (Sorensen, Sousa, and Schaner 2007). Eighteen states charge interest on a regular basis (every month or every other month), and an additional eighteen states charge interest intermittently (for example, interest may not be charged until the TANF case is closed). The increase in arrears has been significantly larger for the states that charge interest regularly than for states that either do not charge interest or only charge interest intermittently.

Given these policies, it is not surprising that low-income NCPs are reluctant to earn market wages, which would qualify them for the EITC, or to enter the formal child support enforcement system. Nor is it surprising that never-married mothers and mothers with TANF benefits are less likely than other mothers to receive the full amount of child support due. In 2007, 51 percent of custodial parents who were divorced and had child support awards received the full amount due, compared with about 40 percent of separated and never-married parents and 34 percent of parents receiving public assistance (Grall 2009).

Policy Recommendations

Short-term: Workforce. In the short term, the administration must see that ARRA funds are used to meet the training needs of low-income workers, particularly less-skilled and less-educated younger men, who have borne the brunt of job losses in the recession (Smeeding, Garfinkel, and Mincy 2009; Sum et al. 2009). As we move out of the recession, many dislocated workers will be prepared to find new jobs immediately; however, many people will need to acquire new skills to find work in new sectors so that they can restore as much of their former earnings as possible. The effects of the 1998 reorganization of the workforce development system, which included a broadening of its reach and successive reductions in funding, will be glaring as both disadvantaged and dislocated workers stream into One-Stop Career Centers. It will be even more difficult to provide training to the many less-educated young men in need. In the rush to create and fill positions and to ensure that former welfare recipients do not lose their foothold in the labor market, states are likely to neglect the training needs of less-educated workers, especially men. To avoid this situation, expenditures of ARRA funds must be carefully monitored to guarantee that the emphasis on training actually occurs.

Long-term: Payroll-tax relief and child support enforcement. A critical near-term goal is to reverse the decline in disposable incomes of childless workers, especially NCPs. Unless we do so, "make work pay," which has been a hallmark of income-security policy for the past decade, will be an unrealized goal for these young men, their children, and families. Reversing declines in income involves policy reform at the intersection of the EITC and child support enforcement, a daunting task because the federal government administers the former, while state governments, for the most part, administer the latter. Thus wide variations could exist across states in the proportion of less-educated NCPs who actually receive an expanded childless worker credit or NCP/EITC. To avoid this discrepancy, much of the policy reform must occur at the federal level.

The most direct method of focusing reform at the federal level is to use the childless worker credit, rather than the NCP/EITC, to increase the disposable incomes of less-educated NCPs. This is the approach many recommend and the approach Representative Davis takes in HR 2979, which is currently before various committees of the 111th Congress (Solomon-Fears, Falk, and Pettit 2009). While the objective of providing greater support to nonresident fathers who have child-related expenses than to truly childless workers is laudable, it is very difficult to do so in practice, largely because the IRS and the OCSE each has independent needs for privacy and data security. The administrative challenges associated with verifying whether the NCP has a formal child support order, whether that order has been paid in full, and whether the father is income eligible and meets the tax requirements, and then rapidly sharing that information across the two agencies, cannot be underestimated. Furthermore, the experience in New York State with the NCP/EITC suggests that few potentially eligible NCPs actually receive the credit (Cade 2008), because filing for the credit is costly and the net benefits are low (Mincy, Jethwani-Keyser, and Klempin n.d.).

Therefore, it might be much easier and more effective to allow all NCPs to apply for an enhanced childless credit. If NCPs owed child support arrears, states could intercept the credit, just as under current law. Wheaton and Sorensen

(2009) argue that an intercepted credit provides little or no incentive for work or child support compliance, but this assumption is untested. According to low-income NCPs and the providers that serve them in New York, even an intercepted credit provides an automatic mechanism to pay down arrears, thereby increasing monthly disposable income (Mincy, Jethwani-Keyser, and Klempin n.d.). One can still question, however, how much of the credit should be intercepted because of arrears.

The answer to that question, like the answer to the question of whether to condition EITC eligibility on full child support compliance, depends on the sensitivity of child support receipt to the business cycle. There is surprisingly little research on this question, but recent reports suggest that child support default rates are rising during the Great Recession (Bosman 2009; Miller and Mincy 2009). It seems merciless to insist on full compliance with child support during the longest recession in the postwar period, especially while forgiving debts accumulated on Wall Street and Main Street. However, the federal government enters the debate about how to manage child support arrears at great peril. State experiments with arrears abatement strategies demonstrate that it is possible to devise such strategies for NCPs with incomes of $20,000 or more, but not for those with lower incomes, who are the NCPs with the highest arrears (Hong 2008; Sorensen, Sousa, and Schaner 2007). Both HR 2979 and Senator Bayh's companion legislation (S 1309) provide demonstration funds for states to work on this and other complicated issues about child support and low-income NCPs. Congress should pass and fund this legislation so that states can use arrears abatement strategies to address the question of tax interception as well as EITC eligibility.

Addressing these questions is important. Defaults on current child support payments would exclude fewer NCPs from the NCP/EITC than not having a formal child support order (Wheaton and Sorensen 2009; Mincy and Miller forthcoming). However, the two conditions may be related. Low-income NCPs and custodial mothers may avoid the formal child support system, because the former cannot afford to comply and therefore do not compile the legal market earnings needed for the EITC (Huang and Pouncy 2005). If so, addressing the range of challenges that child support enforcement poses for low-income NCPs will ultimately determine whether they can access work-based subsidies, which are now the primary antipoverty strategies available to low-income Americans.

Long-term: Unemployment insurance and workforce. In the longer term, policy for low-income men and fathers should address three additional ARRA-related foci. First, we should assemble and build on the lessons we learn from states that have used UIMA funds during the Great Recession to extend unemployment benefits to part-time, part-year, and low-wage workers. Second, ARRA's temporary infusion of WIA training funds could well sunset before the economic recovery creates enough tightness in the labor market to affect the demand for less-educated young male workers. Subsequent budgets must add enough funding to WIA so that training services are available to help to reverse the secular decline in the earnings of less-educated men. Third, we must renew a commitment to the research and development necessary to identify, test, and disseminate a set of effective workforce development strategies for increasing the skills and earnings of less-educated men. Over the past 15 years, little attention has been paid to the improvement and development of such strategies. Programs such as Youth Build and the Job Corps began with private funding for research, development, and advocacy. These programs have become established parts of the Department of Labor's offerings. A few private foundations continue to invest in career, sector-based, and youth development strategies, in the hopes of spurring additional innovations that could advance federal programming. ARRA's funding of training in high-growth and emerging industries and sector-based training could provide additional support to such efforts, but it is unlikely to provide support for the application of these strategies to disadvantaged workers. Funding programs for disadvantaged workers, as well as the advocacy that leads to public adoption of innovations in employment-training for disadvantaged workers, has been the role of private philanthropy. Unless private philanthropy plays this role on a larger scale, how will we identify the Youth Builds and Job Corps of tomorrow?

Meanwhile: Mandated participation in subsidized/transitional jobs programs. A constant theme of this article is that low rates of employment, labor force participation, child support order establishment, and child support compliance dilute the potential impacts of all work-based policies on poverty among disadvantaged men. To have a greater impact, these systems must be expanded to cover workers with weaker attachment to mainstream employment and child support. UIMA and proposals to increase payroll tax relief for NCPs through the childless worker credit take this approach. Given the recent thrust of income-security policy, which predicates assistance on work and responsibility, the more enduring approach will rely on higher rates of employment, labor force participation, child support order establishment, and child support compliance among disadvantaged men. The challenge is finding a strategy that will accomplish this in the face of the secular decline in labor force participation among less-educated men and the sluggish demand for their labor in the next several years, following the Great Recession.

Arguing that culture rather than economic incentives or slack labor markets was the primary reason for low employment rates among poor men, Mead (2007) proposed to reduce poverty among such men by mandating work for parolees and NCPs who do not pay their child support obligations. This recommendation would apply the same paternalistic approach that Mead argues was so critical to the success of welfare reform. Under his proposal, ex-offenders and NCPs who did not pay their child support obligations would be mandated to participate in work programs where their job-search efforts would be closely supervised by case managers. If they were unable to find private sector jobs within 30 days, these men would be required to participate in subsidized jobs and required, in the case of NCPs, to pay child support.

Some of the elements of Mead's (2007) proposal are already in place. We recommend building on these elements by expanding transitional jobs programs for disadvantaged men already subject to work mandates (i.e., some parolees and NCPs who do not pay their child support obligations). Such an approach is appropriate whether the reason for not working is poor soft skills, the upshot of what Mead calls culture, low economic incentives, or low private sector demand for less-educated workers.

Transitional jobs programs employ participants in subsidized jobs and help them to acquire work experience so that they can compete in the labor market and eventually obtain unsubsidized jobs. The Center for Employment Opportunities (CEO) is developing a particularly important model for ex-offenders in New York. Most of CEO's clients are less-educated black and Latino men, with the vocabulary, deportment, and interpersonal relationships that enable them to survive in hypermasculine urban environments. To help them to learn a different set of skills, which they will need to acquire and sustain unsubsidized jobs, CEO provides soft skills training. It also provides case management services and referrals to meet a variety of other needs, including health, housing, food security, and substance abuse treatment. However, many of CEO's clients must find a job as a condition of parole. Many of CEO's clients are also NCPs with child support obligations that grew during incarceration, so CEO also helps clients to modify their child support orders (child support intermediation). These services are typical of workforce intermediaries who serve less-educated men. However, since CEO's clients are ex-offenders, acquiring a job immediately upon release is critical so that they can meet parole requirements, pay for daily expenses, and pay child support. Therefore, CEO combines the foregoing services with subsidized jobs in which CEO is the employer of record (Redcross et al. 2009). This distinguishes CEO from many other workforce intermediaries, who must rely upon unsubsidized jobs in the private sector to place their clients.

Early evaluation results of the CEO model show that it produces short- and long-term reductions in recidivism but only short-term gains in employment and earnings. Long-term gains in employment and earnings probably do not occur because once the period of subsidized employment ends, treatment group clients are able to find unsubsidized jobs at no higher rates (and paying no higher wages) than control group members (Redcross et al. 2009; Bloom 2009). This is consistent with several decades of demonstrations project research involving disadvantaged men (LaLonde 1995). Still, by teaching clients soft skills and helping them to comply with their child support obligations, CEO ensures that disadvantaged men are developing the habits that increase gains to their children and to society from subsidized employment. Along with the long-term reductions in recidivism, the CEO model may yet prove cost-effective in the long run.

This model (i.e., subsidized employment, along with case management, soft skills training, and child support intermediation) should be expanded to serve NCPs who cannot pay their child support obligations. At present we are content to apply the same child enforcement tools to these NCPS as the tools we use to coerce payments from NCPs who are able to pay. Since many never find a stable job or pay the child support due, the result is exponential growth in arrears. Neither NCPs, nor taxpayers, nor custodial families benefit from this approach.

Clearly, these men should not be allowed to continue to shirk their obligations to their children. Whether they are unable or unwilling to find private sector jobs on their own, they should be required to take subsidized jobs, paying the minimum wage. States already have the authority to mandate delinquent obligors to participate in employment services, but the number of states making use of these mandates fell after 2001, when federal subsidies for such programs were eliminated along with funding for the Welfare-to-Work program. Few if any of these programs produced long-term gains in employment or earnings, although they did report gains in the number of NCPs who paid some child support. Moreover, these programs may or may not have provided effective soft skills training.

We agree with Mead (2007) that states should impose (existing) mandates on NCPs who do not pay their child support obligations, but unlike Mead, we think these mandates should be simple: either pay the full amount of the child support order or go to work immediately in a transitional jobs program, combining the core CEO elements: (1) subsidized jobs, (2) case management services, (3) closely supervised soft skills training, and (4) child support intermediation.

We have two reasons for mandating immediate participation in subsidized jobs, rather than using subsidized jobs as "jobs of last resort," as Mead (2007) recommends. First, we are persuaded that slack demand for less-educated workers, mainstream soft skills deficits (the upshot of Mead's cultural explanation), and poor work incentives all play some role in explaining the low employment rates among disadvantaged NCPs. Any or all of these factors could delay job placement in the private sector, after a mandate is imposed. Mandating NCPs to participate in a subsidized job immediately after indicating that they cannot pay their child support obligations would facilitate automatic wage withholding, which would increase income to custodial families and reduce the accumulation of arrears. Second, immediate participation would promote greater child support compliance and lower arrears, which would help to qualify NCPs for a variety of work-based supports, such as the NCP or childless EITC, which presently elude them because they work in the informal labor market, have high unemployment rates, avoid filing taxes, and pay their child support informally, if at all. Thus, our approach puts taxpayers, custodial families, and NCPs on the right long-run path and does so immediately.

NCPs could transition out of subsidized jobs if they found a private sector employer who provided automatic wage withholding. There would be no incentive to take an unsubsidized job, unless it paid more or offered more favorable employment conditions than subsidized employment. Therefore, subsidized jobs should place more demands on participants than jobs in the private sector. However, we would qualify the mandate for subsidized jobs by noting that some NCPs should be exempt from transitional jobs programs, including disabled NCPs, or NCPs who have caregiving responsibilities for family members. Though many disadvantaged men are not fulfilling their responsibilities to their children, they are providing care and support to other family members, especially their mothers, who may be ineligible for disability and Medicaid benefits or who are receiving inadequate support from those programs. Ignoring these other caregiving responsibilities would force these NCPs to ignore their mandates, which would mean further financial or other sanctions for a population that already owes a disproportionate share of total arrears and is overrepresented in the nation's prisons and jails.

Although the cost of subsidized employment is an issue, we have identified two sources of funds to finance our proposal. The first arises from a $45 million (of $50 million proposed in President Obama's fiscal year 2010 budget) appropriation by Congress to the Department of Labor for a transitional jobs initiative to serve individuals with significant barriers to employment. Ex-offenders and NCPs are particular groups targeted by this initiative (U.S. Department of Labor 2009). The second arises from President Obama's fiscal year 2011 budget, which, if approved,[12] would redirect $500 million from the Bush administration's Healthy Marriage Initiative to a new Fatherhood, Marriage, and Families Innovation Fund. Half of this fund would provide competitive grants to states for comprehensive responsible fatherhood programs that rely on strong partnerships with community-based organizations (Administration for Children and Families 2010). Besides funding services, building knowledge about effective practices, which could be replicated by TANF, child support, justice, and other agencies, is central to these new funding opportunities.

Finally, these new federal funds would support competitive state grants, but because few child support or criminal justice agencies have built the capacity to provide the four components of transitional jobs programs, these agencies must develop partnerships with community-based programs. The components of the CEO model have been developed by many community-based ex-offender, workforce development, and responsible fatherhood programs, using sporadic funding from the private donor community. It is time for private donors to increase their funding of these community-based efforts to leverage the federal funds that will be flowing through the states.

Notes

1. ARRA also substantially increases unemployment benefits and the federal share of the costs of operating the unemployment insurance system. We cover this topic in our section on unemployment insurance.

2. At the time this article was submitted for publication, the 2011 budget had not yet been approved. Congress failed to pass the budget before the end of the fiscal year on September 30, 2010, instead voting to extend the 2010 budget through December 3, 2010 (U.S. Congress 2010). Thus, it was unknown whether the EITC expansion for families with three or more children would become permanent.

3. The EITC is calculated based on either earned income or adjusted gross income, whichever is greater.

4. Annual minimum wage (full time, full year) for 2008 calculated as twenty-nine 40-hour weeks earning $5.85 per hour and twenty-three 40-hour weeks earning $6.55 per hour. Minimum wage increased on July 24, 2008.

5. Annual minimum wage (full time, full year) for 2010 calculated as fifty-two 40-hour weeks earning $7.25 per hour.

6. Three other bills were introduced to expand the credit for childless workers around the same time: one by Representatives Yarmuth and Ellison, one by Senator Kerry and Representative Pascrell, and one by Senators Bayh and Obama (Aron-Dine and Sherman 2007). These proposals tend to build upon Representative Rangel's proposal since he is chair of the House Ways and Means Committee.

7. As previously noted, we calculated annual minimum wage based on the maximum number of possible working hours (52 weeks × 40 hours a week = 2,080), rather than the 2,000 formula. Therefore, our calculations are fairly substantially higher: For 2008, $12,812 compared with $11,700. For 2009, $14,268 compared with $13,100. For 2010, $15,080 compared with $14,500. To truly cover all full-time, full-year minimum wage workers, we believe that EITC calculations should account for the maximum number of possible working hours.

8. See Social Security Act, U.S. Code 42 § 657. The Child Support Enforcement Amendments of 1984 (U.S. Congress 1984) amended Title IV-D to require OCSE to provide fee-based services to custodial parents not receiving public benefits (Public Law 98-378, 98th Cong., 2nd sess.).

9. See Social Security Act, U.S. Code 42 § 666.

10. See U.S. Code 15 § 1673(b).

11. See Code of Federal Regulations 45 § 303.72.

12. At the time this article was submitted for publication, it was unknown whether funding for the proposed Fatherhood, Marriage, and Families Innovation Fund was approved.

References

Administration for Children and Families. 2010. Justification of estimates for appropriations committees, Temporary Assistance for Needy Families. Washington, DC: U.S. Department of Health and Human Services. Available from www.acf.hhs.gov.

Aron-Dine, Aviva, and Arloc Sherman. 2007. Ways and Means Committee Chairman Charles Rangel's proposed expansion of the EITC for childless workers: An important step to make work pay. Washington, DC: Center on Budget and Policy Priorities. Available from www.cbpp.org.

Baker, Dean. 2009. Jobs byte: Unemployment edges downward as employment loss slows. Washington, DC: Center for Economic and Policy Research. Available from www.cepr.net.

Baron, Deborah G. 1999. Comment: The many faces of child support modification. *Journal of the American Academy of Matrimonial Lawyers* 16 (1): 259–73.

Berlin, Gordan L. 2007. Rewarding the work of individuals: A counterintuitive approach to reducing poverty and strengthening families. *The Future of Children* 17 (2): 17–42.

Blank, Rebecca M., and Laura Schmidt. 2001. Work, wages, and welfare. In *The new world of welfare*, eds. Rebecca M. Blank and Ron Haskins, 70–102. Washington, DC: Brookings Institution Press.

Bloom, Dan. 2009. The Joyce Foundation's transitional jobs reentry demonstration: Testing strategies to help former prisoners find and keep jobs and stay out of prison. Policy brief. Chicago, IL: The Joyce Foundation. Available from www.joycefdn.org.

Bosman, Julie. 29 March 2009. Fighting over child support after the pink slip arrives. *New York Times*.

Bradley, David H., and Ann Lordeman. 2009. Funding for workforce development in the American Recovery and Reinvestment Act (ARRA) of 2009. Washington, DC: Congressional Research Service. Available from http://opencrs.com.

Burman, Len, and Greg Leiserson. 9 April 2007. Two-thirds of tax units pay more payroll tax than income tax. *Tax Notes*, 173. Washington, DC: Tax Policy Center.

Cade, Scott. 2008. New York State NCP Earned Income Tax Credit: Discern and learn. Presentation to National Child Support Enforcement Association (NCSEA) Policy Forum and Training Conference, 28–30 January, Washington, DC.

Carasso, Adam, Harry J. Holzer, Elaine Maag, and Eugene Steuerle. 2008. The next stage for social policy: Encouraging work and family formation among low-income men. Tax Policy Center Discussion Paper 28, Washington, DC. Available from www.taxpolicycenter.org.

Cooper, Michael. 17 February 2010. Stimulus jobs on state's bill in Mississippi. *New York Times*.

Edelman, Peter, Mark Greenberg, Steve Holt, and Harry Holzer. 2009. Expanding the EITC to help more low-wage workers. Washington, DC: Georgetown Center on Poverty, Inequality and Public Policy. Available from www.urban.org.

Edelman, Peter, Harry J. Holzer, and Paul Offner. 2006. *Reconnecting disadvantaged young men*. Washington, DC: Urban Institute Press.

Ellwood, David T. 1988. *Poor support: Poverty in the American family*. New York, NY: Basic Books.

Freeman, Richard B., and Jane Waldfogel. 2001. Dunning delinquent dads: The effects of child support enforcement policy on child support receipt by never married women. *Journal of Human Resources* 36 (2): 207–25.

Garfinkel, Irwin. 1992. *Assuring child support: An extension of Social Security*. New York, NY: Russell Sage Foundation.

Gitterman, Daniel P., Lucy S. Gorham, and Jessica L. Dorrance. 2007. Expanding the EITC for single workers and couples without children. Policy brief. Chapel Hill, NC: Center on Poverty, Work and Opportunity, University of North Carolina at Chapel Hill.

Grall, Timothy S. 2009. Custodial mothers and fathers and their child support: 2007. Washington DC: U.S. Census Bureau. Available from www.census.gov/.

Greenberg, Mark, Indivar Dutta-Gupta, and Elisa Minoff. 2007. From poverty to prosperity: A national strategy to cut poverty in half. Washington, DC: Center for American Progress Task Force on Poverty.

Griffin, Maureen Anne. 1999. Payroll tax, federal. In *The encyclopedia of taxation and tax policy*, eds. Joseph J. Cordes, Robert D. Ebel, and Jane G. Gravelle, 320–22. Washington, DC: Urban Institute Press.

Holt, Steve. 2006. The Earned Income Tax Credit at age 30: What we know. Washington, DC: The Brookings Institution. Available from www.brookings.edu.

Holzer, Harry J., and Paul Offner. 2006. Trends in employment outcomes of young black men, 1979–2001. In *Black males left behind*, ed. Ronald B. Mincy, 11–38. Washington, DC: Urban Institute Press.

Holzer, Harry J., Paul Offner, and Elaine Sorensen. 2005. Declining employment among young black less-educated men: The role of incarceration and child support. *Journal of Policy Analysis and Management* 24 (2): 329–50.

Hong, Cindy. 2008. Refining arrears forgiveness: How to improve collections and lower accumulation. In *Policy suggestions to improve child support enforcement and child wellbeing*. Princeton, NJ: Princeton University, Woodrow Wilson School of Public and International Affairs Student Policy Task Force: Fathers, Child Wellbeing, and Child Support Enforcement.

Huang, Chien-Chung, Ronald B. Mincy, and Irwin Garfinkel. 2005. Child support obligations in low-income fathers: Unbearable burden vs. children's well-being. *Journal of Marriage and the Family* 67 (5): 1275–86.

Huang, Chien-Chung, and Hillard Pouncy. 2005. Why doesn't she have a child support order? Personal choice or objective constraint. *Family Relations* 54:547–57.

Internal Revenue Service. 2009a. EITC Income limits, maximum credit amounts and tax law updates. Washington, DC: Internal Revenue Service. Available from www.irs.gov.

Internal Revenue Service. 2009b. Individual complete report (Publication 1304). Washington, DC: Internal Revenue Service. Available from www.irs.gov.

Kobes, Deborah I., and Elaine M. Maag. 3 February 2003. Tax burden on poor families has declined over time. *Tax Notes*, 749. Washington, DC: Tax Policy Center.

LaLonde, Robert J. 1995. The promise of public sector-sponsored training programs. *Journal of Economic Perspectives* 9 (2): 149–68.

Legler, Paul. 1996. The coming revolution in child support policy: Implications of the 1996 welfare act. *Family Law Quarterly* 30 (3): 519–63.

Lerman, Robert, and Elaine Sorensen. 2003. Child support: Interactions between private and public transfers. In *Means-tested transfer programs in the United States*, ed. Robert A. Moffitt. Chicago, IL: University of Chicago Press. Available from www.nber.org/.

Mead, Lawrence M. 2007. Toward a mandatory work policy for men. *The Future of Children* 17 (2): 43–72.

Meyer, Daniel R., Yoonsook Ha, and Mei-Chen Hu. 2008. Do high child support orders discourage child support payments? *Social Service Review* 82 (1): 93–118.

Miller, Daniel P., and Ronald B. Mincy. 2009. *The effects of child support arrears on formal and informal labor force participation*. New York, NY: Center for Research on Fathers, Children, and Family Well-Being.

Mincy, Ronald B., Irwin Garfinkel, and Lenna Nepomnyaschy. 2005. In-hospital paternity establishment and father involvement in fragile families. *Journal of Marriage and Family* 67 (3): 611–26.

Mincy, Ronald B., Monique Jethwani-Keyser, and Serena Klempin. n.d. *Hit or miss: Benefits and barriers of the New York State Earned Income Tax Credit*. New York, NY: Center for Research on Fathers, Children, and Family Well-Being.

Mincy, Ronald B., and Daniel P. Miller. Forthcoming. *Barriers to participation in the Federal NCP/EITC.* New York, NY: Center for Research on Fathers, Children, and Family Well-Being.

Mincy, Ronald B., and Elaine Sorensen. 1998. Deadbeats and turnips in child support reform. *Journal of Policy Analysis and Management* 17 (1): 44–51.

Nepomnyaschy, Lenna. 2007. Child support and father-child contact: Testing reciprocal pathways. *Demography* 44 (1): 93–112.

Nightingale, Demetra S., and Elaine Sorensen. 2006. The availability and use of workforce development programs among low-skilled young persons. In *Black males left behind*, ed. Ronald B. Mincy, 185–210. Washington, DC: Urban Institute Press.

NYC Department of Consumer Affairs. 2008. Summary of Mayor Bloomberg's proposed expansion of the Federal Earned Income Tax Credit. New York, NY: Department of Consumer Affairs. Available from www.nyc.gov.

Office of Child Support Enforcement. 2007. *Child Support Enforcement: FY 2006 preliminary report.* Washington, DC: U.S. Department of Health and Human Services. Available from www.acf.hhs.gov.

Office of Inspector General. 2000. Establishment of child support orders for low income non-custodial parents. Washington, DC: U.S. Department of Health and Human Services. Available from www.oig .hhs.gov.

Pearson, Jessica. 2004. Building debt while doing time: Child support and incarceration. *Judges' Journal of the American Bar Association* 43 (1): 5–12.

Pirog, Maureen A., and Katherine M. Ziol-Guest. 2006. Child support enforcement: Programs and policies, impacts and questions. *Journal of Policy Analysis and Management* 25 (4): 943–90.

Primus, Wendell. 2006. Improving public policies to increase the income and employment of low-income nonresident fathers. In *Black males left behind*, ed. Ronald B. Mincy, 211–48. Washington, DC: Urban Institute Press.

Redcross, Cindy, Dan Bloom, Gilda Azurdia, Janine Zweig, and Nancy Pindus. 2009. Transitional jobs for ex-prisoners: Implementation, two-year impacts, and costs of the Center for Employment Opportunities (CEO) Prisoner Reentry Program. New York, NY: MDRC. Available from www.mdrc.org.

Reichman, Nancy E., Julien O. Teitler, Irwin Garfinkel, and Sara S. McLanahan. 2001. Fragile families: Sample and design. *Children and Youth Services Review* 23 (4/5): 303–326.

Rich, Lauren M., Irwin Garfinkel, and Qin Gao. 2007. Child support enforcement policy and unmarried fathers' employment in the underground and regular economies. *Journal of Policy Analysis and Management* 26 (4): 791–810.

Sammartino, Frank, Eric Toder, and Elaine Maag. 2002. Providing federal assistance for low-income families through the tax system: A primer. Tax Policy Institute Discussion Paper 4, Washington, DC. Available from www.taxpolicycenter.org.

Scholz, John K. 2007. Employment-based tax credits for low-skilled workers. Brookings Institution Discussion Paper 2007-14, Washington, DC. Available from www.brookings.edu.

Scott, Christine. 2008. *The Earned Income Tax Credit (EITC): Changes for 2008 and 2009.* Report RS21352. Washington, DC: Congressional Research Service.

Shelton, Alison M., Kathleen Romig, and Julie M. Whittaker. 2009. *Unemployment insurance provisions in the American Recovery and Reinvestment Act of 2009.* Report R40368. Washington, DC: Congressional Research Service. Available from http://opencrs.com.

Smeeding, Timothy, Irwin Garfinkel, and Ronald B. Mincy. 2009. Young disadvantaged men: Fathers, families, poverty, and policy: An introduction to the issues. Paper presented at the Institute for Research on Poverty Working Conference on Young Disadvantaged Men: Fathers, Families, Poverty and Policy, 14–15 September, University of Wisconsin–Madison.

Solomon-Fears, Carmen, Gene Falk, and Carole A. Pettit. 2009. Side-by-side comparison of current law, H.R. 2979, and S. 1309. Washington, DC: Congressional Research Service. Available from www.crs.gov.

Sorensen, Elaine. 2004. Understanding how child-support arrears reached $18 billion in California. *American Economic Review* 94 (2): 312–16.

Sorensen, Elaine, Liliana Sousa, and Simone Schaner. 2007. *Assessing child support arrears in nine large states and the nation.* Washington, DC: The Urban Institute. Available from www.urban.org.

Sum, Andrew, Ishwar Khatiwada, Joseph McLaughlin, and Sheila Palma. 2009. The deterioration in the labor market fortunes of young men in the U.S. and its consequences for family formation, family well being, and the future economic well being of children: No country for young men? Paper presented at the Institute for Research on Poverty Working Conference on Young Disadvantaged Men: Fathers, Families, Poverty and Policy, 14–15 September, University of Wisconsin–Madison.

U.S. Congress. 1982. *Job Training Partnership Act of 1982*. Public Law 97-300, 97th Cong., 2d sess. (October 13, 1982).

U.S. Congress. 1984. *Child Support Enforcement Amendments of 1984*. Public Law 98-378, 98th Cong., 2d sess. (August 16, 1984).

U.S. Congress. 1998. *Workforce Investment Act of 1998*. Public Law 105-220, 105th Cong., 2d sess. (August 7, 1998).

U.S. Congress. 2007a. *Responsible Fatherhood and Healthy Families Act of 2007*. S 1626, 110th Cong., 1st sess. (August 3, 2007).

U.S. Congress. 2007b. *Tax Reduction and Reform Act of 2007*. HR 3970, 110th Cong., 1st sess. (October 25, 2007).

U.S. Congress. 2009a. *American Clean Energy and Security Act of 2009*. HR 2454, 111th Cong., 1st sess. (May 15, 2009).

U.S. Congress. 2009b. *American Recovery and Reinvestment Act of 2009*. Public Law 111-5, 111th Cong., 1st sess. (February 17, 2009).

U.S. Congress. 2009c. *Julia Carson Responsible Fatherhood and Healthy Families Act of 2009*. HR 2979, 111th Cong., 1st sess. (June 19, 2009).

U.S. Congress. 2009d. *Responsible Fatherhood and Healthy Families Act of 2009*. S 1309, 111th Cong., 1st sess. (June 19, 2009).

U.S. Congress. 2010. *Continuing Appropriations Act, 2011*. Public Law 111-242, 111th Cong., 2d sess. (September 30, 2010).

U.S. Department of Labor. 2009. Congressional budget justification: Employment and training administration, training and employment services. Washington, DC: U.S. Department of Labor. Available from www.dol.gov.

U.S. Department of Labor. 5 November 2010. Economic news release: Employment situation summary for October 2010. Washington, DC: U.S. Department of Labor, Bureau of Labor Statistics. Available from www.bls.gov.

U.S. Department of Treasury. 2009. General explanations of the administration's fiscal year 2010 revenue proposals. Washington, DC: U.S. Department of Treasury. Available from www.ustreas.gov.

U.S. Department of Treasury. 2010. General explanations of the administration's fiscal year 2011 revenue proposals. Washington, DC: U.S. Department of Treasury. Available from www.ustreas.gov.

Waller, Maureen, and Robert Plotnick. 2001. Effective child support policy for low-income families: Evidence from street level research. *Journal of Policy Analysis and Management* 20 (1): 89–110.

Wandner, Stephen A., and Andrew Stettner. 2000. Why are many jobless workers not applying for benefits? *Monthly Labor Review* 123 (6): 21–33.

Wheaton, Laura, and Elaine Sorensen. 2009. Extending the EITC to noncustodial parents: Potential impacts and design considerations. Washington, DC: The Urban Institute. Available from www.urban.org.

Award-winning & authoritative reference at your fingertips...

SAGE eReference